P99 HAR.

HARLAXTON MEDIEVAL STUDIES

VOLUME EIGHTEEN

SIGNS AND SYMBOLS

HARLAXTON MEDIEVAL STUDIES

HARLAXTON MEDIEVAL STUDIES, XVIII

SIGNS AND SYMBOLS

Proceedings of the
2006 Harlaxton Symposium

Edited by
John Cherry
and Ann Payne

SHAUN TYAS
DONINGTON
2009
·

© The Contributors
Published in 2009 by
SHAUN TYAS
(an imprint of 'Paul Watkins')
1 High Street
Donington
Lincolnshire
PE11 4TA

ISBN
1 900289 989 (ten digits)
978-1900289-98-6 (thirteen digits)

Typeset and designed from the discs of the authors
by Shaun Tyas

Printed in Great Britain by
the MPG Books Group, Bodmin and King's Lynn

CONTENTS

LIST OF CONTRIBUTORS

Adrian Ailes	The National Archives, London
Mary Carruthers	New York University
John Cherry	British Museum, London
Elizabeth Danbury	University College, London
Christa Grössinger	University of Manchester
Phillipa Hardman	University of Reading
P. D. A. Harvey	University of Durham
Julian Luxford	University of St Andrews
Nigel Morgan	Corpus Christi College, Cambridge
Elizabeth New	Aberystwyth University
Nicholas Rogers	Sidney Sussex College, Cambridge
Andrew Prescott	University of Wales Lampeter
Lucy Freeman Sandler	New York University
Alison Stones	Pittsburgh University
Pamela Tudor-Craig	Society of Antiquaries of London

To Janet Backhouse (1938–2004)

LIST OF PLATES

The plates appear in alphabetical order by author.

1 (Ailes). Cocket seal (Edward III) for delivery of wool and hides at Boston depicting the three lions passant guardant (or 'leopards') of England. TNA E43/649.

2 (Ailes). Custom counterseal (Edward III) for delivery of wool and hides at Boston depicting a lion passant guardant (or 'leopard') of England and a bust of the king. TNA E43/649.

3 (Ailes). Privy seal (1333) of Richard Airmyn, keeper of the house of converts, featuring a single lion's head at the centre of a cross and a fleur-de-lis on each arm. TNA E 43/59.

4 (Ailes). Signet of Richard II depicting the royal crown. TNA CP 51/1/4. Reproduced from Tout, *Administrative History of Medieval England*, 5, p. 202, pl. iv.

5 (Ailes). Seal (1313) of the Great Wardrobe depicting two crossed keys. TNA E 43/559.

6 (Ailes). Seal (1315) of Ralph Giffard, sheriff of Cambridgeshire and Huntingdonshire, featuring a gatehouse or castle between his initials. TNA E 43/669.

7 (Ailes). Seal (1330) of office of Richard de la Pole as the king's butler featuring the broad arrow badge. TNA E 43/63.

1 (Carruthers). Cambridge University Library MS Gg 1.1, f. 490v: diagram of brain functions. English, c.1330 (photo: by permission of the Syndics of Cambridge University Library).

2 (Carruthers). Cambridge, Fitzwilliam Museum, MS Fitzwilliam 11, f. 70. Mnemonic notae in a late 15th-century German, Rhineland (?), bible.

3 (Carruthers). Oxford, Bodleian Library MS Douce 366, f. 147v: Ormesby Psalter. Norwich, betw. 1310 and 1320.

4 (Carruthers). London, BL, Add. MS 54782, ff. 55v–56: Hastings Hours, 1480–83. Flemish. (photo: © British Library Board)

5 (Carruthers). Oxford, Bodleian Library MS Douce 366, f. 9v. Beatus page in the Ormesby Psalter, Norwich, c.1325.

1 (Cherry). Drawing of the chantepleure in Villard de Honnecourt's notebook. Paris, BNF, ms fr. 19093, f. 17. French, between 1225 to 1235. (photo: from Hahnloser, *Villard de Honnecourt,* Tafel 17e)

2 (Cherry). The Corpus Christi silver-mounted mazer. English, fourteenth century. (photo: by permission of the Fellows of Corpus Christi College, Cambridge)

3 (Cherry). Drawing of the Corpus silver mazer with bird. English, fourteenth century. (photo: from *Catalogue of Plate, exhibited at the Fitzwilliam Museum* (1895), no. 11)

4 (Cherry). White-painted pottery chantepleure. English, fifteenth century. British Museum. (photo: by permission of the Trustees of the British Museum)

5 (Cherry). White-painted pottery chantepleure. English, fifteenth century. British Museum. (photo: by permission of the Trustees of the British Museum)

6 (Cherry). Ipswich ware. English, seventh to eighth century. Ipswich Museum. (photo: the author: by permission of Ipswich Museum)

7 (Cherry). The Chantepleure from PS's edition of Paradin's *Devises* (1591).

8 (Cherry). Sheath and set of knives. French early fifteenth century.Watercolour published in *Archaeologia* 60, pt 2 (1906). (photo: the author)

1 (Morgan). Jesus and Mary monograms, Thornford, St Mary Magdalene (Dorset). (photo: the author)

2 (Morgan). Tower base with Jesus, John and Mary monograms, Garboldisham, St John Baptist (Suffolk). (photo: the author)

3 (Morgan). Mary monogram surrounded by roses and lilies, Great Chart, St Mary (Kent). (photo: the author)

4 (Morgan). Jesus and Mary monograms, Ropsley, St Peter (Lincolnshire). (photo: the author)

5 (Morgan). Mary monogram, Bitchfield, St Mary Magdalene Lincolnshire). (photo: the author)

6 (Morgan). Mary monogram, Steeple Ashton (Wiltshire). (photo: the author)

7 (Morgan). Mary monogram on a shield held by an angel, Glastonbury, St John (Somerset). (photo: the author)

8 (Morgan). Mary monogram, Ashill, St Nicholas (Norfolk). (photo: the author)

9 (Morgan). Mary monogram with Annunciation brooch or morse, New College, Oxford.

10 (Morgan). Entrance porch with Mary monograms, Great Witchingham, St Mary (Norfolk). (photo: the author)

11 (Morgan). Entrance porch with Mary monograms, Yaxley, St Mary (Suffolk). (photo: the author)

12 (Morgan). Tower parapet with Mary monogram, Little Stonham, St Mary (Suffolk). (photo: the author)

13 (Morgan). Tower parapet with Mary monogram, Rougham, St John Baptist (Suffolk). (photo: the author)

14 (Morgan). Clerestory parapet with 'STSM', Wortham, St Mary (Suffolk). (photo: the author)

15 (Morgan). Swords of sorrow, Bury St Edmunds, St James (now Cathedral), (Suffolk). c. 1500. (photo: the author)

16 (Morgan). Heart of Mary roof boss, Bristol, Cathedral. c. 1475–1500. (photo: from C. J. P. Cave, *Roof Bosses in Medieval Churches* (Cambridge, 1948), p. 45, pl. 298)

17 (Morgan). Heart of Mary roof boss, Beverley, St Mary (Yorkshire). c. 1475–1500. (photo: from C. J. P. Cave, *Roof Bosses in Medieval Churches* (Cambridge, 1948), p. 45, pl. 297)

18 (Morgan). Heart of Mary shield, Butcombe, St Michael (Somerset). c. 1475–1500. (photo: the author)

19 (Morgan). Heart of Mary badge, Museum of London. c. 1450–1500.

20 (Morgan). Marian shield, Sugar Chantry, Wells Cathedral. c. 1489. (photo: from *Antiquaries Journal*, 11 (1931), pp. 286–8)

1 (New). Sacred Monogram. Cambridge, Fitzwilliam Museum MS 2–1957, f. 41v. (photo: by permission of the Syndics of the Fitzwilliam Museum to whom rights in this publication are assigned)

2 (New): Five Wounds on a shield with the lance, spear and nails. Cambridge, Fitzwilliam Museum MS 2–1957, f. 46. (photo: by permission of the Syndics of the Fitzwilliam Museum)

3 (New): Wounded Heart, hands and feet of Christ, with Calvary cross, scourges and nails. Cambridge, Fitzwilliam Museum MS 2–1957, f. 78. (photo: by permission of the Syndics of the Fitzwilliam Museum)

4 (New): Head of Christ. Cambridge, Fitzwilliam Museum MS 2–1957, f. 50. (photo: by permission of the Syndics of the Fitzwilliam Museum)

11 (Sandler). Bohun Psalter and Hours, Psalm 42. London, BL, Egerton MS 3277, f.32v, detail. (photo: © British Library Board)

12 (Sandler). Bohun Psalter and Hours, Psalm 16. London, BL, Egerton MS 3277, f.13v, detail. (photo: © British Library Board)

13 (Sandler). Hamburg Bible, Prologue to Daniel. Copenhagen, Kongelige Bibl. MS Gl.kgl.S.4 2o, II, f.183, detail.(photo: after C. de Hamel, *Medieval Craftsmen, Scribes and Illuminators* (London, 1992), fig. 8)

14 (Sandler). Omne bonum, 'Colour'. London, BL, Royal MS 6 E vi, f. 329, detail. (photo: © British Library Board)

1 (Stones). Rennes, BM 255, f. 30v. (photo: Lancelot-Grail Project)

2 (Stones). London, BL Add. MS 10292, f. 25. (photo: © British Library Board)

3 (Stones). London, BL Royal MS 14.E.III, f. 36 (photo: © British Library Board)

4. (Stones) Paris, BNF, fr. 9123, f. 38 (photo: Bibliothèque nationale de France)

5 (Stones). London, BL Add. MS 10292, f. 31. (photo: © British Library Board))

6 (Stones). Le Mans, MM 354, f. 110 (photo: Lancelot-Grail Project)

7 (Stones). Rennes, BN 255, f. 46 (photo: Lancelot-Grail Project)

8 (Stones). London, BL Add. MS 10292, f. 31v. (photo: © British Library Board)

9 (Stones). Paris, BNF, fr. 105, f. 65v (photo: Bibliothèque nationale de France)

10 (Stones). Paris, BNF, fr. 9123, f. 53v (photo: Bibliothèque nationale de France)

11 (Stones). Paris, BNF, fr. 19162 f. 65 (photo: Bibliothèque nationale de France)

12 (a and b) (Stones). Berkeley, UCB 106, f. 145v, details from columns a and b (photo: courtesy of The Bancroft Library, University of California, Berkeley)

13 (Stones). Hildesheim, Sankt Godehard, St Albans Psalter, p. 215 (photo: Sankt Godehard)

14 (Stones). London, BL Add. MS 10292, f. 34. (photo: © British Library Board)

15 (Stones). London, BL Add. MS 10292, f. 35v. (photo: © British Library Board)

16 (Stones). London, BL Royal MS 14.E.III, f. 125v. (photo: © British Library Board)

17 (Stones). New Haven, Yale University, Beinecke Library 229, f. 253 (photo: author)

18 (Stones). London, BL Royal MS 14.E.III, f. 128. (photo: © British Library Board)

19 (Stones). Oxford, Bodleian Library, Douce 215, f. 35. (photo: © British Library Board)

20 (Stones). London, BL Royal MS 14.E.III, f. 130v. (photo: © British Library Board)

21 (Stones). New Haven, Yale University, Beinecke Library 229, f. 257v (photo: author)

22 (Stones). London, BL Add. MS 10294, f. 46v. (photo: © British Library Board)

23 (Stones). London, BL Add. MS 10294, f. 47v. (photo: © British Library Board)

24 (Stones). New Haven, Yale University, Beinecke Library 229, f. 262v (photo: author)

1 (Tudor-Craig). Mortuary Roll of Lucy de Vere. London, BL, Egerton MS 2849. (photo: © British Library Board)

2 (Tudor-Craig). Sir John de Wautune and wife. Wimbish, Essex 1347. Brass rubbing by L. A. S. Waller, 1848.

3 (Tudor-Craig). Sir Miles de Stapleton and wife, 1364, formerly Ingham, Norfolk. (photo: from Stothard, *Monumental Effigies*, 1819)

4 (Tudor-Craig). Sir John Harsick and wife, 1384. Southacre, Norfolk.

5 (Tudor-Craig). Peter Halle and wife, c. 1430. Herne, Kent.

6 (Tudor-Craig). Sir William Mauntell and wife, 1487. Nether Heyford, Northamptonshire.

7 (Tudor-Craig). Sir John de la Pole and wife, c. 1380. Chrishall, Essex.

8 (Tudor-Craig). Robert Hatfield and wife Ada, 1409. Owston, Yorks.

PREFACE

The twenty-third Harlaxton Medieval Symposium was held from 17 to 20 July 2006 on the theme of Signs and Symbols. Both the symposium and the collection of essays in these *Proceedings* are dedicated to Janet Backhouse, who died in 2004, as a memorial to her enthusiastic support of the Harlaxton symposia, and her love for the remarkable house which provides their setting. We are grateful to all who attended, gave papers, chaired sessions, and contributed articles for publication; our special thanks go to Andrew Prescott who, in addition to filling all of these roles, compiled the full bibliography of Janet's published works included at the end of this volume (pp. 192–204).

It is sad to record that two contributors died between the conference and the publication. For them too this volume assumes a commemorative aspect. Stephen Medcalf (University of Sussex) spoke on 'The colour blue as symbolic: medieval and modern', and it is a matter of regret that at his death his fine paper was not in a sufficient state of readiness for publication. Christa Grössinger's text was virtually ready and the editors have been able to see it through to publication, although unfortunately it is less fully illustrated than she would have wished. We should like to thank Emma Ferguson for assistance in tracing illustrations among Christa's papers at the John Rylands Library, Manchester, and John Hodgson, Keeper of Manuscripts and Archives there, for enabling us to use them.

Of the twenty-three papers read at the 2006 symposium, fifteen appear in this volume. We have been able to begin and end with general, wide-ranging studies. Signs and Symbols are very dependent on memory, and are often used as indicators for memory, so we are delighted to open the volume with Mary Carruthers's paper 'Thinking with images: the spatial and visual requirements of cognition and recollection in medieval psychology'. Christa Grössinger concludes with a cautionary word against over-interpretation. In between, in the best interdisciplinary tradition of Harlaxton, historians, literary scholars and art historians come together to explore the specific use of signs and symbols in the Middle Ages, both religious and secular, across many media and covering a broad spread of subject; they range, as the Index reveals, from 'Anchors, Angels and Apes', through 'Dogs, Dolphins and Dragons' to 'Woolsacks, Words, and Wyverns'.

We thank Harlaxton College and its staff for their continuing hospitality to the Symposium, and Julian Limentani, Peterborough Cathedral architect, a welcoming host on the conference outing. Christian Steer was the most energetic and efficient organiser of this, his first symposium, as Secretary; Hannes Kleineke expertly compiled the Index; and Shaun Tyas undertook with his customary unflagging enthusiasm both copy editing and publication of the volume: our thanks to them all.

John Cherry and Ann Payne

'Thinking in Images': the Spatial and Visual Requirements of Cognition and Recollection in Medieval Psychology

MARY CARRUTHERS

The arts of memory are firmly associated with a method of making bizarre images, projecting them into locations in actual buildings, and using those links to remember in pre-selected order all the subjects and even the exact words of the speech an orator has composed wholly in advance. While this modern characterization has some truth in it, it is by no means comprehensive, and indeed it seriously misrepresents the primary compositional functions of *ars memorativa*, and misstates its psychological goals. This would be no more than an annoying inconvenience, by no means unique in scholarship, were it not that so much has been claimed for these arts, both by well-meaning practitioners (and sometimes not so well-meaning frauds) and – paradoxically – by modern scholars seeking to diminish or refute the abilities their ancient proponents are alleged to have claimed, to ensure an all-comprehensive and -comprehending human memory. All too often, these writers are knocking over straw-men.[1]

In this essay, I hope to set *ars memorativa* in some of its medieval contexts, in order to clarify what efficiencies were actually claimed for it, and set forth some principles whereby one might now recognize what 'memory-images' were thought to achieve, and work fruitfully with them. It may be useful to begin with what has become since the sixteenth century (but not much before then) the authorized statement of *ars memorativa*; that in the Ciceronian treatise on rhetoric, *Rhetorica ad Herennium*, composed in about 85 BC by someone whose name is unknown, though it was attributed in the Middle Ages to Cicero.[2] Latin

---

[1] For example, P. Ricoeur, *History, Memory, Forgetting* (Chicago, 2004), p. 67, wrote that arts of memory are "an outrageous denial of forgetfulness and ... of the weaknesses inherent in both the preservation of [memory] traces and their evocation."

[2] Recent scholarship still favours an unknown (and probably unknowable) author, a Roman master educated in the Greek tradition, working at about the time Cicero was young. G. Calboli argued in his first edition of the work, *Cornifici Rhetorica ad C. Herennium* (Bologna, 1969), that the author was one Cornificius, and proposed two possible candidates from that family, but he has more recently retreated from this position. The subsequent dissemination of the work is described with admirable clarity by

1

having no articles, this phrase has unfortunately, in English and other European languages, been translated as *the* art of memory, well before Frances Yates adopted it as the title for her justly influential book.[3] The *ad Herennium* description is so well known now that it has over-shadowed most of the rich medieval traditions and even other later, and arguably more influential, traditions from late antiquity, Jewish as well as Greek: indeed for clarity's sake it is better referred to as the 'Herennian' art, for its examples are specific to that work and were not widely known or adopted until, as part of university study of the *Rhetorica ad Herennium*, they were commented on extensively after the mid-thirteenth century.[4]

Yet the Herennian art offers a place to begin because it does demonstrate a couple of the basic principles involved in crafting the sort of images thought particularly useful for remembering those things one must remember, even when under the considerable stress of forensic debate: "For example, the prosecutor has said that the defendant killed a man by poison, has charged that the motive for the crime was an inheritance, and declared that there are many witnesses and accessories to this act."[5]

To remember the main points of this accusation, we might make a scene of the dead man lying ill in bed, with the defendant by his bedside, holding a cup in his right hand, and in his left hand a set of tablets with a pair of ram's testicles hanging off his fourth finger. In this way we have an image for each salient point, the dead man, the defendant accused of poisoning him (the cup in his right hand), the inheritance at issue (recorded in the tablets), and the witnesses or *testes* in the pun on *testiculi* (the ram's testicles). It is important to note that this scene is presented only as an example of a fairly simple, straight-forward principle of marking the subject matters [*res*] of an oration (forensic in this case) with vivid images arranged in a coherent scene, which can serve the speaking orator as ready cues to recall the ordered points of his composition. I stress the banality of the thought-task because the example has proven so durable and memorable that historians have over-emphasized its influence. Making strongly distinctive, one-of-a-kind images to mark material one needs quickly and securely to retrieve is not a

R. Taylor-Briggs in her chapter in *The Rhetoric of Cicero in its Medieval and Early Renaissance Commentary Tradition*, V. Cox and J. O. Ward (eds) (Leiden, 2006), pp. 77–108.

3   F. A. Yates, *The Art of Memory* (London, 1965). Yates's study opened up the field to ancient and early modern historians in a way it had not been before, but it does focus on the Herennian tradition exclusively.

4   See Cox and Ward (eds), *The Rhetoric of Cicero*, esp. the essays by Ward (an overview of medieval teaching of rhetoric and the dissemination of Ciceronian texts), pp. 3–76; Cox (on the early Renaissance Italian dissemination of Ciceronian material), pp. 109–143; and Carruthers, pp. 209–38 (on the medieval teaching of *ars memorativa* both within and outside the Herennian tradition).

5   [Cicero], *Rhetorica ad Herennium* III. 33; ed. and trans. by H. Caplan, Loeb Classical Library (London, 1977).

mnemonic principle that was discovered uniquely by the *auctor ad Herennium*, whoever he was.

This example is itself so memorable that it has a way of obscuring its own underlying principles, and also of dominating and de-familiarizing techniques still known to us, and practiced by us on such a daily basis that we do not even consider them as instruments of our thinking processes. These include distributing our knowledge through a structure of multicompartmented cells (or seats or rooms or pockets or boxes), by means of paired procedures of 'division' and 'collection'. Lengthy and diffuse matters are 'shortened' into chunks (called either *divisiones* or *discretiones*), of a size that can be encompassed by one 'gaze' or *conspectus* of the mind's eye. *Discretio*, which comes from the verb *discerno* 'that which can be seen all at once,' conceptually derives from this basic observation about how we best recollect. These discrete *divisiones* are 'collected' or 'gathered up' – *colligere, collectus* – into 'places', *loci* (a word psychologists still use) within an overall single structure that orders them clearly *in relation to* one another. This is an important characteristic to grasp, and it was much emphasized in practice. Mnemonic places are not conceived of only as singulars but also always in relationship to other mnemonic places; it is this that gives them the quality of 'place' *within* a structured form of which each is a part. The retrieval process addressed in mnemonic art is conceived of as investigation, a rational retrieval and gathering-together of the materials of thought from the various mental places in which they have been located.[6] Recollection, which is reasoning of a kind, requires its methods and instruments – it is not a matter solely of unplanned, irrational inspiration, nor need it always be a chancy, desperate search for ever-elusive prey.

As is often the case with memory procedures, St Augustine best describes recollection:

> Sojourning there [in my memory] I command something I want to present itself, and immediately certain things emerge, while others have to be pursued for some time and dug out from remote crannies. Others again come tumbling out in disorderly profusion, and leap into prominence as though asking "Are we what you want?" when it is something different that I am asking for and trying to recall. With my mental hand I push them out of the way of my effort to remember, until what I want becomes clear and breaks from cover [like a hunted rabbit]. Then, there are remembered items that come to hand easily and in orderly sequence as soon as they are summoned, the earlier members giving way to those that follow and returning to their storage-places, ready to be retrieved next time I need them. All of which happens when I relate [*narro*] anything from memory.[7]

[6]   These various terms are discussed and defined at some length in the preface to M. Carruthers and J. Ziolkowski (eds), *The Medieval Craft of Memory* (Philadelphia, 2002).
[7]   Augustinus, *Confessionum libri XIII*, X. 8; ed. L. Verheijen, CCSL 27 (Turnhout, 1981). Throughout this essay, I have used the translation of M. Boulding (Hyde Park, NY,

Augustine does not imply that his memories are all in the form of vivid images. But the *Rhetorica ad Herennium* certainly says that making memorable images to mark the matters stored in their various memory places is essential. The question is what kind of image is memorable. As usual in ancient and medieval theory, art should take its lesson from nature: *Imitetur ars igitur naturam*. "When we see in everyday life things that are petty, ordinary, and banal, we generally fail to remember them, because the mind is not being stirred by anything novel or marvellous. But if we see or hear something exceptionally base, dishonorable, extraordinary, great, unbelievable, or laughable, that we are likely to remember a long time."[8]

We overlook what is common and familiar to us; indeed, consider how hard it is to remember whether or not you have taken the quota of pills you have every day, or where you left your car in a large, undifferentiated parking lot. As the *auctor* comments, this is why "incidents of our childhood [when all was new] we often remember best." So in crafting memory markers we should seek to make them "as striking as possible." Do not fashion an indistinct crowd of images, but ones that obviously do something (*imagines agentes*); images "of exceptional beauty or singular ugliness," some dressed in crowns and purple, others disfigured by bloody wounds or smeared with mud or red paint – or images that are comic and make us laugh, "for that too will ensure our remembering them more readily."[9] The distinctiveness required of such image-crafting is given it through the stylistic figure known as *enargeia*, 'vividness'. Its power or virtue lies not in its likeness to an object but rather in its ability to strike and impress the viewer in a lasting and distinctive manner.[10] Aristotle's context is rhetoric, so his immediate reference is to verbal 'picturing', but 'vividness' can be also a quality of painting and sculpture. In the famous Horatian maxim, *ut pictura poesis*. And it should be remembered that Simonides, the sixth-century (BC) Greek poet said to have discovered the Herennian art, was also famous for his aphorism that poetry is speaking picture, and painting is silent poetry.[11]

1997). Any changes are indicated by square brackets. Augustine's choice, in this description, of the verb, *narrare*, underscores that memories are related to one another, the fundamental principle of 'location'.

8   *Rhet. ad Her.* III. 36.

9   *Rhet. ad Her.* III. 37.

10 E*nargeia* and its closely related term in rhetoric, *energeia*, are both well discussed by R. Lanham, *A Handlist of Rhetorical Terms*, second edition (Berkeley, 1991); see also K. Eden, *Poetic and Legal Fiction in the Aristotelian Tradition* (Princeton, 1986), pp. 70–5. Aristotle importantly discusses the term in his *Rhetoric*: see S. Newman, 'Aristotle's Notion of "Bringing before the Eyes": Its Contributions to Aristotelian and Contemporary Conceptualizations of Metaphor, Style, and Audience', *Rhetorica* 20 (2002), pp. 1–23.

11 First discussed at length by Yates, *Art of Memory*, pp. 42–4. See also L. Bolzoni, *The Gallery of Memory* (Toronto, 2001), pp. 182–8, who sets the craft of memory images into the larger context of late medieval and Renaissance physiognomic portraiture.

In Scholastic psychology all thinking required mental images, and these were the product of the *vis imaginativa,* whose role in thought-crafting is diagrammed in a fourteenth-century drawing in Cambridge, University Library MS Gg 1.1, f. 490v (Plate 1). Impressions are initially received from the various external senses in the *sensus communis* or *fantasia*, located in the forward part of the brain. The various sense impressions are then brought together mentally by the image-forming ability, *imaginatio* or *vis formalis*, the ability of forming an image from many sensory data. Raw sense data were thought to be composed or 'gathered together' (*colligere*) by the actions of both *fantasia* and *vis formalis* (the power of shaping) into images having formal properties that are perceptible and useful to human thought. The materials for thinking are thus wholly mental creations, *phantasmata*, a word taken by scholastic commentators from Aristotle's treatise, *De anima*, but which occurs as well in Quintilian's rhetoric, translated in Latin as *imagines*.[12] The concept of the *phantasm* or *imago* has as important a life in rhetoric as it does in philosophy.

The Aristotelian criterion of similitude, 'likeness', for memory images should be understood in this context – mental images have 'likeness' not as photographs do, but in the way that a schematic drawing can be said to be 'like' the object it represents. It is equally important to notice that the resulting mental image was considered to be composed of input from all the senses. In the context of thinking, the word *imago* in medieval Latin was not limited solely to the visual sense, though it is also true that the visual was regarded as the primary instrument of cognition for most people. And finally, the images are themselves psychologically fabricated. *Fantasia* and *imaginatio* are agents which put separate bits together into a whole sensory experience – they are not just recording devices.

These *imagines,* as the materials of understanding, are made present to the mind in the activity called *cogitatio*, 'cogitation, thinking', and from them ideas and thoughts are constructed. All thoughts are therefore made of images, and the other name for cogitation in this picture is *vis imaginativa* or 'the ability to imagine'. These human conceptions as phantasms, mental images, are finally retained and recollected by memory, *vis memorativa*, the final stage of this constructive process. The diagram makes clear as well that memory, like thought and imagination, is *vis*, an agent, not a passive receptacle.

The path between memory and thought-making, *vis cogitativa*, must be two-way, because memories have to be recalled as well as stored. So a sort of valve was thought to exist, which would allow images to pass into memory, and also to be recalled for cogitation. This was called the *vermis*, drawn eponymously in the diagram as a little worm-like creature between *cogitatio* and *memoria*. Moreover, it

12 Quintilian discusses the important role of *phantasmata*, both for the orator and the judges (audience) throughout the *Institutio oratoria*, but esp. in Books VI. 2. 29–36 and VIII. 3. 61–73.

had been observed that people often lower their heads in order to think and raise them when trying to recollect something. This was taken as evidence for the action of the *vermis*, opening as needed for recollection, and closing for concentrated thinking once one had received from memory the materials one needed. Without such a control, it was thought, memories could crowd unbidden into the mind, overwhelming and distracting rational thought. The *vermis* is a gatekeeper.

It is striking how entirely the imagination is implicated in cognition and in memory by this medieval analysis. This aspect is the most astonishing, most alien, from the stand-point of our own rationalist psychology. Sensations are collected up at the start of the process in the *sensus communis*, but from the instant they are received in bits and pieces from their various sources, fictive faculties – *fantasia*, *imaginatio*, and *vis imaginativa* – go to work. These may or may not make an image that is accurate or faithful as a representation of something else: the important thing for the process of recollection is that an image is constructed. It is fashioned by bringing or 'gathering' matters into a common 'location' in memory into which it is 'placed'.

There are two kinds of mnemonic image-making described in *Rhetorica ad Herennium*, one for *memoria verborum* and one for *memoria rerum*.[13] This distinction, of *memoria rerum* and *memoria verborum*, belongs to the basic lexicon of memory advice: it is also made by Quintilian, Fortunatianus, Julius Victor, and subsequent writers. Ancient and medieval pedagogy also recognized a crucial, foundational role in learning for rote memorization, or recitation by heart. Confusingly (and this confusion is apparent even in the ancient sources) such recitation was termed *ad verbum* or *verbaliter*, 'word-for-word' as we would now say. The practical distinction between verbatim, rote memory and *memoria rerum*, 'subject-memory', is well made by St Augustine, a master of rhetoric himself. In his work on teaching converts, *De catechizandis rudibus*. Augustine uses two technical terms for recollection, *ad uerbum* and *summatim*, but distinguishes them clearly from one other in respect to their tasks, associating *memoria rerum* (*summatim*) particularly with the task of composition:

> Even if we have memorized verbatim [*ad uerbum edidicimus*], [when we teach] we should neither just recite ... entire books [of the Bible], nor, by retelling in our own words [through paraphrase], explicate every single matter contained in these volumes ... but having grasped them all by their main topics [*cuncta summatim generatimque complecti*] ... we can select certain things as more worthy to be examined closely ... dwelling on something a piece at a time as though to loosen it up and expand it, [and] offer it for inspection and admiration by the minds of the audience.[14]

---

[13] *Rhet. ad Her.* III. 33–4.
[14] Augustinus, *De catechizandis rudibus*, 3. 5; ed. J. B. Bauer, CCSL 46 (Turnhout, 1969); my translation. A new translation by R. Canning, *Instructing Beginners in Faith*, is now

'Subject-memory' is the essential device of composition, the preacher choosing to dilate upon certain matters in the text which he has selected for particular inspection by his audience, while having the entire text at his disposal in order, both verbatim – which is what Augustine means by 'ad uerbum' – and by its subject-matters or *summatim*. But the sort of word-memory Augustine here refers to is not what the *Rhetorica ad Herennium*, in the context of *ars memorativa*, called *memoria verborum*.[15] Verbatim recitation, then as now, meant memorizing and reciting texts by rote – this is clear from what Augustine says in this passage.

Memoria verborum is a distinct application of rhetorical memory technique – utilizing especially the figures of *enargeia* and *homophony* (puns) – to strange words or names one has trouble with, or to phrases which one must recall with immediate accuracy: precisely the matters which one does *not* have by rote, but needs to find safely and trouble-free, even in the stressful situations of debate or *ex tempore* preaching and teaching. The example of *memoria verborum* given in the *Rhetorica ad Herennium* is a hexameter line from a tragic play, and the technique depends on a set of visual puns which mark and cue each syllable of the verse, a rhetorical version of the game of charades. It is presented by the *auctor* as an exercise for budding orators, not as an alternative to *memoria rerum* nor as a technique particularly helpful in composition, though it might have a useful role during delivery. To later writers, the purpose of such 'images-for-words' (when they mention it) is to prompt very specific memories, such as those of a specific verse (in the Herennian example) or the particular theme-text for a sermon (as in Bradwardine's advice, discussed below) or of words or names in unfamiliar languages like Hebrew and Greek. The examples are always brief – single verses or single words – and highly particular. Marker-images like these can also be made to start one going on materials one had already memorized by heart, but for which one might want an additional cue (exactly as stage prompters do still). Another word for them, used commonly by Cicero and in late Roman rhetoric, and also – much later on – by masters like Geoffrey of Vinsauf, is *notatio* or *nota*. In later medieval mnemotechnical writing, the term *imagines verborum* is often superceded by (or interchangeable with) *notae* or *notationes*, a change perhaps made for reasons of clarity, since *ad verbum* memory had been reserved for rote recitation (as in the passage from *De catechizandis rudibus* which I cited earlier). Crafting such markers or *notationes* is a fundamental tool of memory craft, and is counselled by all writers on the subject.

---

available (Hyde Park, NY, 2006). See M. Carruthers, *The Craft of Thought* (Cambridge, 1998), pp. 62–6.

15 See M. Carruthers, *The Book of Memory* (Cambridge, 1990), esp. pp. 80–96, and Yates, pp. 24–31. Yates thought that the category of *memoria verborum* was presented by the *auctor ad Herennium* as an alternative to *memoria rerum*, as a technique for memorizing every word of a prepared speech (pp. 24–5) *instead of* its subject-matters.

Nota is a common term in all the arts of the trivium. The general term means simply a 'marker', a sign placed against a text to distinguish it, locate it, and call it to mind. Quintilian describes the use of *notae* in rhetoric during his discussion of rhetorical *memoria*: one should mark matters that one has particular difficulty remembering, or that one particularly wants to remember, with *notae* of a distinctive character. A single *nota* can mark a lengthy text, or a complex subject. An orator's *notae* mark the subjects of his oration in their appropriate order so that he may easily digress and yet return to his planned topics.[16] In this way, *notae* share one essential characteristic with alphabetical letters: they are the means of calling to mind things that are not immediately present to the senses in forms that can be made into the sort of *imago* which the brain can use in thinking.

Yet in the end, rhetorical *notae* are not like letters. They are not writing, even though some systems can share some features with the *litterae* of writing systems. The *notae* of memory function as abbreviations and prompts. Unlike graphemes and other sorts of writing, they are not primarily representational symbols. This is clear in the teaching of ancient and medieval writers. Memory images are not said to symbolize content at all, in our sense. Rather, they lead to and unlock content already laid away like sorted coins in the cells of memory. Quintilian makes the point plainly: "If some things do not stick easily in the mind, it is quite useful to attach some marks [*adponere notas*] to them, the recall of which will warn and jog the memory ... But if a student is slow at this, let him use the further device (which is quite a useful contribution of the Art of Memory) of suiting his marks to the ideas which he is liable to forget – an anchor ... if he has to speak about a ship, or a javelin if it is about a battle. [Signs] are very effective – and one memory leads to another – just as a ring put on a different finger or tied with a thread reminds us of why we did these things."[17]

In both grammar and rhetoric the craft of making markers, the *ars notaria*, that was taught in connection with the editing, transcription, and transmission of verbal material in antiquity and later, was regarded as the ultimate form of *notae*. But there are many sorts of *notae*–*nota* being a big, baggy word, whose many applications are not completely compatible in all details. That fount of all early medieval knowledge, Isidore of Seville, distinguished among several kinds of *notae*.[18] There are the Tironian *notae*, the shorthand system for whole words and

---

16 *Inst. orat.* XI. 2. 29–30; trans. D. A. Russell, Loeb Classical Library (London, 2001), from the edition of M. Winterbottom (Oxford, 1970). I have quoted throughout from this translation. Quintilian quotes Cicero (*De oratore* II. 358) that "we use the Sites [memory loci] as our wax tablet, the Symbols as our letters [*simulacris pro litteris utamur*]"(*Inst. orat.* XI. 2. 22), the model also used in the *Rhet. ad Her.* III.17.30 (a work Quintilian likely did not directly know).

17 *Inst. orat.* XI. 2. 29. Russell translates Quintilian's *signa* as 'Symbols', which I have changed to the more neutral 'signs'. Since at least Coleridge, 'symbol' has been fraught with literary connotations not appropriate to Quintilian's usage here.

syllables, used by notaries transcribing oral proceedings. The medieval scholastic system of abbreviations is an heir to this system.

Isidore also characterizes as *notae* the acronymic 'juridical notes', such as SPQR or RP (*res publica*). Also 'digital *notae*', hand gestures used for speech in conditions of silence, such as those of soldiers or monks, and *notae litterarum* or cypher writing. But the system to which he gives the greatest attention is *notae sententiarum*, the critical marks that ancient editors used to punctuate and annotate their texts. Many of these served the functions we still associate with punctuation. Some served an editorial function, to indicate missing or faulty text. But a number of them were used to mark ambiguous or difficult language: for example where a word could have several senses, or where the language was particularly obscure and doubtful. They were also used to indicate quotations from sources. In other words, the *notae sententiarum* are not solely grammatical and editorial, but can point up a work's rhetoric too, the figures that produce difficulty and dubious meaning.

In addition to their place in mnemotechnical study, the words *notae* and *notationes* were used in rhetoric also as the name for several topics of verbal *brevitas*. In rhetoric, brevity (abbreviation) is paired with amplification: matters presented in a topic of brevity invite – even require – amplification. Cicero used *notatio* as a name for what was also called *etymologia*, those extraordinary rhetorical etymologies in which a word is divided and twisted and shifted in many ways in order to gather in a host of far-fetched associations to be amplified in a speech. The word *notatio* was used as well for the topic called 'character', such as the stereotypes of the Seven Deadly Sins or of Youth and Old Age. This sort of *notatio* presents a lively picture of a complex concept, frequently used to introduce a passage in which the various characteristics of the *imago* are amplified with gloss and commentary. The pictures of the various liberal arts in Martianus Capella's fantastic dream of *The Marriage of Mercury and Philology* were favorite medieval examples: John of Salisbury uses them to introduce his discussion of the various arts, for example Dialectic, who carries both a serpent and wooden moulds (*formulae*). The serpent may bite the unlearned and incautious, while the malicious (*improbi*) are shaped and corrected by the forms of reasoning.[19]

---

[18] Isidore of Seville, *Etymologiarum libri* I. 21–6; ed. W. M. Lindsay, 2 vols (Oxford, 1911).

[19] John of Salisbury, *Metalogicon*, III.10 (trans. D. D. McGarry [Berkeley, 1962] p. 192; eds J. B. Hall and K. S. B. Keats-Rohan, CCCM 98 [Turnhout, 1998]), referring to Martianus Capella, *De nuptiis philologiae et Mercurii* IV. 328. An interesting change has occured between Martianus's original and John of Salisbury's account of it. In Martianus, Dialectic carries tablets on which appropriate formulae are written in the wax; John, perhaps struggling with an inadequate text, seems to imagine forms like those used to shape things like cheeses, a possible meaning of *formula* at the time.

Plate 2 shows a page from Cambridge, Fitzwilliam Museum MS 11, which makes use of specifically mnemonic sorts of *notae*. The manuscript, a Bible in figures (*figurata*), is one of three exemplars still extant; nothing about the early provenance of any of them can now be traced, though they all appear to be German in origin, and from the later fifteenth century, indeed from about the same time and roughly in the same locations as the more famous compendium of such images, the *Rosarium,* assembled by Georg Simler and printed (twice) in 1502.[20] They all are in a genre of Gospels and Epistles with mnemonic images, designed to be used by preachers needing to invent sermons. Fitzwilliam 11 is small enough to be easily carried about by an individual. Each page in the book is divided into a grid of ten places. These contain pictures of the chapters of the Gospels in numbered order – Plate 2 shows John chapters 1–10. Each cell is identified by the *incipit* of the chapter written at the top. The main matters of the chapter are then mapped out in *notae*, in this case a visual image which draws to mind either its chief words or general themes. So, in the location for chapter one, the titulus *In principio erat* is written across the top. The chapter images are an eye, a dove, an unlaced shoe, a pointing finger, and in the corner a large stone, and a tree, each image pointing in this case to specific language in the text. The eye prompts the words 'vidimus gloriam eius' (v. 14); the dove descending is the Spirit (v. 32); the unlaced shoe 'ut solvam eius corrigiam calciamenti' (v. 27); the pointing finger to 'ecce agnus Dei' (v. 29), all parts of the story of Jesus's baptism. The calling of the first disciples at the end of chapter one is recalled by the rock for Peter (v. 42), and the tree recalls Nathaniel, whom Jesus saw under a fig tree ('vidi te sub ficu', v. 48). It is interesting that all except the first of these images cue words occurring after the best-known part of chapter one, its first fourteen verses, which even a dunce could be expected to know off by heart.

The *notae* for chapter two, *Et tertia die nuptiae sunt*, are linked to its two chief events (the wedding at Cana and the cleansing of the temple). The cell for chapter three, *Erat autem homo ex*, which concerns Jesus's conversation with Nichodemus, contains four images: a water jug for 'renatus fuerit ex aqua et Spir-

---

[20] These books have been studied by J. M. Massing, 'Late Medieval Mnemonic Bibles', in J-J Berns and W. Neuber (eds), *Ars memorativa: zur kulturgeschichtlichen Bedeutung der Gedächtniskunst 1400- 1750* (Tübingen, 1993), pp. 101–15. The xylographic *ars memorandi [ewangelistarum]*, was expanded with verses from various sources and typeset, with woodcuts, in 1502, and reprinted several times after that. The expanded version is called *Roseum memoriale* or *Rosarium* or *Rationarium evangelistarum*, and, depending on the edition, is attributed to Sebastian Brandt, Petrus Rosenheim of Melk, or Georg Simler, though the latter is the originator of the 1502 printed edition. There are also printings of Petrus Rosenheim's *Roseum* verses that do not include the woodcuts. The xylographic text is presented and its publication history discussed (with bibliography) by J. W. Halporn, in Carruthers and Ziolkowski (eds), *The Medieval Craft of Memory*, pp. 255–93.

itu' (5), a serpent "sicut Moses exaltavit serpentem" (14), a lamp 'lux venit in mundum' (19), and ascending feet for 'qui de celo venit' (31). And so on it goes, chapter by chapter, with images for every chapter of the four gospels and the Epistles, those materials from which sermons most commonly were preached. There are also recurring *notae* used as indexers to mark texts that are significant to major themes of the Gospels. The crown that marks the incident with the Samaritan (see the cell for chapter four, *Ut ergo cognovit Jesus quia*) indexes the passages wherein Jesus directly reveals his divine kingship (as in Jn. 4: 26).

This figure Bible would not be of much help to a beginner just learning the words of the text, though most modern scholars have assumed the pictures were made in the first instance for illiterate and novice readers, for children. Absolutely not. *Notae* like these – visual puns and thematic indexers – are useful to people who are already adept, who have the text reliably by heart and who therefore can recognize the visual cues. In short, they are useful for the invention of material from a store already secured by rote, and prepared for instant recollection by the elementary method of division, placement, and marking. In many cases (though not all), the matters selected for notation in this work have some liturgical significance, a feature important to a preacher making sermons appropriate to the church calendar. In fact, in the other two manuscripts of this figurated Bible, various additional texts and comments have been written by their users into the blank spaces around the images. And – tellingly – these ancillary texts are not the same in the two exemplars that have them. In other words, the users of the books have adapted the figures to their own meditations, understanding this book not as an authoritative text to be memorized but as a device for composing and meditation.

The requirement that marker-images be 'vivid' can be analysed further. At least by the time of Quintilian (first century AD), the stylistic quality of *enargeia* or 'distinctness' had become pretty much conflated with another category, *energeia*, used as a category of style by Aristotle in the *Rhetoric*, and defined by him as 'making the lifeless living' or 'vividness'. In memory work 'vividness' is an aspect of the requirement that the *imagines* be *agentes*, that is be doing something, engaged in activity.

Plate 3 shows a page from the Ormesby Psalter (Oxford, Bodleian Library, MS Douce 366, fol. 147v), a manuscript widely known for its lavish, intricate marginal and bas-de-page illumination. It demonstrates a number of qualities expressing stylistic vividness and distinction – 'distinction' being the quality that sets or 'marks out' a composition for both comprehension and recollection. 'Distinguishing' one's texts, in an idiom current from late antiquity, meant to correct, punctuate, and mark them up for further reading. But the character of such reader-friendly 'distinguishing' (*distinctio*) varies considerably during the Middle Ages, and indeed varies even from book to book. Few other aspects of making a book are as readily influenced by (and influence) taste and judgment. The Ormesby Psalter well displays the East Anglian taste for what Margaret Rickert memorably described as a "variety of grotesques which mingle on equal terms with the denizens of field and forest, and which often, especially in the later examples, tend to become gross in size and coarse in humour."[21] Indeed. That taste is on display as well in a treatise composed not long after the Ormesby Psalter was made (in two campaigns, c. 1310 and c. 1325, in the diocese of Norwich).[22]

Applying the qualities of *enargeia* and *distinctio* to making images for subject-matters in his treatise *De memoria artificiali adquirenda* (On acquiring a trained memory) – composed a decade after the Ormesby Psalter was completed, in the diocese of Lincoln, probably while its author was still at Oxford – Thomas Bradwardine gives some examples of how to make vivid groups in a set of backgrounds.[23] He is making a set of *notationes*, images which can serve to mark whatever content one may choose to link to them. Bradwardine does not assign any specific content to these images; they are examples rather than prescriptions. His first example, chosen because these *notae* were so very familiar a part of the rote vocabulary of a basic medieval education, is the Zodiac:

---

[21] M. Rickert, *Painting in Britain: The Middle Ages*, Pelican History of Art (Baltimore, 1954), p. 138.

[22] L. F. Sandler, *Gothic Manuscripts, 1285–1385*, A Survey of Manuscripts Illuminated in the British Isles V, 2 vols (London, 1986), no. 43. Sandler comments that the imagery of this book seems "purposely arbitrary, intended to surprise and delight because of its absurdity" (vol. 2, p. 49): such arbitrariness, surprise, and humour are among the hall-marks of images especially in the Herennian tradition of mnemonic advice, which dominated in university curricula of dialectic as well as rhetoric; see J. O. Ward, *Ciceronian Rhetoric in Treatise, Scholion and Commentary*, Typologie des sources du moyen âge (Turnhout, 1995), pp. 182–92, and Carruthers in Cox and Ward, *The Rhetoric of Cicero*. L. F. Sandler has suggested that Bradwardine was likely to be working within the same aesthetic ambiance as the artists of some of the Bohun manuscripts: see her 'Political Imagery in the Bohun Manuscripts', in A. S. G. Edwards (ed.), *Decoration and Illustration in Medieval English Manuscripts* (London, 2002), pp. 115–53, and in her essay 'Gone Fishing: Angling in the Fitzwilliam Bohun Psalter' in the present volume.

[23] Evidence for authorship and the manuscript sources are discussed in my edition of this text, M. Carruthers, 'Thomas Bradwardine: *De memoria artificiali adquirenda*', *The Journal of Medieval Latin* 2 (1992), pp. 25–43. My translation of it appears in Carruthers and Ziolkowski (eds), *The Medieval Craft of Memory*, pp. 205–14; all quotations are from this translation. It is likely in Oxford as in Paris that the Herennian art at this time was discussed as part of the teaching of natural philosophy (psychology), in lectures on Aristotle's *Parva naturalia*. Albertus Magnus and Thomas Aquinas discussed it in that context, not in rhetoric, and the only complete manuscript of the Bradwardine treatise is part of a book of natural philosophy (Cambridge, Fitzwilliam Museum, MS McClean 169). Bradwardine is unlikely to have commented on the *Rhetorica ad Herennium* except in such a context, and indeed this art of memory nowhere mentions the *Ad Herennium* by name.

Suppose that someone needs to have in mind the twelve signs of the zodiac, that is the Ram, the Bull, etc. So he might, if he wished to, make for himself in the front of the first location a very white ram with golden horns, standing up and rearing on his hind feet. And he might put a very red bull to the right of the ram, kicking the ram with his rear feet; standing erect, the ram with his right foot might kick the bull in his large and super-swollen testicles, causing a copious effusion of blood. And by means of the testicles one will recall that it is a bull, not a castrated ox or a cow.

In a similar manner, a woman may be placed before the bull as though laboring in birth, and in her uterus as if ripped open from her breast may be figured coming forth two most beautiful twins, playing with a horrible, intensely red crab, which holds captive the hand of one of the little ones and thus compels him to weeping and to such signs, the remaining child wondering yet nonetheless touching the crab in a childish way. Or the two twins might be placed there being born not of a woman but from the bull in a miraculous manner, so that the principle of economy of material may be observed. To the left of the ram a dreadful lion might be placed, who with open mouth and rearing on its legs attacks a virgin, beautifully adorned, tearing her garments. With its left foot the ram might inflict a wound to the lion's head. The virgin might hold in her right hand the scales, for which might be fashioned a balance-beam of silver with a cord of red silk, and weights of gold; on her left may be placed a scorpion horribly stinging her so that her whole arm is swollen; and also she could strive to balance the scorpion in the aforementioned scales.

These are certainly active images, *imagines agentes*, kicking, stinging, biting, and generally carrying on in the manner we have become familiar with from many margins in medieval books of materials intended for meditational reading. The margins of the page shown in Plate 3 are filled with such linking images – the scrolling of the foliage, the hybrid creatures (themselves linkages of different materials, human and animal), in the bas-de-page the two hair-pulling wrestlers on beasts that also are biting one another, and animals ride and hunt one another across the top margin. The ways in which such images are made to connect to one another, sometimes violently and sometimes scatalogically, give visual presence in the book to the requirement of linking, grouping, and 'collecting', which is prerequisite to the recollection of meditation. A book motivated by a wholly different taste can achieve the same effect by different means: an example is the recurring motif of linked items including pearls, breads, pilgrim badges, and fish which shapes many of the page borders in the Hours of Catherine of Cleves (New York, Pierpont Morgan Library, MSS 917 and 945). For meditation is an activity that is truly mind-*full*, it draws things in. The traditions of western monasticism are not about emptying thought but rather channeling and directing it for purposes of inventive contemplation. *Meditatio* is not a concept developed solely in monasticism; in Roman rhetoric *meditatio* was the inventive phase of composition.[24]

[24] The relationships of meditation, recollection, and invention are discussed at length in

Agent images also require activity from the reader and viewer and listener. In a passage that has become famous as a rare statement of medieval aesthetic that is not primarily ethical, Richard de Fournival, a canon of Amiens cathedral in the thirteenth century (d. 1260), wrote in the preface to his *Bestiaires d'Amours*, that all vivid language has both *painture* and *parole*, for it has *parole* in the words being read aloud and *painture* both in the paintings of the book and in the vivid pictures which those words and paintings cause the audience to see in their minds as well as hear with their ears:

> When one sees painted a story, whether of Troy or something else, one sees those noble deeds which were done in the past exactly as though they were still present. And it is the same thing with hearing a text, for when one hears a story read aloud, listening to the events one sees them in the present.[25]

Plate 4 shows an opening of the Hastings Hours, made for Lord Hastings in Flanders in about 1480 (London, BL, Add. MS 54782, ff. 55v–56). The text on the recto is a memorial of St. Thomas Becket, the picture on the verso shows his martyrdom. Together they present the common aesthetic principle articulated by Richard de Fournival, for the verso demonstrates the *painture* in the text, the text the *parole* in the picture. The floral margins with nectar-sucking butterflies show a basic trope of meditative reading as gathering nectars from the flowers of text in order to compose the honey of meditative prayer. Margins in other books showing hunting (and fishing) scenes also incorporate a common trope for memory, for recollection is an activity of investigation, as in the passage I quoted earlier from Augustine's *Confessions*, and *investigare* involves tracking down the prey one seeks by means of its *vestigia* or markers. An excellent example (Plate 3) is the hunt in the top margin of folio 147v of the Ormesby Psalter.

Another requirement for effective memorability is that images be made unfamiliar. This is an aspect of making oneself mindful of the book one is reading. 'Difficulty' is a virtue in medieval aesthetic, for it concentrates the mind, requiring

---

The Craft of Thought. Returning to Bradwardine gives me the pleasurable opportunity to acknowledge my large intellectual debts to my colleague, Lucy Freeman Sandler, whose unparalleled knowledge of English manuscripts and sense of fun has provided me with many fresh examples of all these master tropes, and who first encouraged me to consider how Bradwardine's memory text might reflect real artistic practices with which the author was likely familiar. Bradwardine himself in this text invites his students to use images painted in churches and in books as models of memory-images.

25 Richard de Fournival, *Li Bestiaires d'amours*, ed. C. Segré (Milan, 1957); translated by J. Beer, *Master Richard's Bestiary of love and response* (Berkeley, 1986). A number of scholars have studied the aesthetic suppositions presented by this text, including V. A. Kolve, *Chaucer and the Imagery of Narrative* (Stanford, 1984); E. Sears, 'Sensory Perception and its Metaphors in the Time of Richard of Fournival,' in *Medicine and the Five Senses*, eds W. F. Bynum and R. Porter (Cambridge, 1993), pp. 17–39 ; S. Huot, *From Song to Book* (Ithaca, 1987); and Carruthers, *The Book of Memory*.

one's ingenuity and creative attentiveness. Both the Apocalypse and the Song of Songs became favored texts for meditation in part because of their vivid but difficult language. Obscurity in the Bible is valued just because it affords such a delightfully hard chew: this is evident in Augstine's comments on the vivid obscurity of Song of Songs 4: 2: "Your teeth are like a flock of shorn ewes, that have come up from the washing, all of which bear twins, and not one among them is sterile." Augustine commented:

> I don't know how it is, but I find it more delightful to contemplate the saints when I see them as the Church's teeth that cut people off from their errors, and after softening up their hardness by biting them off and chewing them transfer them into its body. I also get enormous pleasure from recognizing who the shorn ewes are … But why I should see this with greater pleasure than if no such comparison were forthcoming from the divine books, it is hard to say.[26]

His delight is intellectual, finding and recognizing the familiar in obscurity, which is the pleasure of most indirect language.

Such rhetorical difficulty and obscurity can reside in page layouts too, which achieve a similar goal. Rote-retained language like that of the psalms is refreshed by being made obscure. As the monks knew well and taught their successors, tedium (*acedia*) is a great enemy of effective prayer. Plate 5 shows the famous Beatus page in the Ormesby Psalter (fol. 9v), made during its second campaign of illustration, around 1325. Even the most evident texts are de-familiarized by a layout like this. The letters on this page are hard to find, even to see, let alone to read. The recto page of this opening gives the words again, but in writing that is much easier to read. The contrast helps to emphasize the extreme difficulty of the words and the attention needed to make profitable sense of them.

There is no better de-familiarizing device than laughter (though fear and surprise are equally as good). Thanks in part to Umberto Eco's *The Name of the Rose*, medieval clerics have a reputation for sour sobriety that is better suited to Cotton Mather's puritans (as presented by Nathaniel Hawthorne). The evident humour in manuscript margins must be the work, we are told, of anti-establishment clerics and rebellious scribes. I doubt it. Bradwardine's memory treatise is filled with very funny, lively images, and no-one could call him a secret rebel. An example taken from his advice on making 'images for words' makes the point. Bradwardine deliberately has chosen a topic that is non-lectionary, secular, and entirely specific. It can thus only serve as an example, and could not be cribbed for other occasions. Pedagogically, this is an effective way to force a student to apply the method, not just to repeat the illustration. Suppose, he says, your sermon topic is the following sentence (he is alluding to the victory of the English over the Scots at the sec-

---

[26] Augustine, *De doctrina christiana* II. 7; ed. J. Martin, CCSL 32 (Turnhout, 1962); translated by E. Hill, *Teaching Christianity* (Hyde Park, NY, 1996).

ond battle of Berwick in 1333): 'Benedictus Dominus qui per regem Anglie Berwicum fortissimum et totam Scotiam subiugavit.' ('Blessed be the Lord who by means of the English king subjugated most mighty Berwick and all Scotland'.) You might proceed to fix the syllables of this sentence in your mind in this manner:

> For the first phrase, if you know someone named Benedict, or even Saint Benedict the Abbot, place him at the front of the first location; and if you have a lord you know, whom you just call "dominus," not using his actual name, place him injured in the face, pulled by the hair, mangled, or, in some way touched by the right hand of Benedict;[27] or you might place there Saint Dominic or Emperor Domitian or someone known to you called by a similar name. For the third word and the fourth, which are monosyllables, proceed according to the technique for syllables; or for "qui" place a very white cow with very large very red teats, erect upon her hind legs, whose right front foot Benedict might hold with his left hand as though dancing with her. For indeed, a cow is called "qui" in northern English. In addition the cow, in a strange manner, holds in her left front foot a partridge [*perdix*], which will give the word "per" to your memory.
>
> Then in the foreground of the second location you should bring together a king, resplendent in a crown and the other tokens of royal majesty, or if you should know well any king, or someone called or surnamed King, or one who in some game was a king, place him there, and let him hold in his right hand an eel [*anguilla*] wriggling about greatly, which will give you "England" [*Anglia*]. And in his left hand he might hold a bear by the tail or foot, which in English would signify the two first syllables of the word "Berwicum," and consequently the whole. From the other side of the bear might come mighty Samson or a lion, and strike that bear; and so this will figure to you "most mighty" [*fortissimum*]. Finally, the rest of this text can be fashioned in a third location in a similar manner, by placing there someone named Thomas, with his right hand subduing like a beast either a Scot or someone so named or surnamed, or someone whom you know to have campaigned vigorously in Scotland; and placing in his left hand an impressive yoke. This technique is for remembering material presented audibly, but certainly for remembering visual matter, such as recalling written things, one may make use of a similar method.

Bradwardine himself preached a victory sermon after the battle of Crécy (1346). If he used this technique to remember his topic sentence on that occasion, he must have had a good time preparing it, though no trace remains in the official Latin version which has survived for us. The practical advantage of this lively method lies in its unique memorability. Having fixed one's topics in order, one can digress with confidence, knowing that, with such a set of vivid images, one would always find

---

[27] In comments from the floor when this paper was read, Dr. Phillipa Hardman of Reading University suggested a possible trilingual pun visualized in the image of 'Benedictus' wounding a lord: French *blessé* (wounded) is a homonym of English *blessed*, the meaning of Latin *benedictus*.

one's way back to the main matter and on to the next quickly and securely, and also would know when one was finished, probably the most important thing to recognize when one is speaking *ex tempore*.

The craft of memory, like its successor investigative arts, including systematic logic, was not fundamentally just an overly complicated procedure for preparing to pass examinations or for memorizing random facts or lengthy texts. Its principles are in fact ill-suited to rote retention and repetition, as people who have written about it have been pointing out for over two thousand years. Perhaps we should finally listen to them. For these authors and their students, 'mnemonics' was a craft for the creation of new knowledge, and for investigating difficult subjects in the forum of debate and commentary. The concepts of place and marker-images were basic to it, because the secure ordering of material in places gave one the flexibility and security necessary to *make something out of* the matters one had learned, whether in the form of lengthy texts or of long lists of historical facts. Manuscript paintings such as the ones illustrated in this essay can imply a whole science of recollection and a comprehensive investigative method. They are gate-houses of the mind for those with the knowledge to use them, those skilled in the arts of memory and possessing the keys of study which those arts provided.

Powerful Impressions:
Symbols of Office and Authority on Secular Seals

ADRIAN AILES

Most government departments today boast some form of logo or badge or symbol. Perhaps the most famous are the portcullis, as used by the houses of parliament, and the crown, as used by HM Revenues and Customs. Even MI5 has an attractive badge incorporating various symbols of government, an heraldic winged 'sea lion', and a *five*-petalled cinquefoil. This paper examines the way in which such symbols, usually heraldic, were employed on secular seals during the Middle Ages to represent an official duty or an administrative post at court or in central and local government.

The Sovereign in Sigillographic Splendour
The most obvious symbolic image of power and authority as represented on seals, and indeed elsewhere, was that of the high office of kingship as clearly portrayed on the double-sided great seals of western European monarchs from the eleventh century onwards. On one side the sovereign was displayed to all, magnificently attired and surrounded by his various symbols of office: crown, orb, and sword or sceptre, and sitting on his royal throne in divinely sanctioned splendour. This was the king very much 'in majesty', the fount of justice, dispenser of the law, supreme governor. On the reverse of the same seal he was usually shown in full armour on horseback – the mounted warrior and military leader, suzerain of his feudal host and defender of the realm, perhaps even, as in the case of William I, a conquering hero.[1] From the late eleventh century lesser men (though still high ranking) began to seal with a single-sided equestrian seal. During the course of the thirteenth century this purely military portraiture was in turn replaced by the knight's *alter ego* – a shield of arms which could symbolize not just his military power and authority but also family pride, feudal, marital and tenurial ties and alliances, patronage, and

---

[1]   For the king in majesty see B. Bedos Rezak, 'The King Enthroned, a New Theme in Anglo-Saxon Royal Iconography: the Seal of Edward the Confessor and its Political Implications', reprinted in eadem, *Form and Order in Medieval France* (Aldershot, 1993), pp. 53–88. For William I's seal see D. Bates, *William the Conqueror* (Stroud, 2004), pp. IV: 171–2. For both seals see M. T. Clanchy, *From Memory to Written Record*, 2nd edn (Oxford, 1993), pp. 310–12.

above all social status. Churchmen, too, portrayed themselves in the specific attributes of their authority: mitre, ecclesiastical vestments, holding their pastoral staff and sometimes gloves. And women were depicted on seals in their long aristocratic dresses and often holding a lily or hawk, symbols respectively of Mary and a noble lifestyle. But even here, amongst the non-combatants of society, heraldry was to intrude, though not to such a great extent.[2]

Devices borrowed from the English royal arms and various other symbols quickly came to symbolise key functions and positions held by officers or agents of the Crown as well as the offices and government departments they served. They are evident on four emerging classes of official seals during the middle ages: the deputed seals used in place of the great seal,[3] the more personal privy and signet seals of the sovereign,[4] the departmental seals of central government,[5] and, finally, the seals of local offices and officials.[6]

[2]   See, for example, Rezak, 'Women, Seals and Power in Medieval France, 1150–1350' reprinted in eadem, *Form and Order*, pp. IX: 61–82; and A. Ailes, 'Armorial Portrait Seals of Medieval Noblewomen: Examples in the Public Record Office', in *Tribute to an Armorist*, ed. J. Campbell-Kease (London, 2000), pp. 218–34.

[3]   During the twelfth and thirteenth centuries government departments such as the Exchequer and Chancery settled at Westminster, where they were staffed by their own bureaucrats and created their own records. They were also given a certain degree of autonomy made effective by possession of their own authenticating seals. Deputed great seals, used for convenience instead of the great seal appeared in the twelfth century. They approximated in size and form to the great seal itself portraying the king on one side, but on the reverse the heraldic symbols of his office, namely the royal arms.

[4]   The history of the single-sided privy and signet seals, the small personal seals of the sovereign can be traced back in this country to the intaglio counterseal used by John in the late twelfth century. Privy seals from the reign of Edward I onwards portrayed the royal arms whilst the earliest signet seals bore a variety of royal badges before settling for the familiar royal shield from the end of the reign of Richard II (*Guide to Seals in the Public Record Office* (London, 1968), p. 46; T. F. Tout, *Chapters in the Administrative History of Medieval England*, 6 vols (Manchester, 1920–33), 5, pls i–vi). Other signets were used, though their exact use is unknown. Edward III used a signet portraying a griffin (one of his many badges), whilst Henry V and VI used an eagle signet (*Guide to Seals*, p. 46 and n. 3 for examples). For Henry VI's eagle signet see 'Examples of Medieval Seals', *Archaeological Journal*, 18 (1861), pp. 47–59 (49–55).

[5]   From the fourteenth century there emerges another group of smaller one-sided official seals: the departmental seals of central government. Like the privy and signet seals they sometimes acted as cogs turning even greater cogs, namely the great seal, in the ever-burgeoning machinery of central government. They often bore the emblems that came to be associated with their departments, emblems that were sometimes repeated on the personal seals of the officials that ran those departments.

[6]   As the Crown and central government spread their influence and power into the provinces so the seals of local office and their officials also began to adopt certain familiar images of royal power thereby sending out strong messages of royal and central authority.

Devices Portrayed

Five devices in particular were used. The first, not surprisingly, was the royal arms, three lions passant guardant or three 'leopards', as they were called when shown full-faced. Often just a single leopard or a leopard's head was borrowed from the arms to convey much the same message as the complete coat. The second was the head or bust of the king. The third, a crown, sometimes appearing on the head of the king, sometimes alone, and sometimes accompanied by another royal symbol or other object. The fourth came to represent government security, the key. And the last was a castle or fortified gatehouse, a symbol increasingly adopted by the king's representative in the shires, his sheriff. Other offices, of course, brought with them their own official seals, but only in one or perhaps two cases (as we shall see later) did the seal bear a device that was to have a lasting impact on the iconography of government.

Royal Arms and Lions' Heads

John Cherry, in a previous Harlaxton symposium, has already demonstrated the use made of the royal arms on seals and elsewhere (such as weights) as a key symbol of the Crown. They not only represented the person and power of the king but also his wider governance and jurisdiction, especially with regard to government administration.[7] The same arms also became powerful iconographic weapons of lordship and dominion.

As far back as the very dawn of heraldry the lion was employed by those in official positions close to the king and serving within his household and court. Reginald II, count of St Walery, was a steward to the future Henry II before his accession in 1154 and after that he was his Justiciar for Normandy. His arms are unknown, but he countersealed with a lion device.[8] Another trusted friend who held high station within the royal household was Warin FitzGerold. He was a chamberlain to both Henry II and Richard I and sealed with the arms two lions passant guardant, arms that Henry II almost certainly bore. From 1200 to 1215 Hubert de Burgh as a chamberlain to King John sealed with a shield of arms bearing three lions passant – a direct reference not only to his royal patronage but also to the royal office he now held. Later he bore the personal lozengy arms more closely associated with him as depicted on his seal as earl of Kent.[9]

---

[7]   J. Cherry, 'Heraldry as Decoration in the Thirteenth Century', in *England in the Thirteenth Century: Proceedings of the 1989 Harlaxton Symposium*, ed. W. M. Ormrod (Stamford, 1991), pp. 123–34 (131–2); and compare C. Beaune, *The Birth of an Ideology: Myths and Symbols of Nations in Late Medieval France*, trans. S. R. Huston, ed. F. L. Cheyette (California, 1991), p. 203.

[8]   P. Bony, *Un Siecle de Sceaux Figurés 1135–1235* (Paris, 2002), p. 45 and Fig. 169 where dated c.1160; J. H. Round, *Calendar of Documents Preserved in France* (London, 1899), 1, p. 374 where dated between 1144 and 1151; A. Ailes, *The Origins of the Royal Arms of England: Their Development to 1199* (Reading, 1982), pp. 60–1.

We know that in the thirteenth century a simple shield of three leopards replaced the *majesty* portrait of the king on Henry III's double-sided seal for Gascony and very probably also on his Exchequer seal.[10] From the reign of his son and successor, Edward I, the same arms replaced the king's *equestrian* portrait on his great seal for Scotland and very probably that for Ireland.[11] His depiction as a military leader was thus replaced by his symbols of overlordship, namely his arms of dominion and authority, the faceless symbols of a powerful occupying force. From at least the reign of Edward III the same combination of majesty portrait and royal arms followed on the seals of the central common law courts at Westminster, where the king continued to be seen in almost Christ-like pose as God's representative, the supreme law-giver and fount of all wisdom and justice.[12] The royal arms also appeared on the king's privy and signet seals as symbols of those royal offices, as we shall see later.

On a local level, the two-sided customs seals belonging to the king's custom houses, and 'cocket' seals introduced for the delivery of wool and hides for various towns after the levy of customs in 1275, initially bore no image of the king at all. Instead, they repeated on both sides the king's *alter ego* – his three leopards depicted either on a shield or covering the face of the seal (Plate 1).[13] The matri-

[9]   *Catalogue of Seals in the Department of Manuscripts in the British Museum*, ed. W. de G. Birch, 6 vols (1887–1900), [hereafter BM plus number of seal] BM 7943; 'On the Seals of Hubert de Burgh and his Son John', *Proceedings of the British Archaeological Association*, 14 (1858), pp. 282-83; P 143. For his later seal: BM 5769.

[10] P. Chaplais, *Piers Gaveston: Edward II's Adoptive Brother* (Oxford, 1994), p. 37 and n. 77; Hilary Jenkinson, 'The Great Seal of England: Deputed or Departmental Seals', *Archaeologia*, 85 (1936), pp. 293–338 (297, 308, 313, pls lxxxiv (1, 2), lxxxix (1, 2)). For Gascony see also M. Vale, *English Gascony, 1399–1453* (Oxford, 1970), pp. 80–1, 107–8.

[11] Jenkinson, 'Great Seal of England: deputed or departmental', pp. 319, 324, pl. xcv (1, 2). The situation for Wales was slightly different. From 1284 there were two deputed great seals for the principality, one for the north and one for the south. Certainly in the reigns of Henry VI the king was depicted riding on the obverse whilst his majesty portrait was replaced on the seal for north Wales by the arms of that division and on his seal for South Wales by the arms of England. See Jenkinson, 'Great Seal of England: deputed or departmental', p. 325ff, and *Guide to Seals*, p. 42.

[12] Jenkinson, 'Great Seal of England: deputed or departmental', pp. 299–303, pls lxxxv (1, 2), lxxxvi (1, 2, 3).

[13] Although impressions can be dated to Edward II's reign (BM 1159–66 and TNA SC 13/D88) the matrices were probably produced in the reign of his father (A B. Tonnochy, *Catalogue of British Seal dies in the British Museum* (London, 1952), nos 31–46 and Cherry, 'Heraldry as Decoration', pp. 131–2; see also P. D. A. Harvey and Andrew McGuiness, *A Guide to British Medieval Seals* (London, 1996), pp. 41–2. Cocket seals were certainly in use in Edward I's reign (T. Madox, *History and Antiquities of the Exchequer of the Kings of England*, 2 vols (London, 1769), 1, pp. 782–3). For their use see T. H. Lloyd, *The English Wool Trade in the Middle Ages* (Cambridge, 1977), p. 62 and see also *Calendar of Close Rolls 1302–7*, p. 137, and *Calendar of*

ces of these customs and cocket seals, almost identical in design, appear to have been produced centrally. The heraldry here was again a powerful reminder of royal authority and control, an important consideration for a duty that was to become the source of a permanent regular addition to the Crown's revenue. Seals of towns, ports and their officials might also include the royal arms on their seals. Medieval examples include Dorchester, Helston, Lyme Regis, Rochester, Shrewsbury, Windsor and London.[14]

From at least the early thirteenth century individual leaders could be referred to by the devices they bore on their shields. Edward I, for example, was known as the 'leopard'.[15] In time such devices came to represent not only the person but also the nation they led. In England a single lion shown either in full or just its head was often adopted on several official seals as a symbol of central or local government control. Under Edward III the reverse of customs and cocket seals, such as that for Boston, often bore a leopard in conjunction with a bust of the king (Plate 2).[16] Following a statute in 1369 special seals were made for new staples for the weighing of wool, woolfells, and leather in various towns. Some of these portrayed woolsacks, but those for Bristol, Exeter, Poole and Southampton included a lion or lion's face.[17]

The seal (1367) of Peter de Belassis, constable of the staple of Lincoln, depicts a shield bearing a merchant's mark incorporating a leopard's face, and the mid-fifteenth century seal of the mayor of the staple of Westminster depicts a leopard's face between two fleurs de lis.[18]

Following the statute of Acton Burnell, *de Mercatoribus*, in 1283 and the *Statutum Mercatorum* two years later, seals were ordered for the recognisance of debts. These statute merchant seals, as they were called, proved remarkably uniform in design, incorporating (from 1312 and perhaps earlier) a bust of the king usually accompanied by a leopard and a castle or castles.[19] Examples can be seen

---

    Patent Rolls 1313–17, p. 4. Edward's seal for the port of London bore the royal arms on a lozenge (Tonnochy, *Seal-dies*, no. 34, BM 1157, cf. TNA SC 13/F163).

14   BM 4870, 4986, 5146, 5331, 5392, 5512, 5068.

15   A. Ailes, 'Heraldry in Medieval England: Symbols of Politics and Propaganda', in *Heraldry, Pageantry and Social Display in Medieval England*, ed. P. Coss and M. Keen (Woodbridge, 2002), pp. 83–104 (85).

16   Boston: TNA E 122/220/51, SC 13/D89, E 43/649.

17   J. H. Bloom, *English Seals* (London, 1906), pp. 234–5. Bristol: BM 4700; Exeter: BM 4922, Southampton: BM 5420.

18   R. H. Ellis, *Catalogue of Seals in the Public Record Office: Personal Seals*, 2 vols (London, 1978–81) [hereafter P and number of seal], P 1012; TNA C 148/26 [1467]; BM 1099, the matrix dates to Richard II's reign.

19   See *Proceedings of the Society of Antiquaries*, 2nd series, 7 (1877), pp. 107–19; 9 (1883), p. 253; 25 (1913), p. 160; Rowland Bretton, 'Seals of the Statute Merchant', *Coat of Arms*, 7 (1962–3), pp. 203–5, and 9, p. 114 ; Bloom, *English Seals*, pp. 233–4; W. de Gray Birch, *Seals* (London, 1907), pp. 68–9.

on seals of Bristol,[20] Northampton,[21] Coventry,[22] and London.[23] That for Gloucester places the lion on the king's chest.[24]

As already noted the three lions became closely associated with royal authority and from the early fourteenth century officials at court and in government occasionally appropriated the royal beast on their own seals, likewise to reflect their
prestigious station and loyalty to the Crown. For example, the 'secretum' or privy
seal of Ingelard de Warley, keeper of the Wardrobe, which he used in 1313, depicts
a cross with five leopards' heads on it between the hand of God, a leopard, a man's
head and a castle.[25] Twenty years later the privy seal of Richard Airmyn, keeper of
the House of Converts, also depicted a cross but with a single leopard's head at
the centre and a fleur de lis on each arm between the emblems of the four evangelists (Plate 3).[26] Walter de Weston, clerk of the works at the palace of Westminster from 1331 to1351, used an armorial seal depicting three crowns and, on a
chevron, the three lions of England.[27]

In 1342 John de Kermon, a clerk of the Exchequer, used a seal depicting a
traceried circle divided by a saltire fusily and in each of the four compartments a
leopard's face.[28] Two years later Ralph de Stafford held the office of Steward and
Marshal of the royal household. His official seal for that high office neatly com-

[20] TNA E 326/10809; BM 1066.
[21] TNA E 326/9225; BM 1081.
[22] BM 1071.
[23] BM 1080.
[24] TNA SC 13/D146; BM 1073.
[25] P 2215; R. C. Fowler, 'Seals in the Public Record Office', *Archaeologia*, 74 (1925), pp.
103–16, pls xxxi–xxv (p. 110) and cf. P 2214. See also Tout, *Chapters in the Administrative History of Medieval England*, 5, p. 135 n. 2. At the beginning of Edward II's
reign Ralph de Stokes, a clerk of the king's Wardrobe, sealed with a cross charged with
Christ's head at the centre and an eagle displayed on each arm; a lion's head denoting
his royal master and official position appears in each of the four spaces (TNA E 43/683).
The seal of John de Bansted, keeper of the king's Wardrobe, of the same date, depicts
a leopard of England walking past a tripartite bush (TNA E 43/7). And the seal [1312/13]
of Robert de Wodehouse, a controller of the Wardrobe depicts a leopard's head with
two bodies sitting in front of an oak tree (TNA E 43/9; DL 25/2184 [1344]); R. Ready,
'Note on the Fourteenth-Century Seal of Robert de Wodehouse', *Archaeological Journal*, 15 (1858), p. 289. William de Dalton, keeper of the Great Wardrobe, sealed [1354]
with a leopard of England with a saracen's head above, between two small roses (TNA
E 43/38).
[26] P 926.
[27] P 2230 [1341]; cf. earlier seal P 2229. For the clerks of the king's works see *The History
of the King's Works: vol. 1, The Middle Ages*, ed. R. A. Brown, H. M. Colvin, A. J. Taylor
(London, 1963), p. 170, and for Weston, p. 172. The crest of Henry de Walton, archdeacon of Richmond and keeper of the king's Wardrobe, as depicted on his seal dated
1359, is a leopard's head and neck (P 2205; Fowler, 'Seals in the PRO', p. 111).
[28] P 1621.

bined personal and official family heraldry by placing the Stafford chevron between the three lions of England.[29] And at the other end of the scale, even Edward II's larderer could manage to combine a pictorial representation of the contents of his food store, namely a leaping dolphin, with a royal lion's face beneath.[30]

As such men 'borrowed' from the royal arms to reflect their official duties and positions so the leopard became more and more associated with the court and government. As Caroline Shenton has noted in her essay on Edward III's use of the leopard symbol, when in 1363 goldsmiths were compelled to use a maker's mark, the leopard's head they adopted became known as 'the king's mark'.[31] The same was true in the provinces and, indeed, overseas. The official seals of sheriffs, the king's representative in the counties, occasionally included a lion's face.[32] Edward III's seal for the office of aulnager (who stamped the cloth to prove that it was of the required size and quality) for Winchester depicted a lion's face and below a fleur de lis, symbols of both his kingdoms.[33] As we have already seen, the 1367 seal of Peter de Belassis, as constable of the staple of Lincoln, incorporated a leopard's face, and the mid-fifteenth century seal of the mayor of the staple of Westminster depicted a leopard's face between two fleurs de lis. During the Hundred Years War the lion of England was frequently referred to in propagandist literature and occasionally appeared on Anglo-Gallic coins. Not surprisingly, it was introduced into the civic seals of French towns occupied by the English as a potent symbol of foreign domination.[34] Occasionally it appeared on the seals of officials abroad. For example, the seal dated 1344 of Nicholas de Huggate, the king's receiver for the duchy of Aquitaine, depicts the miracle of his namesake, St Nicholas, who stands on a couchant leopard,[35] while the mid-fourteenth century seal of Richard de Ecclesall, treasurer of Calais, shows his arms surrounded by three roundels each containing a leopard's head. The symbolism, if not already obvious, is borne out by the seal legend: SCVTVM RICARDI CONSERVENT TRES LEOPARDI.[36]

---

[29] BM 819 and cf. 13641; Birch, *Seals*, p. 60.
[30] P 920 [1316]. Cf the seal [1327] of Benet de F(o)ulsham, pincernarius of the king which includes between two cloves a shield charged with three leopards' heads in bend (TNA E 43/618). The seal used by Robert de Wodehouse as clerk to the royal kitchen from the last few years of Edward I's reign features a pike and rod (TNA C 148/138, E 213/328).
[31] C. Shenton, 'Edward III and the Symbol of the Leopard', in *Heraldry, Pageantry and Social Display in Medieval England*, ed. Coss and Keen, pp. 69–81.
[32] P 1000.
[33] Tonnochy, *Seal-dies*, no. 52, p. 17.
[34] See Ailes, 'Heraldry in Medieval England', pp. 92–3 and refs cited there.
[35] P 1571.
[36] P 1325; TNA E 43/615 [1355], Fowler, 'Seals in the PRO', p. 113.

The King's Head

As already noted, statute merchant seals might include a bust of the king as well as his leopard symbol. The king's head would have been a familiar symbol of royal authority to all, having appeared for many years on the coins of the realm. Under Edward III the reverse or counter seals of customs and cocket seals such as those for Boston, which until then had only featured a leopard or leopards, began to portray the king's head or, in the case of Cornwall, possibly that of the duke (Plate 2).[37] Boroughs that were directly founded and enfranchised by the king such as Dartmouth or Winchester, might incorporate the royal effigy or the king's bust on their seals.[38] The reverse of the fourteenth-century seal of Dorchester in Dorset includes the head of the king surrounded by the legend CAPVT DOMINI EDWARDI REGIS ANGLIE.[39] The king's head was, as we shall see later, used on the official seals of the Exchequer of Receipt.

Crown

Closely connected to the king's head was his crown. This appeared as the main feature on the single-sided seals for the subsidies on cloth, such as in the fifteenth-century subsidies seal for Lincolnshire.[40] It also appears on the same seals adorning the king's head or accompanying the royal arms or other royal symbol.[41] The crowns depicted on William de Weston's seal alongside his three leopards may well allude to his royal patronage. However, the crowns used on the seals of the senior royal heralds, the kings of arms, almost certainly refer to their official post.[42] Needless to say the crown on, for example, signets of Richard II, symbolises the king's royal personage and office (Plate 4).[43] In Richard III's reign yeomen of the crown were to wear the crown in silver gilt on one shoulder as the king's insignia and, still today, the device symbolises government.[44]

Keys

A symbol that was adopted on official seals centrally, and to some extent locally, was the key or keys. Just as St Peter was given the keys of heaven by Christ to bind and unloose, so keys represented the ability to lock and unlock certain resources and power. The king's treasure, including his records like the Exchequer and Chancery rolls, was initially kept in portable locked chests, but in time permanent

[37] TNA SC 13/D89; E 43/649; BM 4842.
[38] Birch, *Seals*, p. 219. BM 4852 (Dartmouth).
[39] BM 4870.
[40] Tonnochy, *Seal-dies*, pp. lv, 11.
[41] Tonnochy, *Seal-dies*, p. lv.
[42] H. S. London, *The Life of William Bruges* (Harleian Society, 111–12, 1970), p. 95; BM 5098.
[43] Tout, *Administrative History*, 5, p. 202, pl. iv.
[44] R. Horrox, *Richard III: A Study of Service* (Cambridge, 1989), p. 245.

repositories had to be found. The Treasury of the Wardrobe and the Treasury of the Exchequer of Receipt were, therefore, housed in St Peter's Westminster Abbey doubtless still under lock and key. During the fourteenth and fifteenth centuries the seal of the office of the Treasury of the Exchequer of Receipt featured two keys either back to back or separated by the king's head. Sometimes they were accompanied by a small royal lion in base.[45] The seal of the Great Wardrobe in Edward II's reign featured two keys crossed in saltire (Plate 5).[46] That of the office of the Wardrobe under Edward II and Edward III featured either a key on its own, or a key or two crossed keys combined with a rod or wand of office, presumably that of the keeper.[47] The key is actually referred to in a somewhat enigmatic legend on the seal of William de Farlee, keeper of the Wardrobe, dated 1360.[48]

This idea of the key representing government security and control might be the reason for its appearing on the official seal of the chamberlain of Scotland in 1310, where it flanks the arms of England.[49] The St Peter connection is again borne out on the 1419 seal for the mayor of the staple of Westminster, which depicts two crossed keys between four woolpacks.[50] Here the keys once again neatly symbolise both government security and its Westminster location.

Castle

Another symbol that was adopted locally was the turreted castle or fortified gatehouse. From the early twelfth century this appeared on civic seals including that of York.[51] Henceforth it appeared on the seals of mayors, provosts, bailiffs and chamberlains.[52] However, it was probably best known for having regularly appeared from the early fourteenth century on the official seals of sheriffs. This was almost certainly because of the sheriff's role as constable of the county castle.[53]

[45]   TNA SC 13/A152, E 43/54; E 43/563; E 30/443 (BM 876); E 43/124. See *Guide to Seals*, p. 49.

[46]   TNA E 43/559.

[47]   TNA E 43/43, Fowler, 'Seals in the PRO', p. 111; TNA E 43/41; E 43/628; E 43/629; E 43/718.

[48]   TNA E 43/628. Fowler, 'Seals in the PRO', p. 111. The seal (1333) of Robert de Tauton, clerk of the Wardrobe, featured the head of Christ surrounded by various symbols including a key and a sword (P 2115) and that of Thomas Cross, keeper, dating to 1342 depicts the martyrdom of Becket with a bust of a praying figure accompanied by a key and a sword (P 1258). The signet (1407) of William Loveney, keeper of the Great Wardrobe, depicts a key (TNA E 43/50). See also H. Stanford London, 'Official Badges', *The Coat of Arms*, 4 (1956-58), pp. 99-100, and *PRO Guide to Seals*, p. 49 for further references.

[49]   BM 17231; cf. the seal of Henry son of Thomas the Marshal depicts two keys erect between two busts facing each other, and in base a lion (BM 17348).

[50]   TNA E 42/169.

[51]   BM 5542.

[52]   Mayor of Bedford BM 4617; provost of Exeter BM 4923; bailiffs of Colchester BM 4830; chamberlain of Norwich BM 5238; and cf. escheator of Northumberland BM 5228.

The castle was often depicted between the two initials of the sigillant's name such as in the seal (dated 1315) of Ralph Giffard, sheriff of Cambridgeshire and Huntingdonshire (Plate 6).[54]

Occasionally the seal also incorporated the sheriff's personal arms with or without the initials, as in the cases of Thomas de Rokeby, sheriff of Yorkshire, and Henry Sturmy, sheriff of Hampshire.[55]

Alternatively the castle might appear without initials but accompanied by some other subordinate charge such as a rabbit or fleur de lis.[56] Sometimes a sheriff would use the official seal of a predecessor even if the initials did not match his own name. The important factor was that all recognised this as the sheriff's seal. Thus William Carent, sheriff of Somerset and Dorset from 1427 to 1428, used the seal of his predecessor, Robert Hill, despite its letters R and H.[57] Sheriffs did, of course, have their own personal seals, usually armorial, which they sometimes used in an official capacity[58] and sometime alongside their official seal.[59]

Apart from these standard symbols, others were employed. In the reign of Richard II, John Archer, the king's archer, not surprisingly used arrowheads on his seal.[60] Adam de Bray, keeper of Edward II's horses, used a horseshoe on his seal, and William Marshal, keeper of Edward III's horses at Reading, depicted horseshoes on his arms.[61] From the late fourteenth century various admirals used ships displaying sails or either their own arms of those of their royal master. This striking image was to be replaced in the sixteenth century by the now familiar symbol of an anchor.[62]

[53] I am grateful to Mr Robert Kinsey for this suggestion.
[54] P 1444.
[55] P 1956; E 40/13641, and see C. H. Hunter-Blair, 'Armorials upon English Seals from the Twelfth to the Sixteenth Centuries', *Archaeologia*, 89 (1943), pp. 1-26, pls I–xvii (pl. xi (s)).
[56] TNA E 101/99/10; BM 5237, Birch, *Seals*, p. 217.
[57] P 1555.
[58] P 1588. For the personal seal of Thomas de Rokeby: P 1957.
[59] Seal [1332] of Peter de Saltmarsh sheriff of Yorkshire (TNA E 43/86).
[60] TNA E 231/396.
[61] TNA E 17/242/122, m.4; P 1716; and cf. Ralph the Farrier (TNA E 40/131 and 134).
[62] Certainly the case in Scotland (BM 14911 and H. Laing, *Ancient Scottish Seals* (Edinburgh, 1866), no. 494). The seal of the Navy Office in 1652 depicted an anchor between two smaller anchors (TNA SP 18/45, f. 131v). For English admirals: BM 1042, 1043, TNA E 30/333 (Edward earl of Rutland and Cork, 1397; see Fowler, 'Seals in the PRO', p. 115); TNA E 101/53/18 for Nicholas Carew, lieutenant of the admiralty in Devon and Cornwall. For John Holand, duke of Exeter (d. 1447). and Richard, duke of Gloucester, as admirals, see *Antiquaries Journal*, 27 (1947), pp. 86–7, and *Archaeologia*, 46 (1881), pp. 366–70. For badges concerned with the navy, including the anchor and ship, see London, 'Official Badges', pp. 93–100, and PRO *Guide to Seals*, p. 49.

That fearsome piece of underhand medieval weaponry, the caltrap, appears along with the three lions and the Tiptoft banner as a badge on the seal of the court of the marshalsea of the household in 1426, when the office was held by John Tiptoft.[63] And the exquisite fourteenth-century matrix of the coroner of the royal household, which today survives in the Society of Antiquaries, London, has for a device a wheel ensigned with a coronet, alongside a coroner's verge or staff of office; the coroner of the household was known as the coroner of the verge.[64] Foresters in the fifteenth century not surprisingly sealed using the device of a stag's head.[65]

On 22 December 1386 a certain Thomas Stokes was ordered to stand in the pillory for one hour. His offence was to pretend to be a taker of the ale for the king's household. As such he had visited several breweries and there marked several barrels full of ale with a mark called the 'arewehede' stating these barrels were for the king's household. Needless to say, he took money for these barrels. This dates the arrowhead or 'broad arrow' badge, one of the most endearing and enduring of official government symbols, to well before its government use by the Sydney family. In fact, the first extant example of its use as a household or government badge can be seen on the official seal of Richard de la Pole as the king's butler dating to as early as 1330 (Plate 7).[66]

As the Stokes episode proves, the broad arrow had very quickly come to symbolise a government office and its authority reminding those who saw it both then and, indeed, through many centuries to come of the same stark message: property of HM Government. It was thus one of a number of symbols of government office, both central and local, depicted on medieval seals. Some, like the broad arrow, have now disappeared but others, especially the crown, still exist – a tangible link with the past all too often replaced by the proverbial rubber stamp of bureaucracy or the ubiquitous logo so beloved by modernity.

[63] BM 820.
[64] H. S. Kingsford, *Seals* (London, 1923), p. 35; BM 821.
[65] London, 'Official Badges', p. 100. A hunting horn appears as a similar badge in manuscripts dating back to the thirteenth century.
[66] P 1890; H.S. London, 'The Broad Arrow as a Government Badge', *Coat of Arms*, 3 (1954–55), pp. 135–6; idem, 'Official Badges', p. 93, citing government use of the broad arrow badge in 1383.

Security and Safeguard:
Signs and Symbols on Boxes and Chests

ELIZABETH DANBURY

'Decus et tutamen' (an ornament and a safeguard) was the phrase chosen in 1983 to be engraved on the milled edge of certain designs of the new pound coins.[1] Security of currency – and the safeguarding of this and of other valuable objects – was and remains of vital importance to individuals, corporations and nations. For many centuries, when most buildings contained relatively little moveable furniture, some of the most important free-standing items, as well as some original parts of the architectural fabric were made or adapted to store precious or important objects such as money, jewellery, clothes, textiles, armour, sacramental objects and ecclesiastical treasures, as well as books and archives. Often, such furnishings were simple and undecorated, reflecting the practical purposes for which they were built, but some had markings, inscriptions or more elaborate embellishments and it is these decorations which are the subject of this paper.

Although most of the objects to be discussed are the chests and boxes in which documents and manuscripts were usually held, archives and books were also kept in wooden armoires or presses ('armoires' is the more commonly used term).

Armoires could be either free-standing or created out of the original fabric of a building.[2] The form of the free-standing armoire changed substantially during the Middle Ages. It began as a simple shelved or unshelved storage space. Later developments included a few drawers instead of shelves, open pigeonholes with no doors in front, or numerous drawers rather than just a few. Eventually the armoire was amalgamated with the open boards used to display plate and cups,

---

[1] The quotation comes from Virgil, *The Aeneid*, Book V line 262. For the coin, see http:www.royalmint.com/Corporate/BritishCoinage/CoinDesign/OnePoundDesigns.a spx (accessed September 2008).

[2] This paper owes much to: P. Eames, *Medieval Furniture: Furniture in England, France and the Netherlands from the Twelfth to the Fifteenth Century* (London, 1977), esp. pp. 1–54 and 108–80 (hereafter Eames). An armoire is the equivalent of the modern cupboard, but the term 'armoire' is used to avoid confusion with the medieval cupboard, which was a flat, open board on which cups and other plate were kept and displayed (Eames, p. 1).

and became the item of furniture known as a buffet, dressoir or dresser. Considerable money, skill and labour were expended on the making of armoires intended for the safekeeping of valuable books and records. The household accounts of Philip le Hardi, Duke of Burgundy, for the year 1364–5, include an entry for the making of three armoires to house the Duke's muniments:

> trois grans armaires de bois de chesne, bon et net, fendu à la resse, et icelles enfoncier et revestir de bonnes aiz de noier et de chesne, bien fenées et courroiées, pour metre en icelles les lettres et chartes qui souloient estre ou Tresor de Talent pour estre là à plus grant seurté et pur les veoir et avoir plus pretement toutes foiz qu'il sera mestier (three large armoires, well made and assembled, built-in and equipped with good shelves of walnut and oak and well banded with ironwork, for storing the letters and charters which used to be at the 'Tresor' of Talent castle. The archives to be kept in these armoires for greater security and so that they may be viewed and taken out more speedily whenever necessary).

These armoires were made by Belin d'Anchenoncourt, master carpenter of Dijon from 1348, who was appointed master of all carpentry works for the Duke of Burgundy in 1367.[3] The inventories of the Prior of Durham for 1446 likewise refer to 'unum Armariolum novum pro Computis conservandis' (one new armoire for storing accounts), while the Privy Purse expenses of Queen Elizabeth of York, the wife of Henry VII, for 1502 record a payment of 10s. to William Trende 'for money by him layed out for the making of a cheste and almorys in the Queenes Counsaille Chambre for to put in the bokes'.[4]

Some medieval armoires built to hold archives and records still survive. Several, including one which can be dated to 1413 by payments made to William Ickenham, the Winchester College carpenter, for making it as a storage place for the College's account books, are in Winchester College.[5] This armoire is a simple, serviceable, plain and undecorated armoire, with a wooden back and partitions between each of the four remaining bays (see Plate 1). Originally, behind each door, there was a bottom board and a shelf to hold the account books. A more elaborate multi-drawer armoire, which may be dated to c. 1458–70, is in the muniment room of the Vicars Choral at Wells. Its drawers were supplied with finger tabs, so that they might be opened more easily.[6] Another multi-drawer armoire with pigeonholes for sixty-one individual drawers of different sizes (the smallest drawers being at the highest level of the armoire) survives in the Aerary (treasury) in St George's Chapel at Windsor Castle. Its original purpose was to store the rolls which recorded financial and legal transactions, and, though described as 'roughly assembled', it retained its original function until 1999.[7] The late medieval free-

3   Eames, p. 5 and n. 44.
4   Eames, p. 5.
5   Eames, pp. 27–8 and n. 89, plate 13B.
6   Eames, pp. 40–1, plates 22A, 22B.

standing armoire in the muniment room at Westminster Abbey, which has recently been dated to the early part of the reign of Richard II, is composed of three bays and five internal compartments.[8] It has been suggested that it was designed with a particular use in mind: namely, the storage of archival rolls. According to Penelope Eames, 'The boards on either side of the doors would tend to prevent the rolls spilling out on the floor when the doors were opened, and yet would hardly interfere with ready accessibility'.[9] The use of armoires to safeguard financial and legal rolls was widespread in medieval England, and remained so in government departments throughout the seventeenth and early eighteenth centuries.[10] A few ecclesiastical archives also retained the use of armoires. For example, the dean and chapter of Hereford Cathedral had two large ranges of armoires made in the late sixteenth or early seventeenth century, both of which had forty compartments.[11] However, outside the departments of central government, armoires were largely superseded in popularity in the later middle ages by the objects referred to variously in contemporary sources as chests, hutches, arks, coffers and coffins.[12]

Chests were among the most common and basic pieces of medieval furniture.[13] They had multiple functions. They could be used to store and transport a wide range of items, to stand as footstools at the side or at the end of great beds – or to sit on. The different designs of chests reflected their various uses. Some had flat lids and rested on four wooden or iron feet. Others rested directly on the ground and had domed lids. For travel and transport, the simple box form, without feet or other projections, was the most suitable, and the domed lids, which were the most popular for travelling chests, were designed to throw off water. Flat-bottomed boxes with domed lids could be and were used for the permanent safe-keeping of valuables, but it was the footed chests which were most frequently used for storage.[14] The feet kept the bottom of the chest clear from the ground, whether

7   Eames, pp. 41–3, plates 23, 24A, 24B, 25.
8   Eames, pp. 30–3, plates 16A, 16B; D. W. H. Miles and M. C. Bridge, *Westminster Abbey, London: Tree-Ring Dating of the Chests and Fittings*, English Heritage Research Department Report Series 3 (London, 2008), pp. 17–18, 24.
9   Eames, p. 32.
10   E. M. Hallam, 'Nine Centuries of Keeping the Public Records', in G. H. Martin and P. Spufford (eds), *The Records of the Nation* (Woodbridge, Boydell Press, 1990), p. 32 and footnote 48; E. M. Hallam, 'Problems with Record Keeping in Early Eighteenth Century London', *Journal of the Society of Archivists*, VI (1979), pp. 219–26 and plates.
11   T. Aston, 'Muniment Rooms and Their Fittings', in R. Evans (ed), *Lordship and Learning: Studies in Memory of Trevor Aston* (Woodbridge, 2004), p. 243 (hereafter Aston).
12   For a recent discussion of the terminology for chests, see D. Sherlock, *Suffolk Church Chests* (Suffolk Institute of Archaeology and History, 2008), pp. 5–6; see also Aston, pp. 239–40.
13   Eames, pp. 108–80: for an illustration of the various chest types, see Eames, figure 17, p. 109.
14   For images and discussion of flat-bottomed and footed chests used for storage in Suf-

of pressed earth or clay and well above floors of wood or stone, and thus preserved the contents from immediate contact with damp, and from access by mice, rats and other *undesiderata*. Footed chests were employed, like armoires, to store all kinds of valuable and important objects, as well as those which needed special protection from vermin and dirt, such as grain, bread and medicines. Wooden chests built to hold valuable items were often bound in iron and provided with multiple locks for additional security. Although not specifically made with this purpose in mind, the so-called 'Domesday Chest', now held in The National Archives, housed the Domesday Book from the time of the chest's construction in about 1500. This chest was kept in the Palace of Westminster and thereafter in the Chapter House of Westminster Abbey. It has three different sets of locks, opened by three different keys, which were originally held by three separate officials. Only if the officials came together, or surrendered their individual keys to a third party, could the chest be opened.[15] This practice and the reasons behind it are clearly explained in the twelfth-century *Dialogus de Scaccario*, which describes the duties of the treasurer's two knights chamberlain in the English royal exchequer:

> Hii claves archarum baiulant, arche enim cuilibet due sere sunt diversi generis; hoc est cuius neutri clavis alterius posit aptari – et hii claves earum deferent. Circum cingitur autem quilibet archa corrigia quadam immobili in qua desuper, firmitatis seris, thesauri sigillum apponitur ut nulli eorum nisi de communi assensu accessus pateat (They keep the keys to the chests, for each chest has two locks of different types, such that the key of one lock cannot open the other locks – and these knights carry the keys to the locks. Moreover, each chest is encircled by a stiff strap which the treasurer seals after the chests are locked, so that none of them can open the chests unless all three agree).[16]

In the *Dialogus de Scaccario,* the writing of which probably commenced in 1177 and was completed a few years later, it is explicitly stated that it was not only money, gold vessels and other precious objects which were held in these chests:

> Verum plura sunt in repositoriis archis thesauro que circumferuntur et includuntur et custodiuntur a thesaurario et camerariis, sicut plenius ostensum est, qualia sunt sigillum Regis de quo queries, liber iudiciarius, rotulus qui exactorius dicitur, quem quidem nominant breve de firmis; item magni annales compotorum rotuli, privilegiorum numerosa multitudo, receptarum recauta ac rotuli receptarum ac brevia Regis de exitu thesauri, et pleraque alia que consedente scaccario cotidianis usibus necessaria sunt (But other things are kept in the storage chests of the treasury that are moved around, locked up, and guarded by the treasurer and chamberlains, as has been shown above;

---

folk churches, see: D. Sherlock, *Suffolk Church Chests*, passim.

[15] TNA E31/4.

[16] E. Amt (ed.), *Dialogus de Scaccario* and S. D. Church (ed.), *Constitutio Domus Regis* (Oxford, 2007), p. 12 (translation p. 13).

these include the king's seal about which you asked, Domesday Book, the roll called the roll of exactions (which some call the writ of farms) the pipe rolls, a great number of charters, the counter-tallies, the rolls of receipts, royal writs from issues from the treasury, and many other things needed every day when the exchequer is in session).[17]

The Liberate Rolls for 1259 contain an entry relating to the purchase of locks for the great chest which held the rolls of the Exchequer.[18] The basic storage units for the records of government in medieval England were great iron-bound chests and massive coffers, secured with three keys.[19] Practices at Westminster were mirrored and adopted by other institutions, such as ecclesiastical corporations, colleges and universities, while wealthy private individuals also used chests to hold their most important records. So popular did the archival chest become that there is abundant evidence that the normal, proper place for the storage of muniments by the high middle ages was the chest.[20]

Founders of educational and charitable foundations laid down rules for the formulation of vital records and for their storage and safe-keeping, sometimes themselves paying for chests in which such archives were to be held.[21] The most important documents relating to the foundation and organisation of Winchester College were placed – and continued to be held until after 1962 – in the two original oak chests made for them and bound with iron in the year 1396–7, almost certainly on the orders of the founder, William of Wykeham (see Plate 2).[22] When Henry VII planned his hospital of the Savoy in London, he specified that in a room, to be known as the exchequer, where the audits of the accounts of the hospital should be heard: 'will be prepared, ordained, situated and disposed boxes, baskets, treasure chests and muniment chests provided in such a number and size as seems sufficient and convenient for the custody of documents; and in them we wish to be placed, kept secure and conserved each and every account, whether in book or enrolled form, of the master, offices and ministers and of all others who are obliged to render them'.[23] In a room above the exchequer, designated as a treasury, were to be stored six chests or coffers, five of which were to hold money,

---

17 Amt (ed.), *Dialogus de Scaccario*, pp. 94 (translation p. 95) and xx.
18 *Calendar of the Liberate Rolls Preserved in the Public Record Office, vol. VI, 1267–1272* (London, HMSO, 1964), p. 271.
19 Hallam, 'Nine Centuries of Keeping the Public Records', p. 30.
20 Aston, p. 239.
21 C. Rawcliffe, 'Passports to Paradise: how English Medieval Hospitals and Almshouses Kept Their Archives', *Archives*, vol. XXVII, no. 106 (2002), pp. 2–6 (hereafter Rawcliffe).
22 J. J. Harvey, 'Winchester College muniments: an introduction with a summary index', *Archives*, vol. V, no. 28 (1962), p. 203 and n. 6. I am grateful to Miss Suzanne Foster, archivist to Winchester College, for information about these chests and their contents.
23 Rawcliffe, 'Passports to Paradise', p. 5 and n. 20.

plate and valuables, while the sixth was to safeguard the royal charters, letters
patent, ecclesiastical confirmations of rights and privileges, deeds of title and other
written records of especial importance to the foundation.[24] A third example comes
from St. John's College, Cambridge, which was founded in 1511 in accordance
with the will of Lady Margaret Beaufort (d. 1509), mother of Henry VII and also
foundress of Christ's College, Cambridge. A series of statutes, made in 1524 for St.
John's College, contained instructions for the proper storage of the records concerning the foundation. A great iron-bound chest was to be placed in the college's
tower: in this chest were to be stored three smaller ones. In one of these smaller
chests the licence and foundation charter of the college, the code of statutes and
the common seal were to be held, while in the other two were to be stored emer-
gency funds and money for purchase of lands and legal expenses. Another chest
was to house papal bulls, royal charters, episcopal charters and letters and records
of ordinations and appropriations, as well as original documents recording bene-
factions made by other important lords and patrons of the college.[25] The prologue
to the statutes De evidentiis of both St John's College, Cambridge and Corpus
Christi College, Oxford, upon which those of St John's College were based, under-
line why the storage of records was so vital to such institutions: 'Moreover, so that
the master and fellows may be prepared when the college becomes involved in
lawsuits, and shall not go into battle unarmed, we ordain that their weapons – that
is their documents of title, charters and other writings – shall be placed in the
upper chamber of the tower'.[26] The documents acted as the fortifications of the
college against attack by greedy predators; protection of the records therefore
preserved the institution from the threat of aggression and potential ruin.

Most surviving chests, boxes and armoires used for the storage of archives
were not decorated at all: one of their main purposes was to protect of the contents, not to serve as ornaments in their own right. However, as one of the other
principal purposes of record storage is to facilitate the recovery and retrieval of
documents, there are examples of archival furniture with markings indicating the
contents. Sometimes the markings were raw and unpolished. Two medieval
chests, known as treaty chests, which were held (and still remain) in the 'Treasurie
of Leagues', namely the Chapel of the Pyx at Westminster Abbey, the most ancient
of all the treasuries used by the Exchequer, have scratched lists of their contents
on the inside of their lids.[27] The more legible of the two reads: 'Francia, Hispania,

24 Rawcliffe, 'Passports to Paradise', pp. 5–6.
25 M. Underwood, 'The Defences of a College: the Law's Demands and Early Record
Keeping in St. John's College, Cambridge', in R. Evans (ed.), Lordship and Learning,
p. 226 and nn. 3 and 4.
26 Underwood, 'The Defences of a College', pp. 226–7.
27 Westminster Abbey Pyx Chamber, Lesser Treaty Chest and Greater Treaty Chest. I am
grateful to Dr Richard Mortimer, Westminster Abbey archivist, and his staff, for advice
on these chests.

Burgundia, Hispania (2), Britannia, Burgundy, Navar' Before HVIII'.[28] The scratched names are scarcely definable as decoration, but they make the contents of the chest clear (see Plate 3). The outside of the drawers of the armoire at St. George's Chapel, Windsor, are painted with the names of the specific properties to which the documents inside the drawers relate.[29] The boxes (pixides) in Magdalen College, Oxford, had labels affixed to them, giving the name of the town or manor whose records they held, so that the correct pyx could be quickly and easily found and retrieved (see Plate 4).[30] At the other extreme of size, on the outside of a pair of large wooden doors, each measuring approximately seven foot high and two foot wide, from an armoire once in the Exchequer of Receipt, in which were kept the receipt and issue rolls and other procedural documents, may still be seen a painted inscription offering a detailed explanation of the room, the armoire and its contents: 'Annis regnorum Phillippi et Marie 2 & 3, this place and the rest of the office were stablyshed by the righte honourable W. Marques of Wynchester and Highe Treasurer of England, for keepynge of all Pelles of Receipts and Exitus of the Court of Receipts called inferius scaccarrium, and of all warrants and wrytynges belonging to the same and accordynge to the aincyent ordre thereof ... Anno Domini 1555'.[31]

Some archives employed a sophisticated alpha-numerical system, recorded either on the chests or (as may still be seen on the surviving records) on the documents themselves, or on both. In the latter half of the fifteenth century, the archives of the Prior and Convent of Ely were stored in, among other containers, in chests, one of which contained two large boxes. The other five chests were divided into subsections, each denoted by letters. In one of these chests, which was divided into seven subsections, royal documents were in subsections A1, A2, A3, A4 and A5, and episcopal *acta* in subsections B1 and B2. Attached to each subsection was a label listing its contents, while the documents themselves were endorsed with the chest number, the subsection number, a reference and the name of the manor or parish to which they related.[32] The label cross-referenced the documents to their numbers in the conventual cartulary, which made for easy and efficient archival retrieval. Such cross-referencing was not just confined to the records of corporate bodies. A list made in July 1535 of the archives of Edward Stafford, third Duke of Buckingham, who had been executed in 1521, explains the system used in his archives: 'Memorandum: that in a boxe signed with this letter 'A' wherein is written Caurs [Shropshire] Dominium ys conteigned xvij pecis of

28   Westminster Abbey Pyx Chamber, Greater Treaty Chest.
29   Eames, *Medieval Furniture*, pp. 41–2, plates 14A, 14B.
30   Aston, 'Muniment Rooms and Their Fittings', p. 241. I am grateful to Dr Robin Darwall-Smith, archivist of Magdalen College, for comments on this subject.
31   TNA E 409.
32   Aston, 'Muniment Rooms and Their Fittings', p. 240.

evidence, the copies wherof are written in a booke under the same title Caurs Dominium. Whiche pecis are suentlye signed on the backes with these numbers 1.2.3.4.5.6.7.8.13.14.15.16.17.18.19.20.21. Wherein the boke and the contentis in the boxe dothe in all thinges agree, xvij pecis'.[33] The same list notes that deeds relating to the Duke's holdings in Wallop (Hampshire) had been stored in a box labelled with the letter B and the name 'Wallop'. One document had been found to be missing from this box, but the entry relating to it in a copy register enabled it to be identified as no. 31 in a series of 37 deeds, and even provided the first words of the missing document: 'Sciant presentes et future quod ego Margaret Bagot etc'.[34]

In some parts of the English royal archives, the use of colours, images and pictograms was preferred to this more sophisticated system. According to *Liber B*, one of two registers of diplomatic documents completed in about 1292, treaties and other records relating to Aragon were kept in a red coffer decorated with a scene showing jousting knights, while Gascon records were appropriately stored in containers marked with the image of grapes being pressed, the latter scene underlining the importance of the Gascon wine trade to England. In 1370, it was recorded that the letters of the king of Scotland were placed in a hamper within a chest in the muniment room at the Exchequer of Receipt under a sign showing an axe. The deployment of pictograms and pictoral labels remained a feature of some central government records and their containers until the 1730s.[35] This usage was mirrored in civic and town archives. In 1612, Henry Manship, a notary and burgess of Great Yarmouth, made a catalogue of the muniments belonging to the corporation. He listed the documents and the boxes in which they were held and noted the marks – crosses, saltires, crosses within circles and other symbols – used to distinguish the individual boxes containing specific records.[36] In national and in civic archives alike, images, colours and heraldry were likely to be used to identify chests containing documents relating to allies, trade partners or even enemies in foreign lands or, on the other hand, to express pride in one's own identity and nation when travelling or working abroad. Demonstrations of personal identity and friendship are illustrated in the book chest, dated to about 1340, of the bibliophile Richard de Bury (1287–1345), successively Chancellor of England and

---

[33] C. Rawcliffe, 'A Tudor Nobleman as Archivist: the Papers of Edward, Third Duke of Buckingham', *Journal of the Society of Archivists*, vol. 5 (1974–7), p. 296 and n. 14.

[34] Rawcliffe, 'A Tudor Nobleman as Archivist', p. 297 and n. 14.

[35] Hallam, 'Nine Centuries of Keeping the Public Records', pp. 32–3.

[36] Norwich, Norfolk Record Office, Y/C1/1, ff. 7–10v: a copy of this manuscript, made in 1763, is BL, Add. MS 23737. I owe this reference, as well as helpful discussions on the subject, to Professor Carole Rawcliffe. See C. Rawcliffe, 'The Cartulary of St. Mary's Hospital, Great Yarmouth' *Norfolk Record Society* vol. LXXI, 2007, pp. 157–230: the career of Henry Manship is discussed on pp. 171–6.

Bishop of Durham. The underside of the lid of the chest is painted with four shields of arms, flanked by heraldic beasts and fighting figures. The shields are those of Bury's family (Aungerville), the arms of his sovereign, Edward III (England quartered with France ancient), and of the family of Neville of Raby (Ralph Neville, fourth Lord Neville of Raby, was a personal friend of Bury's).[37] National pride is illustrated in heraldry on the armoire of the guild of Spanish merchants in Bruges. This armoire, constructed like a slab-ended chest, has been identified as the *arca* which from 1441 until 1596 held the records of the titles and privileges of the guild. In addition to four drawers, marked A, B, C and D, in which to store particular documents, the outside was decorated with heraldic shields bearing the arms of the united realm of Castile and Leon, the arms of Burgos, which was the capital of Castile-Leon, and, on the last shield, a Spanish device showing two dragons' heads with open mouths holding an heraldic bend between them.[38]

As noted above, in English central government archives, it was not uncommon to store special documents, notably treaties and alliances (referred to as 'leagues') and records relating to other countries and states, in special coloured or marked containers. It is almost certainly no coincidence that several of the chests, coffers and forcers (these are small containers of leather and wood, often reinforced by iron) which formerly held important diplomatic documents, have survived and are now either in the Chapel of the Pyx at Westminster Abbey or in The National Archives.[39] Some of these containers carried no decoration or identifying marks at all, even though the muniments they once held were of very great significance. One such is the plain cylindrical forcer of hollowed oak, with leather hinges and copper rivets, said to have once held the so-called 'golden league' of Alfonso X of Castile, who was king of Galicia, Castile and Leon from 1252 to 1284.[40] Nicknamed 'el sabio' (the wise), he was the eldest half-brother of Edward I's first wife, Eleanor of Castile, and the instrument in question was dated at Burgos on 1 November 1254, the day of Edward and Eleanor's marriage there. By this document, one of only three sealed with a solid gold seal which remain in The National Archives, Alfonso ceded all his rights and claims in Gascony to his new brother-in-law, whom he had just knighted. The document is elaborately written and decorated, and of great significance to both donor and recipient. But the container which preserved it was plain and not embellished with any distinguishing marks or decoration. In contrast, two of the so called 'treaty chests' now also held at The National Archives are decorated in a way that attests their purpose, date and con-

---

[37] Glasgow, Burrell Collection, Glasgow Museums and Art Galleries 14/352; J. J. G. Alexander and P. Binski (eds), *The Age of Chivalry* (London, Royal Academy, 1987) pp. 426–7 (no. 523).

[38] Eames, *Medieval Furniture,* pp. 35–7, n. 99, plates 19A, 19B, 20A, 20B, 20C, 20D.

[39] Westminster Abbey Pyx Chamber, Lesser Treaty Chest and Greater Treaty Chest; The National Archives E 27.

[40] TNA E 27/10 (the forcer): TNA E 30/1108 (the 'golden league' of Alphonso X).

tents. These are the Bruce chest and the Calais chest (see Plates 5–8).[41]

The Bruce chest originally housed documents relating to the negotiations concerning the negotiations and ransom payment for King David II of Scotland.[42] David II was the only surviving son of King Robert I (the Bruce) and his second wife, Elizabeth de Burgh.[43] He succeeded his father in 1329, at the age of five, but, in 1334, after Edward III's invasion of Scotland and victory at Halidon Hill in the previous year, he was sent to France for safety. He did not return until 1341, when Edward Balliol, who had meanwhile performed homage to Edward III for Scotland, was deposed. In response to a plea for assistance from France, David invaded England in 1346 (the same year as the battle of Crécy), but was defeated and captured at the battle of Neville's Cross and imprisoned in the Tower of London. He was eventually released under the provisions of the treaty of Berwick, which was concluded on 3 October 1357. The terms of his freedom were rigorous and unsparing. They originally included a promise of homage to Edward III as well as the throne of Scotland if David died childless, and the payment of a ransom of 100,000 marks (£66,000) – a massive sum which it proved impossible for the Scots to pay. The Bruce chest is a rectangular oak coffer, made, like most English chests, out of oak. An early dendrochronology test dated it to 1360; it was made from the same tree as the Calais chest.[44] It is pinned with wooden dowels and has iron hinges. The original iron hasp, lock, lock-plate and handle are missing. Internally, the chest is divided into two compartments. Originally, it seems to have been painted red, and on the front and lid of the chest are shields of arms and an inscription. The arms include those of John de Coupland (the warden of Berwick Castle, who had captured David II in 1346 and, as a result, was knighted, awarded a pension of £500 and a royal pardon for previous border banditry);[45] of John de Colville; the royal arms of England at the time of Edward III (England and France ancient); and of Ralph Neville, fourth Lord Neville of Raby (d. 1367), one of the commanders of the English army at Neville's Cross, who also led the ransom negotiations for the English and whose heraldic arms also figure on Richard de Bury's book chest. The inscription reads: 'Hic continetur obligaciones super deliberacione et redempcione domini David Brus die iij mensis Octobris' (Here are kept the bonds relating to the release and ransom of lord David Brus, on the third day of the month of

---

[41] Bruce chest, TNA E27/9; Calais chest, TNA E27/8. These are always referred to as 'chests', but should probably be defined as coffers, since they were of a much smaller size than most chests, and could be stored in larger chests for safe-keeping (see footnote 47). The present author plans to make the Bruce and Calais chests the subject of a more detailed heraldic and historical study.

[42] TNA E 27/9.

[43] M. A. Penman, *David II: 1329–1371* (Edinburgh, 2004).

[44] C. Jenning, *Early Chests in Wood and Iron: Photographs with Commentary*, PRO Museum Pamphlets No. 7(London, 1974), p. 2.

[45] Penman, *David II*, pp. 135, 138.

October). It is significant that David II is referred to as 'dominus' and not as 'rex', though the terms of the eventual agreement concerning his freedom made no specific claim to English overlordship over Scotland.[46] The continued use of Bruce chest for the storage of documents relating to Scotland after Edward III's reign is illustrated by its retrieval in July 1400, together with a mass of written evidence, both archival and chronicle, to be shown to Henry IV in preparation for his expedition against the Scots.[47] In 1412, by which date the chest held several treaties and other agreements with Scotland, as well as muniments relating to Flanders and a register of archival material, certain of the records were again removed for study. Throughout the fifteenth century, the Bruce chest was used as a place of storage for important documents relating to Flanders as well as to Scotland. The chest itself was locked away in one of the great chests used for the safe-keeping and security of the most valuable records.[48]

The Calais chest also continued to be used for document storage long after it was made. In 1419 documents were taken from the coffer to Henry V in France, perhaps in preparation for the treaty of Troyes, which was ratified in May 1420.[49] Its original purpose, however, was to house records relating to the treaty of Brétigny, finally ratified in Calais on 24 October 1360. By its terms, the French were to pay an enormous ransom – three million gold écus (at that time worth £500,000 and the equivalent of several years annual income for Edward III) for the release of their king, John II, who had been captured by the victorious English army at the battle of Poitiers, on 19 September 1356. The English were to be given Calais, Ponthieu and an enlarged duchy of Aquitaine, the French king being initially obliged to surrender his sovereignty over the ceded territories. In return for all this, Edward III would abandon his claim to the French crown. Since these last two conditions failed to achieve the consent of either side, they were removed from the main text of the treaty and relegated to a separate agreement, which was to be put into effect only after the transfer of the territories. This omission allowed the two sides to confirm the peace on 24 October without fulfilling any terms unacceptable to them.[50] In spite of the fact that John did not surrender his claims to England's newly acquired lands, the agreement at Calais and the military victory to

[46] Penman, *David II*, p. 181; *ODNB*, vol. 17, p. 844 (biography of Edward III).

[47] The importance to medieval Anglo-Scottish relations of relevant archive material is apparent from the mass of surviving records written by the notaries Andrew de Tange and John de Caen for Edward I and Edward II, relating to the issue of the disputed succession to the throne of Scotland ('The Great Cause') and to the claims of Edward I and his immediate successors to be overlords of Scotland. Many of these records are published in: E. L. G. Stones and G. G. Simpson (eds) *Edward I and the Throne of Scotland* 2 vols (Oxford, 1978).

[48] Unpublished introduction to TNA E 27, p. 11 and note.

[49] TNA E 27/8.

[50] *ODNB*, vol. 17, pp. 844–5 (biography of Edward III).

which it bore witness were justifiably considered a triumph, which the chest made to contain the documents celebrated. The Calais chest is constructed almost identically to the Bruce chest, save for the partition, which is now missing. Much of the ironwork has also been lost, but there is evidence that there was an iron handle on the lid. Like the Bruce chest, it was probably originally painted red and decorated with an inscription and with the arms of those involved in the diplomatic processes leading to the making of the treaty. The rubbed and faded inscription on the lid reads: 'Pax facta Cales' inter reges et regna Anglie et Francie die xxiv [mensis Octobris]' (Peace made at Calais between the kings and kingdoms of England and France on 24 day of October). The shields on the lid and front of the chest include the arms of Richard Fitzalan, third earl of Arundel and eighth earl of Surrey, one of the leading English emissaries who attended the formal ratification of the treaty at Calais; the Dauphin, who represented his father at the peace negotiations; the royal arms of England at the time of Edward III; the royal arms of France at the time of John II (France ancient); those of Edward the Black Prince, victor of Poitiers, who acted as plenipotentiary for his father; John de Buckingham, bishop of Lincoln from 1362 until 1398, who was keeper of the Privy Seal between 1360 and 1363, and who also witnessed the ratification; and Sir Guy de Bryan (d. 1390), one of the king's standard bearers and steward of the royal household, who was created a knight of the Garter in 1369.[51]

The instruments held in these chests related to power, money, prestige, victory and sovereignty. It is not surprising that the Bruce and Calais chests themselves have survived, unlike most painted medieval English chests.[52] The heraldic decoration and the inscriptions, which emphasised the historic importance of the chests and their contents, may well have played their part in ensuring this survival; small, plain coffers without heraldry might easily have been discarded or lost. Relatively few other archival containers pre-dating 1600 so far discovered have inscriptions or heraldry. Among them is a small thirteenth-century wooden skippet (round box) in The National Archives is inscribed 'Littera episcopi Heref' pro Johanne de Mawardin et Is[abella] uxore eius' (Letter of the bishop of Hereford for John de Mawardin and Isabel his wife); the surviving letter has been dated to 1284.[53] An oval pyx of thin wood, also in The National Archives, bears a contemporary inscription stating that it contained two deeds relating to a variety of manors and advowsons in Kent, Somerset, Dorset and Wales surrendered to Henry VI on 20 February, 1443.[54] A round pyx, which may have been made in

---

[51]   For Richard Fitzalan: *ODNB* vol. 19, pp. 768–9; John de Buckingham: *ODNB* vol. 8, pp. 511–13; Sir Guy de Bryan: G. E. C[okayne], *The Complete Peerage of England, Scotland, Ireland, Great Britain and the United Kingdom, Extant, Extinct or Dormant* (London, 1910–98, 14 vols in 15), vol. 2, pp. 361–2.

[52]   Alexander and Binski (eds), *The Age of Chivalry*, p. 427; Sherlock, *Suffolk Church Chests*, pp. 27–8.

[53]   TNA SC 16/5: the document is E 42/420.

1553–4, is covered with dark green leather. There is an inscription round its side 'Maria Regina Dei gracia A[nglie] F[rancie] Y[bernie]' (Mary, by the grace of God Queen of England, France and Ireland), while the lid is decorated with a crowned double rose and the inscription 'Maria Regina'.[55] However, on the whole, the systematic marking of archival containers did not usually take place before the seventeenth century, and then only in those institutions anxious to keep and organise archives more effectively, when boxes and archive containers were labelled by notaries, scholars and antiquaries and could be cross-referenced to lists or catalogues.[56]

Nor was elaborate decoration employed on most furniture made to hold archives and records. Armoires, chests and boxes built for this purpose were not regarded as aesthetic objects to ornament a room, but as a strong and durable means of protecting the rights, privileges, lands and revenues of individuals, institutions and governments. They were intended as safe places of deposit to secure their contents from theft, fire, water, the passage of time and man's negligence or carelessness. They also ensured the ready availability of records when they were needed to defend and protect the legal interests of their owners. It was for these purposes that they were created, in these capacities they served and for these reasons some of them still survive.

54   TNA SC 16/7: the documents are E 40/3225–6.
55   TNA SC 16/8.
56   Underwood, 'The Defences of a College', p. 233 and plate 7. I am most grateful to Professor C. T. Allmand, Professor Carole Rawcliffe and Mrs Ann Payne for reading and commenting on an earlier draft of this paper.

Colour in Medieval Maps

P. D. A. HARVEY

Introduction

In 2005, at the International Conference on the History of Cartography, Catherine Delano Smith as Cartographica and Alessandro Scafi as Pictor presented a rehearsed discussion about medieval maps. They reached amicable agreement that 'it is lines that make a map' – colour, however important, is an optional extra. Even the 'silent' world map of Brunetto Latini in the 1260s, which has no inscriptions, still has drawn lines; it cannot rely on its colours alone to tell its story.[1] However, most detailed medieval maps are coloured and there was no dispute over the importance of colour. One of the earliest authors to discuss maps was the Franciscan historian Paolino of Venice, who wrote that without a map it was not so much difficult as impossible to imagine the various divisions of the world:

> There is needed moreover a twofold map, [composed] of painting and writing. Nor wilt thou deem one sufficient without the other, because painting without writing indicates regions or nations unclearly, [and] writing without the aid of painting truly does not mark the boundaries of the provinces of a region in their various parts sufficiently [clearly] for them to be descried almost at a glance.[2]

Despite its unquestioned importance, little has been published on the colour of medieval maps. R. A. Skelton, in an article in 1960 on 'Colour in Mapmaking', scarcely glanced at maps before 1500.[3] In 1970 Anna-Dorothee von den Brincken

---

[1]   A.-D. von den Brincken, 'Die Ausbildung konventioneller Zeichen und Farbgebungen in der Universalkartographie des Mittelalters', *Archiv für Diplomatik, Schriftgeschichte, Siegel und Wappenkunde*, 16 (1970), pp. 333–4, opp. pp. 328, 336.

[2]   'Requiritur autem mapa duplex, picture ac scripture, nec unum sine altero putes sufficere, quia pictura sine scriptura provincias seu regna confuse demonstrat, scriptura vero non tamen erit sufficienter sine adminiculo picture provinciarum confinia per varias partes celi sicut determinat ut quasi ad oculum conspici valeant.' Text from A.-D. von den Brincken, 'Mappa mundi und Chronographia: Studien zur *imago mundi* des abendländischen Mittelalters', *Deutsches Archiv für Erforschung des Mittelalters*, 24 (1968), p. 127; translation by J. Schulz, 'Jacopo de' Barbari's View of Venice: Map Making, City Views, and Moralized Geography before the Year 1500', *Art Bulletin*, 60 (1978), p. 452.

[3]   R. A. Skelton, 'Colour in Mapmaking', *Geographical Magazine*, 32 (1959-60), pp. 544-53.

discussed the development of colour and conventional signs on medieval world maps and Dr Delano Smith, writing in 1985 on the signs used on maps down to 1700, took their use of colour fully into account.[4] Ulla Ehrensvärd in 1982 published an article in Swedish on colour on early maps and another in English in 1987 that is not simply a translation of the first. However, in 1987 she was still able to say that 'the role color plays on maps has yet to receive thorough historical scrutiny'.[5] She was right – and still is, not least of maps from the Middle Ages, though we have had further important work, published in 1998, by Danielle Lecoq, with Jean-Yves Sarazin, who looked at maps in the context of medieval writings on colour.[6]

Dr Ehrensvärd pointed out the difficulties. On some maps colours have deteriorated or have been lost. On the Hereford world map of about 1300 sufficient traces remain to show that the rivers were coloured with a blue pigment that has mostly flaked off, but considerable experience is needed to appreciate that the sea, now uniformly brown, was originally green.[7] Then again, colour reproduction has been the exception rather than the rule; for instance, the huge collection of maps of Africa and Egypt, and of many adjacent areas, that Youssouf Kamal printed in sixteen volumes between 1926 and 1951 is entirely black and white.[8] Where there has been reproduction in colour it has often been unreliable. There is much uncertainty over the colours used on the Ebstorf world map, destroyed in 1943, although a coloured lithograph had been published in successive versions in 1896 and 1900 and a half-size set of photographs had been hand-coloured, copying the map, in 1930.[9]

It is appropriate here to recall Janet Backhouse's comments in an otherwise wholly favourable review of John Williams's splendid edition of the pictures in twenty-seven manuscripts of Beatus of Liébana's Commentary on the Apocalypse

[4] Von den Brincken, 'Ausbildung' (see n. 1), pp. 325–49; C. Delano Smith, 'Cartographic Signs on European Maps and their Explanation before 1700', *Imago Mundi*, 37 (1985), pp. 9–29.

[5] U. Ehrensvärd, 'Färg på gamla kartor', *Biblis*, 1982, pp. 9–56; U. Ehrensvärd, 'Color in Cartography: A Historical Survey', in *Art and Cartography: Six Historical Essays*, ed. D. Woodward (Chicago, 1987), pp. 123-46, quotation from p. 123.

[6] D. Lecoq and J.-Y. Sarazin, 'La terre de toutes les couleurs chez les encyclopédistes et les philosophes naturalistes des XIIᵉ–XIIIᵉ siècles', in *Couleurs de la terre*, ed. M. Pelletier (Paris, 1998), pp. 16–39. A recent account of medieval attitudes to colour, though without particular reference to maps, is C. M. Woolgar, *The Senses in Late Medieval England* (New Haven, 2006), pp. 155–74.

[7] C. Clarkson, 'The Hereford Map: The First Annual Condition Report', in *The Hereford World Map: Medieval World Maps and their Context*, ed. P. D. A. Harvey (London, 2006), pp. 100, 101; N. Morgan, 'The Hereford Map: Art-Historical Aspects', ibid., p. 121.

[8] Y. Kamal, *Monumenta cartographica Africae et Aegypti*, 5 vols in 16 (Cairo, 1926–51).

[9] *Die Ebstorfer Weltkarte*, ed. H. Kugler, 2 vols (Berlin, 2007), i, pp. 5–6; ii, pp. 5–9.

– pictures, be it noted, that include both a world map and a picture-map of the New Jerusalem. She notes that the work contains

> no colour plates beyond a representative group of specimen pages in his introductory first volume. For the general reader the extraordinary excitement engendered by the vibrant, not to say exotic, colouring of these particular manuscripts is entirely lost ... Unfortunately, the traditional colour transparencies still required by most publishers remain very substantially more expensive than black and white prints. Moreover they are, alas, extremely variable in quality... [10]

It was a faulty colour transparency that deceived Professor Von den Brincken by showing the rivers on the Sawley (or Henry of Mainz) world map as blue or violet; they are in fact uncoloured.[11] But in published colour reproductions the printing as well as the photography may introduce variation. Illustrations of the Cotton and Munich world maps in books published by the British Library in 1991 and 2006 probably derive from the same transparencies but the printed colours are markedly different; most notably the seas on the Cotton map, brown-grey in 1991, are deep green in 2006.[12]

Certainly there has been rapid and continuing improvement, certainly in the cost and to some extent in the reliability of colour reproduction. Notable recent examples of books about maps, superbly illustrated in colour, include *Couleurs de la terre* and *Segni e sogni della terra*, produced in connection with exhibitions in Paris and Milan in 1998 and 2001, and *The Map Book*, edited by Peter Barber in 2005.[13] However, we are still at the mercy of less than perfect technology. A ninth-century map of the Promised Land, showing its division between the Twelve Tribes, was twice published in colour in 2005; on one reproduction the River Jordan from the Sea of Galilee to the Dead Sea appears in light red-brown, on the other in dull olive.[14] We cannot use reproductions to assess the finer points of colouring and we should still be very cautious in relying on them even for broad colour ranges – but as we seldom have the chance to see medieval maps from different repositories side by side we depend entirely on reproductions to compare the colours of one with another. It should be borne in mind that much of what follows is based on coloured illustrations in published works; I have almost certainly been deceived at some points by colour changes introduced in photography or printing.[15]

[10]   *Antiquaries' Journal*, 83 (2003), p. 505.
[11]   Von den Brincken, 'Ausbildung' (see n. 1), pp. 326n, 338, opp. p. 336.
[12]   P. D. A. Harvey, *Medieval Maps* (London, 1991), pp. 22, 26; *Hereford World Map* (see n. 7), pp. 6, 7. I am grateful to Miss Kathleen Houghton, of the British Library, for advice on this point.
[13]   *Couleurs* (see n. 6); *Segni e sogni della terra: Il disegno del mondo dal mito d'Atlante alla geografia delle reti* (Milan, 2001); *The Map Book*, ed. P. Barber (London, 2005).
[14]   *Imago Mundi*, 57 (2005), plate 1; *Map book* (see n. 13), p. 41.

All the same, we can reasonably look for some general principles in the ways colour is used in medieval maps. It may be functional, being the sole means of providing certain information. It may be simply decorative. Or it may be realistic, reproducing on the map the colouring of nature. A single map may use colour in more than one of these ways and, as we shall see, the lines of demarcation are not at all precise: a map's functional colour, for instance, may serve a decorative purpose as well. Moreover, some colouring on the maps is wholly conventional, copied from one map to another from force of habit or tradition, and it can be hard to tell whether it was functional, decorative, realistic, or, a further possibility, symbolic in origin.

Functional Colour

Arguably most colour on maps is in a sense functional: at the very least it makes for greater clarity, as Paolino pointed out. Because they are drawn in red, the tiny circles that mark towns on seven copies of the early-fourteenth-century small grid map of Palestine stand out, clearly distinguished from other features.[16] Sometimes, however, colour is used to convey information that is lost if the map is reproduced in black and white. This is unusual on medieval maps but there are cases where it does occur. We see it on portolan charts, navigational maps first recorded in the late thirteenth century that, at first covering little more than the Mediterranean and the Black Sea, expanded to take in the west coast of Europe, Britain, Ireland, and ultimately the Atlantic islands and the west coast of Africa. On many of these charts rocky coasts are marked with black stippling, sandy shoals with red.[17] Even more commonly, the place-names that crowd the coasts are written in red if they are important ports, in black if they are not. Thus in southern England on a chart drawn by Pietro Vesconte of Venice in about 1330, Southampton, Exmouth, and Plymouth are in red, while Portsmouth, Lyme, Falmouth, and many other places are in black.[18]

[15] In the notes that follow I give a reference to the manuscript (along with a reference to a coloured reproduction, if any) only if I have seen it myself; otherwise I give the reference to the reproduction alone.

[16] BL, Add. MS 27376*, ff. 188v–189, reproduced in Harvey, *Medieval Maps* (see n. 12), p. 79; Brussels, Bibliothèque royale, ms 9347–9348, ff. 162v–163, ms 9404–9405, ff. 173v–174; Florence, Biblioteca Riccardiana, ms 237, ff. 142v–143; Oxford, Bodleian Library, MS Tanner 190, ff. 205v–206, reproduced in E. Edson and E. Savage-Smith, *Medieval Views of the Cosmos* (Oxford, 2004), pp. 102–03; Vatican City, Biblioteca Apostolica Vaticana, ms Pal. lat. 1362, ff. 7v–8, ms Reg. lat. 548, ff. 141v–142.

[17] Tony Campbell, 'Portolan Charts from the Late Thirteenth Century to 1500', in *The History of Cartography*, I: *Cartography in Prehistoric, Ancient, and Medieval Europe and the Mediterranean*, eds J. B. Harley and D. Woodward (Chicago, 1987), p. 378.

[18] BL, Add. MS 27376*, ff. 180v–181, reproduced in Harvey, *Medieval Maps* (see n. 12), p. 42.

The same mapmaker used colour in a different way on the small grid map of Palestine. Here the boundaries of the Twelve Tribes are drawn in red, clearly distinguishing them from the green rivers; on a slightly later de luxe version of the same map the boundaries of the Tribes are in gold.[19] Colour is again used to distinguish a boundary on the map of the Isle of Thanet that Thomas of Elmham, monk of St Augustine's Abbey, Canterbury, drew in his chronicle in about 1400. It illustrates his account of the way part of Thanet was given to Domneva, founder of Minster Abbey: she was to have the land demarcated by her pet deer as it ran from one side of the isle to the other.[20] In the text the colours on the maps are explained: "In the foregoing illustration a green line is used for the course of the deer, going this way and that way across [the isle] ... The red lines show the isle's highways from one parish to the next".[21] Without the colours, as well as the explanation, the lines would be hard to interpret. It is unusual to have colour explained in this way, but on his world map of 1448 Andreas Walsperger notes that 'the red spots are cities of the Christians, the black ones in truth are the cities of the infidels', a convention that he did not invent himself for there was a similar note on the now lost chart of the Mediterranean by Giovanni da Carignano in the 1320s.[22]

Perhaps the most remarkable case of the functional use of colour, not least because it is so early, is on the pair of plans of Canterbury Cathedral drawn in about 1150 to show its water system. The pipe bringing the water to the cathedral priory is coloured green up to the water tower in one cloister and the washing place in the other, but the pipes that then distributed the water from these two points to the rest of the priory are all red.[23] Even though there is no text explaining this, it illustrates perfectly what Paolino says of the value of colour in giving clarity to the map.

Decorative Colour

If we can say that most colour on a map is functional in adding to its clarity we can also argue that all colour on a map, however functional its intention, has a deco-

---

19 The seven copies from Vesconte's workshop are listed in n. 16; the copy with gold boundaries is Paris, BnF, ms latin 4939, ff. 10v–11, reproduced in *Couleurs* (see n. 6), p. 39.

20 Cambridge, Trinity Hall, MS 1, f. 42v, reproduced, and discussed by F. Hull, in *Local Maps and Plans from Medieval England*, eds R. A. Skelton and P. D. A. Harvey (Oxford, 1986), plate 8, pp. 119–26.

21 'In ista enim praecedente figura pro cursu cervae notatur viridis linea, huc atque illuc transversaliter intendendo ... Rubeae vero lineae vias regales insulae ab una parochia in aliam manifestant', Thomas of Elmham, *Historia monasterii S. Augustini Cantuariensis*, ed. C. Hardwick, Rolls Series (London, 1858), p. 207.

22 D. Woodward, 'Medieval *Mappaemundi*', in *History of Cartography* (see n. 17), p. 325; Kamal, *Monumenta* (see n. 8), iv, part i, p. 1139.

23 Cambridge, Trinity College, MS R.17.1, ff. 284v–285, 286, reproduced, and discussed by W. Urry, in *Local Maps* (see n. 20), plates 1A, 1B, pp. 43–58.

rative quality as well, enhancing its appearance. Sometimes, though, colour does nothing else; there is no loss of clarity or of information in a black-and-white reproduction. It is colour simply for its own sake.

We see this in the ninth-century map of the Promised Land. We cannot be sure from the two reproductions whether it colours the Jordan red-brown or dull olive, but we can be reasonably sure that it uses red-brown for the Sea of Galilee, the Dead Sea, the coastline, the symbols for towns, and the title at the top, unlike the grey-black of the other wording.[24] Again, on a map of Sherwood Forest in the late fourteenth or early fifteenth century the streams, their names, and the linear framework underlying the map are all in red, while almost everything else is in brown ink.[25] In neither case does the colour add to what the map tells us; no information is lost if the maps are reproduced in black and white. The red and red-brown do no more than enliven what might otherwise seem rather dreary diagrams. At the same time, however, they differentiate certain sorts of information from the rest and to that extent serve a function in adding to clarity. Decorative and functional colour are not opposed alternatives; to a greater or lesser degree the colour is likely to be both.

On a few maps decorative colour is introduced into physical features, On a portolan chart drawn by Angelo Dulcert in 1339 some mountain ranges, like the Alps, are coloured red-brown, others, like the Pyrenees, blue-green, apparently just for the sake of variety.[26] There is earlier precedent on some versions of the Beatus map, that is, the world map in manuscripts of Beatus of Liébana's commentary on the Apocalypse. On one, dating from the early twelfth century, the Alps and Apennines have deep green background colour, the Pyrenees yellow-brown, and on one dated 1047 red, black, blue, and purple are all used for mountains, with differing colours for their outlines and shading.[27] On another version of about 1075 not only are the mountains variously coloured, in dark green, orange, ochre, or red, but a similar range of colours is used for the rivers, only replacing orange with dark blue.[28]

More often, town symbols were vehicles for decorative colouring. On a map of Palestine from about 1200 that was among the Ashburnham Libri manuscripts, the more important towns are marked by squares of gold, criss-crossed with fine red lines.[29] A more usual symbol for a town was a building seen in elevation, rang-

[24] *Imago Mundi*, 57 (2005), plate 1; *Map book* (see n. 13), p. 41.
[25] Belvoir Castle, archives of the duke of Rutland, map 125, reproduced, and discussed by M. W. Barley, in *Local Maps* (see n. 20), plate 10, pp. 131–9.
[26] *Couleurs* (see n. 6), p. 43.
[27] BL, Add. MS 11695, ff. 39v–40, reproduced in Harvey, *Medieval Maps* (see n. 12), p. 23, and in *Map Book* (see n. 13), p. 45; *Beato di Liébana: Miniaturi del Beato de Fernando I y Sancha (Codice B.N. Madrid Vit. 14-2)*, ed. U. Eco (Parma, 1973), pp. 84–5.
[28] *Segni e sogni* (see n. 13), p. 66.
[29] Florence, Biblioteca Medicea Laurenziana, ms Ashburnham Libri 1882.

ing from a simple gatehouse or tower to an elaborate fantasy of turrets, domes, and pinnacles. These buildings might be left uncoloured, as on Matthew Paris's four maps of Britain in the mid-thirteenth century, though on three of these a red line around many of the towns' names adds a decorative element.[30] Often, though, the symbol was coloured. On the one copy of the small grid map of Palestine that shows towns this way, instead of with tiny red circles, each symbol is painted over with a dull yellow wash, and on the Hereford world map one or more of the details on each of the elaborate town symbols is picked out in red.[31] On the large four-teenth-century map of Palestine in the Pierpont Morgan Library the symbols' colouring, in red and green, is as fantastic as their shapes.[32]

On John Hardyng's map of Scotland in the early fifteenth century the town symbols seem no less fantastically coloured, a profusion of vermilion, blue, mauve, and yellow-brown. All the same, there are hints at reality. We cannot believe in the bright red of some obvious stonework, but the blue roofs of the church buildings that mark Glasgow and Dunfermline and the red roofs on some other buildings must be meant to suggest lead and tiles.[33] On Thomas Elmham's map of Thanet the churches appear as line drawings, each in red and blue, a choice of colours that may be meant to echo, however distantly and conventionally, brick and stone with roofs of tiles and slates or lead.[34] The buildings that mark each town on the mid-fourteenth-century Gough map of Britain are uncoloured except for their roofs, painted red.[35] We begin to see that just as functional colouring cannot be sharply distinguished from decorative, neither can we always be sure that there is no real-istic element in what is primarily decorative colouring. Indeed, while we may accept that functional purpose, decoration, the imitation of reality, or symbolism underlies all colouring on maps, it does not follow that we can assign every

[30] BL, Cotton MS Claudius D.vi, f. 12v; Cotton MS Julius D.vii, ff. 50v–53; Royal MS 14 C.vii, f. 5v; Cambridge, Corpus Christi College, MS 16, f. v verso; all are reproduced in *Four Maps of Great Britain Designed by Matthew Paris about 1250*, ed. J. P. Gilson (London, 1928).

[31] Paris, BnF, ms latin 4939, ff. 10v–11, reproduced in *Couleurs* (see n. 6), p. 39; Hereford, Mappa Mundi Trustees, details reproduced in P. D. A. Harvey, *Mappa Mundi: The Hereford World Map*, 2nd edn (Hereford, 2002), frontispiece, pp. 4–12 passim, 40–52 passim.

[32] New York, Pierpont Morgan Library, M.877.

[33] BL, Lansdowne MS 204, f. 226v, reproduced in Harvey, *Medieval Maps* (see n. 12), p. 70.

[34] See n. 20 above.

[35] Oxford, Bodleian Library, MS Gough Gen. Top. 16, reproduced in *The Map of Great Britain circa A.D. 1360 known as the Gough Map*, Royal Geographical Society Reproductions of Early Manuscript Maps IV, Bodleian Library Map Reproductions I (Oxford, 1958); partial or much reduced reproductions are in Harvey, *Medieval Maps* (see n. 12), p. 78, and *Map Book* (see n. 13), pp. 64, 65.

coloured feature to any one of these categories; in much colouring there are elements of two or more of them.

Realistic Colour

Many medieval maps include features realistically coloured. The sea is painted green on our two oldest world maps, the Vatican map and the Albi map, which both date from the late eighth century,[36] and green sea appears on map after map down to the fifteenth century. Clearly it had its origin in nature, though the shades used on some maps are far from realistic. The brown of mountain ranges as seen from afar again occurs on many medieval maps and so too, though less often, do trees coloured green. Buildings, whether or not serving as town symbols, are often coloured realistically. On one version of the Beatus map, dating from about 1300, the ranges of mountains are shown decoratively in crazy-paving patterns of red, green, blue, or yellow, but the buildings that mark towns are painted in the shades of brown that one might expect of varying stonework.[37] Plans of Constantinople and Gallipoli in a copy of Cristoforo Buondelmonti's *Book of Islands* from the second half of the fifteenth century show their buildings in shades of red-brown and olive that again are entirely realistic.[38]

Where there are scenes with figures on a map the colouring is usually more or less realistic. The Earthly Paradise with Adam and Eve on versions of the Beatus map, the groups of figures on the Catalan atlas of 1375, the huntsman presenting a boar's head to King Edward the Confessor on the 1444-6 map of Boarstall in Buckinghamshire, are varied examples.[39] These scenes are pictures, and we would expect them to follow the same colour conventions as pictures in any other context. But it would be a mistake to draw a sharp distinction between the pictorial and the cartographic elements on any medieval map. In medieval Europe there was no word that meant, simply, map, and the whole map will have been viewed as a particular sort of picture or diagram: *tabula*, *imago*, *figura*, are words that are used.

With this in mind we can look at one group of medieval maps that has been systematically reproduced in colour, English local maps and plans. Sixteen of those known from before 1500 are coloured, and among them is a clear division. We have seen how the plans of Canterbury Cathedral make functional use of colour to distinguish the two parts of its water system, and the buildings on these plans, just as on the map of Thanet, perhaps make a gesture towards realistic colouring. Otherwise the colouring on the six maps that are certainly or possibly

[36] *Map Book* (see n. 13), pp. 39, 43.
[37] *Couleurs* (see n. 6), p. 33.
[38] Ibid., p. 58.
[39] The versions of the Beatus map in BL, Add. MS 11695, ff. 39v–40, reproduced as in n. 27, *Segni e sogni* (see n. 13), p. 66, and *Couleurs* (see n. 6), p. 33, all colour the Earthly Paradise realistically; *Couleurs*, p. 45; *Local Maps* (see n. 20), plate 18.

earlier than 1400 is decorative. On the ten certain fifteenth-century maps the colouring is realistic, though we must make exceptions of the red background to each building on the 1430 map of Pinchbeck Fen and of the few green roofs on the plan of Bristol of about 1480.[40]

Medieval local maps from other parts of Europe probably follow a similar pattern. The 1460 plan of villages in the Côte-d'Or comprises realistic views of landscape: the buildings are grey with red, yellow or grey roofs, trees are green with brown trunks. The river Saône and its tributary streams are blue – just as rivers are coloured blue on several of the English local maps and on many other medieval maps of every sort.[41] We might even say that blue rivers and green seas are normal on medieval maps: the green rivers of the Gough map of Britain and the small grid maps of Palestine are unusual, and so too is the blue sea of the Ashburnham Libri map of Palestine.[42] We may even see a hint of tidal waters in the way Matthew Paris extends the green sea some way up the rivers in one version of his map of Britain.[43] But how far is the blue of rivers realistic colouring? There is no difficulty in seeing dull green seas and rivers as based on nature, but while seas and sometimes rivers, even in northern Europe, may appear blue under a bright, clear sky, this is not the colour one first thinks of in imagining a river. This opens the wider question of conventional colour on medieval maps, colour copied from one map to another but of uncertain origin, whether functional, decorative, imitating nature, or symbolic.

Conventional Colour

We are so used to modern maps that colour all water blue that we scarcely see it as a convention and are apt to forget that in real life blue is not the only colour, or even the most frequent colour, of seas, lakes, and rivers. The convention appears on maps before the Middle Ages: sea and rivers are blue in the hand-books of the Roman surveyors (known, admittedly, only in post-Classical copies) and the sea is blue on the Dura-Europos shield of the third century AD.[44] The convention may well take its origin in nature, more likely to produce blue water in Mediterranean lands than in northern Europe. But this is not the only possible explanation. Dr

---

[40] *Local Maps* (see n. 20); the plan of Bristol is plate 28. Of relevant maps that have come to light since this publication in 1986 only the map of Pinchbeck Fen is coloured: TNA, MPCC 7, reproduced and discussed by R. Mitchell and D. Crook, 'The Pinchbeck Fen Map: A Fifteenth-Century Map of the Lincolnshire Fenland', *Imago Mundi*, 51 (1999), plates 3, 4, pp. 40–50, and also reproduced partially in *Map Book* (see n. 13), pp. 68, 69.

[41] Harvey, *Medieval Maps* (see n. 12), p. 95.

[42] References in nn. 35, 16, 29.

[43] P. D. A. Harvey, 'Matthew Paris's Maps of Britain', in *Thirteenth Century England IV*, eds P. R. Coss and S. D. Lloyd (Woodbridge, 1992), p. 116.

[44] *Map Book* (see n. 13), pp. 24, 25, 29.

Ehrensvärd discusses patterns of symbolism in early authors who attached a particular colour to each season, or to each cardinal point, or to each of the four elements; blue might indeed represent water or the sea, but so might purple or yellow.[45] Colours used conventionally on medieval maps may well have had a pre-medieval symbolic origin, linked to nature only obscurely if at all.

The same question arises over another common convention on medieval maps. From the eighth century onwards world maps usually coloured the Red Sea red, and many of them coloured the Persian Gulf red as well, making Arabia a peninsula between two red arms of the sea. Perhaps no explanation is needed: it was called the Red Sea, so it was necessarily painted red. But why did the Middle Ages suppose it was called the Red Sea? Possibly the great heat of the region gave it a red colour.[46] Brunetto Latini is more precise: "Know that this sea is red not of its own nature but by chance, as the sea-bed is of red earth".[47] We should perhaps see the red on the maps simply as realistic colouring: the Red Sea was red just as other seas were green. But again another explanation is possible. Dr Ehrensvärd points out that on one version of the Beatus map not just the Red Sea and the Persian Gulf are red but the whole Indian Ocean as well, that is all the sea on the eastern half of the map. This can be linked to colours given to the cardinal points that saw red as the colour of the east and she suggests that the red of the Red Sea on medieval maps is "a vestigial symbolic association of color with direction".[48]

Another colour convention occurs on portolan charts. From an early stage in their development they coloured small islands overall in a variety of colours. Thus on a pair of maps by Pietro Vesconte in about 1330 Malta is green, Gozo red, Minorca brown, Ibiza green, and Formentera red, while Sicily, Sardinia, Corsica, and Majorca, being larger, are left uncoloured.[49] This persisted throughout the fourteenth and fifteenth centuries, with interesting variations. Thus in the Catalan atlas of 1375 islands are shown not in single colours but in multicoloured patterns.[50] Again, many charts mark cities and regions with appropriately coloured flags, and on some islands this colouring is transferred to the island itself, so that Rhodes is coloured red with a white cross, Lanzarote with the red cross of Genoa – perhaps the only unquestionably symbolic colouring to appear on medieval

[45]   Ehrensvärd, 'Color' (see n. 5), pp. 129–31.
[46]   Von den Brincken, 'Ausbildung' (see n. 1), p. 339.
[47]   'Et sachiés ke cele mers est rouge non mie par nature mais par accident, por les teres ki sont rouges dont il fait son cors', Brunetto Latini, Li livres dou tresor, ed. F. J. Carmody, University of California Publications in Modern Philology 22 (Berkeley and Los Angeles, 1948), pp. 110–11.
[48]   Ehrensvärd, 'Färg' (see n. 5), p. 11; Ehrensvärd, 'Color' (see n. 5), p. 129.
[49]   BL, Add. MS 27376*, ff. 180v–182, reproduced in Harvey, Medieval Maps (see n. 12), pp. 38–9, 42.
[50]   Couleurs (see n. 6), p. 45.

maps.[51] On some charts larger islands are given a coloured outline. A chart of the Atlantic coast by Grazioso Benincasa in 1469 has solid colouring on the Scilly Isles (green and red), the Isle of Wight (red), and the Isle of Man (blue), but outline colouring on Ireland (green), England (red), and Scotland, separated from England by a bridged channel (light brown), while the continental coast is uncoloured.[52] Which islands counted as large, which small, depended on the scope of the chart and the individual mapmaker. Mecia de Viladestes in 1413, on a chart of the Mediterranean, the Black Sea, and the Atlantic coast, showed Crete in solid colour, along with Corsica, Sardinia, Sicily, and Scotland; late-fifteenth-century charts of the Aegean by Nicolo Pasqualini and Benedetto Pesione show Crete and Eubbea outlined in blue and red but all other islands in solid colour.[53] The convention deserves detailed investigation. Its origin may be functional or decorative – or neither.

Conclusion

Islands on portolan charts are not the only aspect of colour on medieval maps that calls for much more detailed work. The difficulties are real; we can have total confidence only in the examination of original maps with colour standards and with knowledge of the way pigments may have changed in the course of time. But colour is a component of nearly all detailed maps that survive from medieval Europe. To ignore this in discussing them is to blind ourselves to a significant part of the mapmakers' work. The historian of cartography, like the patron who commissioned a map in the Middle Ages, should heed the advice of Paolino of Venice: "There is needed moreover a twofold map, [composed] of painting and writing. Nor wilt thou deem one sufficient without the other".

---

[51] Campbell, 'Portolan Charts' (see n. 17), p. 378.
[52] BL, Add. MS 31315, ff. 4v–5, reproduced in Harvey, *Medieval Maps* (see n. 12), p. 63.
[53] *Couleurs* (see n. 6), p. 46; BL, Egerton MS 73, openings 23, 24, reproduced in Harvey, *Medieval Maps* (see n. 12), pp. 66, 67.

The Monograms, Arms and Badges of the Virgin Mary in Late Medieval England

NIGEL MORGAN

The imagery of the Virgin Mary in late medieval England was first and foremost that of her holding the Child, and then a range of narrative scenes from her apocryphal childhood, through that of the New Testament, to her apocryphal final days and eventual taking up into heaven. Although such iconography dominated in all forms of art there is also a very extensive range of signs and symbols relating to her in which her physical form is not a constituent but which to the viewer signified some aspect of her. The most popular of these signs is her monogram, always containing an 'M' but existing in a range of forms. Her symbols are most famously the flowers of the lily and the rose, and the relatively rarely found heart pierced by a sword. The definition, roles and contexts of these 'signs' and 'symbols' is the subject of this paper.

In using this terminology it may be useful to begin by speculating on what signs and symbols might have meant in the visual language of the Middle Ages. From the thirteenth to the fifteenth century they became vastly more important than for the period before 1200. Even, for example, such ubiquitous symbols as the attributes of the saints only began to evolve from the second half of the twelfth century. Before that date, St Peter's key was one of the very few established attributes. Labelling of the saints not by inscriptions, but by animals, birds or objects, which defined them for the viewer will have a long life until eventually in the 'naturalism' of the Renaissance and the Baroque they came to be viewed for the most part as incongruous insertions. Why the art of the thirteenth to sixteenth centuries should be so obsessed by 'symbols' is a difficult question to answer. 'Signs' are also a dominant characteristic of late medieval art, most obviously in the predominance of heraldry, monograms, badges, mottos and emblems. These survive long after the Middle Ages, but it was in the fourteenth and fifteenth centuries that the display of these signs reached an extreme elaboration and range of contextual display never to be exceeded. Again, the question as to why this occurred should be raised, but it is beyond the scope of this paper to provide an answer.

Signs and symbols had of course existed in art of all times and periods and were part of the legacy of the art of antiquity to the Middle Ages. Are they really two different forms of visual language? Heraldry and emblems are signs of individual persons or families, but they may contain symbols such as flora, fauna and inanimate objects which have additional meaning other than being the sign by which the family of an individual is identified. It should, however, be remembered that the majority of heraldic blasons have no symbolic meanings but are just signs of the family. Of course, the context of the heraldry may go beyond this to symbolise the power, prowess or patronage of that family. For the Virgin Mary and the saints, flora, fauna and inanimate objects can be a sign in that they tell the viewer who the saint is, but they can also be a symbol. Peter's key signifies the figure as St Peter but it also is a symbol of the role in heaven of that saint, and in wider terms of the status of the papacy. The red or white rose held by Mary does not need to be a primary sign for her because the Child she holds is the principal signifier that the figure is Mary. The rose if white is a symbol of her purity, and if red a symbol first of her love and secondly, if five-petalled, signifies her five sorrows.[1] Red and white roses of course are widely used as symbols of love and purity in secular art and social custom, and are by no means only readable as symbols if held by the Virgin Mary. For her the rose can be a symbol of much wider aspects of her character as in the famous line of the fifteenth-century carol 'rose of virtue'.[2] Another sign of Mary is the heart pierced by a sword, but it is primarily a symbol because it refers both to her love and her sorrow. The heart, like the rose, has of course a lot of secular and medical 'baggage' which complicates any understanding of its multifarious meanings.[3]

The Marian monograms which will be discussed at some length in this paper are almost completely in the category of 'signs', although various contexts in which they occur, and additional elements within or around the monogram, will impart symbolism to it. Indeed, it will become apparent that hardly ever is the monogram of Mary completely a sign in the same sense as a shield with a blason of abstract forms is. The physical location context of all these signs and symbols in art inevitably determined particular meanings for a medieval viewer, which changed when the same sign or symbol was in a different context.

[1]   Conversely the white rose could be expected to signify her joys, but I do not know of a text to support this. For a general survey of rose symbolism in the Middle Ages connected with Mary see: R. Woolf, *The English Religious Lyric in the Middle Ages* (Oxford, 1968), pp. 287–9, and B. Seward, *The Symbolic Rose* (New York, 1960), pp. 22–4, 43–8, and in secular literature, Idem, pp. 5–42.

[2]   On this and other rose symbolism carols see: R. L. Greene, *The Early English Carols*, 2nd edn (Oxford, 1977), 116–18, 394–5, nos. 173–6, and L. Spitzer, '*Explication de texte* applied to three great Middle English Poems', *Archivum Linguisticum*, 3 (1951), pp. 137–52.

[3]   On the complex symbolism of the heart in the Middle Ages see: A. Walzer, 'Das Herz in Kunst und Geschichte', in *Das Herz*, II (Biberach an der Riss, 1966), pp. 9–62 and K.-A. Wirth, 'Religiöse Herzembleme', in *Das Herz*, II (Biberach an der Riss, 1966), pp. 63–106. For its imagery on monumental brasses see: M. Norris, *Monumental Brasses. The Memorials*, I (London, 1977), pp. 197–8.

Unlike the saints the Virgin Mary has no established single emblem of flora or fauna which she carries or has beside her which specifically defines that it is she, that is excepting the Christ Child which must be considered as her primary emblem. Almost all seated or standing figures of Mary in the Middle Ages have her carrying the Child. There is no established imagery or her standing or rising up alone as in later centuries in the Virgins of the Immaculate Conception, and those of Our Lady of Lourdes or of Guadalupe. The special case of the iconic tradition of the isolated bust of Mary as intercessor gesturing with her hands in the art of Rome and Byzantium seems never to have reached England on the basis of surviving evidence.[4] Even that image was in most cases combined with an icon of the adult Christ signifying her intercession to Him.[5] From the twelfth century onwards in northern Europe she is also usually crowned, and so the crown becomes her attribute, although not a specific attribute, for it only becomes clear that it is Mary if the Child is with her, for of course all royal women saints wear crowns in medieval art.[6] Also, she often holds another royal attribute, the sceptre. Although, what appears on first impression to be a sceptre is quite often a flower or plant symbolising Isaiah's prophecy of the stem from the root of Jesse.[7] As far as English art is concerned there is no established colour symbolism for Mary's garment. She may be in blue, as frequently, but not exclusively, is the case in France and Italy, but sometimes

[4]   See H. Belting, *Bild und Kult. Eine Geschichte des Bildes vor dem Zeitalter der Kunst* (Munich, 1990), pp. 353–66, and G. Wolf, *Salus populi romani. Die Geschichte römischer Kultbilder im Mittelalter* (Weinheim, 1990), pp. 161–70, for further discussion of this image of Mary.

[5]   W. Tronzo, 'Apse Decoration, the Liturgy and the Perception of Art in Medieval Rome: S. Maria in Trastevere and S. Maria Maggiore', in *Italian Church Decoration of the Middle Ages and Early Renaissance*, ed. W. Tronzo (Baltimore, 1989), pp. 167–93.

[6]   For Mary wearing a crown in English art see N. Morgan, 'Texts and Images of Marian Devotion in English Twelfth-Century Monasticism, and their Influence on the Secular Church', in *Monasteries and Society in Medieval Britain, Proceedings of the 1994 Harlaxton Symposium*, Harlaxton Medieval Studies, VI, ed. B. Thompson (Stamford, 1999), pp. 130–32, and N. Morgan, 'Texts and Images of Marian Devotion in Thirteenth-Century England', in *England in the Thirteenth Century, Proceedings of the 1989 Harlaxton Symposium*, Harlaxton Medieval Studies, I, ed. W. M. Ormrod (Stamford, 1991), pp. 86–8. In Italy there is an Early Medieval tradition of Mary wearing a royal diadem which in the twelfth century is transformed into a crown. On this see U. Nilgen, 'Maria Regina – ein politischer Kultbildtypus?', *Römisches Jahrbuch für Kunstgeschichte*, 19 (1981), pp. 3–33, and Wolf, *Salus populi romani*, pp. 119–24.

[7]   T. A. Heslop, 'The Romanesque Seal of Worcester Cathedral', in *Medieval Art and Architecture at Worcester Cathedral*, British Archaeological Association Conference Transactions (1975) (Leeds, 1978), pp. 71–9 and T. A. Heslop, 'The Virgin Mary's Regalia and 12th-century English Seals', in *The Vanishing Past: Studies of Medieval Art, Liturgy and Metrology presented to Christopher Hohler*, British Archaeological Reports, International Series 1111, eds A. Borg and A. Martindale (Oxford, 1981), pp. 53–62, for a discussion of both crown and sceptre.

she is dressed in white and yellow (i.e. gold) and even in red, green or purple, particularly in stained glass. From the thirteenth century in England for the rest of the Middle Ages the 'standard' image of the Virgin in wood or stone, as would be found in every church in the country, was the seated or standing crowned figure holding the Child.[8] A typical example in a manuscript painting, probably reflecting the sort of wooden image omnipresent in English parish churches, is a c. 1250 example in a Psalter made for St Albans Abbey (London, BL, Royal MS 2.B.vi).[9] In painting she often has at her feet the serpent-dragon and lion, to signify her as the new Eve, whose Son will triumph over the sin of the first Eve, as in the Amesbury Psalter (Oxford, All Souls MS 6).[10] This imagery continues into the fourteenth century as in the De Lisle Psalter (London, BL, Arundel MS 83 pt. II), but is rarely, if at all, found in the fifteenth century.[11]

The sign by which Mary came to be represented from the mid-fourteenth century onwards was the initial of her name, 'M' for Maria, often linked with an 'R' for Regina, because in late medieval English art she is nearly always represented crowned. The monograms are often so constructed as to include a horizontal bar in the left hand lobe of the 'M' making an 'A'. If the middle vertical bar of the 'M' is also read as an 'I', the monogram spells out 'MARIA'. Unlike the Name of Jesus 'at whom every knee shall bow' (Philippians 2 v. 10) there is no scriptural reference to support the veneration of the name of Mary. From the mid-fifteenth century onwards there is a liturgical and devotional cult of the Name of Jesus, immensely popular in England, but no counterpart for the name of Mary.[12] However, frequently in the tracery lights in stained glass the monograms of Jesus ('IHC' or 'IHS') and Mary are placed beside each other as in the c. 1350–75 glass at Thornford, St Mary Magdalene (Dorset) somewhat incongruously placed under a lion's head in the top tracery light (Plate 1).[13] Also the Mary monogram is often paired

---

8   On this type of image and contemporary English-influenced examples in Norway see Morgan, 'Texts and Images, Thirteenth Century', pp. 81–2, 82–91, pls. 5, 10, 11.

9   N. Morgan, *Early Gothic Manuscripts 1190–1250*, Survey of Manuscripts Illuminated in the British Isles, 4.1 (Oxford, 1982), pp. 133–4, no. 86, Plate 291, and Morgan, 'Texts and Images, Thirteenth Century', pp. 84–9.

10   N. Morgan, *Early Gothic Manuscripts 1250–1285*, Survey of Manuscripts Illuminated in the British Isles, 4.2 (London, 1988), vol. 1, pp. 59–61, no. 101, Plate 23, and Morgan, 'Texts and Images, Thirteenth Century', pp. 89–92.

11   L. F. Sandler, *The Psalter of Robert de Lisle* (Oxford, 1983), p. 64, pl. 16.

12   C. A. Carsley, 'Devotion to the Holy Name. Late Medieval Piety in England', *Princeton University Library Chronicle*, 53 no. 2 (1992), pp. 157–72, E. Duffy, *The Stripping of the Altars. Traditional Religion in England c. 1400–c. 1580* (New Haven, 1992), pp. 115–16, and E. G. C. Atchley, 'Jesus Mass and Anthems', *Transactions of the St Paul's Ecclesiological Society*, 4 (1905), pp. 163–9.

13   Royal Commission on Historical Monuments England, *An Inventory of Historical Monuments in Dorset, vol. I, West* (London, 1952), p. 250.

with the Jesus monogram in the fifteenth-century flintwork panels in Norfolk and Suffolk parish churches.[14] In these the Mary monogram frequently is crowned as at Garboldisham, St John the Baptist (Suffolk) where it is placed in a frieze at the foot of the c. 1463–70 tower with the IHS and SI monograms, the latter signifying the dedicatory saint, John the Baptist (Plate 2).[15] The location of the flintwork monograms at different positions of the exterior of these churches will be discussed shortly.

Other than the flintwork panels the most extensive location for Marian monograms seems to have been in stained glass in the topmost tracery lights. They are more popular in some parts of the country than others, notably in Lincolnshire, Norfolk, Northamptonshire, Somerset and Suffolk. In Kent, for example, there is only one surviving occurrence, at Great Chart, St Mary, paired with the Jesus monogram. Here the surround of both are the Marian flower symbol of lilies (Plate 3). This symbolism is derived from the pot of lilies frequently depicted in the Annunciation from c. 1300 onwards. The frames at Great Chart are a chaplet of roses for Mary and the Crown of Thorns for Jesus. The pairing of the Jesus and Mary monograms in stained glass tracery lights could just be decorative, but could signify the ejaculatory prayer 'Jesus and Mary have mercy on me'. This might be so when they are placed directly beside each other as in the fifteenth-century glass at Ropsley, St Peter (Lincolnshire) (Plate 4) and Bitchfield, St Mary Magdalene (Lincolnshire) (Plate 5).[16] Such symbolism of combined prayer is less likely when they are placed in corner traceries separated by standing figures of saints, or flanking a central subject such as the Coronation of the Virgin. At Curry Rivel, St Andrew (Somerset) they flank a now lost subject in the two central top lights, and this probably was the Coronation of the Virgin.[17]

A good example of the two monograms associated with many other sign symbols are the tracery lights of the north nave aisle windows of Steeple Ashton, St Mary (Wiltshire) (Plate 6), whose glass probably dates from c. 1480–1500.[18] In one window they flank the chalice and Host, and in another the arms of the Five Wounds. All these signs, including the Mary and Jesus monograms are on shields, as in many other fifteenth-century examples. The precedents for placing devotional and symbolic religious motifs on shields begins in the thirteenth century with the arms of the Trinity as the shield of faith, and with the Arma Christi, the

[14]   J. Blatchly and P. Northeast, *Decoding Flint Flushwork on Norfolk and Suffolk Churches* (Ipswich, 2005), for an excellent discussion, catalogue and series of reproductions of these monograms.

[15]   Blatchly and Northeast, *Decoding Flint Flushwork*, pp. 5, 8, 36–40.

[16]   P. Hegbin-Barnes, *The Medieval Stained Glass of the County of Lincolnshire*, Corpus Vitrearum Medii Aevi, Great Britain, Summary Catalogue, 3 (Oxford, 1996), pp. 37, 248.

[17]   C. Woodforde, *Stained Glass in Somerset 1250–1830* (Oxford, 1946; repr. Bath, 1970), p. 65.

[18]   Woodforde, *Stained Glass in Somerset*, pp. 89–90.

Instruments of the Passion on a shield.[19] These continue to be commonly placed on shields in the fifteenth century. Also, just as angels carry the shields of noble families in stained glass and on the sides of their tombs, so angels hold shields of the monograms. A good example would be in the displaced glass now in the south chancel window of Glastonbury, St John (Somerset) (Plate 7).[20] This interpretation of religious emblems as heraldry is a case of the interplay of secular and religious modes so commonly found in late medieval England.

The example of the monograms at Great Chart has already shown the use of symbolic surrounds to the monograms, in that case flowers. In the stained glass of Ashill, St Nicholas (Norfolk) the 'MR' is set against golden rays (Plate 8).[21] Mary is sometimes surrounded by such rays as she ascends to heaven at her assumption, as in the late fifteenth-century image of the Fraternity of the Assumption connected with the Company of Skinners in London.[22] In this image, as well as the gold rays around the figure of Mary, an angel at the side triumphantly brandishes the 'MR' monogram as Mary rises up to be crowned by the Holy Trinity.

Inscriptions with invocations to Jesus and Mary are at Hoveton St John (Norfolk), Mileham (Norfolk), and Pulham Market, St Mary Magdalene (Norfolk) – Jesu mercy, Lady help'.[23] A common placing of Marian inscriptions was on bells, but these seem always to have full texts and not monograms. In the long catalogue of inscriptions on medieval bells made in the rare publication of Downman some are quite long, whereas others are just 'Ave Maria' or 'Ave gracia plena'.[24] Examples of longer ones would be a prayer for her protection or her prayers: 'Protege virgo pia quos convoco sancta Maria' and 'Sancta Maria ora pro nobis'.

Another form of medieval art which used the monogram was embroidery and tapestry. Little survives, but such textiles are depicted in stained glass and illu-

---

[19] N. Morgan and M. Brown, *The Lambeth Apocalypse, Manuscript 209 in Lambeth Palace Library* (London, 1990), pp. 63–4, 258–9, figs 46, 49, 51, for the Trinity shield. For the Arma Christi see R. Dennys, *The Heraldic Imagination* (London, 1975), p. 96, and dating the earliest occurrence to the supposedly c. 1240 seal of the Cambridge Franciscans.

[20] Woodforde, *Stained Glass in Somerset*, 45, attributing this glass to the Devon school of painting.

[21] C. Woodforde, *The Norwich School of Glass-Painting in the Fifteenth Century* (Oxford, 1950), p. 182.

[22] R. Marks and P. Williamson (eds), *Gothic Art for England 1400–1547*, exhibition catalogue, Victoria and Albert Museum (London, 2003), pp. 58, 271, no. 133, pl. 32.

[23] Woodforde, *Norwich School of Glass-Painting*, p. 182.

[24] E. A. Downman, *Ancient Church Bells in England* (1898). The book was privately printed in only seventy-five copies, and groups inscribed and signed bells according to bell foundry workshops. It seems to be the fullest collection of inscriptions and trade marks on medieval bells. For a selection of Marian inscriptions on bells see also T. E. Bridgett, *Our Lady's Dowry; how England gained that Title*, 3rd edn (London, 1890), pp. 218–20.

minated manuscripts covered with heraldry, badges and monograms. At St Peter Mancroft in Norwich in the stained glass the scene of the Annunciation has the monogram on the red curtained bed.[25] The altar curtain in the Mass of St Gregory scene in the c. 1460–70 Hours of John and Agnes Brown of Stamford (Philadelphia, Free Library, Widener MS 3) also has it.[26] A splendid example is in the stained glass of St Peter Mancroft in the scene of Mary's funeral on her pall, as the procession is arrested by the Jew who laid his hands on her coffin and became fixed.[27] This parallels funeral palls of ecclesiastics and the laity which were decorated with their heraldry, badges or monograms, just as was their secular attire.[28] Mary's monogram likewise is her family sign.

Jewellery too used the monogram. An elaborate example is the late four-teenth-century brooch or morse of a cope given to New College Oxford by Peter Hylle, a citizen of Winchester in 1455 (Plate 9).[29] It has the Annunciation set in the lobes of a bejewelled 'M' and is very similar to a French example, once in the treasury of St Denis.[30] At the simple end of the jewellery spectrum are the plain lead badges, which could also have existed in finer examples in silver or even gold. The use of the 'M' or 'MR' on these badges and brooches, usually surmounted by a crown, raises the issue as to whether this sign was considered amuletic.[31] The issue of charms and amulets in the late Middle Ages is fraught with difficulties of inter-pretation, and I have found no proof that the monogram badges had an apotropaic function. Certainly girdles inscribed with the Magnificat served to secure safe deliv-ery. One such object is described 'In a curious MS of the fifteenth century in the possession of the Rev. James Dallaway entitled 'The Knowying of Woman Kynde' one recipe in difficult cases is to wryte the salme of Magnificath in a longe scrow and gyrdit abowte her, and sche shal be delyvert'.[32] The same issue will come up

[25] D. King, *The Medieval Stained Glass of St Peter Mancroft Norwich*, Corpus Vitrearum Medii Aevi, Great Britain, V (Oxford, 2006), pp. 4–5, col. pl. 2.

[26] Marks and Williamson, *Gothic Art for England*, pp. 274, 278, no. 140, pl. 113.

[27] King, *Stained Glass of St Peter Mancroft*, pp. 73–5, col. pl. 9.

[28] E.g. the funeral pall with dolphins of the Norwich fishmonger, John Reede: *Medieval Art in East Anglia 1300–1520*, ed. P. Lasko and N. J. Morgan, exhibition catalogue, Norwich Castle Museum (Norwich, 1973), pp. 63–4, no. 99. Also, for heraldry, the c. 1516 Fayrey Pall: Marks and Williamson, *Gothic Art for England*, p. 455, no. 349, pl. 31.

[29] J. J. G. Alexander and P. Binski (eds), *Age of Chivalry. Art in Plantagenet England 1200–1400*, exhibition catalogue, Royal Academy of Arts, London, 1987, p. 483, no. 640.

[30] B. de Montesquiou-Fezensac, *Le Trésor de Saint-Denis. Inventaire de 1634* (Paris, 1973), p. 157; B. de Montesquiou-Fezensac and D. Gaborit-Chopin, *Le Trésor de Saint-Denis. Documents divers* (Paris, 1977), pp. 139–40; B. de Montesquiou-Fezensac and D. Gaborit-Chopin, *Le Trésor de Saint-Denis. Planches et notices* (Paris, 1977), p. 47, pl. 29c.

[31] For 'M' badges see M. Mitchiner, *Medieval Pilgrim and Secular Badges* (London, 1986), pp. 90, 104, nos 197, 238–41a, and B. Spencer, *Pilgrim Souvenirs and Secular Badges* (London, 1998), pp. 155–7.

[32] E. Waterton, *Pietas Mariana Britannica. A History of English Devotion to the Most*

later in this paper when the heart with wings is considered, because this also existed as a lead badge.

The problem of the Marian monogram as a protective sign is particularly apposite for the exterior decoration of churches with the flintwork monograms, and their equivalents in relief sculpture. Their positions in the architectural structure are significant, flanking or surmounting doors, on the enclosing parapets of porches and clerestories, on towers both at their bases and their top parapets. These particularly locations suggest a protective function of entrance points and framing the building at its perimeters. At Elmswell, St John the Evangelist (Suffolk) the Mary monogram and the St John monogram flank the tower west door. St John the Baptist or Evangelist is the dedicatory saint of Elmswell church.[33] For churches dedicated to Mary herself the most elaborate use of her monogram is found. Not only do these monograms flank the main door but multiple 'M's' are placed in a horizontal band above it as at Great Witchingham, St Mary (Norfolk) (Plate 10) and Yaxley, St Mary (Suffolk) (Plate 11).[34] These suggested a repeated invocation of the name of Mary as was the case in devotional practice for the name of Jesus. Whether this suggests invocation for protection or devotion is unclear. Repeated invocations of Mary in prayers such as the Ave Maria had been established since the twelfth century and may have originated much earlier.[35] Little Stonham, St Mary (Suffolk) tower parapet indeed has three large crowned monograms on the east, north and west faces spelling out MARI(A) and D(OMI)N(U)S T(E)CU(M) and PLENA (Plate 12).[36] Unfortunately, the fourth tower face does not allow further phrases from the prayer because it is covered by a stair turret. It could either have begun the invocation with AVE or ended it with GRATIA. West Tofts, St Mary (Norfolk) also has a prayer invocation on the south face of the tower which only partially remains.[37] It would have read 'Ihesus, Maria, orate pro nobis'. Helmingham, St Mary (Suffolk) had on its tower an inscription referring to Mary as from the root of Jesse and her rising to heaven in her Assumption: 'Scandit ad ethera virgo puerpera virgula Jesse'.[38] On towers the use of the monogram is again most elaborate in churches dedicated to Mary such as Rougham, St John Baptist (now St Mary) (Suffolk) (Plate 13).[39] Very large 'MR' monograms are on the parapet at the top of

---

Blessed Virgin Marye, Mother of God (London, 1879), p. 207, quoting N. H. Nicolas, *Privy Purse Expenses of Elizabeth of York: Wardrobe Accounts of Edward IV* (London, 1830), pp. 197–8.

33   Blatchly and Northeast, *Decoding Flint Flushwork*, pp. 9, 30.

34   Blatchly and Northeast, *Decoding Flint Flushwork*, pp. 8, 93, 104, 106.

35   Morgan, 'Texts and Images, Twelfth Century', pp. 126–7.

36   Blatchly and Northeast, *Decoding Flint Flushwork*, pp. 8, 74–5.

37   Blatchly and Northeast, *Decoding Flint Flushwork*, pp. 8, 83. This church is located in a restricted access military area and I have not been able to visit it.

38   Blatchly and Northeast, *Decoding Flint Flushwork*, pp. 2, 8, 45–6.

39   Blatchly and Northeast, *Decoding Flint Flushwork*, pp. 8, 67–9.

the 1458–88 tower of Rougham with the relatively rare incorporation of lily pots as mentioned earlier in the stained glass of Great Chart (Kent). Another example of architectural placing of monograms is at the level of the clerestory parapet as at Wortham, St Mary (Suffolk) where 'S T S M' in four panels signifies 'Sancta Trinitas, Sancta Maria' (Plate 14).[40]

The protective and intercessory function of the Mary monogram is clearly evident in the flint flushwork inscriptions on the church of Stratford St Mary (Suffolk) which Julian Luxford discusses in his paper in this volume.[41] The Maria Regina monogram is used for the 'M' in the donor's name, Edward Morse. One of the inscriptions starts with the prayer 'Jesus, Mary, pray for the souls of ...'. The most significant aspect in terms of Marian devotion is that the 'MR' monogram is used for all the 'M's'. The 'MR' is used for Morse in his initials flanking his trade mark – the family were involved in the cloth trade. There is also an example at Stratford St Mary of an unusual monogram incorporating all the letters of MARIA.[42]

The other 'sign' associated with Mary is the symbol of the sword piercing a heart, the prophecy of Simeon at the Presentation of the Christ Child in the Temple ' and thy own soul a sword shall pierce, that, out of many hearts, thoughts may be revealed' (Luke 2 v. 35). This is a prophecy of Mary's suffering in compassion with her Son. The imagery of the sword striking her breast seems never to be found in scenes of the Presentation in English art, but on occasions is found in Crucifixion scenes.[43] This emphasis on the loving and suffering heart of Mary, pierced by a sword, is a counterpart to the medieval devotion to the pierced heart of Christ in his Passion, rather than the post-medieval devotion to the Sacred Heart which emphasises more the love of Christ rather than the Passion.[44] Similarly, the Immaculate Heart of Mary, a relatively modern cult with the feast celebrated on the day following that of the Sacred Heart, is different, although cannot completely be excluded from medieval devotion.

These hearts of Mary are normally set on shields, and occur mainly in sculpture on roof bosses, although occasionally they are found in stained glass and lead badges. This image has received very little study. The only article known to me, and it is a very short article, is by Dom Ethelbert Horne, a monk of Downside, pub-

---

[40] Blatchly and Northeast, *Decoding Flint Flushwork*, pp. 9, 88.
[41] Blatchly and Northeast, *Decoding Flint Flushwork*, pp. 76–7. I would like to thank Julian Luxford for drawing this example to my attention. See below, pp. 119–32, esp. p. 125.
[42] Blatchly and Northeast, *Decoding Flint Flushwork*, p. 77 with Plate
[43] L. F. Sandler, *Gothic Manuscripts 1285–1385*, Survey of Manuscripts Illuminated in the British Isles, 5 (London, 1986), pp. 109–10, no. 99, Plate 254.
[44] N. Morgan, 'Longinus and the Wounded Heart', *Wiener Jahrbuch für Kunstgeschichte*, 46/47, 1993/94, pp. 507–18 and N. Morgan, 'An SS Collar in the Devotional Context of the Shield of the Five Wounds', in *The Lancastrian Court, Proceedings of the 2001 Harlaxton Symposium*, Harlaxton Medieval Studies, XIII, ed. J. Stratford (Donington, 2003), pp. 147–62, on English devotion and imagery of the heart of Christ.

lished in 1931, and to this must be added Brian Spencer's brief discussion of lead badges of this emblem.[45] The other image associated with the sword is the Seven Sorrows of the Virgin, in which seven swords pierce her breast.[46] This occurs particularly in late fifteenth-century Flemish art, and must have been known in England from the many imported Flemish Books of Hours of that period. One fragmentary example in stained glass is in Bury St Edmunds, St James (now the Cathedral) of the early sixteenth century, probably by Flemish glaziers. It is in the top of one of the lights of the westernmost south nave aisle windows and shows the hilts and part shafts of three swords pointing downwards (Plate 15). Nothing remains of the figure of Mary herself. This imagery of the swords of sorrow, in representing the whole figure of Mary, cannot be considered as a sign or symbol, even though its iconographic meaning is symbolic. The image of the sword piercing the heart did become a 'sign' of Mary, but very late in the Middle Ages, probably not before c. 1450 at the earliest. Most examples in England are c. 1475–1525, exactly the same time as the Virgin of the Seven Sorrows was becoming known in England through imported Flemish works or Flemish artists working in England. The heart pierced by the sword occurs in a number of forms. There are two roof bosses in Bristol Cathedral with two different forms.[47] One shows two swords piercing a heart, and I have not found any other examples. Could it be an emblem of an individual patron rather than a sign of Mary? The other is a more conventional type of the sword piercing the heart set against wings (Plate 16), although it could be asked why there are wings. At Beverley, St Mary (Yorkshire), the framing of the wings and the central vertical of the sword make it seem as if the 'M' for Mary is an intentional aspect of the design (Plate 17).[48] At Butcombe, St Michael (Somerset) a shield from a tracery light is now placed in the east window of the south aisle.[49] In this the wings are attached to the heart pierced by the sword, and drops of blood come from the heart (Plate 18). In roof bosses at Hereford Cathedral and Canterbury Cathedral cloister the sword has disappeared and there is only a

[45] E. Horne, 'A Wings, Sword and Heart Badge', *Antiquaries Journal*, 11 (1931), pp. 286–8 and Spencer, *Pilgrim Souvenirs*, pp. 159–61.

[46] C. Schuler, *The Sword of Compassion: Images of the Sorrowing Virgin in Late Medieval and Renaissance Art*, unpublished Ph.D. thesis, Columbia University, New York, 1987, is the only detailed study of this theme.

[47] C. J. P. Cave, *Roof Bosses in Medieval Churches* (Cambridge, 1948), pp. 45, 184, figs 298–9.

[48] Cave, *Roof Bosses*, 45, Plate 297.

[49] Horne, 'A Wings, Sword and Heart Badge', p. 288, Plate 6. The suggestion that this, and the bosses at Bristol, are the rebus of Abbot Newland (Nailheart) of Bristol is not acceptable. His rebus shows a heart pierced by three nails, not a sword: F. Were, 'Bristol Cathedral Heraldry', *Transactions of the Bristol and Gloucestershire Archaeological Society*, 25 (1902), pp. 129, 132; I. M. Roper, 'Effigies of Bristol', idem, pp. 26, 1903, 230; H. Jenner-Fust, 'Hill, Gloucestershire', idem, pp. 53, 1931, 162. I would like to thank Nigel Ramsay for sending me these references.

winged heart.[50] There is perhaps some cross influence with secular art because in French inventories brooches as winged hearts are described.[51] The best explanation of the wings is that these signs originated as a winged angel bust or head holding a heart, just as angels sometimes hold the monogram (Plate 19).[52] Alternatively, Spencer has suggested that the wings are beside the heart to distinguish the heart of Mary from the wounded heart of Christ.[53] In 1463 John Baret bequeathed a 'broche herte of gold ... with aungells and a ruby' to be set on the shrine of St Edmund at Bury.[54]

Wings in Marian signs occur in different contexts, such as in the Sugar Chantry in Wells Cathedral of c. 1489 where two wings flank a lily pot on a shield held by an angel (Plate 20).[55] Presumably they refer to the angel of the Annunciation. Their occurrence in this context does not help to explain their association with the heart. A roof boss over the north aisle doorway to the cloister in Gloucester Cathedral has a shield with two wings, a sword piercing a heart, and what is probably a lily, flanking a tau cross, a sort of Marian counterpart to the Arma Christi.[56] It is in the period when emblems and badges become popular that this imagery of Mary's heart emerges, and doubtless interconnections between secular and religious imagery emerge in forms multilayered in meaning. The heart has a rich symbolism in both secular and religious cultures, and its meaning in a variety of contexts is very elusive. The badge or brooch pierced by two arrows, which Spencer considers a devotional badge, seems to me perhaps to be a secular brooch referring to the arrows of love.[57]

In contrast to these problems of interpreting heart emblems, the monograms of Mary in their various forms have been relatively easy to explain. In some cases they have a devotional function and in others they clearly serve as protective signs. The imagery mixes sign with symbol in both the monograms and the hearts, but one doubts from the viewpoint of a medieval onlooker that any such distinction would be meaningful.

[50]   Cave, *Roof Bosses*, pp. 45, 194, Plate 296.
[51]   R. W. Lightbown, *Medieval European Jewellery* (London, 1992), pp. 184–6.
[52]   Spencer, *Pilgrim Souvenirs*, pp. 159–60, no. 176d.
[53]   Spencer, *Pilgrim Souvenirs*, p. 159. Mitchiner, *Medieval Pilgrim and Secular Badges*, p. 175, no. 558, seems to be an angel holding the heart of Mary, not the Sacred Heart as he suggests. The heart of Christ is usually pierced by the five wounds, for which see the references in n. 44.
[54]   Spencer, *Pilgrim Souvenirs*, p. 159, quoting S. Tymms, *Wills and Inventories from the Registers of the Commissary of Bury St Edmunds and the Archdeacon of Sudbury, 1370–1650*, Camden Society, 49 (1850), p. 35.
[55]   Horne, 'A Wings, Sword and Heart Badge', p. 288, Plate 4.
[56]   Horne, 'A Wings, Sword and Heart Badge', p. 288, Plate 3.
[57]   Spencer, *Pilgrim Souvenirs*, p. 159, no. 176c. For secular betrothal and love badges see Mitchiner, *Medieval Pilgrim and Secular Badges*, nos. 318–19a, and Spencer, *Pilgrim Souvenirs*, pp. 322–3.

Dieu y voye: Some Late Medieval and Early Modern Instances of Divine Vision

NICHOLAS ROGERS

In a Sarum book of hours in Sidney Sussex College, Cambridge,[1] is one of the most striking images of God's regard for mankind to be found in medieval art (Plate 1). Kathleen Scott, in her survey of English illuminated manuscripts of the fifteenth century, describes it as 'Holy Heart with Wound', which does not begin to tackle the oddity of this image.[2] The Sacred Heart is shown, as usual, with a gaping wound,[3] fit for St Thomas to place his hand within, but here the wound takes the form of an eye, from which flow tears.

The initial containing this surreal image prefaces an English translation of the Fifteen Oos, a series of fifteen meditations on the Passion, each beginning with an O, commonly (though wrongly) attributed in the rubrics to St Bridget.[4] This prose translation is part of a section of devotions in English, the other items being verse prayers to various saints that have been assigned to the Lydgate canon.[5] In one of these a prayer for Henry VI has been altered, suggesting a post-1461 date.[6] The Fifteen Oos are usually illustrated either by a Christological subject, often Christ as

---

[1] On Sidney Sussex MS 37, see M. R. James, *A Descriptive Catalogue of the Manuscripts in the Library of Sidney Sussex College, Cambridge* (Cambridge, 1895), pp. 24–5.

[2] K. L. Scott, *Later Gothic Manuscripts 1390–1490*, 2 vols (London, 1996), II, p. 383 (Table III).

[3] An example of the normal iconography of the Sacred Heart occurs on f. 95 of Sidney 37, in an initial at the start of the Psalms of the Passion.

[4] On the origins of the Fifteen Oos, see N. Rogers, 'About the Fifteen "O"s, The Brigittines and Syon Abbey', *St. Ansgar's Bulletin*, 80 (1984), pp. 29–30.

[5] H. N. MacCracken, The Minor Poems of John Lydgate, Part I, EETS, Extra Series, 107 (London, 1911), pp. xxvi–xxviii. The items are: Prayers to Ten Saints (MacCracken 145), ff. 142–145; Prayer to St Leonard (MacCracken 122), ff. 145v–147; Prayer to St Ursula (MacCracken 130), ff. 147–148; Prayer to St Zita (MacCracken 125), ff. 148–148v. Also included in 'O sterre of Iacob', on the Five Joys (MacCracken 140), ff. 148v–150.

[6] The invocation of St George, in the Prayers to Ten Saints, reads 'Pray for us and this region', not 'Pray for sixte Herry and al this regioun'.

[7] On the use of the Salvator Mundi image in this context, see N. Rogers, 'Die Ikonographie des Salvator Mundi', *Hermann Wessel Festschift*, ed. R. Lamp (Emden, forthcoming).

Salvator Mundi,[7] or by St Bridget writing.[8] Sidney 37 also contains the Latin text of the Fifteen Oos.[9] There is no passage in the Fifteen Oos that could have suggested the image of the eye in the heart directly. However, there are several biblical passages that refer to God's omnivoyance. St Peter, in his first Epistle, observes: 'the eyes of the Lord are upon the just, and his ears unto their prayers: but the countenance of the Lord upon them that do evil things'. The association of the gaze of the Lord with judgement is explicit in several texts; for example in Psalm 138 (Domine probasti me) we read: 'Thy eyes did see my imperfect being'. But this psalm also refers to the protection of God's providence, which is also the theme of Psalm 16, v. 8: 'from them that resist thy right hand keep me, as the apple of thy eye'.

In his idiosyncratic survey of northern English manuscripts, John B. Friedman suggests a northern origin for Sidney 37, based on the presence of Cuthbert and John of Beverley in the calendar, although they cannot be regarded as regional indicators at this date.[10] In fact, as Kathleen Scott notes, this book fits neatly into a London stylistic milieu of the 1470s.[11] The heavy figural modelling suggests a link with Anglo-French artists of the mid-century, such as the Fastolf Master (Plate 2).

For whom was this remarkable image intended? At the beginning of the prayer *O beata et intemerata* the owner is depicted kneeling before the Virgin and Child (Plate 3). Although the illumination is not of the highest quality, her appearance points to a high social rank. Over a sideless cote, at this period a fashion associated with peeresses, she wears a heraldic mantle with the arms (*Gules three lions passant guardant or within a bordure azure semy de lis or*) of the Holand family. The identity of this lady can be established with some degree of certainty. There are four women who are possible candidates, all called Anne: Anne Montagu, the third wife of John Holand, first Duke of Exeter;[12] Anne of York, the wife of Henry, second Duke of Exeter and later, even before her first husband had conveniently fallen overboard in 1475, of Thomas St Leger;[13] Anne Holand, the daughter of the second Duke of Exeter; and Anne Holand, sister of the second Duke. Anne Dowden, in her study of depictions of women in heraldic mantles, has observed that, when only one coat-of-arms is shown, this is invariably the paternal arms.[14] This would appear to eliminate the wives of the two Dukes of Exeter, the first of whom, Anne Montagu, would have been discounted on chronological

---

[8]   An early example is Aberdeen University Library, MS 25, f. 50, of *c*. 1415–24.

[9]   Sidney Sussex MS 37, ff. 101–08.

[10] J. B. Friedman, *Northern English Books, Owners, and Makers in the Late Middle Ages* (Syracuse, N. Y., 1995), pp. 240, 327 n. 26. St William, *pace* Friedman, does not occur in the calendar.

[11] Scott, *Later Gothic Manuscripts*, II, p. 330.

[12] *Oxford Dictionary of National Biography* (ODNB), 61 vols (Oxford, 2004), 27, p. 678.

[13] ODNB, 27, p. 662.

[14] A. Dowden, 'Towards a Complete List of Known Heraldic Effigies', *Monumental Brass Society Bulletin*, 62 (1993), pp. 42–5; 63 (1993), pp. 57–64.

grounds, since she died in 1457, which is a date earlier than the style of the manuscript suggests. The headdress is of the form described by Olivier de la Marche as 'les haulx bonnetz coeuvre chifz a banieres' or by costume historians as the butterfly headdress.[15] This fashion first appears on the continent in the late 1450s, but in England, to judge by monumental evidence, it is in vogue from the late 1460s to the early 1480s. An early form of the headdress appears on the brass of Margaret John, d. 1466, now at Ingrave, Essex.[16] The more usual form, closer to that in the manuscript, can be seen on the brass of Lady Elizabeth Say, at Broxbourne, Hertfordshire, of 1473.[17]

Of the two most likely candidates for ownership of the book, one, Anne Holand, daughter of the second duke of Exeter, married Thomas Grey, son of Queen Elizabeth Woodvyle, in October 1466 but died by February 1474,[18] which would provide an almost inconveniently tight *terminus ante quem*. The other, Anne Holand, sister of the second Duke, married firstly John Neville, the heir apparent of the second Earl of Westmorland, but this marriage had apparently not been consummated when he died in March 1450. She then proceeded to marry her first husband's uncle Sir John Neville, by whom she was the mother of the third Earl of Westmorland. After her second husband had been killed at Towton she married James, ninth Earl of Douglas, who had been driven into exile in England. She died on 26 December 1486.[19] Of the two she is the more likely candidate for ownership.

To the best of my knowledge the fusion of Sacred Heart and All-seeing Eye in Sidney MS 37 is unique in medieval art. However, a close parallel exists in the work of Hieronymus Bosch. In the Prado Tabletop,[20] most probably produced *c.* 1490, the Seven Deadly Sins are arranged in a ring around the pupil of an eye, at the centre of which can be seen the Man of Sorrows, emerging from the tomb, with below the monitory inscription 'Cave cave Dominus vidit'.[21] The Passion and God's view of mankind are similarly linked. The Prado Tabletop, with its lively evocation of the sins of mankind, makes clear the cause of the tears in Sidney 37. Gibson, in his excellent analysis of this painting, cites the conversion experience of the German humanist Jakob Wimpheling, which was prompted by the sight in a church in Erfurt of the inscription, in large letters: 'Sin not, God sees'.[22] Wimpheling's text makes no mention of any associated image, but it is plausible that there was one.

[15] M. Scott, *Late Gothic Europe, 1400–1500* (London, 1980), p. 173.
[16] W. Lack, H. M. Stuchfield and P. Whittemore, *The Monumental Brasses of Essex*, 2 vols (London, 2003), I, p. 416, illus. on p. 414.
[17] M. Rensten, *Hertfordshire Brasses* (Stevenage, 1982), Plate 14.
[18] *ODNB*, 27, p. 662.
[19] G. E.C[okayne], *The Complete Peerage*, XII, pt. II (London, 1959), pp. 550–1.
[20] R. H. Marijnissen and P. Ruyffelaere, *Hiëronymus Bosch: Het volledige œuvre* (Antwerpen, 1987), pp. 329–45.
[21] For a good illustration of this detail, see Marijnissen and Ruyffelaere, *Bosch*, p. 335.

I am indebted to Anne Sutton and Livia Visser-Fuchs for directing me to another English manuscript of the third quarter of the fifteenth century containing related eye iconography.[23] MS Staple 2 in the Borthwick Institute, York, is a Register of Royal Grants to the Company of the Merchants of the Staple of England, datable on codicological grounds to between 1463 and 1467. The first example is on f. 5v, where the initial to a charter of Edward III has an eye in a sunburst above, and a rose below (Plate 4). On f. 8, another charter of Edward III has a sun, labelled 'sol' above a bar inscribed 'pax in terra nostra'. Below is an eye shedding copious tears (Plate 5). The eye in the sun evokes Christ as 'sol iustitiae', and the tears may refer to the judicial powers conferred by the second charter. The third image, on f. 15v, is more complex, consisting of thirteen eyes (Plate 6). The texts associated with it point to a judicial interpretation. The scroll above the eyes reads 'Equitatem vidit vultus eius' (His countenance hath beheld righteousness) (Ps. 10, 8) and the left stave 'Honor regis iudicium diligit' (The king's honour loveth judgement) (Ps. 98, 4). The eyes are, therefore, presumably divine, but their multiplicity is puzzling. The capitals used in the left-hand stave are of a type uncommon in England at this date, although similar forms had been used in France since the 1450s.[24] One of the additions to MS Staple 2 is signed by a Calais scribe, and it is possible that the original manuscript is a product of a Calais workshop, at the crossroads between English, French and Flemish art.

The eye as a heraldic charge is virtually unknown in English heraldry, but there are instances of its use in continental heraldry, chiefly in canting arms.[25] An example which closely resembles the Sidney image is the coat-of-arms of the Dutch family of Hartoog, *Or on a heart gules a human eye proper.*[26] In the well-known rebus of Abbot Islip, found in both sculpted and stained glass forms in his work at Westminster Abbey, the eye simply refers to the first syllable of his name, just as the hand holding an oak slip refers to the second, and the man slipping from a fig tree to the whole, but it is possible that the juxtaposition of eye and accident suggested a providential interpretation to some onlookers.[27]

[22] W. S. Gibson, *Hieronymus Bosch* (London, 1973), p. 37; J. Knepper, *Jakob Wimpfeling (1450–1528). Sein Leben und Seine Werke* (Freiburg im Breisgau, 1902), p. 12.

[23] For further discussion of this manuscript, see A. Sutton, 'An unfinished celebration of the Yorkist accession by a Clerk of the Merchant Staplers of Calais', *The Fifteenth Century*, 8, ed. L. Clark (Woodbridge, 2008), pp. 135–61.

[24] E.g. in the Hours of Étienne Chevalier, by Jean Fouquet, of c. 1452–60 (*Jean Fouquet, peintre et enlumineur du XVᵉ siècle*, ed. F. Avril, exhibition catalogue, Bibliothèque Nationale de France (Paris, 2003), no. 24).

[25] J. Woodward and G. Burnett, *A Treatise on Heraldry British and Foreign*, intr. L. G. Pine (Newton Abbot, 1969), pp. 201–02.

[26] J. B. Rietstap, *Armorial Général*, 2nd edn, 2 vols (Gouda, 1884), I, p. 895.

[27] RCHM, *London*, I, *Westminster Abbey* (London, 1924), pp. 35a, 88a, pl. 7. For a good illustration of the rebus, see L. E. Tanner, *Unknown Westminster Abbey* (Harmondsworth, 1948), pl. 64.

Although less immediately startling, the image of divine vision which occurred on an incised slab of 1451, formerly in the Oratorian church at Dijon, is no less singular than that in the Hours of Anne Holand. Its appearance, like that of many of the lost funerary monuments of medieval France, is known from a drawing in the collection compiled for Roger de Gaignières (Plate 7). The slab had a marginal inscription stating 'Here lies Perrin de Laule son of the late Gille de Laule of Salins and of Guillemine daughter of the late Master Odart Donay, the which Odart founded in this chapel a daily Mass and with this the said Perrin has founded an anniversary for a year, the which died the ninth day of November 1451'. In the centre was a pair of spectacles, of the commonest medieval type, with a pair of lenses with straight frame arms riveted together. Associated with them was the inscription 'Dieu y voye' (God sees). The spectacles were shown inverted, underlining the heavenly origin of their owner.[28] The church which the Oratorians took over in 1621 had been a house of the obscure Valliscaulian order, envisaged as a cross between the Cistercians and the Carthusians, which had a handful of priories in Burgundy, as well as two foundations in Scotland.[29] A survey of published material relating to late medieval Burgundy has not revealed anything more about the persons named on the slab.

To the modern viewer the use of a device for correcting defective vision as an attribute of God is bizarre, even heretical. However, this image can be understood if it is placed in its iconographic context. Spectacles were invented in Italy at the end of the thirteenth century,[30] and it is in northern Italy that they first appear in art, in the sequence of famous Dominicans in the chapter-house of S. Nicolò at Treviso, painted in 1352 by Tomaso da Modena. Cardinal Hugues de St Cher is shown wearing a riveted pair of lenses as he writes.[31] Spectacles are part of the impedimenta of the creative process of writing, along with books, pens, inkwells, scissors, rulers. In fifteenth-century groups of apostles one of them is sometimes distinguished by his wearing of spectacles. A fine early example occurs on the Niederwildungen Altarpiece by Conrad von Soest.[32] As in Tomaso da Modena this genre detail serves to reinforce the wisdom of the wearer.

[28]   Cf. The inversion of the Virgin's response to Gabriel, to indicate that it is intended for God, in the Annunciation of the Ghent Altarpiece and Jan van Eyck's 'Washington Annunciation' (E. Dhanens, *Hubert and Jan van Eyck* (Antwerp, 1980), pls 58, 221).

[29]   *Ordinale Conventus Vallis Caulium: the Rule of the Monastic Order of Val-des-Choux in Burgundy*, ed. W. De Gray Birch (London, 1900), pp. xviii, xxvi n. 1.

[30]   They are referred to in a sermon preached by the Dominican Giordano da Pisa at S. Maria Novella in Florence on 23 February 1306 as having been invented less than twenty years previously. He described 'the art of making glasses which help you to see well' as 'one of the best and most necessary skills in the world' (R. Gibbs, *Tomaso da Modena* (Cambridge, 1989), p. 83).

[31]   Gibbs, *Tomaso da Modena*, pl. 19.

[32]   B. Corley, *Conrad von Soest: Painter among Merchant Princes* (London, 1996), pl. XIX.

In Jan van Eyck's 'Madonna of Canon van der Paele', of 1436, the Canon's spectacles may be a realistic depiction of a necessary reading aid for an elderly cler-gyman.[33] Van Eyck clearly revels in their optical properties, just as he delights in depicting the reflections in St George's armour. But Canon van der Paele's spec-tacles also have a symbolic value, representing his wisdom. Similarly, the specta-cles clutched by Simon Bening in his self-portrait are not only a reminder of the detailed work of a miniaturist, but represent the process of creating those minia-tures. With these examples in mind, it is possible to view the spectacles on the tombstone of Perrin de Laule as an image of the Eternal Wisdom of the Creator.

One possible reason for the failure of this symbol of divine vision to catch on is that spectacles soon acquired a negative iconographical connotation. In the work of Bosch they are used to symbolise sham erudition or hypocrisy.[34] A good example of this is in *The Conjurer*, by a follower of Bosch and probably repro-ducing a composition by the master himself, where a man on the left, with an inno-cent air, gazes upwards through the spectacles perched on his nose while he takes the purse of one of the gullible onlookers.[35] In sixteenth-century iconography spectacles are often a sign of folly. Typical of this is Pieter Bruegel the Elder's *Elck*, of 1558, a bespectacled lantern-bearer who searches in vain in a world turned upside down.[36] With the possible exception of the apotropeic examples carved on seventeenth- and eighteenth-century German domestic buildings,[37] there are no further instances of spectacles as symbols of divine vision.

No less outré than the Sidney and Dijon examples is the Divine Eye device developed by Alberti. This first appears in a self-portrait bronze plaque, made *c*. 1435,[38] but in its fullest form occurs on Matteo de' Pasti's medal of about 1450 (Plate 8). The eye is shown as winged above the rhetorical inscription 'Quid tum', within a laurel wreath. Like many Renaissance *imprese*, this takes on the charac-ter of a riddle. In his short tract *Anuli* Alberti has a tantalisingly brief discussion of the 'oculus alis aquilae insignis', in which he observes: 'The ancients likened God to an eye seeing all and everything. Thus we are admonished ... to conceive of God as ever present, seeing all our deeds and thoughts. At the same time we are also reminded that we must be vigilant and circumspect'. A passage in his *De re aedi-ficatoria* suggests that he may have been inspired by Egyptian hieroglyphs: 'The Egyptians employed the following sign language: a god was represented by an eye,

[33] Dhanens, *Hubert and Jan van Eyck*, pl. 143.
[34] H. Janssen, O. Goubitz and J. Kottman, 'Everyday Objects in the Paintings of Hierony-mus Bosch', in *Hieronymus Bosch: New Insights Into His Life and Work*, ed. J. Kold-eweij, B. Vermet and B. van Kooij (Rotterdam, 2001), p. 187. For details of devils wearing spectacles, see Marijnissen and Ruyffelaere, *Bosch*, pp. 191, 233, 291.
[35] Marijnissen and Ruyffelaere, *Bosch*, p. 450.
[36] R. H. Marijnissen, *Bruegel: Tout l'œuvre peint et dessiné* (Anvers, 1988), pp. 100–02.
[37] W. Schulte, 'Die "Brille" als Sinnbild', *Germanien*, XIII (1941), pp. 311–14.
[38] R. Tavernor, *On Alberti and the Art of Building* (New Haven, 1998), Plate 24.

Nature by a vulture'.[39] It is probable that Alberti's interest in the symbolic value of hieroglyphs was stimulated by the rediscovery of the late classical text of Horapollo's *Hieroglyphica* in 1422, which was brought to Florence by Cristoforo Buondelmonti. The numerous sixteenth-century editions of Horapollo bear witness to the spread of interest in the interpretation of hieroglyphs.

At some point the Divine Eye was combined with the Trinitarian symbol of the triangle, examples of which can be found as early as the Uta Codex.[40] The earliest example of this combined symbol is sometimes cited as that in Pontormo's 'Supper at Emmaus' of 1525, now in the Uffizi, but it is clear even to the naked eye that this area of the canvas has been restored.[41] A recent scientific examination of Pontormo's work for the Charterhouse at Galluzzo revealed a tricephalous Trinitarian image underneath. A similar overpainting was carried out on Jacopo da Empoli's reduced copy of the painting, also made for Galluzzo.[42] It is likely that this alteration was carried out in response to Urban VIII's decree of 1628 ordering the destruction of tricephalous images of the Trinity.

It may be significant that the earliest securely datable example of the Trinitarian eye occurs in the frontispiece to a work by the Jesuit Athanasius Kircher, who wrote at length on the meaning of Egyptian hieroglyphs as part of his investigation into hermetic knowledge.[43] His *Musurgia Universalis*, published in Rome in 1650, shows an eye, accompanied in this instance by three ears, in a radiate triangle.[44] The standard form of the image occurs in the frontispieces to *Arithmologia*, of 1665, and *Ars Magna Sciendi*, of 1669.[45] Curiously, an early work of Kirchner's, his *Magnes, sive de Arte Magnetica*, of 1641, provides an independent re-creation of the image in Sidney 37. At the centre of a table representing magnetic declination is a heart with a radiate eye in it, inscribed 'Just as the magnet slopes towards a centre, so do our hearts point towards God.[46] That the Trinitar-

[39]   Tavernor, *Alberti*, p. 32. See also M. Barasch, 'Renaissance Hieroglyphics', in *Hieroglyphen: Stationen einer anderen abendländischen Grammatologie*, ed. A. and J. Assmann (München, 2003), p. 175.

[40]   On the triangle as a Trinitarian symbol, see R. Teufel, 'Dreieck', *Reallexikon zur Deutschen Kunstgeschichte*, IV (Stuttgart, 1958), pp. 406–07. On the Hand of God superimposed on a triangle in the Uta Codex (Munich, Bayerische Staatbibliothek, Clm. 13601), see A. S. Cohen, *The Uta Codex: Art, Philosophy, and Reform in Eleventh-Century Germany* (University Park, Pa., 2000), pp. 28–33, Plate 10, col. pl. 2.

[41]   P. Costamagna, *Pontormo: Catalogue raisonné de l'œuvre peint* (Paris, 1994), no. 46 (pp. 178–81).

[42]   M. Bietti, 'Pontormo copiato', in C. Acidini Luchinat et al., *Da Pontormo e per Pontormo: Novità alla Certosa*, exhibition catalogue (Firenze, 1996), pp. 89–94.

[43]   For an introduction to this aspect of Kircher's work, see J. Godwin, *Athanasius Kircher: A Renaissance Man and the Quest for Lost Knowledge* (London, 1979), pp. 56–65.

[44]   Godwin, *Kircher*, pl. 59.

[45]   Godwin, *Kircher*, pl. 76, pl. on p. 8.

[46]   Godwin, *Kircher*, pl. 67.

ian eye soon became a well-known device is demonstrated by the Flemish medal-list Jan Roettiers' medal commemorating the landing of Charles II at Dover in 1660. Above three figures with regalia awaiting the King's ship is an eye in a radiate tri-angle, with the defiant motto: 'Si Deus est custos quis meus hostis erit'.[47] The sym-bol was a useful compositional device for medallists working within the confines of a circle. It also became a popular motif in ecclesiastical decoration, particularly in southern Germany and Austria. A particularly striking example is J. F. Fromiller's ceiling fresco of the Trinitarian Eye surrounded by putti at Stift Ossiach.[48]

The most widely circulated image of divine vision is that which occurs on American dollar bills (Plate 9). It is widely assumed that this device, an All-Seeing Eye forming the apex of an unfinished pyramid of thirteen steps, is Masonic, and there is an amusing body of literature, much of it web-based, which attempts to reveal hidden mysteries in the iconography of the dollar bill. It is true that F. D. Roosevelt and Henry A. Wallace, the President and Vice-President at the time of the inclusion of the obverse and reverse of the Great Seal of the United States on dollar bills in 1935, were prominent Masons and would have placed a Masonic interpretation upon the design.[49] However, in their exhaustive study of the iconog-raphy of the Great Seal of the United States Patterson and Dougall demonstrate that there is no evidence that any of the men directly responsible for the design adopted in 1782 was a Freemason.[50] The textual and visual elements of the Great Seal derive from the common fund of knowledge available to classically-educated eighteenth-century Americans. The Masonic adoption of the All-Seeing Eye, usu-ally not shown within a triangle, thereby differentiating it from the Trinitarian sym-bol,[51] is an example of their participation in a common European iconographic tradition. The Trinitarian Eye can be found in contexts of unimpeachable ortho-doxy, such as the scudo coin of Pope Leo XII, minted in 1825.[52] Penetrating beyond ecclesiastical decoration and scholarly discourse,[53] this symbol became common currency in the popular iconography of Central Europe, as illustrated by a Bavar-ian bedstead of 1798 from Neubeuern, in which the Trinitarian eye is placed above

[47] D. Fearon, *Spink's Catalogue of British Commemorative Medals 1558 to the Present Day* (Exeter, 1984), no. 111.3.

[48] Teufel, 'Dreieck', Abb. 2.

[49] R. S. Patterson and R. Dougall, *The Eagle and the Shield: A History of the Great Seal of the United States* (Washington, 1976), pp. 402–7.

[50] Ibid., pp. 529–32.

[51] For examples see J. S. Curl, *The Art and Architecture of Freemasonry: An Introduc-tory Study* (London, 1991), figs. 40, 171. For its meaning in Freemasonry see ibid., p. 233.

[52] J. Coffin, *Coins of the Popes* (New York, 1946), pl. XIV, no. 71. The engraver was Giuseppe Cerbara.

[53] For examples of this iconography, see G. Stuhlfauth, 'Auge Gottes', *Reallexikon zur Deutsche Kunstgeschichte*, I (Stuttgart, 1937), cols. 1243–8.

an image of the Christ child holding the Sacred Heart,[54] and a painted panel depicting St Isidore, the patron saint of farmers, from an early nineteenth-century piece of Carinthian furniture (Plate 10).[55]

The three types of image of divine vision considered in this paper were all *sui generis* and for varying reasons did not become established iconographic forms. The eye in the heart of Sidney 37 was devoid of any particular textual relationship and had to contend with a well-rooted standard iconographic form of Sacred Heart. The Dijon spectacles lost their iconographic value as other less positive interpretations of the device were developed. Alberti's *impresa* was not intended to be disseminated widely but only to be understood fully by the cognoscenti, perhaps even only by Alberti himself. Yet, paradoxically, it was the iconographic current of which Alberti's winged eye was an early product that resulted in the creation of an image that eventually established itself in the popular iconographic vocabulary.

[54]   T. Gebhard, *Die volkstümliche Möbelmalerei in Altbayern* (München, 1937), p. 46, Abb. 31.
[55]   K. Eisner and O. Moser, *Kärntner Bauernmöbel: Ausstellungskatalog zur Möbelsammlung in der Propstei Maria Saal* (Klagenfurt, 1982), p. 44, pl. on p. 27.

Symbols of Devotion and Identity in The Shaftesbury Hours (Cambridge, Fitzwilliam Museum, MS 2–1957)

ELIZABETH NEW

The Book of Hours under discussion does not contain miniatures or extensive decoration, and most of the limited attention it has received has focused on its six-teenth-century provenance.[1] It is however a remarkable and important manu-script, because, while not lavish, the text and decoration were carefully chosen by the original owner, and contain coded signs of religious and social identity in both a public and private context.

I. *Original Owner and Early Provenance*
The decoration and a number of inscriptions, which are discussed at length below, clearly demonstrate that the Shaftesbury Hours was made for Elizabeth Shelford, (d. 1528) penultimate abbess of the Benedictine abbey of Shaftesbury in Dorset.[2] In addition to several instances of Shelford's initials and rebus, the Calendar records the date of Elizabeth's election as abbess, her benediction and her investi-ture with the temporalities of the abbey on 25 June, 12 July and 21 July respec-tively.[3]

After Shelford's death the Shaftesbury Hours passed into the hands of Richard Marshall, rector of the parish of St Rumbold, Shaftesbury, and it is possi-ble that Shelford gave or bequeathed it to him.[4] An inscription records that the manuscript was then sold to Alice Champenys, a nun at the abbey.[5] The inscrip-

---

[1] The decoration of the manuscript is recorded in F. Wormald and P. Giles, *A Catalogue of Manuscripts in the Fitzwilliam Museum* (Cambridge, 1982), pp. 516–21, although with some errors and omissions; Luxford discusses the decoration in the general con-text of the manuscript, J. M. Luxford, *The Art and Architecture of English Benedictine Monasteries, 1300–1540: a Patronage History* (Woodbridge, 2005), pp. 5, 32, 44, 46, 70.

[2] Shelford was elected by 50 nuns in 1504, W. Page (ed.), *VCH Dorset* (1975), 2, pp. 78–9.

[3] FM 2–1957, ff. 4, 5v, 6.

[4] No will has yet been identified for Elizabeth Shelford and, a religious, she is unlikely to have made one. I am grateful to Dr Martin Heale for clarification on this point.

[5] FM 2–1957, f. 132v. Champenys was a nun when Shelford was elected, J. Hutchins, *The History and Antiquities of the County of Dorset* (London, 1774), vol. 2, p. 19; she was listed twelfth after the Sub-Prioress on a pension list of March 1542, London, TNA,

tion is undated, but the book was probably acquired by Champenys before 1535, when Marshall moved away from Shaftesbury.[6] The scribe who recorded the sale, possibly Marshall himself, also added Psalm 11, a number of petition prayers headed *pro sorore defuncta*, and versicles and responses for the Penitential Psalms, suggesting that Champenys bought it because she required a manuscript made for use at Shaftesbury. It is also likely that the manuscript would have been imbued with a certain sentimental value, particularly with the addition of prayers for departed sisters. Champenys' will, if she made one, has not been traced, and at the time of writing it is still unclear what happened to the manuscript between the mid-sixteenth and mid-nineteenth centuries.

Fascinating though it is, the provenance of the Shaftesbury Hours is not central to this paper. Instead, the programme of decoration and textual contents of the manuscript form the focus of discussion. The symbolism of the Shaftesbury Hours can roughly be divided into religious and secular, although as with most things medieval the two are frequently interconnected. The decorative elements in the manuscript will be considered in the context of the semiotics of identity, before conclusions are drawn regarding what this manuscript can tell us about the reasons for its manufacture, and about Elizabeth Shelford herself.

II. *Religious and Devotional Symbolism*

The religious imagery in the Shaftesbury Hours is largely Christocentric, although there are Marian elements and a few images which are rather more involved, one in particular relying for a correct interpretation upon the accompanying text.

The popularity of Christocentric devotions in late medieval England is well attested.[7] Books of Hours made in England or for the English market frequently

---

E315/245, Court of Augmentations, f. 140; Champenys was still alive in 1553 when she appears in the Pension Roll for the abbey, W. Dugdale, *Monasticon Anglicanum: a History of the Abbies and Other Monasteries, Hospitals, Frieries, and Cathedral and Collegiate Churches, with their dependencies, in England and Wales*, new edn, ed. J. Carley (London, 1846), vol. II, p. 474, n. 9.

6   Marshall received a BCL from Oxford University, was ordained a priest to the title of St Frideswide's, Oxford, in 1499, and was rector of St Rumbold's, Shaftesbury, 1506–1535. He was last recorded as vicar of Baschurch, Shropshire, in 1535, and is presumed to have died at about this time, A. B. Emden, *A Biographical Register of the University of Oxford to A.D. 1500*, 3 vols (Oxford, 1957), vol. 2, p. 1230. In 1509 Marshall received dispensation to hold more than one benefice, M. Haren (ed.), *Calendar of Entries in the Papal Registers Relating to Great Britain and Ireland. Papal Letters. Vol. XIX, 1503–1513* (Dublin, 1998), no. 118.

7   For general discussions of Christocentric cults, especially the Holy Name, see R. Pfaff, *New Liturgical Feasts in Later Medieval England* (Oxford, 1970), pp. 62–83; H. Blake, G. Egan, J. Hurst† and E. A. New, 'From Popular Devotion to Resistance and Revival in England: the Cult of the Holy Name of Jesus', in D. Gaimster and R. Gilchrist (eds), *The Archaeology of Reformation, 1480–1580* (Leeds, 2003), pp. 175–203.

had cycles of the Passion of Christ in addition to or rather than Marian imagery for the Hours of the Virgin, especially when Hours of the Cross were intermixed.[8] Therefore finding Christological images in the Shaftesbury Hours is not in itself surprising; what is rather more unusual is the form that they take.

The Sacred Monogram, the three letter abbreviation for 'Jesus', is usually written in clear letters, but is here formed in a complex manner from the stems of daisies[9] (Plate 1). It is probable that there were deliberate and theologically sophisticated reasons for this depiction of the Sacred Monogram. The viewer would have to concentrate on the image to identify the Monogram, literally seeking out 'Jesus', with the flowering stems perhaps reminiscent of the Rod of Jesse or *lignum vitae*. The small Wounded Cross below the main decorated initial has Eucharistic and Passion connotations, reflecting the human and divine nature of Christ, dual themes of the late medieval devotion to the Holy Name.[10] Very similar iconography occurs on a fifteenth-century Norfolk Rood screen, which depicts a flowering Crucifix springing from the figure of Jesse and the Sacred Monogram with rose stems intertwined.[11]

The Five Wounds on a shield appear twice in the Shaftesbury Hours, once on the same leaf as the Sacred Monogram and once with the Crown of Thorns as a crest (Plate 2). The Wounds were often depicted as 'charges' on a shield, but the placement of the Crown of Thorns and the crossed lance and sponge are rather less common and deliberately armorial.[12] It is even possible to suggest a model which might have inspired this image. A number of devotional woodcuts of the Five Wounds and the 'arms of Jesus' (Christ's wounded hands, feet and heart on a shield) were produced by the Sheen Charterhouse.[13] Although there are some

---

[8] See for example J. Harthan, *Books of Hours and their Owners* (London, 1977), p. 26; Duffy suggests that St Edmund of Abingdon's linking of the Canonical Hours with events of the Passion had a significant influence on the decoration of Books of Hours, E. Duffy, *Marking the Hours. English People and their Prayers, 1240–1570* (New Haven and London, 2006), pp. 13, 15.

[9] Lower-case letters were used almost exclusively before the mid-sixteenth century, the forms 'ihs' and 'ihc' being favoured in England, Blake et al., 'Cult of the Holy Name', pp. 177–8, n. 23.

[10] See for example the writings of Richard Rolle, in particular *Ego Dormio, Richard Rolle: The English Writings,* ed. R .S. Allen (London, 1989).

[11] The screen is now at the back of East Harling church. Much of the fabric and fittings of the church, including the screen, were replaced in the fifteenth century under the patronage of Anne Harling.

[12] Setting the Five Wounds on a shield became increasingly common from the mid-fifteenth century, N. Morgan, 'An SS Collar in the Devotional Context of the Shield of the Five Wounds', in J. Stratford (ed.), *The Lancastrian Court*. Harlaxton Medieval Studies Series XIII (Donington, 2003), pp. 147–62, p. 151.

[13] London, BL, Egerton MS 1821, f.7, and Oxford, Bodleian Library, Arch. G. f. 14, commented upon in C. Dodgson, 'English Devotional Woodcuts of the Late Fifteenth Century', *Walpole Society* 17 (1928/29), pp. 95–108, pp. 98, 102, pl. XXXVI c. It is of interest

differences between the woodcuts and the Shaftesbury Hours image many elements are remarkably similar and some details, including the rather pointed handle of the lance, (on the lower left) are almost identical, suggesting that the artist was familiar with such devotional leaves. The Wounded Heart, which accompanies an indulgenced Christocentric prayer (Plate 3), has a similarly quasi-armorial feel to it and echoes a number of images in devotional books.

The Head of Christ is a prominent image in the manuscript (Plate 4). It depicts Christ crowned with thorns, connecting the image with the iconography of the suffering Jesus so prevalent in late medieval English art and literature. The jug in the initial below can be interpreted as the 'bitter cup' accepted in Gethsemane, the ewer with which Pilate washed his hands, the vinegar offered during the Crucifixion, a pot of oil for anointing Christ's body, or even an allusion to the Fountain of Life. Similar jugs appear in manuscripts and woodcuts at this date as part of the Instruments of the Passion, again indicating a familiarity with the idioms of contemporary devotional iconography.[14]

The overt Marian imagery in the Shaftesbury Hours is limited to two shields of arms, one quartering roses and lilies (Plate 5), the other with three lilies. The placement of the shields within the Hours of the Virgin, coupled with the charges of roses and lilies, flowers associated with Mary, identify them as the pseudo-armorial charges of the Mother of God.[15] The iconography is somewhat unusual, and additional layers of meaning may be encoded within them, particularly in relation to the roses. There is another rose in the Shaftesbury Hours, a Tudor-style rose at the start of the Penitential Psalms. This can be interpreted in several ways, and perhaps provides the key to understanding these multi-faceted images. The rose is in fact Tudor-style only in its shape, as the five petals are arranged in a different manner to the normal Tudor rose, while the usual sequence of colours are reversed with white dominating. This probably alludes to the Virgin Mary, the 'rose without a thorn' who intercedes for humanity. Other interpretations are however possible, related to more worldly matters discussed below.

One initial, beneath the quartered Marian arms on fol. 37v (Plate 5), would initially appear to be purely decorative, with wavy lines in the centre. The blue-green highlighting is however used mainly for historiated initials, and when one reads the text an interpretation presents itself. The initial is for Ps. 92, *Dominus regnavit gloria*; the third verse of the Psalm continues *levaverunt flumina Domine, levaverunt flumina voces suas* ('The rivers have lifted up, Lord, the

---

to note that the 'arms of Jesus' woodcut was removed from a 1495 printed Book of Hours from Sheen Abbey, now Oxford, Bodleian Library, Douce 24.

14   See for example Cambridge, Fitzwilliam Museum, MS 40–1950, f. 81.

15   Giles suggested that they are Marian 'arms', Wormald and Giles, *Catalogue of Manuscripts*, p. 520; Nicholas Rogers has also stated that they are the 'assumed arms of the Virgin', pers. comm.

rivers have lifted up their voices'). In this context, the odd down-flowing blue-green lines make sense, transformed into the Psalmist's rivers.

III. *Secular Iconography*

The remainder of the decoration in the Shaftesbury Hours is primarily secular. A large historiated initial at the start of the Office of the Dead contains the arms of the Abbey (*azure, a cross fleury and five martlets or*).[16] This was an appropriate place for a prominent image of corporate identity, as the Office of the Dead formed part of the liturgical round where the departed of the community were among those remembered. Elizabeth Shelford may have used the manuscript for some services where the Abbey's arms would have been seen and appreciated, while the image would have acted as a good 'corporate logo' if Elizabeth took the book with her when away from Shaftesbury.

Other elements of the decoration may also relate to the Abbey, albeit in a rather veiled manner. Pen-flourishing in later medieval manuscripts often contains identifiable elements, such as faces or grotesques. Shelford's Book of Hours is no exception, but prominent among the recognisable images are eagles (Plate 5). These might be purely decorative, but there is another possibility. Geoffrey of Monmouth mentions the story of an eagle which perched on the walls of Shaftesbury, speaking prophesies, an episode repeated and expanded upon in the *Brute* chronicles so popular in the later middle ages.[17] This legend may be the reason for such clearly-defined eagles in the Shaftesbury Hours. If so, it is a sophisticated piece of symbolism, relying upon the viewer's knowledge of the textual tradition for a correct interpretation.

It was suggested earlier that the Tudor-style rose may have had other meanings, and one such layer is as a symbol of the abbey. Not only was the Virgin Mary, for whom the rose was a symbol, patron of the abbey, but two roses appear above

[16] A stone with these arms was excavated in 1761 near the abbesses' lodgings in Shaftesbury, Hutchins, *Dorset*, p. 20; an early sixteenth-century civic mace also includes a version of them, *RCHME Dorset*, vol. 4, pl. 26 and p. 66. There is unnecessary confusion about the arms of the abbey, which are on occasion given as 'argent, on a pale cotised sable, three roses of the first', J. W. Papworth, *Ordinary of British Armorials* (London, 1874), p. 1009, quoted in *Notes and Queries for Somerset and Dorset*, 10 (1907) p. 33; these arms are very similar to those used by Shelford and her mother (see below), and the author of the *Notes and Queries* article indeed questions why these arms with the pale and roses were assigned to Shaftesbury Abbey.

[17] *Ibi tunc, ut dicitur, aquila locuta est, dum murus fabricaretur, cuius sermons, si veros esse putarem, sicut cetera memoria dare non diffugerem*, Geoffrey of Monmouth, *Historia regum Britanniae*, ed. J. Hammer (Cambridge, Mass., 1951), p. 45, Bk. 2 Ch. 8; *E le chastel de Cestrebire lei fu el monte de Paladur. A cel chastel clorre de mur uns aigles, ço dit l'on, parla*, I. Arnold (ed.), *Le Roman de Brut de Wace* (Paris, 1938), Tome 1, p. 89, lines 1614–18; Lagamon, *Brut, or Hystoria Brutonum*, eds W. R. J. Barron and S. C. Weinberg (Harlow, 1995), lines 1410–12 and p. 75.

the Abbey's arms on an early-sixteenth century civic mace.[18]

Other imagery in the Shaftesbury Hours is more personal. Three of the historiated initials depict Elizabeth Shelford's initials accompanied by a crozier. These need no interpretation, and are unequivocal statements of Shelford's ownership of the manuscript and her position as abbess. Her initials with crozier also appear on roof bosses in Tisbury parish church, Wiltshire, a possession of Shaftesbury Abbey.[19]

Two sets of ES initials are fairly plain, but at the start of the Hours of the Virgin – a place of particular prominence – a rebus forms part of the design (Plate 6). It is not clear why the 'S' is formed by wyvern or dragon, but the shells on water – the 'ford' – are quite clear. Shells also abound in the border surrounding this initial; scallops appear elsewhere, acting as Shelford's 'badge' throughout the manuscript.[20] A striking use of a shell is to be found in the pen-flourishing of a minor initial (Plate 7). Here, towards the end of Prime in the Hours of the Virgin, is what must surely be a sketch (or perhaps rather more of a caricature) of the abbess herself, nose pointing towards a scallop shell.

Shelford's use of initials and a badge as personal symbols in a manuscript containing heraldic devices may suggest that she did not have the right to armorial bearings. Although little documentary evidence concerning Elizabeth Shelford survives, and her tomb has disappeared, it is possible to trace part of her family. This is something which elucidates a number of elements in the manuscript, and also relates to Shelford's decision not to depict personal arms.

Elizabeth Shelford's mother Gwen is commemorated by a brass in Bramley parish church in Hampshire.[21] (Figure 8) The inscription informs us that Elizabeth's father John was from Hereford, and terms him an esquire, but he has not further been identified with any certainty.[22] The surviving shields of arms have similarly been the subject of much speculation but so far have not been firmly attrib-

[18] RCHME Dorset, vol. 4, pl. 26 and p. 66.
[19] L. Sydenham, *Shaftesbury and Its Abbey* (Lingfield, 1959), pp. 60–61; the bosses are, however, not mentioned by the VCH or Pevsner. The manor and advowson of the church of Tisbury belonged to Shaftesbury; part of the manor grange and the north aisle of the church were rebuilt in the early sixteenth century, D. A. Crowley (ed.), *VCH Wiltshire* (London, 1987), vol. 13, pp. 198–9. Initials become significant badges of identity during the 15th century, frequently found on personal seals for example, P. D. A. Harvey and A. McGuinness, *A Guide to British Medieval Seals* (London, 1994), p. 93.
[20] There are no known impressions of a personal seal belonging to Shelford, but a design with initials or rebus would have been typical for the period. The use of such devices, including by senior ecclesiastical figures, are discussed in J. A. Goodall, 'The Use of the Rebus on Medieval Seals and Monuments', *Antiquaries Journal* 83 (2003), pp. 448–71.
[21] *Transactions of the Monumental Brass Society* 5 (1904–09), pp. 261–2 and *Notes and Queries,* pp. 32–3. The More family lived in nearby Sherfield-upon-Loddon; it is unclear whether Gwen was a More by birth or through a second husband.
[22] *Notes and Queries*, p. 32; Sydenham, *Shaftesbury Abbey*, p. 61.

uted.[23] The most likely suggestion, particularly because they are impaled, is that they are the arms of Gwen herself, and could have been adopted by her daughter.[24] In this context, the roses on the figure's belt-clasp appear deliberately to echo the roses on the shield of arms and, if the rose was her mother's symbol, then a further layer of meaning may be revealed in the Tudor-style rose in Elizabeth's manuscript.[25]

The hypothesis that Shelford adopted her parental arms is supported by the fact that the arms appear elsewhere in places associated with the abbess; they are found, along with the initials ES, on the bosses of Tisbury church, and may have adorned the entrance to the almshouses known as the 'Maudlens' in Shaftesbury.[26] The fact that these arms are not in Elizabeth Shelford's Book of Hours does not prove that they were not hers, but simply that she chose to represent herself in a non-armorial manner in her manuscript.

IV. *Text*

Although Books of Hours are often associated with the laity, a number of women in religious orders owned them.[27] Other nuns at Shaftesbury possessed personal manuscripts, so even within her community Elizabeth Shelford was not unique, although as far as we know she was the only one for whom a manuscript was specially commissioned.[28]

---

[23]   The dexter arms are similar to those attributed to Schoffield and Schefeld and to Talcott, while the sinister impalement may be the Edwards of Flintshire, *Notes and Queries*, p. 32; Sydenham, *Shaftesbury*, pp. 60–1, assumes the arms are those of Gwen More-Shelford; Luxford states that the arms are those of Elizabeth herself, Luxford, *Art and Architecture*, p. 191.

[24]   The dexter may be the arms of Gwen's father rather than her husband. As an unmarried woman, Elizabeth Shelford may have adopted them from her mother without further differencing.

[25]   While most figures on brasses were fairly generic, individual preferences could be catered for, N. Saul, 'Bold as Brass: Secular Display in English Medieval Brasses', in P. Cross and M. Keene (eds), *Pageantry and Social Display in Medieval England* (Woodbridge, 2002), pp. 169–94, pp. 185–7.

[26]   Sydenham, *Shaftesbury*, pp. 60–61, 88; E. Towry Whyte, 'Tisbury Church', *Wiltshire Archaeological and Natural History Magazine* 34 (1910), pp. 599–614, p. 611; Hutchins, *Dorset*, p. 224.

[27]   Nine other extant Books of Hours have so-far been identified as belonging to nuns in later medieval England, while Avelina Cowdrey, Abbess of Wherwell, was depicted holding a 'small devotional book', D. N. Bell, *What Nuns Read: Books and Libraries in Medieval English Nunneries* (Kalamazoo, 1995), pp. 103–217, List of Manuscripts; Luxford, *Art and Architecture*, p. 44.

[28]   Joanne Mouresleygh (fl. 1441–60) owned a devotional compilation, while Bishop Edmund Audley bequeathed a Psalter to his niece Anne in 1524, Bell, *What Nuns Read*, pp. 163–8; the Psalter, now London, Lambeth Palace Library, MS 3285, was made in c. 1430–1440 and not for Edmund Audley as Bell suggests.

Even if the decoration had been lost, there would be little doubt that the Shaftesbury Hours was made for Elizabeth Shelford, largely from the Calendar. There is however a puzzle regarding these entries; they are by the main scribe, but the date given for Shelford's elevation to abbess as 1405, although Shelford was elected in 1504. Why the discrepancy? Unfortunately there is no clear answer to this important question. It may simply be that the error was not noticed until after the manuscript was completed and, even though erasures can be very neat, it might have been decided to retain the erroneous date rather than risk spoiling the finished product.

Shelford is not the only abbess mentioned in the Calendar; three others are recorded, two, Agnes Ferrar and Margery Auchier, by name. Ferrar became abbess in 1246, and Auchier was elected in 1315.[29] Why did these two abbesses warrant special mention? They might have been in an earlier Calendar which served as a model, but it may be suggested that the significant factor is that it is the date of their benediction, rather than election or death, which is recorded.[30] Shelford's benediction by Bishop Edmund Audley receives special attention in the Calendar, with a longer entry than her election, and Ferrar and Auchier may simply have been two previous abbesses for whom the date of benediction was well known. This suggestion is supported by the third entry relating to an abbess. On 13 February the benediction of *domine me abbatisse* is noted in red; there is no name, but Margery Twyneho, Shelford's predecessor, received the benediction on 14 February 1496, and is without doubt the abbess in question.[31] It seems that Shelford wanted to highlight the date upon which she was spiritually invested with the leadership of the community, something echoed in her use of the crozier in conjunction with her initials. This has implications for the reasons behind the commissioning of the manuscript, a matter discussed at length below.

Liturgically, the Calendar is specific to Shaftesbury and includes the various Feasts of Edward, King and Martyr, the abbey's second patron, and the commemoration of SS Elgiva and Modwenna.[32] Though there may have been an earlier model the later medieval feast of St Zita features in the Calendar, suggesting a desire to follow modern devotional trends.[33] There is however little beyond the

29 Ferrar's initial election was quashed on the grounds that her kinsman William de Marisco had been executed for piracy, Sydenham, *Shaftesbury*, p. 20; Ferrar renounced her first election in September 1243, was examined by a royal clerk after re-election in July 1246, and royal assent was granted for her to become abbess in January 1247, *CPR. Henry III; 1232–1247* (London, 1906), pp. 396, 484, 496.

30 Nicholas Rogers has suggested that the Calendar in FM 2–1957 was following an earlier model, pers. comm.

31 Dugdale, *Monasticon*, II, 474.

32 Elgiva was an Anglo-Saxon queen buried at Shaftesbury; Modwenna was a hermit at Burton-on-Trent, a Shaftesbury possession.

33 For St Zita see for example S. Sutcliffe, 'The Cult of St Sitha in England: An Introduction', *Nottingham Medieval Studies* 37 (1933) pp. 83–9, and C. M. Barron, 'The Trav-

notes concerning Shelford to personalise the Calendar; it is instead a firmly institutional record, emphasising the venerable lineage of Shaftesbury Abbey.

The manuscript is devotional, with a number of prayers and collects in addition to the various Hours, but it also contains formal liturgical texts. The Psalms at Prime for the week and musical notation in the Office of the Dead and Commendations of the Soul would have allowed this manuscript to be used for some services. It is also rather large for a Book of Hours, a feature which would have made it easier to read in Choir. Perhaps most telling of all, the Commendations of the Soul contains rubrics noting the feasts of SS Elgiva and Brithelm, with instructions concerning the procession to the latter's tomb after Mass.[34] There was no point including such passages unless it was intended for use within Shaftesbury Abbey.

V. *Interpreting the Shaftesbury Hours*

The style and contents of the Shaftesbury Hours indicate that it was compiled between July 1504 and 1528, most probably soon after Shelford was confirmed as abbess. It was intended for use within the communal life of the abbey, but had a personal devotional function. The rather rough nature of the figural decoration suggests an inexperienced or reluctant artist, possibly the scribe. This strongly suggests that the manuscript was made locally, perhaps in-house.

Most of the texts are standard, but there are a few which are rather more unusual, including an invocation to the Virgin for protection from plague, and the indulgenced prayer *O nuda humanitas*.[35] Several additions were clearly made when Alice Champeneys acquired the manuscript, but there are a couple of others which are dateable only to the first few decades of the sixteenth century, possibly while it was in Shelford's possession. One of these is the prayer 'O swete Jhu the son of God the endles swetnesse of hevyn', an expression of Christocentric piety which recalls the imagery found in the manuscript.[36]

Shaftesbury Abbey had a number of prebends and chantry priests, and appointed clergy for most of the town's churches.[37] One of the parish priests was Richard Marshall, who sold the Shaftesbury Hours. He was an educated man who had studied at Oxford, and his subsequent possession of the manuscript might

---

elling Saint: Zita of Lucca in England', in P. Horden (ed.), *Freedom of Movement in the Middle Ages*, Harlaxton Medieval Studies, XV (Donington, 2007), pp. 186–202. It is, however, surprising, particularly in the light of the Christocentric imagery in the manuscript, that the Holy Name (7 August) added to the Province of Canterbury in 1489 and very popular in the late fifteenth and early sixteenth centuries, was not included.

[34]   FM 2–1957, ff. 122, 126v. Unlike Abbot John Islips's heavily worn book of devotions, (Manchester, John Rylands University Library, Western MS 165) the Shaftesbury Hours is however clean and in good condition.

[35]   FM 2–1957, ff. 52v–53, *Stella celi extripavit*, and f. 78.

[36]   FM 2–1957, f. 10v; the script is documentary cursive.

[37]   *VCH Dorset*, p. 76.

suggest him as a likely candidate as an advisor to Abbess Elizabeth, and possibly even as the scribe or artist of the Shaftesbury Hours.

Shelford may have received guidance, but she was surely the driving force behind the manuscript. The decision to use her initials and rebus, as well as a sophisticated array of secular and sacred imagery, appear to be the deliberate choice of someone seeking to express themselves on their own terms. There are some very personal elements in Shelford's manuscript, such as the possible allusion to her mother through the prominent rose, Elizabeth's initials, and the sketch of the nun within the pen-flourishing. But though Shelford may have been from the much-discussed later-medieval gentry rising in the world, her identity would instead appear to have been bound up not so much with her blood relations but the family of the abbey, whose spiritual ancestors included queens and saints.[38]

Shaftesbury Abbey was one of the great Anglo-Saxon foundations, patronised by royalty before and after the Conquest.[39] As early as the fourteenth century it was however experiencing some financial difficulties, and from the early fifteenth century was eclipsed in wealth and royal favour by the Brigittine house of Syon.[40] The abbess could not, as a woman, sit in Parliament and in the later middle ages fewer royal and noble women chose to be enclosed at the abbey, reducing its national significance. In addition, by the later fifteenth century the town of Shaftesbury was beginning to assert its corporate identity, challenging the abbey's local power.[41] There is some evidence that the late fifteenth and early sixteenth centuries saw attempts to reverse this decline, and this perhaps provides the key to the Shaftesbury Hours.

This revival included programmes of rebuilding both at Shaftesbury and Tisbury in the early sixteenth century, for example. Of perhaps greater significance were actions taken during the abbacy of Margery Twyneho. Unlike her successor Twyneho was of noble descent, and was instrumental in establishing a chantry for her aunt, Margaret St John (d. 1491) a previous abbess of Shaftesbury.[42] In 1500

---

[38] For discussions of the gentry in later medieval England, see P. Coss, *The Origins of the English Gentry* (Cambridge, 2003) and R. Horrox, *Fifteenth Century Attitudes: Perceptions of Identity in Late Medieval England* (Cambridge, 1994). It has been suggested that the commissioning of manuscripts by the gentry reflected their growing political and social importance, C. M. Meale, 'The Politics of Book Ownership: The Hopton family and Bodleian Library Digby MS 185', in F. Riddy (ed.), *Prestige, Authority and Power in Late Medieval Manuscripts and Texts* (Yale, 2000), pp. 103–31, p. 103.

[39] *VCH Dorset*, vol. 2, pp. 73–5.

[40] *VCH Dorset*, vol. 2, pp. 73–5; M. Oliva, 'Patterns of Patronage to Female Monasteries in the Later Middle Ages', in J. G. Clark (ed.), *The Religious Orders in Pre-Reformation England*. Studies in the History of Medieval Religion, XVIII (Woodbridge, 2002), pp. 155–64, p. 155.

[41] Sydenham, *Shaftesbury*, p. 57.

[42] St John's parents were recorded as Sir Oliver St John and Margaret, Duchess of Som-

Twyneho ordered a new register of abbey lands to sort out financial and administrative mismanagement and reaffirm the rights of Shaftesbury Abbey.[43] This manuscript is not a rough check-list, but is in effect a new cartulary, written in a good bookhand and drawn up by Christopher Twyneho, Margery's brother and a successful career cleric, and Alexander Cator, a canon lawyer with close connections to the abbey.[44]

It is within this context that Shelford's Book of Hours should be viewed. Twyneho's estate book provides evidence that fairly high-quality manuscripts were produced within the ambit of Shaftesbury at the start of the sixteenth century, and suggests a renewed sense of purpose among those who ran the abbey. Shelford's manuscript may therefore been seen as part of this move to reassert the spiritual and temporal position of the abbey, in this case through the emphasis upon the authority of the abbess and her exalted corporate lineage.[45]

VI. *Conclusions*

Elizabeth Shelford's Book of Hours can be interpreted, and was almost certainly intended to function, in several different ways; as an expression of devotion and as a liturgical aid, as a book imbued with familial association and personal identity, and as a symbol of renewed corporate vigour. There are still many unanswered questions and discoveries to be made about the Shaftesbury Hours, but it is, ultimately, a rare survival, containing as it does the numerous and many-layered symbols of identity of a devout and powerful woman.

---

erset and Countess of Kendale, in the *CPR* entry concerning the establishment of this chantry, *CPR. Henry VII, 1494–1509* (London, 1916), pp. 142–3.

[43] London, BL, Egerton MS 3098. This manuscript, still in its original brown leather binding with a pink chemise over, comprises 34 parchment folios, neatly ruled and written in a good Gothic bookhand (hybrida) with red penwork linefillers and highlighting of initials.

[44] BL, Egerton MS 3098, ff. 1–1v. Christopher Twyneho, born c. 1460, was a scholar at Oxford and, among other benefices, was a canon at Wells, Salisbury and Hereford; he had died by December 1509, Emden, *Alumni*, vol. 3, pp. 1919–20. Alexander Cator held degrees in Canon and Civil Law from Oxford, and was Master of the Hospital of St John in Shaftesbury from 1504 until his death in 1516, Emden, *Alumni*, vol. 1, p. 371.

[45] Erler discusses how manuscripts could play a significant role in what she terms the 'struggle for power between monastic houses and local magnates', although she emphasises that this struggle would appear to have been at its most bitter in Kent, M. Erler, 'The Abbess of Malling's Gift Manuscript (1520)', in Riddy, *Prestige, Authority and Power*, pp. 147–57, pp. 147–8.

APPENDIX

Main decoration in the Shaftesbury Hours (all decoration is within or surrounding initials):

Fol. 11, Psalms at Prime for the year; Ps. 1 ES monogram and crozier.

Fol. 34, Hours of the Virgin, Matins, ES monogram over scallop-shells on water; Scallop shell.

Fol. 37v, Lauds Shield of arms, (quarterly argent a rose gules, sable a fleur-de-lis argent) with eagle; Ps. 92, Flowing rivers(?).

Fol. 41v, Matins of the Cross (end) Shield with Five Wounds; Hours of the Virgin, Prime Sacred Monogram; Wounded Cross.

Fol. 43v, Hours of the Virgin, Prime (end), Scallop shell, with veiled female head.

Fol. 45, Hours of the Virgin, Sext, Shield of arms, (sable, three fleurs-de-lis argent) with eagle's head.

Fol. 46, None, Five Wounds on shield, Crown of Thorns above, with spear, sponge on rod, nails and rope.

Fol. 47v, Vespers, Wounded Tau cross; Crown of Thorns.

Fol. 50, Compline, Head of Christ; Jug.

Fol. 53v, Penitential Psalms, Tudor-style rose.

Fol. 78, Prayer *O nuda humanitas,* Wounded heart, hands and feet of Christ with Calvary cross, nails and scourges.

Fol. 78v, Office of the Dead, Shield of arms (azure, a cross patonce between five martlets or; Shaftesbury Abbey).

Fol. 105v, Commendations of the Soul, E intertwined with main initial S and a crosier.

Provenance inscription:
Iste liber pertinet domine Alicie Champnys moniali Shastonie quem dicta Alicia emit pro summa decem solidorum de domino Richardo Marshall Rectore ecclesie parochialis sancti Rumbaldi de Shastina predicta (f. 132v).

Sign Language: Seeing Things
in Middle English Poems

PHILLIPA HARDMAN

In this paper my aim is to explore some of the ways in which words perform the function of signs in medieval texts, ranging from the simplest type of example, where the reader sees the word itself as a sign, to more complex instances in which the reader is required to produce a mental picture of a symbolic image or sign in response to verbal prompts or instructions in the text. My interest is in the extent to which such visualizing activities are more than a merely pictorial, illustrative adjunct to the words, and actually contribute towards constructing the meaning of the sign or symbol, as the reader is co-opted into collaboration with the text.

There is a large class of fifteenth-century didactic lyrics that deliver their teaching with the use of a proverbial or moral refrain, often in Latin, and often in the form of a phrase unexpectedly overheard, or voiced by a bird endowed with human speech, upon which the lyric persona may then meditate.[1] In some cases, however, the phrase is not heard, but is seen as a visible written message. For example, in one well-known lyric, the narrator, standing in a chamber among lords and barons, sees a knight wearing a hood with a 'reson', or motto, written on it in gold, as it might be a badge: 'Servyse in none heritage'.[2] The narrator then ponders on the words and sees their truth borne out all around him. In this case, the effect is not much different from a heard phrase, except for the subtle way in which the golden badge-like motto comments subversively on the service of the knight

---

[1] For example, see the following refrain lyrics from the Vernon MS (Oxford, Bodleian Library MS Eng. Poet. a. 1): 'Mercy Passes All Things', 'Deo Gracias', 'Merci God and Graunt Merci', 'Always Try to Say the Best', 'Make Amends', 'Mane nobiscum Domine'; in 'Ever More Thank God of All', the message is seen written on a wall (ed. C. Brown, *Religious Lyrics of the XIVth Century,* 2nd edn, rev. G. V. Smithers (Oxford, 1957), pp. 125–208). For discussion of the Vernon lyrics, see V. Gillespie, 'Moral and Penitential Lyrics', in *A Companion to the Middle English Lyric,* ed. T. G. Duncan (Cambridge, 2005), pp. 68–95 (pp. 85–9); J. Burrow, 'The Shape of the Vernon Refrain Lyrics', in *Studies in the Vernon Manuscript*, ed. D. Pearsall (Cambridge, 1990), pp. 187–99; J. J. Thompson, 'The Textual Background and Reputation of the Vernon Lyrics', in *Studies in the Vernon Manuscript*, pp. 201–24.

[2] IMEV 1446; ed. H. E. Sandison, *The 'Chanson d'Aventure' in Middle English* (Bryn Mawr, 1913), pp. 119–20.

wearing the hood.[3]

More interesting in terms of its visual impact is a lyric that hinges on the refrain word 'Revertere!'.[4] There are three manuscript versions of this poem, varying considerably in length, but all begin with the same three stanzas in which the narrator goes out hawking, stumbles and becomes entangled in a briar.

> My fawkon flewe fast vnto her pray,
> My hownd gan renne with glad chere,
> And sone I spurnyd in my way:
> My lege was hent in a breer.
> This breer, forsothe, yt dyde me gref,
> Ywys yt made me to turn ayé,
> For he bare wrytyng in euery leff
> This Latyn word, *Revertere*. (Oxford, MS Balliol 354, st. 2)

Each following stanza concludes with the same word *Revertere*, with the consequence that, for the reader or listener, the lyric becomes equivalent to the briar: a structure in which every constituent part – stanza or leaf – is inscribed with the same legible sign. This word that both narrator and reader see or visualize has an obvious practical function, like a road-sign bearing a symbolic U-turn arrow to make drivers turn back. The fact that it is specifically designated a Latin word, though, besides giving it attributes of authority, learning and power, implies that its meaning may not be immediately intelligible.[5] However, the narrator has already been forced to enact the backward-turning sense of the sign – 'yt made me to turn ayé' (l. 14) – before the word is seen on the leaves; and even the reader is involved in this enactment of meaning, for by recognizing the Latin word as a sign commanding the same action that was narrated in the earlier line, the reader is in a way imitating the narrator's backward turn. So while a gloss in a later stanza reveals '*Revertere* is as myche to say | In Englische tunge as turne ayen', this translation is to some extent redundant, for the meaning of the word as sign is already constructed by the active reading of the text.

Word and sign are equally closely related in a text that has been described as 'a rudimentary emblem poem'.[6] This is the brief lyric 'O man unkynde', or vari-

---

3   A hood, like a collar or badge, was an item commonly given as livery to the followers of a lord.

4   IMEV 1454; ed. D. Gray, *A Selection of Religious Lyrics* (Oxford, 1975), pp. 82–3 (four stanzas); T. G. Duncan, *Late Medieval English Lyrics and Carols* (London, 2000), pp. 120–23 (eleven stanzas).

5   There is an interesting comparison with 'Service is none heritage', where the intelligibility of the word seen is also an issue: 'That word fast I can be hold | Wheþer it were engliche or what langage' (ll. 5–6).

6   Douglas Gray, *Themes and Images in the Middle English Religious Lyric* (London, 1972), pp. 52–4; T. W. Ross, 'Five Fifteenth-Century "Emblem" Verses from Brit. Mus. Addit. MS. 37049', *Speculum* 32 (1957), 274–82 (p. 276).

ously 'O mankynde', found in three fifteenth-century manuscript versions.[7]

Add. MS 37049	MS Tanner 407	MS Trinity O.2.53
O mankynde	Man vnkynde	O man unkynde
hafe in þi mynde	haue thow in mynde	Haue thow yn mynde
my passion smert	my passion smerte	My passyon smert
And þu sal fynde	And thow schall me ffynde	Thow shall me fynde
me ful kynde	to the ryght kynde	To the full kynde
Lo here my hert.	lo here myn [herte].	Lo here my hert.

In two of these three copies, the text is illustrated with a symbolic, conventional heart shape. The image in BL, Add. MS 37049 includes supplementary details – the wound, drops of blood – and explanatory words; while Oxford, Bodleian Library MS Tanner 407 replaces the word 'heart' with a small heart sign drawn in the space, in the same brown ink as the text.

The lyric has usually been discussed in relation to the image – indeed, Rosemary Woolf, in her magisterial study of the medieval English religious lyric,[8] reproduces a folio from BL, Add. MS 37049 to illustrate her discussion of the text, and claims that the poem does not really work without the image: 'The illustration is far more emotive than the verse: the one is affective on its own, the other is not' (p. 185). Actually, the poem shown in her illustration (Woolf, pl. 1) is not the same text in a 'longer version', as she states, but a different, though similar text, that lacks the crucial line 'Lo here my hert'.[9] The first six lines of the longer text read: 'O man unkynde | hafe in mynde | My paynes smert | Beholde 7 see | þat is for þe | Percyd my hert', and in the second part of this dialogue poem, Man's reply begins: 'O lord right dere | þi wordes I here | With hert ful sore'. The figures of the wounded Christ and the penitent man are shown, as is conventional, beside their speeches as identifying images of each speaker, while between them hangs a huge heart image, marked with the five wounds of Christ and including an explanatory gloss on the measure of the side wound. The function of this image is made clear in the inscription on the scroll above it: 'þies woundes smert . bere in þi hert . 7 luf god aye | If þow do þis . þu sal haf blys . wt owten delay'. Thus it seems that the image must signify both the pierced heart of Christ, offered to the eye of the beholder, and at the same time a responsive human heart compassionately commemorating the sufferings of Christ. The image provides a parallel, symbolic representation of the conversion of the human heart sought by the voice of Christ and performed in Man's words in the dialogue poem alongside it.

---

[7]   BL, Add. MS 37049 (Carthusian miscellany), f. 24; Oxford, Bodleian Library, MS Tanner 407 (commonplace book), f. 52v; Cambridge, Trinity College Library, MS O.2.53 (late-fifteenth-century notebook), f. 69. IMEV 2507; ed. Gray, *A Selection of Religious Lyrics*, p. 25.

[8]   Rosemary Woolf, *English Religious Lyric in the Middle Ages* (Oxford, 1968).

[9]   IMEV 2504; ed. Duncan, *Late Medieval English Lyrics and Carols*, pp. 80–81.

The image in this manuscript that does accompany the brief lyric (f. 24) works in a similar way.[10] Again the heart image stands between the figures of Christ and man (in this case, a Carthusian monk), and here the layout constructs two brief and otherwise separate lyrics as a dialogue, like that in the previous poem. The symbolic heart clearly supplements the text of the first lyric, actualizing the claim 'Lo here my hert', and perhaps indicating in the prominent wound, traditionally understood as the proof of Christ's love for mankind, the token of Christ's promise to be 'ful kynde'. But, as before, the wounded heart image can also signify the responsive heart of the desiring contemplative, for the speaking voice in the second lyric asks of Christ: 'Þi parfite luf close in my breste | ... | And wounde my hert in þi luf fre | Þat I may reyne in ioy euer more wt þe'. The visual symbol thus conveys an alternative version of the heart-to-heart dialogue of compassion created on the manuscript page between these two lyrics.

The crowded design of this page betrays a characteristic anxiety that no opportunity should be lost for elaborating and improving the didactic potential of the symbolic heart. The pious ejaculation 'ihu mercy' is strategically placed on either side of the wounded heart to emphasize its implication of Christ's merciful judgement, while the heart itself is inscribed with the precise number of Christ's wounds and drops of blood, and attempts at versifying these numbers have been squeezed into the space below each of the two lyrics. The simple connection between the verbal prompt 'Lo here my hert' and the answering visible image of the heart has thus been so heavily overlain with additional meanings that it is difficult to separate the functioning of the 'O mankynde' lyric from the total effect of this texts-and-images composition.

The second copy, in MS Tanner 407, presents a much more direct instance of verbal and visual interaction. Here, a successful reading of the text depends on the instant legibility of the conventional representation of the heart – the sign is functioning as a word. There can be no doubt, such as Rosemary Woolf suggests in relation to the Add. MS 37049 images, as to whether we are seeing 'a heart or a heart-shaped shield' (p. 185).[11] Of course, the expectation of a rhyme with the third line, 'My passion smert', guides the reader's ear and eye; none the less, the rebus-like substitution of the sign for the word implies its immediate recognizability.[12] This question gets more interesting when it is turned around: the sign can supply the place of the word, but did the word also produce the corresponding visual sign to the mind's eye?

[10] This image is reproduced in Ross's article (see note 6), pl. 2, which is available online via JSTOR.

[11] In fact the numerous shields in BL, Add. MS 37049 such as the Arma Christi shield (f. 46v) are carefully distinguished by their different outline from these typical heart shapes.

[12] For discussion of the 'rebus' in this poem as distinct from an 'emblem', see Gray, p. 244, n. 77.

This question is relevant to the third manuscript copy, the unillustrated text in Cambridge, Trinity College Library, MS O.2.53. The text still requires visualization – it still declares 'Lo here my hert', but in this case the reader or listener must supply the visual image to complete the meaning of the text. Are the illustrations in the Tanner MS and Add. MS 37049 copies necessary guidance for the reader's imaging faculty, or are they simply representations of a mental image that everyone would be able to produce? The evidence indicates the latter – the exploitation of the symbol for didactic purpose in the one case and the easy substitution of sign for word in the other both imply the universal familiarity of the representational shape standing for the heart. But it is not, of course, the same symbol as in the popular tradition of using the heart shape to signify love, as seen reversed in the humorous formula 'I heart X'. For although, as Rosemary Woolf suggests, the line 'Lo here my hert' may be taken to mean 'Look on my heart, the proof of my love' (p. 186), this does not imply, as it would in a secular context, that the heart is to be understood metaphorically as standing for the idea of love. On the contrary, the literal materiality of the heart is the source of the symbolic heart's power, a conventional image representing the actual heart of Christ wounded through His side, pierced with the spear; and this is clearly shown in those depictions of the 5 Wounds of Christ in the form of His wounded hands, feet, and heart.[13]

In this respect I would differ from Christiana Whitehead, who offers this poem as an example of 'strained' seeing, where 'the thing that we are asked to see proves visually inaccessible'.[14] She writes: 'Christ's ... exhortation, "Lo here my hert", for all its apparent simplicity, actually necessitates an abrupt hermeneutic shift, since "seeing" Christ's heart entails extracting it from the realist context of the crucifixion ... and resituating it in a symbolic or emblematic context' (p. 109). But the poem already assumes a devotional context outside the historical reality of the crucifixion, in which Christ's plea to Man to 'have in mind' His 'passion smert' probably implies an expectation of just such a mnemonic device as the Arms of the Passion to call it to mind. It is noteworthy that the only two lines that remain stable across all three versions of the lyric are the third and the sixth, linking the remembering of Christ's 'passion' with visualizing His 'hert'. As Rosemary Woolf observes, the 'emphasis upon Christ's heart and its widespread depiction in fifteenth-century art derives from a devotion that was to lead directly into the later cult of the Sacred Heart' (p. 186); and central to both the cult and the earlier devotion is the visibility of the heart of Christ to the contemplation of the faithful.[15] Thus the three manuscript copies of the lyric 'O man unkynde', in different

---

[13] See, for example, the devotional prayer card on the Five Wounds produced by the Carthusians of Sheen and reproduced in Eamon Duffy, *The Stripping of the Altars: Traditional Religion in England 1400–1580* (New Haven, CT, 1992), pl. 99.

[14] 'Middle English Religious Lyrics', in *A Companion to the Middle English Lyric*, pp. 96–119 (p. 109).

[15] 'The devotion [to the Sacred Heart] is based entirely upon the symbolism of the heart.

ways, all indicate that the poem operates on the expectation of a readily available mental image of the heart of Christ in the form of a familiar, conventional symbolic shape that the reader or listener will be able to 'have in mind', as the key to His Passion, both in the sense of 'see with the mind's eye' and 'remember, keep in mind'.

At the other extreme from the simple verbal prompt 'Lo here my hert', we can find instances of 'sign language' in medieval poems in which the reader or listener is provided with elaborate and precise textual instructions for the visualization of a symbolic image. A good example is the passage concerning the carpenter's L-square inscribed with the letters P-A-X in *The Pilgrimage of the Life of Man*, John Lydgate's translation of Guillaume de Deguileville's *Pèlerinage de la vie humaine*.[16]

> ffyrst ye shal a squyre take,
> A Squyre off a carpenter;
> And ye shal vse thys maner:
> ffyrst, to done your bysynesse,
> The ton ende vp-ward to dresse
> Hih a-loffte, ryht as lyne;
> And ferthermor to determyne,
> The tother ende lower doun,
> So that (in conclusioun)
> The angle corner in your syht,
> Wych ioyneth the endys lyne ryht;
> In wych corner (yiff ye lyst wyte),
> Ther ys in soth an 'A' ywryte.
> Than lynealy, yiff ye descende
> Doun vn-to the lower ende,
> Ye shal fynde wryte a 'P',
> And alderhyest ye shal se
> In that ende an 'X' yset;
> And whan thys lettrys ben yknet,
> Ioyned in on, who kan espye,
> Parfyt pes they sygnyfye. (ll. 4906–26)

In all versions of the poem, this image of the lettered carpenter's square has a special status: it is a sign of great authority, its meaning established by Christ himself in the words of His Testament of Peace. Unlike the many allegorical *picturae* seen and vividly described by the dreamer throughout the text, and unlike the

It is this symbolism that imparts to it its meaning and its unity, and this symbolism is admirably completed by the representation of the Heart as wounded. ... A visible heart is necessary for an image of the Sacred Heart, but this visible heart must be a symbolic heart' (J. Bainvel, trans. C. J. Murray, in *The Catholic Encyclopedia*, VII (New York, 1910), online at http://www.newadvent.org/cathen/07163a.htm).

[16] *The Pilgrimage of the Life of Man*, ed. F. J. Furnivall, EETS ES 77, 83 and 92 (London, 1899, 1901, 1904).

metaphorical image of peace as a jewel that runs throughout Christ's testament, this is called a 'figure' or 'patroun' or 'exaumpleyre': a design for practical use. Susan Hagen emphasizes the need to visualize the figure, 'for inherent in that shape is the suggestion of other meaning and the stimulus to recollection'.[17] But though scribes or illustrators in some manuscript copies of the text have shown their recognition of the visual importance of the figure by providing a drawing (described by Michael Camille as a 'line-drawn *figure*, more text than image'),[18] and modern editions reproduce such a drawing, it is not the case that the illustration is absolutely necessary to supplement the words, for the verbal image is sufficiently clear for any reader of the unillustrated text to produce an adequate mental picture capable of being recollected and understood. The description of this figure first assumes that the reader can picture in the mind's eye a carpenter's square,[19] and then consists of minutely detailed instructions for setting it up, inviting the reader to see the letter A in the angle joining the two sides of the L-square, then to look to the far end of the horizontal side to see the letter P, and up to the extremity of the vertical side for the X. There follows an explanation of the L-square's significance as a figure of the peace Christ gives to Man, stressing the details of the diagram that have been highlighted in the description: the two sides being joined, to show the unity or indivisibility of this triple peace; the superiority of the side marked X, for Christ; the equal degree of the two points on the lower side marked A, for the individual soul *(anima, âme),* and P, for one's neighbour *(proximus, prochain).* Despite the assumed familiarity of the L-square's appearance, then, it would not be effective simply to state that the letters P-A-X should be imagined at the three sites, for it is the implied physical action of turning one's gaze upwards to Christ, and then of looking to see one's neighbour on literally the same level as oneself, that creates the meaning of the figure for each individual reader or listener. In Lydgate's translation the purpose of this symbolic image is explicitly said to be remembering: 'Yt ys good that the exaumple be | Off pes yput in Remembraunce': it functions as a practical mnemonic device in which the activity of calling the figure to mind will inevitably enact the meaning of the Pax Christi.

---

[17]   Susan K, Hagen, *Allegorical Remembrance: A Study of 'The Pilgrimage of the Life of Man' as a Medieval Treatise on Seeing and Remembering* (Athens, GA and London, 1990), pp. 57–60.

[18]   'The PAX or carpenter's "L-square", a didactic mnemonic image carefully described in the text ... below. Referred to as a *signe figure*, this tool helps the pilgrim in Deguileville's narrative to memorize the proper relationship that the soul or l'Âme at the centre has to negotiate between its love towards Christ above (X) and its love towards its adjacent neighbour, or prochain (P)' (Michael Camille, *Master of Death: The Lifeless Art of Pierre Remiet, Iluminator* (New Haven, CT, 1996), p. 14).

[19]   A neat connection is thus made with the heavenly origin of peace, described in ll. 4888–92 as made by 'thylke souereyn Carpenter | That syt aboue the sterrys cler'.

A similar instance can be seen in the late-fourteenth-century alliterative poem, *The Quatrefoil of Love*, or, *The Four Leaves of the Truelove*.[20] It survives in two manuscripts, neither of which is illustrated; but visualizing the image of *Paris quadrifolia*, the four-leaved herb that gives the text its modern name, is crucial to a reading of the poem.

> Whare þou fyndis grewande a trewlufe grysse,
> With iiij lefes es it sett full louely aboute.
> The first lefe we may lyken vnto þe kynge of blisse,
> Þat weldis alle þis werlde within and withowte;
> He wroghte heuen with his hande and alle paradise,
> And þis merie medilerthe withowtten any dowte;
> Alle þe welthe of þis werlde hally is his,
> In wham vs aw for to leue, loue hym and lowtte
>   Full wele.
> Halde this lefe in 3our mynde,
> Till we his felawes fynde,
> of þat trewlufe and þat kynde
>   Þat nevermore sall kele. (ll. 66–78)

As with the PAX L-square, it is first assumed that the reader will recognize the actual four-leaved herb when it is seen growing. The text than takes the reader or listener through a leaf-by-leaf analysis of the symbolic significance of the plant, configuring it anew as each leaf in turn is 'found' with its new meaning: 'The firste lefe we may lyken vnto þe kynge of blisse' (l. 68), 'Halde this lefe in 3our mynde, | Till we his felawes fynde' (ll. 75–6); 'bi this ilk seconde lefe I lyken goddis son, | Vnto þis ilke firste lefe es felawe and fere; | The thirde vnto þe holy gaste' (ll. 79–81), until the three leaves of the Trinity 'togedir are done' (l. 81),[21] and finally the fourth leaf for the Virgin Mary is added, and all four are seen to be joined 'One a righte rote' (l. 143). There is an interesting subtlety in the sequencing of the analysis, which, contrary to the symmetrical structure of the quatrefoil, sets the addition of the fourth leaf carefully apart from the union of the first three, separated by three stanzas that narrate the events of the Creation, the Fall, and the Incarnation – thus expressing both the unfolding of history and the distance in status between the Godhead and the human Mother of God. As Susanna Fein points out, the word

---

[20]   *The Quatrefoil of Love*, eds I. Gollancz and M. M. Weale, EETS OS 195 (London, 1935). The alternative title is proposed in Susanna Fein, 'Quatrefoil and Quatrefolia: The Devotional Layout of an Alliterative Poem', *Journal of the Early Book Society*, 2 (1999), 26–45, and in her critical edition of the poem in *Moral Love Songs and Laments*, TEAMS Middle English Texts Series (Kalamazoo, MI: 1998). All quotations are taken from the EETS edition.

[21]   The reading 'are done' is that of BL, Add. MS 31042, the base manuscript of the EETS edition, but is rejected by both the EETS editors and Fein in favour of the alternative reading 'þay wone'. It has been preferred here on the principle of *difficilior lectio*, and as contributing to the poem's extended metaphor.

'lefe' in line 75 puns on the two meanings, 'leaf' and 'belief', of the homonyms,[22] and this has especial significance in relation to the three leaves/beliefs of the Trinity, for of course they correspond to the articles of the Creed separately expressing belief in God the Father, Son, and Holy Ghost. At the same time, though, the reader's conventional narrative expectations place a cumulative emphasis on the fourth, final leaf, in line with the poem's eventual presentation of Mary, 'þat ilke ferthe lefe gracyouse and gude' (l. 515), as focus of the penitent's devotion and prayer, and mediatrix for mankind before the Trinity: 'þat scho speke for oure lufe … | Vnto þase ilke iij leues' (ll. 512–13).

In the light of this text's sophisticated design, it seems possible that there may be a visible analogue for its uniquely asymmetrical four-leaf truelove plant in the layout of the verse in both manuscripts where, at the end of each stanza, the three rhyming lines of the wheel are bracketed together and set alongside but apart from the fourth, final line.[23] However, with or without this diagrammatic stimulus, the text itself ensures that, as the reader or listener follows the instructions for visualizing and holding in mind each leaf, and gradually assembles the three-plus-one structure of the four-leaved truelove, the proper theological meaning of the image is constructed by this active process of visualization.

Perhaps the most celebrated symbolic sign described in Middle English literature is the pentangle on Gawain's shield in *Sir Gawain and the Green Knight*, his cognizance and the token of 'trawþe'.[24] The text names the subject of the description in apparent expectation that it will be recognized, and in this case readers are offered three alternative names by which the design is said to be known: the pentangle; the sign of Solomon; and the endless knot.

> Then þay schewed hym þe schelde, þat was of schyr goulez
> Wyth þe pentangel depaynt of pure golde hwez.
> He braydez hit by þe bauderyk, aboute þe hals kestes,
> Þat bisemed þe segge semlyly fayre.
> And quy þe pentangel apendez to þat prynce noble
> I am in tent yow to telle, þof tary hyt me schulde:
> Hit is a syngne þat Salamon set sumquyle
> In bytoknyng of trawþe, bi tytle þat hit habbez,
> For hit is a figure þat haldez fyue poyntez,
> And vche lyne vmbelappez and loukez in oþer,
> And ayquere hit is endelez; and Englych hit callen
> Oueral, as I here, þe endeles knot. (ll. 619–30)

[22] 'Quatrefoil and Quatrefolia', p. 29. Fein also explicates the highly complex structure and symbolic patterning of the text.

[23] For a reproduction of the layout of the poem in BL, Add. MS 31042, see the frontispiece to the EETS edition, or J. J. Thompson, *Robert Thornton and the London Thornton Manuscript*, Manuscript Studies 2 (Cambridge, 1987), pls 19b and 20a.

[24] All quotations are taken from *The Poems of the Pearl Manuscript*, eds M. Andrew and R. Waldron, rev. edn (Exeter, 2002).

After naming the pentangle, the text describes it by three key features: it is a figure 'þat haldez fyue poyntez', of which 'vche lyne vmbelappez and loukez in oþer', and it is 'endelez'. A little later, Sir Gawain's virtues are portrayed with reference to the symbolic form of the pentangle, and the figure is by implication described again, more elaborately:

> Now alle þese fyue syþez, for soþe, were fetled on þis kny3t,
> And vchone halched in oþer, þat non ende hade,
> And fyched vpon fyue poyntez, þat fayld neuer,
> Ne samned neuer in no syde, ne sundred nouþer,
> Withouten ende at any noke I oquere fynde,
> Whereeuer þe gomen bygan, or glod to an ende. (ll. 656–61)

Again, the same three features are picked out – the five points, the interlocking structure, and the endlessness of the design – and again the figure is called a knot and named the pentangle (ll. 662, 664). These alternative names highlight two crucial aspects of the form: its interweaving lines and its five prominent angles. However, the text invites the reader or listener not simply to see this form, but to visualize the pentangle in a more active way, to invent the form anew in the mind's eye, following the particular detail and order of the description. Thus one is led to imagine the process of constructing it as a geometric figure, starting with five points – a word which then as now meant both an angular extremity and a dot marking a position – and going on to produce the lines connecting these points in such a way that the lines cross each other, but make an unbroken whole, a closed shape. The three-dimensional nature of the form – the fact that its lines must not only cross, but also interweave with each other – is prescribed by its repeatedly being called a knot.

By engaging in this active visualization of the pentangle, the reader or listener encounters precisely those elements – the five points, the five interconnected lines, and the endlessness of the tracing – that are central to the poem's treatment of 'trawþe', the virtue that Gawain embodies. And the repetition of the procedure, when the figure is described the second time, enacts something of the complexity of that virtue, for each of the five separate ways in which aspects of Gawain's faithfulness express the nature of 'trawþe' itself has five components: five wits, five fingers, five wounds, five joys, and five special virtues. The endlessness of the pentangle knot enables one mentally to retrace the diagram five times, contemplating each of the five points in relation to each of the five sets of five, in a manner not unlike the use of a pair of rosary beads; while the interwoven structure of the traced lines presents a visual analogue to the crucial interrelatedness of all the elements in Gawain's defining quality of 'trawþe'. Thus the meaning of the pentangle symbol within this text is created through collaboration between the poem's verbal description and the reader's active visualization of the form.

The visibility of the complex pentangle symbol is ensured for modern readers by the provision of a printed illustration of the geometric shape in editions of the text. Less obvious perhaps is the visibility of another powerful symbolic shape – the Cross, a sign which, unlike the pentangle, Gawain does actually invoke and use in the narrative. On two occasions Gawain is said to 'sayne him', to make the sign of the cross upon himself, once as he prays on his winter journey, and once as he faces the enigmatic lady in his chamber. The phrase 'sayne him' is usually translated 'crosses himself', but the older usage interestingly foregrounds not the action of the hand tracing the shape of the cross, but the function of the action as a sign, and it assumes a culturally embedded recognition of this sign as the cross of Christ. We can readily picture to ourselves Gawain performing this pious act, but I think there may be more for the reader to see.

On the first narrative occasion, Gawain is praying in penitential mode: as well as saying his Pater, Ave and Creed, he 'cryed for hys mysdede', at which point 'he sayned hym in sythes sere' (ll. 759–61). This sequence of prayers and actions represents normal penitential procedure; it is an interesting detail in the confession of Sloth in *Piers Plowman* that, while he can scarcely remember his Pater noster, he retains the habit of repeatedly making the sign of the cross: 'Sleuthe … seyned hym swithe' (V. 456).[25] The purpose of this repeated action, as explained in a sixteenth-century Scots handbook on Confession, was to bring vividly to mind the image of the cross of Christ as part of the penitential practice: the author exhorts his readers 'to saine ws aft, putting beffoir our eyes Christ Iesus crucifiede, and al bloudy for oure sinnes'.[26] Gawain then concludes his prayers with a version of the familiar formula of the primer: 'And sayde cros krist me spede' (l. 762),[27] which would remind every literate person of the visible sign of the cross, symbol of Christ crucified, set at the start of the traditional teaching alphabet, the 'criss-cross row'.[28]

---

[25] William Langland, *The Vision of William concerning Piers the Plowman*, Text B, ed. W. W. Skeat, EETS OS 38 (London, 1869), p. 82. His 'two slymy ei3en' (l. 392) hint that Sloth does not see the meaningful image.

[26] Adam King, 'Of Confession', f. 15v, in *Ane catechisme or schort instrvction of Christian religion drawen out of the Scripturs and ancient doctours compyled be the Godlie and lerned father Peter Canisius ... With ane kallendar perpetuale ... maid be M. Adame King ... and ane schort method whairby euery man may exame his conscience* (Paris, 1588). The examination of conscience is foliated separately from the catechism. For an account of the editions and translations of Canisius's text, see Paul Begheyn, SJ, 'The Catechism (1555) of Peter Canisius: the most published book by a Dutch author in history', *Quaerendo* 36 (2006), 51–84.

[27] See J. J. Anderson, 'Gawain and the Hornbook', *Notes and Queries*, ns 37 (1990), 160–63.

[28] The cultural context of these prayers is complex, and the formula with its Latinate word order may also recall popular 'magical' prayers beginning 'Crux Christi', which in written form include numerous cross signs to indicate where the reader should cross him or herself (see Phillipa Hardman, 'Gawain's Practice of Piety in *Sir Gawain and the Green Knight*', *Medium Ævum*, 68 (1999), 247–67).

Thus the reader or listener is prompted to see in Gawain's crossing or 'signing' himself an actual representation of the cross of Christ as well as the enactment of a pious gesture.

The same is true in the different circumstance of the chamber scene, where, either in earnest or as a means of dissimulation, Gawain crosses himself for protection from evil (l. 1202). In just the same way, the Brigittine nuns of Syon are advised in *The Myroure of Our Ladye* to use the sign of the cross to protect themselves: 'And then ye bless you with the sygne of the holy crosse, to chase away the fiend with all his deceytes. For, as Chrysostome sayth, wherever the fiends see the signe of the crosse, they flye away, dreading it as a staffe that they are beaten withall'.[29] The operative word here is 'see': the action of making the sign of the cross is understood as making Christ's cross visible and turning it against evil spirits in precisely the same way that an exorcist uses a crucifix. Eamon Duffy quotes the popular prayer 'Deus propicius esto' to illustrate the widespread, everyday use of this powerful apotropaic symbol: 'Behold + the cross of the Lord, begone you enemies. ... Cross of Christ, defend me from every evil'.[30] Here again, with the command 'Behold', the emphasis is on the visibility of the sign of the cross.

Brief as the verbal prompts are in the text of *Sir Gawain and the Green Knight*, the invitation to visualize the cross each time Gawain is said to 'sayne' himself can contribute helpfully to our understanding of the religious culture in which the poem works, where penitential and protective crosses are to be seen everywhere, both materially present and visible to the mind's eye. In this cultural context, both the meticulously described pentangle and the familiar sign of the cross require the reader to visualize the sign in order to see its meaning.

It seems to me that there is a similar juxtaposition in Chaucer's *Pardoner's Tale* between a complex symbolic figure, described in particular detail, and a brief verbal prompt indicating a conventional emblematic image.[31] These are the richly enigmatic character of the Old Man on the one hand, and on the other, the figure of Death, simply and briefly introduced into the narrative by the boy in the tavern. I do not propose to discuss the Old Man, whom critics have variously interpreted as symbolizing old age, death, fallen humanity, and divine justice, or have associated with such figures as the Wandering Jew and the devil.[32] The defining element of this character's imaginative power is surely its resistance to interpretation. The figure of Death, by contrast, is almost too easy to interpret as the simplest kind of personification allegory. The boy explains the circumstances in which a man has lately died:

[29]   *The Myroure of our Ladye*, ed. John Blunt, EETS ES 19 (London, 1873), p. 80.
[30]   *The Stripping of the Altars*, pp. 269–71.
[31]   All quotations are taken from *The Riverside Chaucer*, ed. L. D. Benson, 3rd edn (Oxford, 1987).
[32]   For references to such interpretations, see *The Riverside Chaucer*, p. 905.

> Ther cam a privee theef men clepeth Deeth,
> That in this contree al the peple sleeth,
> And with his spere he smoot his herte atwo,
> And wente his wey withouten wordes mo. (ll. 675–8)

The reader scarcely needs to visualize the personified figure of Death before trans-lating it into a metaphor for the fact that the man died suddenly and unexpectedly, and the text seems to flatter the reader's superior interpretative skill by contrast with the literal-minded rioters, who rush off on a fool's errand to find and kill Death: 'And we wol sleen this false traytour Deeth. | He shal be slayn, he that so manye sleeth' (ll. 699–700).

However, the spear with which Death has killed his victim does of course call to mind the traditional iconography of Death as a skeleton figure wielding a spear. The moment of death was often symbolically shown much as Chaucer's tavern boy narrates it, with the skeletal form of Death piercing the body with his spear, as in the scene illustrating the 'Debate for the Soul' in the fifteenth-century BL, Stowe MS 39, f. 32v,[33] or in the striking image of a man on his death-bed for the Office of the Dead in the fourteenth-century Macclesfield Psalter.[34] Or the representation of Death might be configured as a menacing warning, as in Lydgate's lyric spoken in Death's own voice: 'Afore be redy or I my belle rynge. | My dredefull spere [that ys] full sharpe ygrounde | Doth yow now, lo, here thys manace', 'Wherefore be redy, and haue no dysdeyne | Yef of my commyng the tyme be vncertayne' (ll. 7-9, 13-14).[35] (Chaucer neatly puts this standard moral lesson into the mouth of the boy in the *Pardoner's Tale* (ll. 680–84) as he repeats his mother's teaching.) In two of the three manuscript copies of Lydgate's text, the lyric is accompanied by an illustration of Death, very clearly identified in one case by name as well by his skeletal form and his attributes of spear and bell (Oxford, Bodleian Library, MS Douce 322, f. 19v). The miniature includes nineteen careful inscriptions of the word 'deth(e)'/'deþ(e)' on the patterned surface around the skeleton figure, and critics have been interested by its appearing so many times;[36] perhaps it stands for

---

[33] For a reproduction of this image, see the online British Library Digital Catalogue of Illu-minated Manuscripts: http://blpc.bl.uk/catalogues/illuminatedmanuscripts/welcome. htm. Death is given the words: 'I hafe soght þe many a day · for to take þe to my pray'.

[34] Cambridge, Fitzwilliam Museum MS 1–2005, f. 235v; for a reproduction of this image, see the Fitzwilliam Museum website: http://www.fitzmuseum.cam.ac.uk/gallery/mac-clesfield/gallery/, and Stella Panayotova, *The Macclesfield Psalter* (Cambridge, 2005), p. 30.

[35] 'Death's Warning', ed. H. N. MacCracken, *The Minor Poems of John Lydgate*, Part II: *Secular Poems*, EETS OS 192 (London, 1934), pp. 655–7.

[36] Woolf, pp. 338–9; Camille, p. 243. For a reproduction of this image, see Woolf, pl. 3a; Camille, Plate 189; and Otto Pächt and J. J. G. Alexander, *Illuminated Manuscripts in the Bodleian Library Oxford*, 3: *British, Irish and Icelandic Schools* (Oxford, 1973), pl. CIII.

the tolling of the death-knell. Whatever it may represent, though, the reiteration certainly achieves an obsessive identification of this symbolic image with the name of Death, and this in turn suggests that an eye accustomed to seeing the armed skeleton as the picture of death would naturally visualize this same image when Death is named elsewhere in Chaucer's text.

Among Death's characteristics, mentioned in Chaucer's and Lydgate's texts, are his close association with old age and his indiscriminate taking of old and young alike, and this creates an enigma when the Old Man in the *Pardoner's Tale* complains that Death will not take him:

> Ne Deeth, allas! ne wol nat han my lyf
> Thus walke I, lyk a restelees kaitif,
> And on the ground, which is my moodres gate,
> I knokke with my staf, bothe erly and late,
> And seye leeve mooder, leet me in! (ll. 727–31)

The irony of the Old Man's situation is increased if Death is visualized here and is seen to be reversing his normal predatory behaviour, as expressed in conventional images such as the scene in Stowe MS 39 or the well-known theme of the Dance of Death, by rejecting the Old Man and not taking the opportunity to strike him dead with his spear.

Another site of tension between literal and figurative interpretations occurs when the Old Man sends the rioters to find Death, saying:

> 'Now, sires,' quod he, 'if that yow be so leef
> To fynde Deeth, turne up this croked wey,
> For in that grove I lafte hym, by my fey,
> Under a tree, and there he wole abyde;
> Noght for youre boost he wole him no thyng hyde.' (ll. 760–64)

The rioters, arriving at the tree, see the heap of gold and at once heedlessly put aside all thought of death: 'No lenger thanne after Deeth they soughte' (l. 772). Again, the text invites the reader's more sophisticated understanding of the gold as symbolically representing death by being both an occasion of mortal sin and a motive for murder. But the meaning of the Old Man's words as expressing the certainty of death is perhaps enhanced if, instead of simply interpreting the reference to death as a piece of proleptic narrative irony, the reader is also prompted to visualize the iconographic figure of Death lying in wait under the tree, unrecognized by the rioters ogling the gold.

Keeping in mind the traditional symbolic image helps the reader or listener to appreciate the subtle way in which death haunts the whole of Chaucer's tale. The pathos of the Old Man's state is encapsulated in his account of his body's decay: 'Lo, how I vanisshe, flesh and blood and skin. | Allas, whan shal my bones been at reste?' (ll. 732–3), where the transformation he describes produces an imitative picture of the Death he so desires. And finally, by the end of the narrative, the homicidal rioters themselves are transfigured into images of death in a darkly ironic twist, for as two of them plan to 'sleen' their fellow with a knife, the text produces an imitation of the original iconic action of Death: 'And I shal rive him thurgh the sides twaye' (l. 828).

The 'image' that started me thinking about the question of visualization was the iconic absence discussed in Michael Camille's *Master of Death* – an empty space in a manuscript of Deguileville's *Pèlerinages*, where, instead of a miniature illustrating the carpenter's L-square described in the adjacent text, the reader sees blank parchment and a marginal note instructing the artist: 'ne faites rien'.[37] I think one can argue that its continued emptiness – the fact that such absent images, however simple and obvious, are so rarely supplied by manuscript owners or readers – suggests that the kind of active visualization I have been exploring here was experienced as sufficient on its own.

---

[37]   Paris, BNF, ms. fr. 823, f. 18v, reproduced in *Master of Death*, Plate 1.

Inventing Symbols and Traditions: The Case of the Stonemasons

ANDREW PRESCOTT

Janet Backhouse was fascinated by the history of the Department of Manuscripts of the British Museum and, like all of us who have worked there, frequently felt at her elbow the imposing ghost of the Keeper of Manuscripts from 1837 to 1866, Sir Frederic Madden. In a paper inscribed to the memory of Janet, there is no better place to start than Madden's study in the British Museum on a dark and rainy autumn day. On 12 October 1859, Madden received a mysterious visitor called Caroline Baker. He afterwards noted in his diary that she had 'a small vellum MS. for which she asked £10'.[1] Madden was unimpressed with both Mrs Baker and the price she asked for her manuscript, offering her just four pounds. Mrs Baker was at first unwilling to part with her treasure for such a small sum, but she apparently needed the money and on the following day agreed to accept Madden's offer. Madden was very pleased with his new acquisition. He wrote in his diary that:

> This MS. is of some little interest, since it contains a treatise in prose on the "Science of Gemetry" or Masonry, of the 15th century, and corresponds partly with the Poem on the same subject in MS. Reg. 17.A I printed by Halliwell in 1841[2] [2nd edn 1843[3]], particularly in regard to the *Articles*. It would be curious to ascertain which was the *earliest* form of the tract, *prose* or *verse*. The former is the fuller of the two, and at the beginning seems to agree with what Halliwell calls the 'Ancient Constitutions', and the Legend quoted from MS. Harl. 1912 and Lansd. 98 the earliest copy of which is stated to be about 1600.

The manuscript purchased by Madden from Caroline Baker is now London, BL, Add. MS 23198. It had already had a varied career before it came into Madden's hands. Following the formation of the first Grand Lodge of Freemasons in 1717, the officers of the Grand Lodge attempted to gather together manuscripts describ-

---

[1] Madden's diary is Oxford, Bodleian Library, MS Eng. hist. c. 140–182.
[2] Madden's memory seems to have been at fault here. Halliwell reported his discovery to the Society of Antiquaries in April 1839: 'On the Antiquity of Free Masonry in England', *Archaeologia*, 28 (1840), pp. 444–7. The first edition of Halliwell's book was published in 1840: *The Early History of Freemasonry in England* (London, 1840).
[3] Although Halliwell's preface to the second edition of his book was dated 1843, it was not published until the following year.

ing the legendary history of the craft of stonemasonry.[4] On 24 June 1721, George Payne, a civil servant who was a former Grand Master, produced at a meeting of the Grand Lodge the very manuscript afterwards purchased by Madden. Payne stated that he had found it in the west of England and alleged (wrongly) that it dated from at least the early thirteenth century.[5] One of the reasons for the popularity of the new Grand Lodge was that educated men like Payne were fascinated by the esoteric legends still current among working stonemasons. The appearance of a document which seemed to suggest that these legends had been circulating for more than five hundred years caused great excitement among the well-to-do members of the Grand Lodge. William Stukeley, who had recently became a freemason in the hope that it would teach him the secrets of the ancients,[6] made a drawing of the manuscript, which is preserved in the Bodleian Library.[7] The Grand Lodge commissioned the Scottish presbyterian clergyman and royal genealogist, James Anderson, to produce a printed edition of these ancient legends which would rescue them from the corruption introduced by 'Gothick ignorance' in the 'dark illiterate ages'.[8] Anderson's printed version of these constitutions, decking them out in a Palladian dress suitable for the early eighteenth century, eradicated many traces of the medieval exemplars, but one line survived, the concluding phrase 'Amen So Mote It Be'.[9] It is one of the most curious of the many byways associated with the collections of the Department of Manuscripts of the British Museum (and a connection of which Janet Backhouse was aware) that this phrase from one of its manuscripts, 'So Mote It Be', is still repeated every day at meetings of freemasons all over the world.

Additional MS 23198 remained in the possession of the Grand Lodge and in 1728 two calligraphic transcripts were made of the manuscript.[10] However, shortly

4   James Anderson, *The New Book of Constitutions of the Antient and Honourable Fraternity of Free and Accepted Masons...* (London, 1738), p. 110.

5   This meeting of the Grand Lodge and Payne's production of the Cooke MS was described by William Stukeley: Douglas Knoop, G. P. Jones and Douglas Hamer, *The Two Earliest Masonic MSS.* (Manchester, 1938), p. 55; David Boyd Haycock, *William Stukeley: Science, Religion and Archaeology in Eighteenth-Century England* (Woodbridge, 2002), p. 176. A pen trial on f. 39v of the manuscript suggests that in the seventeenth century it was owned by William Rand: Knoop, Jones and Hamer, *Earliest Masonic MSS.*, p. 54. William Rand (or Rant), a member of the London College of Physicians who was Gulstonian Lecturer in 1637 and Censor in 1640, 1645, 1647 and 1650, dedicated a translation of Gassendi's life of Nicolaus Claudius Fabricius published in 1657 to John Evelyn and was a correspondent of Samuel Hartlib, both of whom were interested in the esoteric legends associated with stonemasons: *ODNB*.

6   Hancock, *William Stukeley*, pp. 174–80.

7   Knoop, Jones and Hamer, *Earliest Masonic MSS.*, p. 55.

8   Anderson, *New Constitutions*, p. 113.

9   James Anderson, *The Constitutions of the Free-Masons* (London, 1723), p. 56.

10   These are the manuscripts now known as the Supreme Council MS and the Woodford MS, made by Reid in 1728 for William Cowper, the Clerk of Parliament and afterwards

afterwards the manuscript left masonic custody. In 1781, it was in the possession of one Robert Crowe, perhaps in view of the later Norfolk connection of the manuscript to be identified with the solicitor of that name who lived at Swaffham in Norfolk and died in 1786.[11] In 1786, the volume passed into the possession of the Norfolk antiquary Sir John Fenn, best known for his publication of the Paston letters.[12] After Fenn's death in 1794, the manuscript disappeared from sight until Caroline Baker produced it in Madden's office. It is not clear how the reappearance of this manuscript in 1859 came to the attention of masonic scholars. Madden himself was not a freemason;[13] but perhaps he mentioned it to his colleague John Harris, the artist who produced remarkable facsimiles of incunabula for the Museum and who also created the modern form of masonic tracing board.[14] By 1860, the manuscript had come to the attention of the self-styled 'Organist, Clerical Amanuensis, Public Lecturer and Sub-Editor', Matthew Cooke, who was a regular user of the British Museum, falling foul of Panizzi for refusing to obey new rules requiring readers to return their books when they had finished with them.[15] In 1861, Cooke published an elaborate transcript and pseudo-facsimile of the manuscript, made using specially cut types.[16] The manuscript has ever since been known as the Cooke manuscript.

As Madden had immediately noticed, there were similarities between the Cooke manuscript and another medieval manuscript in the British Museum, Royal MS 17 A.I. While the Cooke manuscript is in Middle English prose, Royal MS 17 A.I is in English verse and incorporates extracts from other Middle English poems. Nevertheless, as Madden appreciated, like the Cooke manuscript Royal MS 17 A.I also contains a legendary history of the origins of the craft of stonemasonry and gives ordinances for stonemasons. Madden knew about this poem because it had been printed earlier in the nineteenth century by James Orchard Halliwell (afterwards Halliwell-Phillipps),[17] with whom Madden had had a titanic dispute after

---

owned by Sir Francis Palgrave, now owned by Quatuor Coronati Lodge and on loan to the Library and Museum of Freemasonry: Knoop, Jones and Hamer, *Earliest Masonic MSS.*, pp. 55–7.

[11] Ownership note on f. 2: Knoop, Jones and Hamer, *Earliest Masonic MSS.*, p. 54.

[12] Ibid.

[13] This is apparent from a series of articles and comments on the administration of the Department of Manuscripts made in *The Freemason's Magazine* after the publication of N. E. S. A. Hamilton's attack on John Payne Collier in 1860. Madden also made pejorative comments about Freemasonry in his diary.

[14] See the entry on Harris by Janet Ing Freeman in the *ODNB* and Toshiyuki Takamiya, 'John Harris and the Facsimile Pages [of Caxton's Chaucer]' at http://www.bl.uk/treasures/caxton/johnharris.html.

[15] P. R. Harris, *A History of the British Museum Library 1753–1973* (London, 1998), p. 230. Cooke was also a friend of Halliwell.

[16] *The History and Articles of Masonry (now First Published from a Manuscript in the British Museum)* (London, 1861).

Halliwell had attempted to sell to the British Museum manuscripts stolen from Trinity College Cambridge. Royal MS 17 A.I was known in Madden's time as the Halliwell Manuscript, but at the beginning of the twentieth century at the suggestion of the masonic scholar Robert Freke Gould (who was perhaps piqued that Halliwell was not a freemason and also concerned at Halliwell's scandalous reputation as a manuscript thief) the manuscript began to be referred to as the Regius Manuscript, by which name it is generally known today.[18] The Regius manuscript contains 794 lines of Middle English verse which have been localized by the *Linguistic Atlas of Late Medieval England* to Shropshire.[19] The dating generally given for the manuscript of c. 1390 is based on outdated assessments by David Casley and Halliwell.[20] Edward Augustus Bond proposed a dating for the manuscript of the second quarter of the fifteenth century, and comparison with, for example, London, British Library, Cotton MS Claudius A.II, a manuscript of John Mirk's *Instructions for Parish Priests*, suggests that Bond was broadly right. Bond suggested that Regius and Cooke were not very far separated in date and again it seems he was broadly right.

The key to understanding the function and character of the texts in the Regius and Cooke manuscripts lies, as Madden noted, in the relationship between the poem of Regius and the prose text in Cooke. One of the most striking features of Regius is the inclusion of a number of other texts, including extracts from John Mirk's *Instructions for Parish Priests* on behaviour in church, a popular poem on etiquette called *Urbanitatis*, and an account of the *Quatuor Coronati*, four stonemasons said to have been martyred in Rome. The appearance of these texts is intriguing, suggesting that Regius was at one level intended to provide a small manual on etiquette for use by the fifteenth-century stonemason. However, these additional texts are very much secondary components of the Regius text. At the heart of the Regius manuscript is an account of the origins of the craft of stonemasonry and a series of ordinances regulating the craft which were said to have been promulgated by the Anglo-Saxon King Æthelstan. It is this legendary and highly symbolic history which forms the main thrust of Regius. The poem describes how the great clerk Euclid devised geometry and gave it the name of masonry in order to provide employment for the children of great lords and ladies living in Egypt. Euclid ordained that, although there were masters among the masons, they should nevertheless treat each other as equals, 'neither subject nor

---

[17] See n. 2, above.

[18] R. F. Gould, *A Commentary on the Masonic Poem, Urbanitatis and Instructions for a Parish Priest*, Quatuor Coronatorum Antigrapha 1, pt. 3 (1889), p. lv.

[19] A. McIntosh, M. I. Samuels and M. Benskin, *A Linguistic Atlas of Late Mediaeval English*, 4 vols (Aberdeen, 1986), i, pp. 115, 233–5; ii, pp. 424–38.

[20] For a fuller discussion of the dating issues, see A. Prescott, 'Some Literary Contexts of the Cooke and Regius Manuscripts', in *Freemasonry in Music and Literature*, ed. T. Stewart (London, 2005), pp. 1–36.

servant'. Regius states that masonry came to England in the reign of Æthelstan. To regulate the craft, Æthelstan made a series of ordinances, which the poem describes. Æthelstan's ordinances instructed that a general assembly of masons should be held and ordered all masons to attend it. Æthelstan enjoined that the masons were to receive fair pay. According to Regius, Æthelstan echoed Euclid by declaring that the masons should always remember that they were fellow workers, helping each other in their work, serving each other at meals and avoiding recourse to litigation.

The Cooke manuscript is in prose, which has been localized by Douglas Hamer to the south west Midlands.[21] In the Cooke manuscript, the supplementary material in Regius, such as the extracts from Mirk and the poem *Urbanitatis*, is omitted. On the other hand, the legendary history of stonemasonry has been hugely expanded. It opens with an elaborate invocation to God, who had made all things to be subject to man. God had given man knowledge of crafts, including geometry. The seven liberal arts are then listed. Clearly, the author declares, geometry is at the root of them all, since geometry means measurement of the earth, and all tools involve measurement and are made of materials from the earth. All the crafts of the world, he continues, were founded by the sons of Lamach, who were mentioned in Genesis, with Lamach's eldest son Jabal inventing geometry. Lamach's sons wrote their discoveries on two pillars of stone to survive fire or flood. After the flood, Pythagoras found one stone and Hermes the other. Ham, Noah's son, revived the practice of masonry. Nimrod, Ham's son, sent masons to Assyria and gave them charges which, declares the Cooke manuscript, survive, just as those given by Euclid have survived.

The Cooke manuscript then repeats the story of Euclid in much the same way as Regius, but with more biblical references and the addition of circumstantial information about Egypt. The Cooke author describes how stonemasonry came to Europe. He states that a king was elected in France called Charles II, who loved masons, and gave them charges which were still in use in France. Shortly afterwards, 'Saint Ad Habelle' came to England and converted St Alban to Christianity. Alban also gave charges to the masons and 'ordeyned conuenyent [wages] to pay for þer trauayle'.[22] Cooke then gives a slightly different version of the Æthelstan story. He states that Æthelstan's youngest son himself became proficient in masonry and that the prince gave the masons ordinances. The prince ordered that the masons should have reasonable pay, and procured a charter from the king which stated that the masons might hold an assembly at whatever time they thought reasonable. Cooke then repeats the story of Æthelstan's grant in the same terms as Regius, and repeats the various ordinances. The order of the articles is slightly different, and some of the more general articles in Regius are omitted. The

21 Knoop, Jones and Hamer, *Earliest Masonic MSS.*, p. 63.
22 Ibid., p. 103.

effect of the rearrangement is to give greater prominence to the masons' assembly, and Cooke concludes by stressing that any mason who failed to attend the assembly would be arrested by the sheriff and cast into prison.

Cooke thus elaborates the legendary history of stonemasonry in order to strengthen the claims of stonemasons. The central character of these claims is clear: that the masons should have reasonable pay and that they should be permitted to hold an annual assembly: 'þey schulde haue resonabulle pay' and 'they schulde make a sembly whan thei sawe reasonably tyme a cum to-gedir'. In Regius, it is claimed that these demands were warranted by the charter of Æthelstan. In Cooke, the first regulation that masons should be properly paid is extended back to the time of St Alban, and Æthelstan is presented as confirming these ancient provisions and authorizing the assembly. The way in which the story is subtly manipulated in Cooke to strengthen the claims of the stonemasons is strikingly illustrated by the introduction of the figure of Æthelstan's supposed son (there is no evidence that Æthelstan had any children). Æthelstan's son was apparently invented by the author of Cooke in order to extend his roll-call of royal masons and also to establish more firmly the right of masons to hold their own assembly. According to Regius, the masons' assembly was held by Æthelstan and was attended by the king and many nobleman. Cooke makes a subtle but important change. The introduction in the Cooke manuscript of the figure of Æthelstan's son who becomes a mason changes the character of the assembly. In the Cooke manuscript, the masons' assembly becomes a gathering convened and held by the masons for their own regulation. In other words, the Cooke manuscript introduces the figure of a king's son to the story in order to help establish the right of stonemasons to meet together and regulate their craft.

By manipulating the legendary history of stonemasonry, the compiler of the Cooke manuscript sought to provide a stronger historical warrant for the claim of the masons to hold an annual assembly. Similar concerns are also evident from the way in which Cooke treats the 'articles and points' governing the craft. The ordinances as presented in Regius have been reorganized in Cooke so as to give greater prominence to the assembly. Although Cooke contains fewer articles, it considerably strengthens a number of the provisions. For example, Regius declared that apprentices could be paid less while they were learning their craft, providing they received full wages when their training was complete. Cooke puts this slightly differently, enjoining the master to pay the apprentice a fair wage for the work he undertakes. Cooke apparently represents a shrewdly edited version of the articles from Regius in which the less important articles, such as the injunction that masons should not criticize each other's work, have been omitted in order to emphasize more pressing issues, such as the need for fair pay and the importance of the general assembly.

All this suggests a context for the compilation of these two manuscripts. As is well known, wage pressure was particularly acute in the building trades after the Black Death, and much of the labour legislation in the late fourteenth and fifteenth centuries sought to restrain the wage levels of building workers.[23] In the 1425 parliament, the commons presented a petition complaining that the annual congregations and confederacies made by the masons in their general chapters and assemblies were publicly violating and undermining the statutes of labourers.[24] The commons asked the king and lords to ordain that the holding and gathering of such chapters should be utterly forbidden and judged a felony, and asked that the justices of the peace should be given authority to enquire into these chapters and assemblies. The king replied that such chapters and congregations should not be held, and those who convene such chapters should be adjudged felons. Any masons who go to such congregations should be imprisoned without fine or ransom at the king's will. A statute to this effect was duly enacted. The stories in Regius and Cooke were intended to authorize the continued holding of such assemblies notwithstanding the statutory provision.

As such, the Regius and Cooke manuscripts are striking examples of the way in which medieval fraternities of different types invented and manipulated myths, legends and symbols to provide a historical warrant for various claims. The masons denied the authority of parliament to prohibit the annual assemblies of masons, because these meetings had been authorized by Æthelstan (perhaps chosen for no other reason that his name, meaning 'noble stone', was a credible one for a patron of stonemasons). When Æthelstan was found not to be a sufficiently high authority, the story was extended back to Nimrod. The manipulation of legends and symbols to construct historical identities and to provide invented warrants for claims to property or status is a familiar theme of the middle ages. The Regius and Cooke manuscripts, however, are unusual and important because they allow the process of manipulation to be traced in great detail. Moreover, these manuscripts are associated with a relatively humble group of artisans rather than such élite bodies as monasteries or urban oligarchies. The appearance of such legends among the stonemasons has been taken as suggesting that there was something unusual and distinctive about this craft. This idea that the masons preserved by word of mouth ancient legends and esoteric truths has in modern times led to the construction of dizzying esoteric edifices – one need only think of the various legends of the survival of the Templars, of Rosslyn Chapel and of the *Da Vinci Code*. A more prosaic explanation of the legends in Regius and Cooke is that the stone-

---

[23]   See, for example, C. Given-Wilson, 'The Problem of Labour in the Context of English Government, c. 1350–1450' in *The Problem of Labour in Fourteenth-Century England*, eds J. Bothwell, P. Goldberg and W. M. Ormrod (York, 2000), pp. 85–100; 'Service, Serfdom and English Labour Legislation, 1350–1500', in *Concepts and Patterns of Service in the Later Middle Ages*, ed. A. Curry and E. Matthew (Woodbridge, 2000), pp. 21–37.

[24]   D. Knoop and G. P. Jones, *The Mediaeval Mason* (Manchester, 1938), p. 183.

masons were in the first part of the fifteenth century subject to severe legislative pressure which restricted their wages and right of assembly. The legends were invented and articulated to justify the claims of groups of (probably relatively junior) stonemasons to hold assemblies to agitate for better wages.

However, the stonemasons were not the only artisan group which developed such legends and symbols to help protect their status. It is only because of the intense interest of modern freemasons in the origins of their fraternity that the texts in Regius and Cooke have been identified and so carefully analyzed. Other groups apparently developed similar mythologies which are not documented in the same detail. For example, in 1396 the wardens of the Saddlers' Company in London appeared before the mayor and aldermen and claimed that the serving men in that trade (described using the English term yeomen) 'against the consent, and without leave, of their masters, were wont to array themselves all in a new and like suit once in the year, and oftentimes held divers meetings, at Stratford and elsewhere'.[25] The six 'governors of the serving men' were summoned and declared that:

> time out of mind the serving-men of the said trade had had a certain Fraternity among themselves, and had been wont to array themselves all in like suit once in the year, and, after meeting together at Stratford, on the Feast of the Assumption of the Blessed Virgin Mary, to come from thence to the Church of St Vedast, in London, there to hear Mass on the same day, in honour of the said glorious Virgin.[26]

The master saddlers hotly denied this claim, saying that the fraternity and procession had only existed for thirteen years 'and even then had been discontinued of late years'. They alleged that the fraternity was being used as a cover for plots to secure better wages: 'under a certain feigned colour of sanctity, many of the serving men of the trade had influenced the journeymen among them, and had formed covins thereon, with the object of raising their wages greatly in excess'.[27] The activities of the fraternity were also causing absentecism:

> the serving-men aforesaid, according to an ordinance made among themselves, would oftentimes cause the journeymen of the said masters to be summoned by a bedel, thereunto appointed, to attend at the Vigils of the dead, who were members of the said fraternity, and at making offering for them on the morrow, under a certain penalty to be levied; whereby the said masters were very greatly aggrieved, and were injured through such absenting of themselves by the journeymen, so leaving their labours and duties, against their wish.[28]

[25] H. T. Riley, *Memorials of London and London Life in the XIIIth, XIVth and XVth Centuries* (London, 1868), p. 542.

[26] Ibid., pp. 542–3.

[27] Ibid., p. 543.

[28] Ibid.

The mayor and aldermen forbade the serving men from holding their procession and instructed them to return, with representatives of the master saddlers, to hear judgement. The representatives of the serving men afterwards presented a petition in which they asked the wardens of the saddlers 'that they may have and use all the points which heretofore they have used'.[29] The mayor and aldermen decided that the serving men should indeed be under the control of the masters and should not have a separate fraternity. But they also firmly enjoined the masters to treat the serving men fairly.

It is interesting to note that the term 'points' was also used in the Regius and Cooke manuscripts, where Æthelstan's supposed ordinances were divided into 'articles' and 'points'. Other features of the fraternity of the yeomen saddlers are also reminiscent of the case of the stonemasons as depicted in the Regius and Cooke manuscripts. Although the yeomen fraternity was apparently relatively recent, its members claimed it was an ancient body. Doubtless they would have been able to name figures equivalent to the Anglo-Saxons Æthelstan and Edwin to substantiate the claim of their fraternity to great antiquity. The 'feigned colour of sanctity' adopted by the fraternity likewise recalls the claims of the Cooke manuscript to biblical precedent and warrant. The yeoman saddlers' fraternity possessed written ordinances and it would be fascinating to know how they compared to the manuscripts of the stonemasons. The fraternity had a clearly defined hierarchy of officers and, since penalties were levied, presumably also had a common chest. The insistence that journeymen should attend assemblies of the fraternity for funerals and other occasions recalls similar injunctions in Cooke and Regius that masons should attend assemblies of stonemasons, under pain of imprisonment and forfeiture. The fraternity of yeoman saddlers looks very similar in character to (and perhaps even in some respects more developed than) the associations of junior stonemasons which produced Regius and Cooke.

In 1387 it was claimed that at the Dominican priory of Blackfriars in London, the serving men of the cordwainers gathered

> a great congregation of men like unto themselves, and there did conspire and confederate to hold together; to the damage of the commonalty, and the prejudice of the trade aforementioned, and in rebellion against the overseers aforesaid; and there, because that Richard Bonet, of the trade aforesaid, would not agree with them, made assault upon him, so that he hardly escaped with his life'.[30]

The yeomen cordwainers had hatched a novel scheme to secure approval for their fraternity. They had agreed to pay one of the Dominicans at Blackfriars, Brother William Bartone, to go to Rome to seek papal confirmation of the fraternity. They hoped that papal support would discourage any attempt to prevent them meet-

29 Ibid., p. 544.
30 Ibid., p. 495.

ing in the future.[31] This reference is particularly interesting in that it shows junior craftsmen seeking to purchase clerical support to secure some kind of legal authority for their meetings. It has been a matter of debate whether groups like stonemasons were sufficiently literate to produce texts such as the Regius poem. Douglas Hamer, for example, was insistent that Regius could only have been the work of a clerk, and suggested a connection with Llanthony Priory.[32] However, such a view probably underestimates the extent of urban lay literacy at this period. The yeoman saddlers, for example, had compiled a set of ordinances and presented a written petition to the mayor and aldermen. The case of the yeomen cordwainers illustrates another means by which artisans could gain access to literate culture. It is tempting to wonder how far Brother William also drew the attention of the yeomen cordwainers to legends and stories which would support their case for a separate fraternity. The fact that the meeting took place at Blackfriars also illustrates how the formation of these fraternities of junior craftsmen was due to a variety of motives apart from such material questions as wages and economic status. The procession of the yeomen saddlers seems to have been largely a religious occasion and doubtless this was also a component in the holding of the meeting of the cordwainers at Blackfriars. Mutual aid was also another consideration, as is apparent from the stress of the saddlers on attendance at funerals.

While the two abortive fraternities of yeomen saddlers and cordwainers look very similar in character to the kind of bodies which apparently produced the Regius and Cooke manuscripts, we do not have any direct evidence that they engaged in the invention of legends and symbols. However, in the case of some more prestigious trades, there is clearer evidence of the development of such mythologies. One of the most celebrated of the civic legends of the city of London is the story that the wealthy vintner Henry Picard, who was mayor of London in 1357, entertained five kings in his mansion.[33] The legend of this royal feast has become central to the folklore of the Vintners' Company. The company still uses the toast 'The Vintners Company, may it flourish root and branch for ever with the Five and the Master', followed by five rousing cheers. The feast is depicted in a stained glass window in Vintners' Hall and in 1903 Albert Chevallier Tayler produced a flamboyant painting of the feast as one of the series of murals celebrating London's history installed in the ambulatory of the Royal Exchange.[34] The modern

---

[31] Ibid., pp. 495–6.
[32] Hamer, 'Further Consideration of the Regius MS.', *Ars Quatuor Coronatorum*, 94 (1981), pp. 166–9.
[33] On the history of this legend, see C. L. Kingsford, 'The Feast of the Five Kings', *Archaeologia*, 67 (1916), pp. 119–26, and A. Crawford, *A History of the Vintners' Company* (London, 1977), pp. 263–7.
[34] C. A. P. Willsdon, *Mural Painting in Britain 1840–1940* (Oxford, 2000), p. 67, notes that the choice of this subject by the Vintners in donating this mural deftly added

office block owned by the Vintners' Company, which houses the Wine Standards Board and other bodies connected with the wine trade, is called Five Kings House. According to Joshua Barnes's *History of Edward III*, published in 1688, the guests at the feast comprised Edward III of England, John II of France, David II of Scotland, Peter de Lusignan, King of Cyprus and Waldemar IV of Denmark, together with 'the Duke of Bavaria, the chief hostages of France and King Edward's sons (excepting the Black Prince then in Aquitaine').[35] Barnes's source seems to have been John Stow. However, Stow lists only four kings, omitting the King of Denmark, and states that the Black Prince was in fact present. Stow was also uncertain about the date of the event, placing it in 1357 (the year when Picard was mayor) in his *Annals*, but giving 1363 in the *Survey of London*. In fact, it was impossible for the five kings listed by Barnes to have been present in the same house at the same time in England and it was probably Barnes who added the names of the King of Denmark and the Duke of Bavaria to the guest list. The legend of a great royal feast, however, does go back to the middle ages. Stow's source was the collection of Westminster Abbey documents called the *Liber Niger*, which dates from c. 1485.[36] It has been suggested that story of the feast as reported by Stow was an echo of an incident described in the contemporary continuation of the *Eulogium Historiarum*, which reported how Peter of Lusignan, when he arrived in London in 1363, brought with him as a prisoner the pagan king of Lecco and another great lord called the Lord of Jerusalem, also a pagan who was converted and received at his baptism by Edward III, whose name he took. Shortly afterwards, David of Scotland arrived in London, 'and so before the end of the parliament there were five kings present in London ... such a thing had never been seen since the time of King Arthur, for whose feast at Caerleon six kings were present with himself as the seventh'.[37]

Intriguing though the parallels between the Vintners' legend and the incident reported in the continuation to the *Eulogium Historiarum* seem, it is by no means certain that a feast patronized by five kings took place at that time. The chronicler is simply struck by the presence of five kings in London as an event of Arthurian proportions; he does not explicitly say that the kings feasted together. Moreover, the chronicler makes no direct reference to Henry Picard or the Vintners. Martin Walsh makes the intriguing suggestion that the legend of the feast is an echo of an extravagant celebration of the feast of the patron saint of the vintners, St Martin, on 11 November,[38] but again in the absence of any evidence that

---

another layer to the symbolism – on the occasion of her Diamond Jubilee celebrations a few years previously in 1897, Queen Victoria had entertained four kings in the city of London.

35 Crawford, *Vintners' Company*, p. 263.
36 Kingsford, 'Five Kings', pp. 120–1.
37 Crawford, *Vintners' Company*, p. 266.
38 M. W. Walsh, 'Medieval English "Martinmesse": The Archaeology of a Forgotten Festival', *Folklore*, 111 (2000), pp. 243–4.

the feast took place it is difficult to speculate with any certainty. All that can be said is that the *Liber Niger* establishes that the story that Picard entertained a number of kings in his house had gained currency by the end of the fifteenth century. The genesis of this story and its progressive annexation by the Vintners' Company in a process which continued to the end of the seventeenth century appears strikingly similar to the way in which the stonemasons claimed that they received special treatment for Æthelstan. Both vintners and masons used legends of this kind to affirm that they practiced royal arts.

The use by a London guild of less fanciful historical analogies to enhance its prestige is also apparent from the four Tudor frescoes discovered at Carpenters' Hall in London in 1845 and now preserved in the Museum of London.[39] These emphasize the biblical connections of carpentry in a way that echoes the subsequent masonic annexation of the biblical stories of the Temple. The first fresco from Carpenters' Hall shows Noah receiving the command to build the ark. The second depicts King Josiah ordering the repair of the temple. The third shows Joseph at work as a carpenter, with Christ gathering the chippings. The sequence concludes with Christ teaching in the synagogue with the inscription 'Is this not the carpenter's son?' Each picture had an elaborate caption to reinforce the message about the prestigious character of the craft of carpentry. The symbolism of the Carpenters' Hall frescoes is clear and obvious, but carpenters were also fond of much more elaborate allegorical musings on the character and practice of their trade. This is illustrated by a fascinating late fifteenth-century text published by Edmund Wilson in 1987, *The Debate of the Carpenters' Tools*.[40] This is a lively comic debate between the various tools of the carpenter's trade: the saw, the rule, the plane, the compass and so on. A typical exchange is that between the rule stone and the gouge. The rule stone declares that his master will rule the roost; the gouge says the rule stone was not worth an old shoe: 'You have been an apprentice for seven year, but all you have learnt is how to leer'.[41] Wilson suggests that the *Debate of the Carpenter's Tools* was intended for recitation at a guild feast. The most striking feature of the poem is the technical awareness shown of the various carpenters' tools. If the author was not himself actually a carpenter, he had absorbed a great deal of arcane knowledge of the carpenter's craft.

The *Debate* is not unique; it has been pointed out that the presumably clerical author of the shipwrights' play of the Building of Noah's Ark in the York mystery cycle also displays similar technical knowledge of the shipwright's craft.[42] *The*

---

[39] Drawings of the frescoes by F. W. Fairholt are illustrated in J. Ridley, *A History of the Carpenters' Company* (London, 1995), pp. 26–7.

[40] E. Wilson, 'The Debate of the Carpenter's Tools', *Review of English Studies*, New Series, 152 (1987), pp. 445–70.

[41] Ibid., p. 459.

[42] Ibid., p. 453.

Debate of the Carpenters' Tools makes an interesting comparison with the stone-masons' texts of the Regius and Cooke manuscripts. The *Carpenters' Tools* shows how men who were versed in the arcane technical mysteries of a particular craft were capable of producing complex texts which engaged in elaborate reflections on their craft. The *Carpenters' Tools* demonstrates that there was not an unbridge-able gulf between artisan practice and literate culture, and in this context the pro-duction by stonemasons of the self-serving historical fantasies of the Regius and Cooke manuscripts seems less surprising. However, there is a striking contrast between the *Carpenters' Tools* and the texts in Regius and Cooke. While the *Car-penters' Tools* poem shows a marked ability to use images of a craftsman's tools to make moral points (in a way that almost anticipates later freemasonry), there is no reference in the poem to any legendary history of the sort which is so prominent in Regius and Cooke.

Regius and Cooke were compiled in the West Midlands, and suggest that the process of invention and construction of historic identities was not confined to larger towns. Indeed, one of the best documented examples of the development of such a legend is associated with the Palmers' Guild in Ludlow, not far from where the Regius manuscript was compiled.[43] The earliest records of this guild date back to the 1270s and it was incorporated in 1329. By the beginning of the fif-teenth century, however, a legend had sprung up which claimed a much older ori-gin for this body. It was claimed that the three palmers who supposedly brought back a ring of St John the Evangelist to Edward the Confessor were palmers from Ludlow. This legend was depicted in the palmers' window in St John's chapel in Ludlow Church, which dates from the mid-fifteenth century. It was repeated in the reredos of the chapel, dating from c. 1525, and was still current in Leland's time. The emergence of this legend may be linked to the first description of the guild as 'the guild of Palmers of St. Andrew' in 1377. In general, it is striking that the late fourteenth and early fifteenth centuries appear to have been a fertile period for the emergence of such legends.

The historical invention and manipulation of the Regius and Cooke manu-scripts was not simply a distinctive or aberrant feature of the stonemasons' craft but a more general characteristic of urban artisan culture. In a masterly recent sur-vey, Gervase Rosser has illustrated the richness and variety of civic myths in medieval England and has emphasized that the process of constructing historical identities was as vigorous and complex in the medieval period as in subsequent centuries.[44] Moreover, he suggests that these myths were not passive offshoots of

---

[43] For the following, see C. Liddy, 'The Palmers' Guild Window, St Lawrence's Church, Ludlow: A Study of the Construction of Guild Identity in Medieval Stained Glass', *Shrop-shire History and Archaeology*, 72 (1997), pp. 26–35.

[44] G. Rosser, 'Myth, Image and Social Process in the English Medieval Town', *Urban His-tory*, 23 (1996), pp. 5–25.

political events but profoundly shaped the cultural and social development of medieval urban life. In the context of the types of examples cited by Rosser, the legendary histories of stonemasonry developed in Regius and Cooke appear less exotic. The most familiar example of such an urban myth is undoubtedly the tale of Godiva's naked ride through Coventry. The twelfth-century legends of Godiva had been annexed by the mayor and council as a means of securing greater autonomy from the monks of the priory by the late fourteenth century, when a stained glass window commemorating the claim that Leofric made Coventry toll-free was installed in the civic church of St Michael. By the fifteenth century, the story of Godiva was being used by common townsfolk of Coventry in order to protest against taxes imposed by the town government.[45] Rosser shows that similar processes occurred in many other towns. For example, in Grimsby, the story of Grim and Havelock was adopted as a civic history, while by 1340 Ipswich had developed its own myth of its foundation by a pagan King Ypus.[46]

Rosser largely confines his attention to civic myths associated with particular towns and cities, but it is evident that such shared mythologies were also important bonds between the bodies known variously by such terms as *fraternitas, gilda, compaignie, congregation* and *confrarie*[47] which made up the associational culture of the medieval English town. A major theme of recent historiography of English medieval urban life has been to emphasize how the distinctions drawn by Victorian scholars, particularly the division between craft and religious gilds, have little basis in medieval terminology and practice. As Elspeth Veale has observed, 'The distinction drawn [by historians of medieval England] between fraternity – an association which concerned itself particularly with religious ceremonies, especially the rites of burial, and with the social activities which its members enjoyed – and organised mistery may well have been drawn too sharply'.[48] Although various fraternities, fellowships, crafts and mysteries were an all-pervading feature of medieval town life, there was no rigid legal categorization of them – they were loose and flexible organisations. The more trade-oriented fraternities emerged from religious associations. Thus, by the late twelfth-century, St Martin le Grand in London had emerged as the favoured place of worship of a *congregatio* of saddlers, and the saddlers made an agreement with the canons which provided that they could share in church services, that prayers would be said for them by the canons, and that St Martin's bell was to be tolled for their funeral processions.[49] It was from religious associations of this kind that the more trade-ori-

---

45   Rosser, 'Myth, Image and Social Process', pp. 15–17; Daniel Donoghue, *Lady Godiva: The Literary History of a Legend* (Oxford, 2003).
46   Rosser, 'Myth, Image and Social Process', pp. 11–13.
47   Cf. E. Veale, 'The "Great Twelve": Mistery and Fraternity in Thirteenth-Century London', *Historical Research*, 64 (1991), p. 238.
48   Ibid., p. 262.
49   Ibid., p. 238.

ented fraternities emerged. For example, a fraternity at the church of All Hallows Bread Street in London was founded by a mercer and a salter. Most subsequent bequests came from salters. Eventually, Salters' Hall was built on land owned by the fraternity and the chapel of the guild became known as the Salters' Chapel. A similar process occurred in York, where during the fifteenth century the fraternity of St John the Baptist became associated with the tailors and the guild of Holy Trinity in Fossgate with the mercers.[50]

This approach to the development of medieval guilds has however left a problem in that it is difficult to establish the process by which craft-regulating fraternities emerged from their original religious foundations. This in turn has made it difficult to establish why forms of craft organisation varied from town to town. As Barrie Dobson has recently observed in respect of Durham, 'one is left with the overwhelming impression that, had it not been for the need to impose a procession and sequence of plays on the crafts of the city at their own expense, there would have been no formal guild regulations at all'.[51] Discussions of this issue have focussed primarily on legislative and economic pressures. Elspeth Veale saw the emergence of organisations in London with more specific craft regulation responsibilities as reflecting the need of both the royal and city government to have specific organisations which would assist in the administration of regulations. Thus, royal control of the fish trade meant that the fishmongers were one of the first trades to establish an organisation to control a craft activity, which impressed contemporaries by its spectacular pageants with gilt sturgeons, salmon mounted on horses and forty mounted knights representing 'luces of the sea'.[52] Other scholars have pointed to particular legislative pressures to account for the development of craft-regulating guilds. For example, Sarah Rees Jones has forcefully argued that increasing urban resentment of the powers of the JPs led to an enactment in 1363 stating that craftsmen were to join a single trade and that they were to be regulated by members of their crafts.[53] She suggests that this gave a major impetus to the assumption of regulatory powers by crafts. However, it is possible that a focus on legislative and regulatory pressures is too narrow. In the case of the yeoman saddlers, it is evident that religious and social needs were just as important in the formation of their abortive fraternity as dissatisfaction with wages and conditions

---

50   C. M. Barron, 'The Parish Fraternities of Medieval London', in *The Church in Pre-Reformation Society: Essays in Honour of F. R. H. Du Boulay*, eds C. M. Barron and C. Harper-Bill (Woodbridge, 1985), pp. 14–17.

51   R. B. Dobson, 'Craft Guilds and City: the Historical Origins of the York Mystery Plays Reassessed' in *The Stage as Mirror: Civic Theatre in Late Medieval Europe*, ed. A. E. Knight (Cambridge, 1997), p. 100.

52   Veale, 'The Great Twelve', p. 242.

53   S. R. Jones, 'Household, Work and the Problem of Mobile Labour: the Regulation of Labour in Medieval English Towns' in *Problem of Labour*, eds Bothwell, Goldberg and Ormrod, pp. 133–53.

of work. Within this process, just as cultural factors such as the need to organize processions had an impact on the development of craft organizations, so the development of shared mythologies and legends, which probably took place in the course of social gatherings such as feasts and church services, was also of fundamental importance. Rosser has stressed how we should see urban mythologies not simply as a reflection of political and economic processes but also as a force which helped shape these developments.[54] The explanation for the emergence of craft guilds may not be purely social and economic; it may, as Barrie Dobson hints, reflect the impact of the emergence of a shared and invented history.

The stonemasons who compiled the Regius and Cooke manuscripts clearly had a strong sense of shared history and this in itself may have been powerful enough to encourage them to seek new forms of craft organization which they felt were appropriate to their heritage. The potency of these legends is reflected in their continuity.[55] The legendary history of the stonemasons continued to be developed and articulated throughout the fifteenth and sixteenth centuries. Versions of the Cooke manuscript appeared which claimed to have been sanctioned by Henry VI, a clear attempt to counteract the effect of the 1425 legislation. In response to a labour dispute at York in 1552 and to renewed attempts to control building wages, a version of the legendary history of stonemasonry was developed in which the assembly held in Æthelstan's reign was placed at York. From the end of the sixteenth century, further versions of this legendary history circulated widely in England and Scotland.

Again, this continuity in the craft and fraternal legends of the masons is not unique. One of the most striking examples of such continuity occurs close to Harlaxton, at Stamford, where a 1387 return of the Guild of St Martin states that, on the Feast of St Martin in November, a bull was baited in the streets of the town by dogs, and, after it was killed, the brothers and sisters of the guild sat down to feast on the meat.[56] As such, the Stamford bull running is apparently a vestige of a celebration of the Feast of St Martin, which in turn had pagan overtones. As such, it is not a very remarkable event. However, as Martin Walsh has vividly described, it was to prove a tenacious feature of Stamford life, continuing until the nineteenth century. Throughout its history, the ceremony responded directly to local cultural and social pressures, constantly reinventing itself. The bull running was described by a local writer Richard Butcher in 1646, who emphasized the most disreputable aspects of the event, such as the way in which the runners smeared themselves

51   Rosser, 'Myth, Image and Social Process', pp. 19–25.

55   A. Prescott, '"Kinge Athelston that was a Worthy Kinge of England": Anglo-Saxon Myths of the Freemasons', in *The Power of Words: Anglo-Saxon Studies Presented to Donald Scragg on his Seventieth Birthday*, ed. H. Magennis and J. Wilcox (Morgantown, 2006), pp. 397–434.

56   M. W. Walsh, 'November Bull-Running in Stamford, Lincolnshire', *Journal of Popular Culture*, 30 (2004) , pp. 233–47.

with the bull's excrement. As Walsh notes, Butcher's description of the event clearly links to the wider Puritan attack on popular festivities at this time. The bull running survived, however, partly because it became an emblem by which the town asserted its claim to autonomy against the control of the Burghleys. The ceremony acquired additional carnivalesque components during the seventeenth and eighteenth centuries, with the appearance of a 'bull woman' dressed from head to toe in blue who collected money from spectators. During the later part of the eighteenth century, the ceremony became bound up with political arguments about reform of the town government, with attempts by reformers to suppress the ceremony sparking riots. The growth of nonconformity in the town and the 'reformation of manners' led to renewed attacks on the ceremony in the 1830s, with the newly formed Society for the Prevention of Cruelty to Animals taking a lead, the campaign against the Stamford event becoming a national *cause célèbre*. Eventually, the national government intervened, and troops were used to suppress the bull running, which took place for the last time in 1840.

Such continuities run counter to the current orthodoxy that traditions tend to be constructed and invented and that they are frequently relatively modern fabrications. The *locus classicus* in English historical literature for such a view has been the collection of essays edited by Eric Hobsbawm and Terence Ranger called *The Invention of Tradition*.[57] The essays in this book argue that many of the traditions thought to characterize the British nation are of very recent origin and were often deliberately manufactured. Thus, David Cannadine shows how the British enthusiasm for royal ceremonial was to a very large degree a creation of the early twentieth century, while Hugh Trevor-Roper argues that many aspects of the Scottish 'highland tradition' date back no further than the beginning of the nineteenth century. In his introduction, Hobsbawm points out that this process of inventing tradition appears to have gained considerable momentum during the period between 1850 and the First World War, and suggests that it is linked to the growth at that time of modern ideas of the nation. As Hobsbawm puts it, invented traditions 'are highly relevant to that comparatively recent historical innovation, the nation, with its associated phenomena: nationalism, the nation-state, national symbols, histories and the rest. All these depend on exercises in social engineering which are often deliberate and always innovative'.[58] *The Invention of Tradition* focuses on the creation of nationalist mythologies and symbols, and argues that this process of invention is largely driven by ethnic or nationalist aspirations. Again, this is put succinctly by Hobsbawm elsewhere: 'History is the raw material for nationalist or ethnic or fundamentalist ideologies, as poppies are the raw material for heroin addiction. The past is an essential element, perhaps the essential element in these ideologies. If there is no suitable past, it can always be invented.

[57] *The Invention of Tradition*, eds E. J. Hobsbawm and T. Ranger (Cambridge, 1983).
[58] Ibid., p. 13.

Indeed, in the nature of things there is usually no entirely suitable past, because the phenomenon these ideologies claim to justify is not ancient or eternal but historically novel'.[59]

The Regius and Cooke manuscripts and the other examples discussed here illustrate that the process of the invention of tradition as an aspect of historical legitimisation for groups of various kinds was not purely a recent medieval phenomenon but reaches back to the middle ages. In this sense the interpretation of the 'invention of tradition' as a chiefly modern phenomenon linked primarily to the development of the modern nation state is an over simplification. Various scholars such as Peter Burke have argued that in early modern Europe there was a process whereby popular traditions and myths were appropriated by clerical and secular élites and filtered back in forms designed to support existing hierarchies.[60] Reynolds has examined the medieval myths of *origines gentium* as a significant factor in developing an early national consciousness.[61] Such a process may indeed reach back to the earliest stages of European consciousness. The genealogies of, for example, Anglo-Saxon kings allege fictitious lineages reaching back to such Germanic Gods as Woden and are one of the few expressions of an ethnic consciousness in the medieval period.[62]

Within this context, it is perhaps slightly unfair to stigmatize Hobsbawm as seeing traditions as purely modern and purely collected with nationalism. This has been the most common reading of Hobsbawm's book, but a more careful reading suggests a more nuanced view.[63] Hobsbawm stresses that invented traditions frequently make use of older materials, in just the way that eighteenth-century freemasons made use of the medieval traditions. Moreover, Hobsbawm points to the importance of invented tradition within other forms of social community apart from nation states. Finally, Hobsbawm stresses the significance of ruptures and fissures in continuity, of the sort found in the seventeenth-century attacks on the Stamford bull running. While Hobsbawm stresses the importance of invented traditions within the study of modern nationalism, he also indicates the significance of the study of tradition beyond the modern period and beyond its connection with nationalism. The way in which Hobsbawm's work has become chiefly read in

---

[59] E. J. Hobsbawm, 'A New Threat to History', *New York Review*, 15 December 1993, p. 63.

[60] P. Burke, *Popular Culture in Early Modern Europe* (New York, 1978); *The Historical Anthropology of Early Modern Italy* (Cambridge, 1987), pp. 223–38.

[61] Susan Reynolds, 'Medieval *Origines Gentium* and the Community of the Realm', *History*, 68 (1983), pp. 375–90.

[62] On these genealogies see, for example, D. Dumville, 'The Anglian Collection of Royal Genealogies and Regnal Lists'. *Anglo-Saxon England*, 5 (1976), pp. 23–50, and the relevant entries in L. Webster and J. Backhouse, *The Making of England: Anglo-Saxon Art and Culture, AD 600–900* (London, 1991).

[63] This is particularly evident in the introduction: *Invention of Tradition*, pp. 1–14.

connection with the debate on nationalism means that these other aspects of his interpretation have been neglected.

The Regius and Cooke manuscripts stand as emblems for the richness of the process of the invention of mythology and tradition in the middle ages and as a challenge to the view which sees such inventions as a product of modernity. Moreover, they show that this process reached down to the humblest craftsmen and was not simply a means by which élite power groups reinforced their position. By representing the invention of tradition as linked to the growth of nationalism, there has a been a tendency to suggest that it was a top-down process, a means by which figures like Sir Walter Scott in Scotland or Lady Llanover in Wales imposed their vision of national identity. The Regius and Cooke manuscripts show that medieval artisans could also be potent protagonists of myth, legend and symbol. As Gervase Rosser has put it, 'no one social group could effectively claim a patent on the interpretation of the myth. The urban myth was, rather, contested territory, the focus and arena for debate about the true identity of civil society'.[64] The power of the legends in the Regius and Cooke manuscripts to transform perceptions of civil society has remained a potent one to the present day. Through their role in the emergence of freemasonry in the early eighteenth century, they contributed to Enlightenment debates about the nature of civil society, particularly in countries such as France, where figures such as Voltaire and Montesquieu were freemasons, and America, where Benjamin Franklin published the American edition of Anderson's *Book of Constitutions*, whose origins lie ultimately in the Cooke manuscript. In France and America, Freemasonry continues to play an active part in promoting discussions about civil society. There is no better illustration of the power of invented myth and legend profoundly to transform culture and society.

[64]   'Myth, Image and Social Process', p. 6.

Symbolism in East Anglian Flushwork

JULIAN M. LUXFORD

In the preface to the second edition of his *The Stripping of the Altars*, Eamon Duffy describes later medieval English Christianity as 'a coherent religious symbol-system'.[1] Its structure, he believes, is to be comprehended only through sympathetic and historically rooted analysis of 'traditional' religion's physical and abstract characteristics, and their interconnections, both rational and mystical. This paper examines flint flushwork, an aspect of Duffy's system which, after years of scholarly neglect, has recently attracted a flurry of attention. Three books devoted to the subject have now been published.[2] Specifically, it is the local meanings of particular motifs and inscriptions in flushwork which have generated interest. In deference to the theme of this volume, the following pages will also concentrate upon aspects of symbolism. However, while there will inevitably be some overlap with work already done, I will be more concerned with the broader context and implications of this symbolism than other authors have been. Nobody has yet attempted to locate flushwork in the history of English art and architecture, or analyse its relationship to late medieval religion. It is important to do so, for the bearing it has on such weighty issues as the decorum of ecclesiastical decoration as opposed to secular, the definition of regional aesthetics, and attitudes to the function, appearance and contemporary understanding of church exteriors. It is hoped that this paper will contribute towards a more comprehensive and integrated conception of the medium, and, by extension, its artistic and intellectual contexts.

'Flushwork' is a nineteenth-century term for a type of external decoration which combines motifs in freestone with knapped flints, all elements being outwardly set on a single plane (that is, set *flush*).[3] We do not know what term or

[1] E. Duffy, *The Stripping of the Altars: Traditional Religion in England, 1400–1580*, 2nd edn (London and New Haven, 2005), p. xvi.

[2] M. Talbot, *Medieval Flushwork of East Anglia and Its Symbolism* (Cromer, 2004); J. Blatchly and P. Northeast, *Decoding Flint Flushwork on Suffolk and Norfolk Churches* (Ipswich, 2005); S. Hart, *Flint Flushwork: A Medieval Masonry Art* (Woodbridge, 2008). Stephen Hart's *Medieval Flint Architecture of East Anglia* (London, 2000) also contains a chapter on flushwork.

[3] I first find the term in J. L. André, 'The Perpendicular Style in East Anglia, chiefly Illustrated by Examples from Norfolk', *Archaeological Journal*, 46 (1889), pp. 377–94, at 380. The *Oxford English Dictionary* has it used earlier of jewellery.

terms, if any, were used for it in the middle ages. Simple chequer-board and striated flushwork exists right along England's chalk-belt, but only religious buildings in Norfolk and Suffolk, with a handful of outliers in Cambridgeshire and Essex, exhibit the more complex iconography which will occupy us here. Flushwork's parameters are thus more rigidly regional and ecclesiastical than any other well-represented category of English medieval art. It is found in one form or another on over 400 East Anglian parish churches and gatehouses, and it featured prominently on conventual churches as well. As a phenomenon of the fourteenth, fifteenth and sixteenth centuries, it is as distinctive an aspect of the great parish church rebuilding of the period as the clerestorey, the Perpendicular east window, and the ambitious nave porch. It clung on in a rudimentary manner after the Reformation, and enjoyed an ecclesiologically inspired renascence in the second half of the nineteenth and the early twentieth centuries, but I will not be concerned with its post-medieval manifestations here.

Formal Categories

For current purposes, existing flushwork can be divided into three formal categories, to be discussed in turn with particular reference to symbolism. There is a fourth category, incorporating the basic striated, chequer and lozengy patterns referred to above, which I will not discuss, because it seems to lack more than the most general symbolic connotations.[4] While this taxonomy is grounded in convenience rather than medieval understanding, it neatly accounts for the surviving material. The first category comprises architectural motifs, ranging from friezes of simple panels to elaborate dummy fenestration and tracery. The second takes in inscriptions and ciphers in the form of either monograms, trigrams, or single letters, and the third includes non-literal motifs such as shields, geometrical figures, merchant and trade emblems, saints' attributes, and eucharistic symbols. The last two categories elide to some extent, because their motifs tend to be combined and displayed in series, and also because, as Margaret Aston has pointed out, alphabetic letters clearly possessed pictorial as well as literal designations for medieval viewers.[5]

Architectural Motifs

Our first category, architectural motifs, is much the largest, occurring on around 300 East Anglian buildings. For about a hundred years after its commonly estimated (but probably specious) invention in the first quarter of the fourteenth century, all flushwork seems to have been either simply patterned or else of this type. In most cases, architectural designs are confined to panels, which are often but

---

[4]   It is the exception to the rule, being found in secular as well as ecclesiastical contexts.
[5]   M. Aston, *Lollards and Reformers: Images and Literacy in Late Medieval Religion* (London, 1984), pp. 108, 116, 118.

not always cusped. A single register of such panels on a tower plinth or parapet, a clerestorey parapet, tower buttresses, or around the lower stages of a porch is entirely conventional. Tower parapets carrying flushwork panels are particularly common. The church of St Mary at Mendlesham demonstrates the effect of a high, freestone-dense band of flushwork in this position (Plate 1). In combination with stepped crenellations it suggests, deliberately I would argue, a crown. 'Crowning' a building in this way, as over 160 East Anglian churches were crowned, constituted a straightforward expression of the sanctity of those in whose name(s) it was consecrated.[6] The ubiquity of the crown as a motif denoting sanctity in East Anglian ecclesiastical art of the period, not least in flushwork itself, made coronation of the church both comprehensible and appropriate. It was also suitable in light of the tower's symbolic status as a material manifestation of the name of God, according to the familiar passage in the Book of Proverbs (18: 10): 'Turris fortissima nomen Domini, ad ipsum currit iustus, et exaltabitur'. The same interest in 'crowning' towers exists in different forms elsewhere in late medieval Britain, perhaps most obviously in the richly decorated parapets of Gloucestershire and Somerset, and the 'crown' spires found in Scotland and at St Nicholas in Newcastle.[7] When a sixteenth-century poet remembered the 'golden glittering tops' of the towers of Walsingham priory, whose church was generously embellished with flushwork, he would appear to have had just this symbolism in mind.[8]

Registers of panels on either side of a porch or processional entrance are also relatively common. They are sometimes combined with three-dimensional sculpted niches, as at Hilborough in west Norfolk. Occasionally the panelling is more ambitious, particularly around portals. Parish church porches like those at East Harling, Hitcham, Ixworth, Pulham St Mary, and Woodbridge have all-over panelling. This was also a characteristic of some conventual gatehouses, outstandingly the late-fifteenth-century gatehouse facades of St Osyth and St John at Colchester, in Essex (Plate 2). Both are clothed in elongated panels from plinth to parapet. In these conventual examples the delicacy and attenuation of the flushwork subverts the notion of the gatehouse as a show of strength. The Church Triumphant as well as the Church Militant is suggested, and by extension the heavenly dwelling places reserved for the saved (John 14: 2), which it is often argued are symbolised wherever aedicular forms are multiplied in ecclesiastical architecture.[9] In both cases, the likely associations of high, tabernacled facades of

6   Pevsner's *Buildings of England* volumes list 165 flushworked tower parapets in Norfolk and Suffolk.

7   See I. Campbell, 'Crown Steeples and Crowns Imperial', in *Raising the Eyebrow: John Onians and World Art Studies*, ed. L. Golden, British Archaeological Reports, international series 996 (Oxford, 2001), pp. 25–34.

8   Perhaps Philip, Earl of Arundel, *A Lament for Walsingham*, lines 26–7 (reproduced in Duffy, *Stripping of the Altars*, p. 377).

9   The classic statement is J. Summerson, 'Heavenly Mansions: An Interpretation of

lustrous flint with the description of the New Jerusalem in Revelation 21:18-21 should be borne in mind. Either building can be profitably considered in light of the chevalier Tondal's response to his epiphany of heaven (c.1470): 'this wall was so bright and shiny that it would ward off any displeasure or trouble, and it would inspire with consolation and joy the hearts of those who looked upon it.'[10]

Where it is combined with substantial traceried windows, such comprehensive panelling suggests an extension of the fenestration amounting to partial or complete dissolution of the solid wall surface. Originally, the intention was probably to create a genuine illusion. With exposure, knapped flints lose their darkness and shine, but when first executed, dummy panels and windows in flushwork must have seemed, at least from certain perspectives, to be actually glazed and mullioned.[11] The west tower of Eye parish church, the south nave elevation at Long Melford, and the embellishment of the Thorpe chapel at St Michael in Coslany, Norwich, are prominent examples of plane surfaces illusionistically articulated by flushwork (Plate 3). In the monastic sphere, this concept influenced the embellishment of conventual church presbyteries at Leiston and Walsingham, of which large sections survive. During the fourteenth century, dummy windows were designed as discrete motifs rather than components of all-over decorative programmes. Extensions to round towers, such as those at Mutford, Theberton, and Old Buckenham, have perhaps the earliest examples, displaying simple Y-form tracery. A more complex flushwork window with the 'four petalled flower' motif characteristic of East Anglian Decorated exists on the south side of the nave at Attleborough, while the clerestories at Great Witchingham and Stratford St Mary have late, Perpendicular examples. Such dummy windows form the main decorative emphases of the two monastic gatehouses generally reckoned the *fons et origo* of flushwork, the Ethelbert gate of Norwich cathedral, started in 1316/17, and the north and south faces of the gatehouse of Butley priory in Suffolk, probably begun during the 1320s.[12] Here the intention to suggest glazed windows seems particularly obvious.

Gothic', in idem, *Heavenly Mansions and other Essays on Architecture* (New York, 1963), pp. 1–28; see also C. Wilson, *The Gothic Cathedral: the Architecture of the Great Church, 1130–1530* (London, 1990), pp. 130, 168.

[10]   T. Kren and R. S. Wieck, *The Visions of Tondal from the Library of Margaret of York* (Malibu, FL, 1990), p. 59.

[11]   Cf. E. Fernie, *The Architectural History of Norwich Cathedral* (Oxford, 1993), p. 180.

[12]   In fact, and notwithstanding the calibre of the masons involved, the flushwork of both gatehouses is too well understood for one to credit them with primacy. J. T. Mac-Naughton-Jones, 'Saint Ethelbert's Gate, Norwich', *Norfolk Archaeology*, 34 (1966), pp. 74–84, dated the Ethelbert gate c.1300 (p. 76), but cf. *The Early Communar Rolls of Norwich Cathedral Priory*, ed. E. Fernie and A. Whittingham (Norwich, 1972), p. 91. Dating Butley's gatehouse has proven controversial. Stylistically, the flushwork tracery supports Pevsner's suggestion that the building was started c.1320–5. Cf. in particular

In terms of symbolism, the illusionistic production and multiplication of such architectural features has much in common with blind tracery carved in relief. It manifests the same awareness of the importance and prestige of regular window tracery, which can be understood by turns as status symbol, aesthetic exercise, and, where suitably complex (as at Butley), reflection of the intricacy and symmetry of Creation. The late medieval aesthetic and intellectual interest in panel-work, tracery and window motifs is demonstrated by their appearance in most other media, particularly woodwork: one of the bench-ends at Ufford serves as a convenient local example. In certain contexts, panels and windows, like portals, were considered both attractive and symbolically resonant in their own right. For example, dummy niches immediately suggest not only heavenly mansions, but also the tabernacles in which saints were represented in glass, panel painting and sculpture. This is clearest on the west tower facade at Southwold, to be mentioned further at the end of this paper, and is also apparent where, as on the tower at Hilborough, three-dimensional niches designed for sculpture are combined with flushwork panels. The association with sanctity leads ultimately to the Virgin Mary, so widely and enthusiastically celebrated in our second flushwork category. In the language of late medieval devotion, Mary was not only the 'porta cœli', but the 'fenestra cœli' as well. John Lydgate, the Bury monk-poet, addressed her more than once as 'heavenly fenestrall'.[13] Over and above the conventional application of architectural metaphor to Christ's mother, this reminds readers of the familiar equation of sunlight passing through glass with Mary's virginity, so often expressed in contemporary painting and verse.[14] While dummy windows such as those at Great Witchingham and Stratford St Mary were plainly intended to suggest little more than symmetry alongside their glazed neighbours, it is potentially revealing to consider the richer manifestations of architectonic flushwork according to such frames of reference; particularly where the dedication is to the Virgin.

The juxtaposition of white tracery and the jet-black cores of freshly split flints is a late manifestation of the English architectural taste for contrasting light stones with dark, resonantly expressed by Gerald of Wales and Henry of Avranches in their praise of St Hugh's choir at Lincoln. What impressed these authors about this

---

J. N. L. Myres et al., 'Butley Priory, Suffolk', *Archaeological Journal*, 90 (1933), pp. 177–281, at 238.

[13] *The Minor Poems of John Lydgate*. Part I, *The Lydgate Canon and Religious Poems*, ed. H. N. MacCracken, Early English Text Society, e.s. 107 (London, 1911), pp. 300, 304. On the *fenestra cœli* concept in art see C. Gottlieb, '*En ipse stat post parietem nostrum*: the Symbolism of the Ghent Annunciation', *Bulletin des Musées Royaux des Beaux-Arts de Belgique*, 19 (1970), pp. 75–100.

[14] See in general J. Tasioulas, '"Heaven and Earth in Little Space": the Foetal Existence of Christ in Medieval Literature and Thought', *Medium Ævum*, 76 (2007), pp. 24–48, esp. 26, 45 n. 6; *The Early English Carols*, ed. R. L. Greene (Oxford, 1977), pp. 29, 33, 35, 45, 116, 131, 135 (*bis*), 156.

contrast, over and above its visual impact, was its demonstration of St Hugh's devotion to God and the Virgin Mary: it represented an 'aesthetic oblation' to rival the richest shrine, choir cope or altarpiece.[15] This attitude, which is broadly familiar to us in the words of the eighth verse of Psalm 26 (Vulgate 25), so often proffered as a motive for art and architectural patronage in medieval writing, provides a clear context for understanding the black-and-white aesthetic of flushwork as well.[16] 'Domine dilexi decorem domus tuæ et locum habitationis gloriæ tuæ' has a straightforward relevance to the beautification of otherwise dark, penitential church walls with architectonic displays of flushwork. That embellishment of exteriors was considered a duty as well as an oblation is suggested in a fourteenth-century legal opinion solicited by the abbot of Bury, according to which his church would be unsuitable for consecration until its presbytery chapels were fittingly revetted in freestone.[17] Few East Anglian churches possessed the splendour or the obligations of Bury, of course, but the idea that the appearance of ecclesiastical exteriors in general should be of a standard appropriate to local means was plainly current, and helps us understand the expense lavished on buildings like Holy Trinity at Long Melford, the Thorpe chapel at St Michael in Coslany, and the conventual presbyteries and gatehouses mentioned above, whose flint construction obviated extensive sculptural programmes.

Inscriptions and Ciphers

Our second flushwork category, which is found only on churches, apparently emerged early in the fifteenth century. The catalyst for its appearance more than a hundred years after the invention of flushwork is unclear; certainly, its motifs were current before 1400. In the case of ciphers at least, it may well relate to the off-site manufacture of flushwork elements by specialist craftsmen. As in the case of angel roofs, fonts, altarpieces, and other ecclesiastical componentry, the relatively small freestone panels which are the basis of flushwork letters and symbols are likely to have been made in centralised workshops for distribution on demand. As such they would have belonged to the 'ready-made' architectural category whose rise in the fifteenth century attracted John Harvey's attention.[18] It seems

---

[15] *Lateinische Schriftquellen zur Kunst in England, Wales und Schottland vom Jahre 901 bis zum Jahre 1307*, ed. O. Lehmann-Brockhaus, 5 vols (Munich, 1955–60), II, p. 26 (no. 2367); *The Metrical Life of St Hugh*, ed. and trans. C. Garton (Lincoln, 1986), pp. 54–9. For analysis see P. Binski, *Becket's Crown: Art and Imagination in Gothic England, 1170–1300* (London and New Haven, 2004), pp. 55–7.

[16] For medieval occurrences see e.g. *Lateinische Schriftquellen*, I, pp. 4 (no. 14), 412 (no. 1524), 548 (no. 2054); II, pp. 480 (no. 4054), 522 (no. 4181).

[17] A. Gransden, 'The Question of the Consecration of St Edmund's Church', in *Church and Chronicle in the Middle Ages: Essays Presented to John Taylor*, ed. I. Wood and G. A. Loud (London and Rio Grande, 1991), pp. 59–86, at 80.

[18] J. H. Harvey, *An Introduction to Tudor Architecture* (London, 1949), p. 12; cf. idem, *The Perpendicular Style* (London, 1978), p. 237.

improbable that this repetitive, specialised and small-scale work was done on the building site. In any case, it is rather puzzling that the manifest advantages of flush-work in terms of durability and visual prominence were not exploited for inscriptions and literal ciphers in the fourteenth century, and it is possible that some early examples have been lost.

Flushwork inscriptions are usually in Latin, registering the acknowledged sacral nature of the language and its appropriateness to ecclesiastical contexts. They fall broadly into two categories, which may be called commemorative and votive, the former being more numerous. Commemorative inscriptions are almost always in Gothic script, while votive ones are often in the more honorific and decorative Lombardic. In the case of the former, crowns over individual letters are rare, whereas they are the rule for the Lombardic letters of votive inscriptions and ciphers. Although there are counter-examples in both categories,[19] this division is clear, and notable for the indication it gives of perceived spiritual and artistic hierarchies. Both classes of inscription are interesting as external, and thus particularly prominent, instances of the 'textualization' of late medieval parish churches, a phenomenon more thoroughly represented internally.

About the symbolism of commemorative inscriptions there is relatively little to say. As with intramural inscriptions, they are predominantly memoranda of good works and petitions for prayers. Occasionally they are visually prominent, as for example at Badwell Ash, Botesdale, Long Melford, Northwold, and Stratford St Mary, at the latter of which members of the Mors[e] family are commemorated in two inscriptions on the north aisle dated 1499 and 1530, the earlier in Latin, the later in English. A large panel occupying the central crenellation on the south tower parapet at Rougham exhorts viewers to 'Pray for the sowle of roger Tillot': here the clarity and durability of flushwork is exploited to maximum personal effect. Indeed, in all such cases the virtues and privileges of the commemorated, and the religious influence this could procure, are unmistakeably registered. Other memorial inscriptions in flushwork are relatively small, and are found set into the walls of aisles (e.g. Bacton) and clerestories (e.g. Saxmundham), and the plinths and battlements of towers (e.g. Great Waldingfield and West Tofts). As one might expect, individuals are sometimes celebrated by inscriptions displayed on architectural elements for which they paid or helped to pay.[20] The Morse family, patrons of Stratford's north aisle and Trinity chapel, is a case in point. Elsewhere, as at Needham Market and West Tofts, the commemoration is collective: 'Alle The Begyners of þe werke' are remembered at the latter.

Votive inscriptions occur both as continuous series of words and as individual letters set on plaques and arranged along base courses or parapets. Much more

19   For example, the uncrowned black letter votive inscriptions at Garboldisham (porch) and Helmingham (tower).
20   Blatchly and Northeast, *Decoding Flint Flushwork*, pp. 33, 40, 43–4 etc.

can be said about their symbolism. In general, the use of Lombardic script and crown motifs for each letter indicates a widespread belief that words addressed publicly to God and His saints, as opposed to those addressed to men, required special visual distinction. Some votive inscriptions are so prominent that they influence our thinking about a building and its custodians, and this must have been true for medieval observers as well. The 'ihc NAZARENUS' above the porch entrance at Swannington, whose letters are in this instance not crowned, is a perfect advertisement of the parish's collective piety (Plate 4). Like the titulus on the plinth of a statue or rood-screen figure, it identifies the portal beneath it as a simulacrum of Christ according to John 10: 9: 'Ego sum ostium; per me, si quis introierit, salvabitur, et ingredietur, et pascua inveniet.'[21] The ejaculatory 'GLORIA TIBI TR[INITAS]' (the 'Trinitas' abbreviated to its first two letters) above the porch entrance at nearby East Tuddenham is no less graphic a declaration of collective devotion. Between the south clerestorey windows at Grundisburgh, 'Ave Maria' and 'ihc merci' are spelled out in crowned letters, and 'ihc haue merci' also adorns the north aisle parapet at Fornham All Saints. The most striking example is the 'S[AN]CT[US] EDMUND[US] ORA P[RO] NOBIS' which follows the arch of the west window at Southwold. Here a wealthy parish broadcast in ostentatious terms its allegiance to both its spiritual protector and the church through which his intercession was mediated. The inscription's relation to the Sarum litany, which will have been obvious to *horæ*-toting medieval viewers, locates the parishioners of Southwold squarely within the literate devotional culture of the day.

The compartmentalised Lombardic text beneath the east window at Blythburgh apparently constitutes a sentence reduced to the first letters of its constituent words, a phenomenon found in both commemorative and votive flushwork inscriptions. The letters in sequence are: A, N, SI in a monogram, B, the monogram St, T (engorged with a miniature *scutum fidei*), the Marian monogram, the St monogram again, A, H, K, and R. One supposes that its signification was recognizable to some people in the middle ages, perhaps with reference to a written notice in the church. In any case, there is no reason why the normal medieval viewer should have been better at such puzzles than we are, and to the uninformed, and even to those who recognized their meaning, the letters must have appeared at once esoteric and symbolic of the chancel's special status as the domain of the literate priest, wherein the Latin of the Mass was incanted. While the suggested expansion of the inscription, 'A[d] N[omina] S[ancti] J[ohannes] B[aptiste,] S[anc]t[e] T[initatis,] Marie [et] S[anc]t[e] A[nne] H[ic] K[ancellus] R[econstructus est]', is the most cogent of several proposed alternatives, it leaves one rather unhappy about the precedence given the Baptist over both the Virgin

---

[21]   For doors as symbols of Christ see e.g. BL, Additional MS 35298, f. 168v (mid-later fifteenth-century manuscript); '*Magnificencia ecclesie*', ed. H. N. McCracken, *Proceedings of the Modern Language Association*, 24 (1909), pp. 687–98, at 695.

and Holy Trinity, to whom the church is dedicated.[22] As interesting is the unique black letter flushwork alphabet set into the north aisle wall and buttresses at Stratford St Mary. Like the Blythburgh lettering, it has intrigued numerous writers, but in this case the primary meaning at least is quite straightforward. According to late medieval sources, the alphabet was one of the 'þingis shorth touched to [the] helþe of euery persoone þat þenkiþ to be saued'.[23] As such, it often appeared as a preface to the Pater noster, Ave Maria and creed in books of hours and devotional miscellanies. From it could be made the words of all sacred writings, prayers and holy names. Thus the Stratford alphabet encouraged those travelling along the main London road, which ran beside the church, to pray according to their inclination. Specifically, given the church's dedication to the Virgin, an association with such texts as the 'Alphabetum laudatorium beate marie' which existed at Syon abbey in the fifteenth century is possible. A fifteenth-century Latin copy of the *Pilgrimage of the Soul* which belonged to John, duke of Bedford contains a short treatise in which the letters of the alphabet congregate to spell out a crown of honour for the Virgin and her son, further demonstrating the idea's currency.[24]

This alphabet qualifies as a devotional inscription, but it leads us to consider the literal ciphers which are displayed like stone sacramentals on approximately eighty East Anglian parish churches. Here there is opportunity only to hint at their formal, iconographic and semantic range. (Most have been catalogued by John Blatchly and Peter Northeast, who convincingly interpret some obscure examples.) Some churches have ciphers of unusual or unique appearance. Stratford St Mary itself has a formally unique, and rather clumsy, version of the Marian monogram. It is designed to indicate where the 1499 inscription ends and that dated 1530 begins, and makes use of a pale grey cement rather than flint. Colour and form combine to distinguish it from the script on either side, and it is thus an interesting example of a site-specific solution to a particular problem. In most cases, however, the ciphers used in flushwork were of a few standard iconographic types, although formal variations exist which may indicate manufacture by different workshops. Much the commonest are the sacred trigram (either IHC or IHS) and

---

[22] Blatchly and Northeast, *Decoding Flint Flushwork*, p. 19; cf. W. R. Gowers, 'The Flintwork Inscription on Blythburgh Church', *Proceedings of the Suffolk Institute of Archaeology*, 11 (1903), pp. 51–8; H. Roberts et al., *Holy Trinity Blythburgh: Cathedral of the Marshes* (Blythburgh and Norwich, 1994), p. 13.

[23] These words preface the alphabet, Pater noster, Ave Maria, creed, and blessing in a fifteenth-century devotional miscellany, now Manchester, John Rylands Library, MS English 85 (see f. 2). See *Medieval Manuscripts in British Libraries*, ed. N. Ker et al., 5 vols (Oxford, 1969–2002), III, p. 409, for an indication that the manuscript is East Anglian.

[24] *Syon Abbey with the Libraries of the Carthusians*, ed. V. Gillespie and A. I. Doyle, Corpus of British Medieval Library Catalogues 9 (London, 2001), p. 39; M. R. James, *A Descriptive Catalogue of the Manuscripts in the Library of Lambeth Palace* (Cambridge, 1930), p. 429.

the Marian monogram (a cipher in which all five letters of the Virgin's name can be read). Other ciphers signify patron saints, normally those to whom churches were dedicated. Instances include the crowned M for St Michael at Great Cressingham and St Michael at Plea, Norwich, the crowned L for 'Sanctus laurentius' at Hunworth, and the row of crowned letters I for 'Iohannis' above the porch entrance at Coltishall. The usual setting of such ciphers around doorways and windows, or else on tower parapets, advertised a parish's collective piety and religious orthodoxy to all observers. They can be understood, according to the mentality of the period, as the insignia of spiritual livery, proclaiming a parish's allegiance to its protector saint(s). They also provided a devotional focus outside the church to complement the many contained within. The letter M for Maria, Marian monogram and/or sacred trigram repeated above porch entrances, as at Rickinghall Superior, Yaxley and Great Witchingham, relate to the ubiquitous and constant repetition of the Ave Maria and Pater noster (Plate 5). One could count one's prayers here as one did on a string of beads.

From the location of flushwork ciphers, and their multiplication, it seems reasonable to suppose that they carried apotropaic associations as well as devotional ones. On towers they defended against lightning strike, and bear comparison with the 'fulgura frango'-type inscriptions found on some medieval bells.[25] Around doors and windows, where sacred and profane space intersected, they may have been thought to work against malign influences, just as parish rogationtide processions did. Their symbolism in this regard would thus have been similar to that of gargoyles, the Michael-and-Dragon scenes often represented in portal spandrels, and the figures of woodwoses which guard numerous porches and fonts (e.g. Mendlesham and Butley). This aspect of their symbolism needs further consideration. However, given the widely documented and contemporaneous apotropaic use of such ciphers elsewhere (in Germany for example the sacred trigram defended against lightning strike and sorcery, while in England the Holy Name was the basis of charms),[26] and the application to buildings of such prophylactic charms as 'Mentem Sanctam Spontaneum Deo et Patrie Liberacionem',[27] which protected against fire and is found on west country paving tiles of the period, it is relevant to propose it here.

[25] Cf. BL, Additional MS 35298, f. 169: 'by the ryngyng of halowid bellis thondryng lightning and other tempestis ben put awaye fro us'.
[26] B. Scribner, 'Popular Piety and Modes of Visual Perception in Late-Medieval and Reformation Germany', *The Journal of Religious History*, 15 (1989), pp. 448–69, at 453–5; Duffy, *Stripping of the Altars*, pp. xx, 71–4, 295–8.
[27] Examples in the British and South Wiltshire museums are catalogued by Elizabeth Eames: see e.g. her *Catalogue of Medieval Lead-Glazed Earthenware Tiles in the Department of Medieval and Later Antiquities, British Museum*, 2 vols (London, 1980), I, p. 253; II, no. 1429. On charms in general during our period see Duffy, *Stripping of the Altars*, pp. 266–98.

As the commonest non-architectonic motifs in flushwork, the Marian monogram and sacred trigram deserve some additional comment. In them the devout medieval viewer was confronted with shorthand expressions of his or her most urgent religious preoccupations. Both names, like the church itself, had immediate Eucharistic connotations: these are underscored emphatically where, as at March in Cambridgeshire, Gedding, Quidenham, Stanton Downham, and Worlingworth, a small disk signifying the host is inserted between the Marian monogram and the crown over it (Plate 6). Marian and Christocentric feasts, including the Feast of the Holy Name, were initiated in England during the period in which these ciphers were being most enthusiastically applied to church exteriors.[28] The name of Mary was not the object of a liturgical feast, but had been venerated since at least the twelfth century, and was clearly accorded the highest importance.[29] Lydgate's *Ave, Jesse Virgula!*, which belongs to a class of devotional poem which Professor Duffy says 'proliferated at every level of society',[30] contains a verse perfectly distilled in these Marian ciphers:

M. in Maria, betokyneth Eek meknesse,
A. next in Ordre, tokne of attemperaunce,
R. [is] remedye, our surffectys to redresse,
I. betoknyth Iesus, helpe for al our grevaunce,
A. is for Amor, moost sovereyn of pleasaunce,
Al set in Oon tu sola puerpera,
This name shall nevir [be] out of our remembraunce,
Callyd fflos campi, O Ave Iesse virgula.[31]

This candid, theologically accessible celebration of Mary's name no doubt expresses many of the connotations which Marian monograms in flushwork elicited in pious minds. The monogram, and the sacred trigrams, were omnipresent in other media, of course, but the public location and large size of their flushwork manifestations emphasize their importance and devotional utility in a particularly obvious way. As with all ciphers and inscriptions in the medium, we should consider them as encouragements to oral declamation as well as silent meditation.

Non-Literal Motifs

Our third formal category, which again we must deal with briefly, contains considerable variety, including many unique motifs. As suggested previously, these typically occupy the same contexts as the ciphers of category two: base courses, buttresses, the interstices between clerestorey windows, and tower parapets.

---

28 R. W. Pfaff, *New Liturgical Feasts in Later Medieval England* (Oxford, 1970).
29 G. M. Gibson, *The Theater of Devotion: East Anglian Drama and Society in the Late Middle Ages* (Chicago and London, 1994), p. 138.
30 Duffy, *Stripping of the Altars*, p. 223.
31 *Minor Poems of John Lydgate*, p. 303 (emphasis mine).

Many, such as the merchant marks at Elmswell and Stratford St Mary, De Vere mullets at Lavenham, Tyrell knots at Gipping, and the device of Robert Scott, abbot of Bury from 1467 to 1484, at Ixworth, relate to individual people or families. Where, as at Rickinghall Superior, Woodbridge, Ufford, and elsewhere, blank shields occur, an intention may have been the apotropaic repulsion of evil from vulnerable parts of the church (e.g. windows, doorways and towers). It seems very unlikely that they were ever intended to bear arms. Heraldry itself is curiously uncommon in flushwork; only a handful of examples have been identified, to go with the Trinitarian shields at Blythburgh, Northwold, Rattlesden, and Worlingworth.[32] Saints' emblems are found in iconographically conventional forms, including saltire crosses for St Andrew at Barton Bendish, Brockley, Northwold, and Walberswick, spiked wheels for St Catherine at Elmswell, Ixworth, Northwold, and *ex situ* at South Elmham St Peter, cockle shells for St James at Southrepps, the gridiron of St Laurence at Hunworth (Plate 7), an arrow-impaled crown for St Edmund at Charsfield, Rattlesden and Grundisburgh, crossed keys for St Peter at Rattlesden and Thetford, a papal tiara for the same at Bacton, crossed swords for St Paul at Griston and Thetford, and the sword of St Michael at Great Cressingham and Hilborough. The lily-pot of the Virgin Mary (Elmswell, Eye, Grundisburgh, Helmingham, Rougham, Thetford, West Tofts, and Worlingworth), and a four-petalled flower supposed to allude to the Mother of Christ (Bacton, Elmswell, Garboldisham, Ixworth, Northwold, and Wortham) also appear.[33] Some sacred trigrams are accompanied by components of the *arma Christi* (e.g. Badwell Ash, Garbolisham, Worlingworth), and at Quidenham there is a crown of thorns engorged with three nails.

Chalice and host motifs deserve individual attention for their symbolism. The porch at Ufford displays a representative example, and others occur at Badwell Ash, Bunwell, Charsfield, Elmswell, Eye, Worlingworth, and Woodbridge (Plate 8). As generally symbolic of spiritual authority, this motif is found in numerous contexts, including the stained glass of chancels and the so-called 'chalice' brasses used for the tombs of priests.[34] In an extended sense it is also associated with the Eternal Mass at which Christ Himself will celebrate; and one late-medieval treatise designates it the most important of all images in art.[35] This is general symbolism, but we

---

[32] See e.g. Blatchly and Northeast, *Decoding Flint Flushwork*, p. 11.

[33] Ibid., p. 9; Talbot, *Medieval Flushwork*, p. 35. Both call the flower a rose, but the Marian rose usually has five petals and five thorns, for the Virgin's Joys and Sorrows. People may nevertheless have understood it thus, but (in the spirit of Lydgate) *flos campi* seems a better name for it.

[34] C. L. S. Linnell, 'East Anglian Chalice Brasses', *Transactions of the Monumental Brass Society*, 8 (1951), pp. 356–65.

[35] Gibson, *Theater of Devotion*, pp. 170–76; K. Kamerick, *Popular Piety and Art in the Late Middle Ages: Image Worship and Idolatry in England 1350–1500* (New York, 2002), pp. 38–9.

must also consider its particular significance for individual viewers if we are to understand fully the motif's location and prominence. Something of this can be suggested with reference to 'personalised' examples in other media, such as the adventitious representations sometimes found in medieval manuscripts, and their use in texts and iconography dealing with the fate of the individual soul.[36] In a luxury manuscript of Lydgate's translation of the *Pilgrimage of the Soul*, Prayer shows Pilgrim his anticipated salvation in the form of a chalice and host, and indicates its postmortem efficacy with reference to two cadavers (Plate 9).[37] The illustration, probably executed in Suffolk and datable to the first half of the fifteenth century, preserves for us something of the flavour and vitality which the motif must have possessed for the parishioners of Ufford, Woodbridge and Worlingworth, who noticed its representation in flushwork each time they approached their church porch.

Finally, geometrical, star-shaped and foiled motifs in flushwork are also common, and exist in some variety. Churches such as St Andrew at Cotton, All Saints at Hawstead and St Mary at Ixworth are particularly rich in them. They rarely mirror contemporary fashions in English tracery, but some are stylistically similar to decorative motifs found in late medieval English and Netherlandish woodwork, especially chests. They seem to be largely if not wholly decorative in function, although a locally circumscribed symbolism may have attached to some. One example in particular, a square panel containing a quatrefoil in a circle with two mouchettes above, deserves particular comment, as it has been identified by Blatchly and Northeast as the trademark of the Aldryche 'workshop' of North Lopham in Norfolk.[38] I think it unlikely at best that Thomas Aldryche and his 'firm', documented only in a surviving contract of 1488 which does not mention flushwork, were in fact responsible for the very numerous projects ascribed to them.[39] However, that one or more of these apparently decorative flushwork panels were in fact flint-workers' trademarks is possible.

Conclusion

In conclusion I wish to suggest that despite the analogues which can be found for some of its motifs in other media, flushwork has its own particular visual language,

[36] For adventitious drawings of chalices see e.g. BL, Royal MS 7. E. IX, f. 86; Oxford, St John's College, MS 129, f. 15.

[37] BL, Cotton MS Tiberius A. VII, f. 102v. Discussed in K. L. Scott, *Later Gothic Manuscripts 1390–1490*, 2 vols (London, 1996), II, pp. 251–3.

[38] Blatchly and Northeast, *Decoding Flint Flushwork*, pp. 3–4: they ascribe 'the majority' of flushworked elements on sixty-six churches in Suffolk to Thomas Aldryche and his 'firm'. I think expert flint-workers more likely than regular masons to have been responsible for most flushwork, although large workshops may of course have included such specialists. I am grateful to both John Blatchly and Richard Fawcett for discussing the matter with me.

[39] For the contract see L. F. Salzman, *Building in England down to 1540* (Oxford, 1997), pp. 547–9.

which is more closely allied to the forms and ideas of architecture than representational art. To interpret this language we must consider the medium's physical, institutional and social settings as carefully as its iconography. At Worlingworth, a Marian monogram with host over it, inscribed, as actual hosts may have been, with the sacred trigram, encapsulates the differences between flushwork's vocabulary and that of mainstream art (Plate 6).[40] This motif is the flushwork equivalent of a painted or sculpted image of the Virgin and Child, or of the Pietà. The idea of the *Theotokos* is just as clearly expressed, but the mode of expression is abstract and symbolic rather than naturalistic. Similarly, the sacred monogram with raguly bar at Old Buckenham is with one exception the closest flushwork gets to the Crucifixion. A striking but previously un-remarked fact is that, with one obscure exception, figural iconography does not exist in flushwork. (The outstanding case is an amorphous motif on the porch at Worlingworth, which has been identified by analogy with the stained glass example in the Clopton chapel at Long Melford as a Lily Crucifix.[41]) We do not even find the Evangelistic tetramorphs; there is nothing beyond a few small and schematic fish and bird motifs.[42] That the idea of representing figures in flushwork occurred to medieval East Anglians is strikingly demonstrated by a row of image plinths represented within flushwork 'tabernacles' on either side of the west door at Southwold (Plate 10). Yet despite their popularity within East Anglian churches, figures never became part of the repertoire, even though they constituted such an important aspect of external embellishment in other parts of England.[43] Flushwork, for all its variety, is an art of the symbol rather than the image.

Acknowledgements

I wish to thank the many people who have heard and commented on what I have to say about flushwork over the past eight years, particularly in this instance Fabio Barry, Paul Binski, John Blatchly, Richard Fawcett, and David King.

---

[40] For the possible inscription of the trigram on medieval hosts see H. Blake et al., 'From Popular Devotion to Resistance and Revival in England: the Cult of the Holy Name of Jesus and the Reformation', in *The Archaeology of Reformation 1480–1580*, ed. D. Gaimster and R. Gilchrist (Leeds, 2003), pp. 175–203, at 181.

[41] Blatchly and Northeast, *Decoding Flint Flushwork*, pp. 67–9.

[42] Notably, All Saints at Hawstead has a Pelican of piety on the east tower parapet, and St Nicholas at Rattlesden a diminutive dragon in a circle.

[43] Perhaps the idea of two-dimensional images on church exteriors was thought unattractive for some reason, although with the popular acceptance of the monumental brass, coincidental with and in many respects analogous to flushwork, one might expect a relaxed attitude to two-dimensional figures. Facial and other features could easily have been added in lines of pitch.

Effigies with Attitude

PAMELA TUDOR-CRAIG

In general, as the inoffensive tombs to our ancestors, memorials have survived better than other artefacts of their time; but too often they have been moved, despoiled, pared down to the bare bones of the effigy. As we study their dates, identity, and their stylistic grouping, we can forget the further dimensions that were all important to their subjects: how they wanted to be remembered and, above all, how they wanted to present themselves at the Throne of Judgement. All too often we have only the sculpted figure, bereft of its colour and its original surroundings. However certain fragmentary survivals can afford clues of the further dimensions. There is much to be learnt, for instance, by studying the positions effigies occupy (where they have not been moved), and, since most medieval effigies have open eyes, upon what was their gaze fixed. Prayer with the eyes closed is a Protestant habit. The double image (Plate 1) at the beginning of the Mortuary Roll of Lucy de Vere, prioress of the Benedictine convent at Hedingham in Essex, illustrates our difficulty in confronting the great inheritance of medieval monuments: the problem of comprehension.[1] Again and again, there survives in our churches only the equivalent of the lower scene in Lucy de Vere's Roll, the outstretched figure on its marble tomb, but not the vision of the soul carried by angels through the border that represents in this Roll the Firmament of Heaven.

The hope of resurrection and the help of angels in the ascent to heaven, the primary statement of Lucy de Vere's Mortuary Roll, has left traces on a number of tombs. It was painted on the recess housing a thirteenth-century knight at Winchelsea – and on how many more now painted-over recesses? It was carved in relief on the back of the niche in which lies the effigy of Bishop William de la Marcia, died 1302, at Wells. He was a possible candidate for sanctity: Wells was in need of a saint. The three figures have lost their heads, but they represent the Bishop as he rises sedately to heaven, flanked by two rather solid angels. A most unusual variant, with angels hauling up the praying torsoes of Sir John and Lady Harrington into the canopy, is carved into the cusping on either side of the first surviving, though now ruinous, Chantry Chapel of 1347 at Cartmel in Lancashire.

Almost every Gothic tomb includes a pair of carved angels, one either side of the head or heads. Sometimes they swing censors perilously close to the

[1]   BL, Egerton MS 2849, part. I. See *Sacred*, ed. J. Reeve (London, 2007), p. 195.

deceased, but usually they plump cushions. They come in pairs, so cannot be identified with guardian angels, of whom we have only one each according to scriptural tradition, as cited by Christ himself (Matthew 18, 10). Honorius of Autun codified the matter in the early twelfth century: each soul, as it entered the body, was entrusted to an angel. Alone among English medieval monuments, the Tournai marble slab in Ely Cathedral of a Bishop, perhaps Nigel who died in 1169, conforms to Honorius' one-to-one. Despite the popularity of guardian angels they did not acquire their own feast day till the end of the Middle Ages – recorded in Portugal in 1513 – and finally acknowledged by the whole Roman Church in 1670. So it is not surprising that in a funereal context they appear in pairs, censing, comforting, acting as supporters for shields of arms, and ultimately carrying the soul in a napkin to heaven. William Blake's copy of the painting in the trefoil above the tomb of Aveline, Countess of Lancaster, died 1273, to the north of the main altar of Westminster Abbey, records this element in her funeral iconography:[2]

> Matthew, Mark, Luke and John,
> Bless the bed that I lie on.
>> Four corners to my bed,
>> Four angels round my head;
>>> One to watch, and one to pray
>> And two to bear my soul away.

There are many versions of this prayer, possibly the *White Paternoster,* to which Chaucer refers in the *Miller's Tale*, and certainly related to a German version learned as a child by Johannes Agricola, b. 1492. It descends from Jewish Cabbalistic protection prayers against the terrors of the night.

So much for the role of angels. There is much still to be done in identifying how many later medieval tombs played the double role of Easter Sepulchres; to appreciate that the sometimes agitated pose of knightly effigies expressed their eagerness to respond to the Summons; or where the carrying of a miniature building conveys reliance upon a generous building campaign to tip St Michael's scales in their favour. There is material for a dozen articles on these topics. Within the confines of these pages one only of these avenues can be explored, and the depiction of married fidelity as the strong suit upon which a couple might rely at the Bar of Heaven has been chosen.

Married Fidelity

Sir Hugh Hastings, who died in 1347 at the siege of Calais, was proud subject of the grandest of all surviving brasses at Elsing in Norfolk.[3] He did not depend for

---

[2] Illustrated by P. Binski, *Westminster Abbey & the Plantagenets* (London, 1995), pp. 113–14.

[3] See Lynda Dennison and Nicholas Rogers, 'The Elsing Brass and its East Anglian Connections', in *Fourteenth Century England*, I, ed. N. Saul (Woodbridge, 2000), pp.

his immortality upon his gilt and enamelled and glass inset brass with eight weepers, tied to him by links of comradeship in the French Wars as well as by kinship. His soul rises in its napkin held by angels past his patron Saint George towards the coronation of the Virgin in the canopy. According to Weever, his eyes gazed upon the *sun, the moon and the stars, all very lively set forth in metal beholding the face of the earth*. In other words, the vault above his brass, set out like the vault above John Baret in St. Mary's, Bury St. Edmunds, a century later, is intended to suggest the Firmament of Heaven, through which Hugh's soul must pass to gain its destination. His hope of success was portrayed in the east window where, flanked by a row of scenes of the Annunciation, Nativity, with on the other side probably the Resurrection and the Ascension, he and his wife kneel, holding up a detailed model of the church he had built. It was upon his prowess as a builder of the church that he relied, as the sum and symbol of his Good Deeds. The long inscription struck a new note: he referred to his wife as 'consors carissima'.

Of the same year, and by the same outstanding artist, is the strange and beautiful brass of Sir John de Wautune (1347) and his wife Ellen at Wimbish in Essex (Plate 2).[4] Within the centre of a cruciform brass, standing on an elephant, the little figures of Sir John and his wife scarcely fit. Clearly the outlined cross had been designed to enclose a single figure, perhaps of a priest, and was pressed into service for this couple. With typical fourteenth-century elegance, they turn and sway towards one another, and they look out of the corner of their eyes at each other, with what still reads as a tender and almost shy glance, such as young lovers give. This fresh, and apparently never repeated, composition stands on the threshold of a group of effigies where the couple hold hands. Rendered in brass or freestone, they date from 1356 till the mid-fifteenth century, but with the majority clustered in the years around 1400. The earliest example is the brass at Great Berkhampstead, Herts., of 1356. Then came in brass, the lost Sir Miles de Stapleton and his wife, formerly at Ingham, Norfolk (1364) (Plate 3), Sir John Harsick and his wife at Southacre, Norfolk (1384) (Plate 4), Thomas de Freville and his wife at Little Shelford, Cambridgeshire (1410). There followed Thomas Baron Camoys and his wife at Trotton, Sussex (1421), Peter Halle and his wife at Herne, Kent (c. 1430) (Plate 5) and the outflier, Sir William Mauntell and wife (1487) (Plate 6) at Nether Heyford, Northamptonshire.[5] This brass and the brass of Sir John and Lady de la Pole of c. 1380 at Chrishall, Essex (Plate 7), have the husband on his wife's left, giving him the awkward gesture of stretching his armoured right arm across his armoured body, and making any attempt to draw his sword (sometimes nervously

---

167–94. Nigel Saul is the pioneer in our wider understanding of the intent of most brass memorials. See, for example, his masterly study of a group of largely brass memorials in *Death, Art and Memory in Medieval England* (Oxford, 2001).

[4]   N. Saul (ed.), *Fourteenth Century England*, I, p. 170 & pl. 5.

[5]   All illustrated by Malcolm Norris, *Monumental Brasses*, II (1964).

fingered by a left hand) quite impracticable.[6] Among freestanding effigies with the same motif are the alabaster monument to Thomas, Earl of Warwick and his wife (1375-80) at St Mary's, Warwick[7], and the lively tomb of Ralph Greene and Katherine Mallory carved in 1419-20 by Thomas Prentys and Robert Sutton, at St Peter's Church, Lowick, Northamptonshire[8]. This list is in no way definitive, but it points up the wide geographical, and fairly close dating, range of the gesture.

At the heart of the theme lie the gilt bronze effigies of Richard II and his first wife, Anne of Bohemia, whose death in 1394 broke her husband's heart. The arms, which were of solid metal, were promptly stolen, likewise the crowns, and orb, but the contract between the king and Nicholas Broker and Godfrey Prest, citizens and goldsmiths of London, survives.[9]

> Two images of copper and brass, gilt, and crowned, *close together and with right hands joined* … and holding sceptres in their left hands, and a ball and cross between the said images. The one image a likeness of our lord the King, the other, of that excellent and noble lady Anne…

Poor Queen Phillippa had wanted to share a double tomb with Edward III, but he did not allow it, so Richard II and Anne of Bohemia were the first royal double tomb in England. They still gaze at the Trinity and Coronation of the Virgin on their tester. Of Richard's love for Anne we have eloquent testimony.

Nigel Saul has established beyond peradventure that this new composition is deliberately intended to convey the devotion between husband and wife by his note on the brass of Robert Hatfield, a Lancastrian estate official, and his wife Ada at Owston, Yorks. (Plate 8).[10] Hatfield commissioned the brass on his wife's death in 1409, and his own date of death remains blank. The inscription reads:

> Robert Hatfield gist ycy et Ade sa femme ousque lui en droiturel amour foies plein …

These monuments with the couple right hand in right hand reflect the marriage vows to which they have been faithful. In a late thirteenth-century manuscript of Gregory's Decretals, a Bishop is joining a couple together by placing their right hands in one another's.[11] In the first scene of the panel painting of the history of

6   See L. Stone, *Sculpture in Britain: the Middle Ages* (Harmondsworth, 1955), Plate 5, p. 183.
7   Illustrated in ibid., pl. 139 and p. 182.
8   *Gothic, Art for England 1400–1547,* ed. R. Marks and P. Williamson (London, 2003), pl. 8 and cat. entry 330 by J. C. Bayliss.
9   Rymer's *Foedera,* VII, pp. 795–6.
10   N. Saul, "'Till Death Do Us Part": Robert Hatfield and his Wife Ada at Owston, Yorks', *Monumental Brass Society Bulletin,* 85 (2000), pp. 505–6, illus. I am grateful to Derrick Chivers for this reference and for collecting all my brass illustrations. This brass is of an importance quite out of scale with its modest format.
11   Hereford Cathedral Library MS 0.7.vii.

St Etheldreda of c. 1455 in the Society of Antiquaries the Saint and her husband are holding right hands while the Bishop blesses their union.

The Sarum marriage rite is an extraordinary document. Neither party says anything at all, but they hold one another's right hands as the Priest prays over them. This gesture was developed in the Book of Common Prayer, where first the man takes his betrothed's right hand in his and makes his promises, and then the lady takes his right hand in hers and makes her pledges. After that, in both Sarum and later liturgies, the man takes the lady's left hand to put on it the ring. In the Sarum liturgy at that point the priest prays:

> Et in amore tuo vivat et crescat et senescat et multiplicetur in longitudinem dierum.

The period spanned by tombs showing the hand-holding gesture corresponds with the first flowering of English writing in the vernacular. Chaucer was an eloquent defender of long and good marriages as blessed by the Church. As the Miller declares:

> Ther been ful goode wyves many oon.
> And ever a thousand goode agayns oon bade...

The Franklin prefixes his tale of the fidelity between a knight and his wife with a description that could not be bettered of happy marriage:

> Ther was a knight, that loved and foughte amain
> In Armoryke, that clepèd is Britéyne,
> To serve a lady in his beste wise; ...
> ... at the laste she for his worthinesse
> And chiefly for his meke obéisance,
> Hath suche a pitee felt for his penaunce
> That privily she felle into accord
> To take him for her housbonde and her lord,
> (Of such lordshipe as men have over their wives);
> And, for to lede the more in blisse their lyves,
> Of his free wille he swor it as a knight,
> That never in his wille by day or night
> Wolde he upon him take the mastery
> Against her wille, nor guard her jealously,
> But her obey, and follow her wille in al,
> As eny lover to his lady shal;
> Save that the name of sovereynetee
> That wolde he have because of his degree.
> She thanketh him, and with ful grete humblenesse
> She sayde; "Sir, since of your gentilnesse
> Ye profre me to have so large a reyne,
> May never God, I pray, betwixte us tweyne,
> For guilt of mine, bring eyther war or stryfe.
> Sir, I wil be your humble trewe wife,

137

> Here have my trothe, til that myn herte fail" ...
> Love wil nought be constreined by mastery.
> When mastery cometh, the god of love anon
> Beteth his wynges, and fare wel, he is gon ...
> Love is a thing, as any spirit, free ...[12]

The delicate balance between mastery and free will within the marriage state was addressed, not always so happily, by John Mirk, the famous preacher and Augustinian Prior of Lilleshall in Shropshire in his late fourteenth-century text:

> To preach them also you might not hesitate
> Both to wife and each husband
> That neither of them no penance take
> Nor no vow to chastity make,
> Nor no pilgrimage take to do
> But if both assent ther-to.[13]

Chaucer, was only seven years old when Sir John de Wautune and his wife Ellen turned towards one another in their brass at Wimbish, only sixteen when the couple at Great Berkhamstead were perhaps the first to take one another by the hand on their brass.

It cannot be that no married couples had been devoted to one another before Sir Hugh de Hastings and Sir John de Wautone and their ladies in 1347. What is fundamentally new is that these couples saw steady love not only as their delight in this life, but their chief hope of an honourable reception in heaven: the brightest aspect of themselves that they could offer at the seat of judgement. How many double effigies of men and women predating the Black Death remain? There are single effigies of women of consequence : the queens at Fontevrault; the first brass of a woman, Margaret de Camoys d. 1310 (if it is her), in the nave of Trotton in Sussex; and, of course, Aveline, Countess of Lancaster, who died, aged fourteen or fifteen, in 1273, but may not have been commemorated until c. 1295.[14] But there are virtually no joint tombs.

There may have been a great shift in the perception of the opportunities for holiness within the married state in the century leading up to 1340, a new consciousness of the value of faithful marriage as a road to the heavenly kingdom, and a new appreciation of the status of wives. In this matter the role of two powerful and intelligent queens, Eleanor of Provence and Eleanor of Castile, was crucial. Eleanor of Provence spent her very last years in seclusion, but the conspicuous display of mourning occasioned by the death of Edward I's queen in 1291 marked a

[12] I am grateful to the late Stephen Medcalf for this most apt quotation. He insisted this was the first passage in English literature to explore the happily married state.

[13] See B. A. Burr, 'Gendering Pastoral Care: John Mirk and his Instructions for Parish Priests', in *Fourteenth Century England*, IV (Woodbridge, 2006), ed. J. S. Hamilton, pp. 93–108.

[14] See Binski, *Westminster Abbey*, in note 2, pp. 113–14.

turning point. From that date ladies of consequence could expect to be memorialised.

I would suggest this changing status of women may have been encouraged by the friars. The dating evidence for the mortuary Roll of Lucy de Vere hangs on the inclusion among those asked to pray for her of the Franciscans, established in Cambridge in 1226, two years after their first arrival in England and in the year of their Founder's death. The Dominicans had arrived already in 1221.[15] As St Francis died, one of his brothers saw his soul ascend to heaven, the scene to be painted in the Upper Church at Assisi, and already painted on Lucy's Mortuary Roll. The fact that they were not bound by rules of enclosure meant that friars were not only free to preach to the laity, but to become confessors, initially in royal and noble households. Eleanor of Provence favoured Franciscans, Eleanor of Castile Dominicans. The lively circle of aristocratic literary women who associated with these queens has been discussed by Nigel Morgan.[16] By the early fourteenth century, the friars had extended their range, not only in what they appear to have taught their penitents, but in the households where they had become established. The Holkham Bible Picture Book, famous for its rough but highly original imagery of Biblical scenes interwoven with contemporary life, has an introductory colophon by the Dominican Friar who owned it, exhorting his artist: *Now do it well, and thoroughly, for it will be shown to rich people.*[17] Note that the book belonged to a Dominican. The Order, whose terrain had included from the beginning the Universities, had no problem about book ownership. It was otherwise among the Franciscans. So the manuscript with the clearest evidence of Franciscan teaching was undoubtedly paid for by the patron. The Psalter of Robert de Lisle (1288–1344), was bequeathed by its owner to his unmarried daughters, and then to the nuns of Chicksands, in the year 1339 when his wife died and he entered the Greyfriars in London.[18] Among the exquisite illuminations are a series of diagrams for meditations by the late thirteenth century Franciscan theologian, John of Metz, plus a Tree of Life worked out by St Bonaventura.

The great household of the de Bohuns at Pleshey in Essex was home at one time to three Austin Friars: William de Monkland, Chaplain to Humphrey de Bohun (died 1361), and two illuminators, 'frere John de Teye', and from 1381 Henry Hood.[19] The lively and friendly art of de Teye and Hood would have made biblical instruction very enjoyable to the family.

[15] See M. Robson, *The Franciscans in the Middle Ages* (Woodbridge, 2006), pp. 30 36. See also *Eleanor of Castile 1290–1490*, ed. D. Parsons (Stamford, 1990), pp. 38–9.

[16] E.g. in *The Lambeth Apocalypse: MS 209 in Lambeth Palace Library* (London, 1990), esp. pp. 94–6, and note 31.

[17] BL, Add MS 47682. See *Sacred*, ed. J. Reeve, p. 125.

[18] Bound, with the Howard Psalter/Hours in BL, Arundel MS 83. See Lucy Sandler, *The Psalter of Robert de Lisle in the British Library* (London, 1983).

[19] See L. F. Sandler, *Gothic Manuscripts 1285–1385*, Survey of Manuscripts Illuminated in

The style adopted in another family with an allegiance to the Dominicans harks back to the graphic realism of the Holkham picture book: the famous Luttrell Psalter of c. 1340.[20] That Psalter is not only remarkable for the popular series of scenes of agricultural life that have invaded the margins of the Psalms from the Calendar, and for its outrageous grotesques, but for its images of happy family life. A banquet which goes far beyond the usual January calendar scene of the goodman and his wife warming their toes by the fire is the occasion for two Dominican friars to join the family festivities which the staff are frantically preparing. This must be the Feast of Fools in the Christmas Season since father has donned a cap with ass's ears.

Alas, such was the success of the Friars in their role as chaplains to great or even moderately great households that too many of them were themselves corrupted by the soft life, and by the later fourteenth century their Orders were not held in high honour in this country. But in 1340 their popularity was still widespread.

It would be useless for the Friars to guide married couples, perhaps more often married women, in terms of piety founded on the three monastic vows, which they were unable to obey. A way had to be found where the virtues of matrimony could lead to holiness. Such a path might be that of fidelity, one of the most valued virtues of the medieval knight. Many mottoes, including Richard III's, referred to loyalty; and it was loyalty that all those knights prepared to leap from the bed of death at the last trump were demonstrating. If marriage was enduring, and, alas, death in childbirth often overcast such a prospect, then the virtue of fidelity could be extolled in that context too. Sir Geoffrey and Lady Agnes de Luttrell shared forty years, and he only survived her another five. William Langland would declare at the outset of *Piers Plowman*, probably drafted by 1362:

> Meed shall no more be master on earth
> But love and lowliness and loyalty together.

Nicholas Love (died 1423–4) was Prior of the Carthusian house of Mount Grace, Yorkshire, from 1410. The Carthusians, with their vow of silence, remained faithful to their austere ideals to the end of the Middle Ages. His translation of the Franciscan text, *The Mirrour of the Blessed Lyf of Jesu Christ*, then thought to have been written by Saint Bonaventura, but now attributed to the fourteenth-century Johannes de Caulibus, was one of the most popular books of the later Middle Ages.[21] As the author followed the Gospel narrative, particularly of St John, so he

---

    the British Isles (Oxford, 1986), vol. 1, pp. 34–6.

[20] BL, Add. MS 42130. See Janet Backhouse, *The Luttrell Psalter* (London, 1989).

[21] *The Mirrour of the Blessed Lyf of Jesu Christ/ a translation ... by Nicholas Love/Prior of the Carthusian Monastery of Mount Grace*, ed. Lawrence F. Powell (Roxburghe Club; Oxford, 1908).

gently associated the events with domestic life, particularly that of women. For instance, he opened the marriage at Cana by supposing that the Virgin had moved into her sister's house to help organise the feast:

> [She was] in hir sistres house homely as in her owne hous ordeynynge and mynistryinge as maistresse therof ...[22]

The author put a dubious twist onto the event by suggesting the bridegroom was St John, and that Christ invited him at the end of the feast to desert his new wife to follow him. However Love's comment on the woman at the well of Samaria must have given pause to the most misanthropic man:

> He spake so homely with that symple woman alone and of so grete thinges as though it hadde been with many grete wise men the pride and the presumpcioun of many clerkes and prechoures is confounded and reproved.[23]

His narrative ended with an image of Christ attracted as much to the family hearth as to the heroic abnegations of the proudest monastery:

> He wolde be beden of us to dwelle with us and drawen with fervent desires devoute prayeres and holy meditaciouns. And therfore as he hath taught us it byhoveth evere to praye and nought faill: but that we take in mynde the werkes of pitee and hospitalite.[24]

On the west wall of Trotton church, Sussex, is a painting of a Good Man, with the virtues of Hope and Charity, and surrounded by the seven Works of Mercy, all of them within the range of the most humble. In the same church, before the High Altar, lies the brass of Thomas, Lord Camoys, who died in fact in 1421, though the inscription reads now 1419. This is the second brass we have met with where the husband and wife hold hands, and where there is confusion on the date of death of the husband. Is it possible that Elizabeth Mortimer, widow of Henry Hotspur, Camoys second wife, died before him, that her husband commissioned the tomb immediately, and that the date was a later addition? The inscription describes him as a 'zealous Knight of the Garter'. He commanded the left wing of Henry V's army at Agincourt, proudest of battles. So he was faithful to his king, and, his gesture proclaims, to his wife. He has earned the lion at his feet. We might well expect at the hem of her skirts a dog, emblem of fidelity as well as household pet. The dog on the brass at Deerhurst of Sir John Cassy, c. 1400 looking longingly up at his mistress, has his name, Terri (which means faithful, hence terrier) inscribed on his cushion. Numerous wives, in freestone or brass, have their dogs sporting round their ankles, quite unabashed by their husbands' lions. But Lady Camoys shelters a little boy, her husband's son Richard by his first marriage, under her cloak. If their

[22] Ibid., p. 104.
[23] Ibid., p. 127.
[24] Ibid., p. 275.

joint marriage was childless, this was indeed her good deed.

> Hond by hond we shullen us take,
> > And joye and blisse shullen we make,
> For the devel of helle man hath forsake,
> And Goddes Sone is maked oure make ...

> Synful man, be blithe and glad,
> For youre mariage thy pees is grad
> Whan Crist was born! ...[25]

Medieval monuments ran through the whole gamut of aspiration, from the hope that deep penance would absolve from horrors of Purgatory, though confidence in the prayers of family and benefactors, to trust in angelic support, to the proximity of saints, both literal and figurative, to the virtue of the Sacraments, to the sacrifice of celibacy and, in the monuments demonstrating mutual affection, to the achievement of a happy marriage. The only thing never considered was the possibility that death might be the end of all things.

[25] A poem of c. 1350 in the miscellany, Oxford, Bodley MS 26. See Carlton Brown (ed.), *Religious Lyrics of the Fourteenth Century* (Oxford, 1957). It must have enjoyed wide and long popularity. Surely the last stanza *Synful man, be blithe and bold, For hevene is bothe boghte and sold...* is parodied in the note pinned to the tent of John Howard, Duke of Norfolk, on the eve of the Battle of Bosworth, August 1485: *Jockey of Norfolk, be not so bold, Dickon thy master is bought and sold.*

La Chantepleure: a Symbol of Mourning

JOHN CHERRY

In his will, dated November 1259, Martin of St Cross, warden of the leper hospital at Sherburn in county Durham, left among fine silver and rings, a bequest to the Bishop of Salisbury, of a bowl of silver with a gilded foot that was called 'chantepleure'.[1]

This article will examine the use of the word to define an object and its subsequent use as a device and a badge used by a family in the early fifteenth century, firstly for mourning and subsequently for ornament. It will also pose the question of the distinction between definition, medieval symbol and Renaissance emblem. Since Martin's 'chantepleure' is described as a bowl, we can turn to the sketchbook of Villard d'Honnecourt prepared in 1225–35 to enable us to visualise its appearance. This drawing (Plate 1) of a mazer shows a tower arising in the centre of the bowl, on which stands a bird, almost certainly a swan, who appears to drink from the column. This was a drinking or puzzle jug where the wine was poured into the cup and a series of tubes in the middle, gave the appearance that the swan, which was made hollow, was drinking the water through his beak which must be held low.

Villard's text 'Vesci une cantepleure co'on peut faire' may be translated:

> This is a chantepleure that may be made in the form of a drinking cup. In the middle of the cup is fixed a little tower and in the middle of the tower is a tube that extends to the bottom of the cup and the length of the tube is equal to the depth of the cup. There must be also three little cross pieces to the tower touching the bottom of the cup so as to allow the wine to enter the tube. On the top of the tower must be a bird holding his beak so low that he seems to drink when the cup is filled. Then the wine will run through the tube, and through the foot of the cup, which is double. It must be understood that the bird must be made hollow.

Hahnloser, in his publication on the sketch book, alludes to the classical and Arabic tradition of making and writing about ingenious contrivances and automata, which lay behind this, but this aspect of the subject will not be pursued here.[2]

---

[1] *Wills and Inventories of the Northern Counties*, ed. J. Raine, *Surtees Society*, 2 (1835), p. 7. 'Item Domino Sarum chipum argenti cum pede deaurato qui vocatur Chanteplure'.

[2] H. R. Hahnloser, *Villard de Honnecourt* (Graz, 1972), pp. 48–9, Tafel 17e.

A later example of this type of vessel (Plate 2) was given to Corpus Christi College, Cambridge, by John Northwode, who was admitted a fellow before 1388. A drawing (Plate 3) shows how it works.[3]

The possession of a chantepleure of silver by Charles V, King of France, in 1380, probably, though not certainly, indicates that the term continued in use in this sense until the late fourteenth century.[4]

The name used both in Durham and by Villard in the thirteenth century indicates singing and weeping. It was applied as the title of a French thirteenth-century poem to those who sing in this world and weep in the next.[5]

It is in this sense that the word was used by Chaucer, who wrote (c. 1374) in The Compleynte of Fair Anelida and False Arcite (lines 320–1):

> I fare as doth the songe of Chantepleure;
> For now I pleyne and now I pleye.

It is not until the early fifteenth century that the chantepleure was specifically used in connection with mourning. The occasion was the murder of Louis, Duc d'Orléans in Paris in 1407 and the subsequent mourning for his death by Valentina, duchess of Orléans. This 'chantepleure' was not a silver vessel with a swan, but a pottery vessel popular in the fifteenth and sixteenth centuries. Simpler than Villard's example, it functioned on the same principle of water flowing through, but which could be held back by a vacuum, in this case with a thumb over the top (Plates 4 and 5).[6]

This vessel type had a long existence in England, since an example, in Ipswich ware, was found in Ipswich dating from the seventh or eighth century (Plate 6).[7] The principle occurs in earlier vessels, of classical date, which were used as water sprinklers either for gardens for laying dust or dampening linen.

The source for the Orléans use of the chantepleure as a mourning emblem in the early fifteenth century is contained in Claude Paradin's *Devises heroïques*, a collection of emblems first published in 1551. This was one of the most popular of French sixteenth-century emblem books. In the second edition of his work (1557) Paradin illustrates a watering pot with the letter S above the neck and a band twined around the neck on which there are the words *plus ne me riens*,

3   *Catalogue of a Loan Collection of Plate Exhibited in the Fitzwilliam Museum* (Cambridge, 1895), pp. 7–9, no. 11.

4   J. Labarte, *Inventaire du mobilier de Charles V* (Paris, 1879), no. 2225. It had the arms of d'Aussement.

5   F. Godefroy, *Dictionnaire de l'ancienne langue française* (Paris, 1883), tome 2, 57 sub chantepleure.

6   The most recent publication of the type of vessel is in the exhibition catalogue *Sur La Terre Comme Au Ciel*, Cluny Museum (Paris, 2002), no. 67 and 68, p. 168.

7   N. Smedley, 'A 16th-Century Sprinkler from Ipswich,' *Proceedings of the Suffolk Institute of Archaeology,* 27.2 (1956), pp. 124–5. The Ipswich ware example is mistakenly described in this article as thirteenth century, but is otherwise unpublished.

which is the second part of the title inscription *Riens ne m'est plus, Plus ne m'est riens.*[8] The work was translated into English in 1591 by the unidentified PS, and in his words:

> She used for her cognizance an earthen pitcher in fashion like a water pot, on the mouth whereof was the character of this letter S. signifying perhaps these words concerning the same Dutches: Solam Sæpe seseipsam sollicitari, suspirareque, that is, being alone shee accustomed to mourne and to sigh with her selfe, togither with these words subioyned, Nil mihi præterea mihi nil Which is, nothing remaineth to me, nothing have I more.[9]

Similar wood cuts were used in this edition and the 1591 illustration is shown here (Plate 7). Valentina Visconti, daughter of Gian Galeazzo Visconti of Milan, was born at Pavia in 1366 and married Louis, duke of Orleans in 1389. She was caught up in the problems created by the madness of her brother in law, Charles VI, king of France. Although she had great ability to soothe the king in his madness, the difficulties of the situation caused her to leave Paris in April 1396 and she did not return to Paris until eleven years later.[10]

On November 23rd 1407, her husband, Louis of Orleans was killed by followers of the Duke of Burgundy. Valentina was overwhelmed with grief at her loss, and during the following years she attempted in vain to secure the condemnation of her husband's murderers. She died on 4th December 1408, aged 38, and was buried initially in the Lady Chapel of the church of Saint Sauveur in Blois. According to Paradin, the walls of the chapel where her bronze tomb lay, and the choir of the church were painted with chantepleures and the motto. Her body was later moved to the church of the Celestins at Paris, where she lay in a tomb supported by four lions.[11]

Was the chantepleure as used by Valentina a badge, or 'a devise' as suggested by Paradin's title or an emblem as used to describe the type of books that flourished in the sixteenth and seventeenth century and of which Paradin's book was a notable example? Here I will use the word 'badge' to designate a simple figure without a motto, such as the Dunstable Swan Jewel, and 'device' to mean a simple emblematic composition comprising both an image and a motto. The association of the motto with an image indicates that Valentina's badge can be considered a device rather than a badge or emblem.[12]

8   C. Paradin, *Devises heroïques*, 2nd edn (Lyons 1557), pp. 91–2.

9   PS, *The heroicall devises of M. Claudius Paradin* (London, 1591), pp. 113–15.

10   D. Muir, *A History of Milan under the Visconti* (London, 1924). R. C. Famiglietti, *Royal intrigue: Crisis at the Court of Charles V 1392–1420* (New York, 1986).

11   N. L. Goodrich, *Charles of Orleans* (Geneva, 1967), p. 107.

12   J. D. D'A Boulton, 'Insignia of Power: The use of Heraldic and Para-Heraldic Devices by Italian Princes', in Charles M. Rosenberg (ed.), *Art and Politics in late Medieval and early Renaissance Italy 1250–1500* (Notre Dame, 1990), pp. 103–28.

In choosing such a device, Valentina may have been influenced by her father's use of devices. Gian Galeazzo used a device, allegedly composed for him by Petrarch, of a burnished gold sun with eight rays that has at its centre a small white dove carrying the motto ' a bon droit'. Devices occur among the jewels that she brought from Milan in 1389. There was a white hart brooch with the scroll 'qui dient plus haut' set with four rubies and four pearls. She used badges and images soon after her arrival in France.[13]

Alternatively she may have been influenced by the widespread use of badges with mottos used in the courts of Charles V and VI of France. Bernard de Vaivre suggested the fashion may have been derived from Edward III's badges, through the intermediary of the Duke de Bourbon. Colette Beaune has shown how badges were employed to emphasize royal power in the reign of Charles VI.[14]

The earliest surviving use of the chantepleure as a badge is on a leather sheath for knives, which may be dated to the early years of the fifteenth century (Plate 8). The sheath bears the chantepleure shedding water or tears (without any inscription), the interleaved gothic initials OY, and the figure of a peasant or gardener bearing tools for hedging and hoeing. He walks resolutely forward with the black letter inscription *J'endure* above his head. O and Y refer to Olivier and Ysabel. Ysabel was the daughter of John the Fearless, Duke of Burgundy, who at the age of six was married to Olivier, Count of Penthièvre, in July 1406.[15] However, the four knives contained within the sheath bear the arms of John, Duke of Touraine, son of Charles VI, who married Jacqueline of Hainaut in July 1406. John was dauphin of France from 1415 to his death in 1417. There are two possible explanations. The imagery on the sheath, if it is contemporary with the knives, predates the adoption of the chantepleure by Valentina, and therefore the imagery may not have any mourning connotations. It may simply be wishing that the marriage endures and is fertile. This seems to be a more straightforward explanation than assuming that the knives were recased in 1412. If the knives were recased in 1412, then iconography of the sheath must play on the previous use by Valentina of the device, although here it is used as a badge. The phrase 'J'endure', meaning

13   K. Sutton, 'Giangaleazzo as Patron', *Apollo*, cxxxvii (February, 1993), p. 93. The arrival of Valentina in France is studied by M. J. Camus, *La venue en France de Valentine Visconti* (Turin, 1890); R. W. Lightbown, *Medieval European Jewellery* (London, 1991), p. 165. See also F. M. Graves, *Deux inventaires de la maison d'Orléans 1389–1408* (Paris, 1926), and *Quelques pièces relatif à la vie de Louis Duc D'Orléans et de Valentine Visconti, sa femme* (Paris, 1913).

14   C. Beaune, 'Costume et pouvoir en France à la fin du moyen age: les devises royals vers 1400', *Revue des Sciences Humaines*, LV (1981), pp. 136–7. B. de Vaivre, 'A propos des devises de Charles VI', *Bulletin Monumental*, 141 (1983), pp. 92–5.

15   Olivier was the son of Jean, Count of Penthièvre and Marguerite de Clisson. He married Ysabel (or Isabella) of Burgundy on 22nd July 1406 at Arras. See Richard Vaughan, *John the Fearless* (London, 1966), p. 247.

either 'I survive' or 'I endure', may indicate mourning but not necessarily so. Malcolm Jones thought it meant that the labourer survives or persists through time in contrast to the aristocrats, such as Louis d'Orléans, who were prone to die out in spectacular fashion. Whatever its exact meaning, the importance of the sheath is the complexity of images that it provides. Here are letters as a sign of ownership, the chantepleure as a badge rather than a device and the labourer as a device. With the addition of an inscription that gives a moral quality, the labourer foreshadows the later use of the device as an emblem.[16]

The badge of the chantepleure continued to be used in the jewellery of the Orleans' family in the mid fifteenth century, though no examples of such jewellery have ever been found. Charles of Orléans, the poet, son of Louis and Valentina, was captured at Agincourt in 1415. He spent most of his life in England, and returned to France in 1440, where he married Mary of Cleves. She adopted her mother in law's badge, which she may have seen it in Blois, where Valentina was buried. She had jewels made using the badge as a decorative device. There was a gold ring enamelled with tears and in 1455–6 her accounts record a payment of some 15 livres and 15 sols to Jehan L'essayeur for making a chantepleure of gold that she gave to Adolf of Cleves, her favourite brother, in order to wear a feather in his hat. In the inventory of the jewels of Charles and Mary, made on the 4th February 1456, there occurs a chain of gold doubled four times adorned with three chantepleures and three letters from Mary's device. And to this entry there are two additional notes added. She also had a large gold ferrure or stomacher made with the device *Riens ne m'est plus* and chantepleures.[17]

The use of both badge and device by Mary of Cleves shows a more formal hereditary use of the image. In the case of Valentina there was considerable grief and the use of the badge was a very real mourning symbol. However there was no reason for Mary to mourn. When she used the badge, Charles was alive and well. Even when Charles did die, far from finding that she had no more joy, she married le Sire de Rabodanges, a man whose only claim to fame, according to a rather snobbish French historian, was that he was governor and bailiff of St Omer.[18]

The Tapestry

The well-known tapestry in the Musée des Art Decoratifs in Paris shows a man and woman in elegant dress standing in front of a tent held open by two angels the

[16] O. M. Dalton, 'On a Set of Table Knives in the British Museum made for John the Intrepid, Duke of Burgundy', *Archaeologia* 60, pt 2 (1906), p. 423. The identification of the arms by Dalton was incorrect. There is a more recent discussion of the iconography in *Sur la terre, comme au ciel*, ex. cat. (Paris, 2002), p. 169, no. 69, where the research of Monsieur Dominique Delgrange on the heraldry is incorporated.

[17] L. de Laborde, *Les Ducs de Bourgogne* (Paris, 1849–52), vol. 2 (1851), 353 (no. 6732), 378 (no. 6949), and 379 (no. 6954).

[18] E. Collas, *Valentine de Milan* (Paris, 1911), p. 419, fn. 1.

man plays with a dog with a stick. The lady holds a watering pot watering the flowers growing in the flowerpot beneath.

The identity of the two figures has long been a matter of debate. The letters A L on the belt of the lady have been thought to indicate that part of Valentina's name. But if the tapestry referred to Valentina and Louis, it would have been made some forty to fifty years after their deaths. The date of the tapestry would suit Charles and Mary of Cleves, but the letters on the belt are not acceptable for this.[19]

Conclusion
This shows four stages of the symbol:

(1) The vessel plus sound suggesting a verbal play on noise. The same word could be applied to two different objects. One might have thought that the name chantepleure applied to the watering pot reflected the sound it made. Although the emptying of the pot sounds like weeping, the slight gurgling noise produced by the entry of water through the holes at the bottom can hardly be thought of as singing. The most convincing explanation is that there is a double meaning. It is used as a vessel through which water runs, but it also takes in the poetical use of the term referring to the emotional change between joy and grief, particularly with the allusion of the latter to death, the application of the name to the watering pot becomes a sort of pun.

(2) The adoption of the device in extreme personal grief as a mourning symbol by Valentina d'Orléans.

(3) The badge used by others in the family in the fifteenth century.

(4) The appearance in the emblem tradition of the sixteenth century.
The badge stands halfway between the medieval badge which might or might not have a hidden significance and the later emblems of the sixteenth century which are visual expressions of moral allegories. As an emblem in the sixteenth century, 'la chantepleure' did not have a successful career. It only appears in Paradin's work, and even that was thought of as one of the less significant emblem books since the comments were in prose rather than rhyming couplets.

---

[19]   The identification of the two people in the tapestry as Louis of Orleans and Valentina was first made in 1892 in the exhibition in Madrid, see *Las Yogas de la exposicion Historico Europea de Madrid* (Madrid, 1892), tafel 165–6. B. Kurth, *Die Blütezeit der Bildwirkerkunst zu Tournai und der Burgundische Hof* (Vienna, 1917) firmly rejects this identification on grounds of chronology and subsequent writers on tapestries have followed her. G. J. Demotte, *La Tapisserie Gothique* (Paris, 1924–6), also rejects the suggestion that the tapestry represents Charles of Orléans and Mary of Cleves, and in this he was followed by E. Mcleod (op. cit., p. vii) who says that there are no grounds for supposing that the figures represent Charles and Mary. The latest note on this tapestry and an excellent illustration of it is in *Sur la Terre comme au Ciel*, ex. cat. (Paris, 2002), p. 170, no. 70.

As far as I am aware, the device never achieved a representation in any other media, such as plaster overmantels or ceiling decoration or embroidery, as so many emblems did. Alison Saunders notes that Paradin claims the original purpose of the *Devises Heroïques* was to promote virtue rather than to act as a visual source, since something visually depicted can fasten an idea in the mind, which would otherwise be ephemeral. Stressing the widespread use of such devices among the aristocracy, Paradin hoped that in bringing such devices to the attention of a wider audience, he might bring that audience to greater virtue. He concluded on a firmly moral note by pointing to the didactic value of his work as well as its decorative value.[20]

A vessel that wept, and when it had finished weeping, was empty inside, was and is, a very apt symbol for those who mourn for the departed, whether it was for Louis of Orléans, Isabella of Penthièvre, or Janet Backhouse.

---

[20]   A. Saunders, *The Sixteenth-Century French Emblem Book* (Geneva, 1988).

Signs and symbols in the Estoire del saint Graal and the Queste del saint Graal

ALISON STONES AND †ELSPETH KENNEDY[1]

The *Lancelot-Grail* romance in French prose holds a special place among vernacular texts and manuscripts of the Middle Ages. Surviving in whole or in part in some two hundred copies,[2] most of them illustrated, the stories of King Arthur and his knights, their chivalric exploits and their quest for spiritual fulfilment, were appreciated by audiences of a variety of social classes and ages. Indeed, these

---

[1]   This article is based on work done in collaboration with the late Elspeth Kennedy as part of the Lancelot-Grail Project. I am deeply indebted to Elspeth for her contributions to the project in general and to this study (see http://ltl22.exp.sis.pitt.edu/lancelot/ WhatisLancelotGrail.htm); A. Stones, 'Teaching and Research on the Web: Three Sites', in *Computing and Visual culture: Representation and Interpretation*, ed. T. Szrajber (Fourteenth Annual Chart Conference; London, 1999), pp. 111–22; Stones, 'The *Lancelot-Graal* Project', in *New Directions in Later Medieval Manuscripts*, ed. D. Pearsall (York Medieval Studies) (Woodbridge, 2000), pp. 167–82.

[2]   The most complete list is still in B. Woledge, *Bibliographie des romane et nouvelles en prose française antérieurs à 1500* (Geneva, 1954, repr. 1975), *Supplément 1954–73*, Geneva, 1975), although several manuscripts have come to light since 1975, most notably the Turin and Bologna *Estoire* fragments, Bologna AS b.1 bis, n.9 and Turin BN L.III.12, see M. Meuwese, 'De omzwervingen van enkele boodschappers en een jongleur. Van Bologna via Oxford en Parijs naar Vlaanderen,' in *Maar er is meer. Avontuurlijk lezen in de epiek van de Lage Landen. Studies voor Jozef D. Janssens*, ed. R. Sleiderink, V. Uyttersprot, B. Besamusca (Leuven, 2005), pp. 338–57. Text editions referred to are for *Estoire*: E. Hucher, *Le Saint Graal*, 3 vols (Le Mans, 1877–8), vols II and III, based on Le Mans 354 (H); H.O. Sommer, *The Vulgate Version of the Arthurian Romances*, 7 vols (Washington, DC, 1909–13), vol. I (hereafter S I), based on BL, Add. MS Add. 10292; J.-P. Ponceau, *L'Estoire del Saint Graal*, 2 vols (Paris, 1997) (hereafter Pon), based on Amsterdam, Bibliotheca Philosophica Hermetica MS 1 to f. 63, then on Rennes BM 255. For *Queste:* H.O. Sommer, *The Vulgate Version of the Arthurian Romances*, 7 vols (Washington, DC, 1909–13), vol. VI 3. 1–199.5 (hereafter S VI), based on BL, Add. MS 10294; A. Pauphilet, *La Queste del Saint Graal,* (CFMA) (Paris, 1923), (Long Cyclic Version, based on Lyon, BM, Palais des Arts MS 77, siglum K); we refer to *La Queste del Saint Graal* (CFMA) (Paris, 1965) (hereafter Pau); *La quête du Saint-Graal, roman en prose du XIIIe siècle*, ed. F. Bogdanow, tr. A. Berrie (Livre de poche. Lettres gothiques, 4571) (Paris, 2006), based on Berkeley, UCB 73, appeared too late to be taken into account here.

romances address the human condition on multiple levels, where chivalric values of valour and prowess, loyalty and fidelity in friendship and love, take their place alongside treachery and betrayal, cowardice, deceit and adultery. In the telling of the adventures, the reality of contemporary society is coupled with allegory and symbolism in the Quest for the Holy Grail and the events and elements that surround the search for spiritual purity that the quest embodies.

Two branches of the five-part cycle focus particularly on the Grail and share many elements in common. Among these is the episode of Solomon's enchanted ship and its miraculous contents, whose discovery foreshadows and anticipates the mysteries of the Grail itself, bringing peril and danger to the unworthy as well as salvation to the chosen. The ship is discovered in the *Estoire del saint Graal* by Nascien, one of the first converts of Joseph of Arimathea and his son Josephé the first Christian bishop according to the story. In the *Queste del saint Graal* the ship appears again, and there it is found by the three chosen Grail knights Perceval, Boort and Galahad, and its meaning and that of its contents is interpreted by Perceval's (nameless) sister, a seer who will become a Grail martyr, an allegory of the redemptive powers of death and sacrifice, leading up to the achieving of the Grail Quest by the three knights. How the manuscripts illustrate these episodes and what can be made of their similarities and differences are the focus of this paper. We select in particular the three copies that form the core of the *Lancelot-Grail* Project, a collaborative effort to interpret these copies, which were produced in the same scribal and artistic environment in the early years of the fourteenth century in northern France; two earlier copies of the *Estoire* and two Parisian stylistically related copies of the second or third decade of the fourteenth century; and some images from other manuscripts are included for comparative purposes.[3] These manuscripts are referred to by abbreviation of place or collection.[4] Many

---

[3]   Add. = London, British Library, Additional MSS 10292-4; Amsterdam = Amsterdam, Bibliotheca Philosophica Hermetica MS 1; BNF, fr. = Paris, Bibliothèque nationale de France, français; Douce = Oxford, Bodleian Library, MS Douce 215; Le Mans = Le Mans, Médiathèque Louis Aragon, MS 354; Rennes = Rennes, Bibliothèque municipale MS 255; Rylands = Manchester, The John Rylands University Library, MS French 1; Royal = London, British Library, Royal MS 14.E.III; Yale = New Haven, Yale University, MS 229. A comparative tabulation of these events discussed here is to be found on http://vrcoll.fa.pitt.edu/stones-www/lancelot-project.html .

[4]   For the date and place of these manuscripts see A. Stones, 'Another Short Note on Rylands French 1', in *Romanesque and Gothic, Essays for George Zarnecki*, ed N Stratford (Bury St Edmunds, 1987), pp. 185–92. The comparative approach to *Lancelot-Grail* iconography in tabular form was pioneered by Susan A. Blackman, 'The Manuscripts and Patronage of Jacques D'Armagnac Duke of Nemours (1433–1477)', Ph.D. thesis University of Pittsburgh, 1993, Appendix, and eadem, 'A Pictorial Synopsis of Arthurian Episodes for Jacques d'Armagnac, Duke of Nemours', in *Word and Image in Arthurian Literature*, ed. K. Busby (New York and London, 1996), pp. 3–57. For the three early fourteenth-century manuscripts see also M. Meuwese, 'Three Illustrated

other manuscripts could eventually be drawn upon for further comparison, some of which are mentioned in the notes, and eventually we hope to achieve fuller pictorial coverage of these and other manuscripts on our web site.

I.1. *Estoire del saint Graal*

In the *Estoire del saint Graal* the episode of Nascien on Solomon's ship is preceded and prepared for by the maritime adventures of King Mordrain, another of Joseph and Josephé's early converts, who is miraculously transported to an island. There he is visited by Christ, who names himself 'Tout-en-Tout', and by the devil. They arrive in turn, in boats of different colours, and Tout-en-Tout assures Mordrain he will be saved by the sign of the cross. The narrative then turns to Nascien, transported from Calafer's prison to the Turning Island from where he encounters Solomon's ship, boards it and examines its contents, with dire results. Between the adventures of Mordrain and Nascien comes the abduction of Nascien's son Celidoine, and at the end of the sequence all three heroes are reunited. After other adventures, the sea-crossing of Joseph, Josephé and their followers to England, bearing the Holy Grail, concludes the maritime sequence.

The manuscripts vary considerably as to which aspects of these events are selected for illustration and where in the text the pictures, or markers in the form of champie initials (gold letters against a party-coloured pink and blue background), are placed. Among the manuscripts compared here, Royal and Amsterdam are closest to each other in their positioning of eight markers for the sequence as a whole (not counting the Hippocrates story and the Tomb commission made by Nascien's wife Flegentine which interrupt the sea-adventure episodes), eight champie initials as favoured in Amsterdam and eight miniatures in Royal; Rennes gives fewest illustrations, five historiated initials, four of them corresponding in position to Le Mans and Add. MS 10292, and one without parallel. Le Mans has five champies and two historiated initials, all corresponding in position to a miniature in the Additional manuscript. Add. MS 10292 has more markers than the other manuscripts: thirteen miniatures and two champie initials, allowing for a much more expansive pictorial treatment than in any of the other manuscripts. This is characteristic of the approach to pictures taken in general in

---

Prose Lancelots from the same Atelier', in *Text and Image: Studies in the French Illustrated Book from the Middle Ages to the Present Day* (*Bulletin of the John Rylands University Library of Manchester* 81/3), ed. D. J. Adams, A. Armstrong (Manchester, 1999), pp. 97–125. To the late Elspeth Kennedy is due the realization of the importance of the placing of miniatures in relation to the text rather than a consideration of the similarity of pictorial subjects alone. What emerges is that differing principles of picture-text structure were used by the designers – whether the pictures serve to introduce an episode (if placed at the beginning of an episode) or to accompany a textual descriptions (if placed immediately above or adjacent to the relevant text passage). Different strategies were chosen even among the manuscripts made in the same atelier.

Add. MSS 10292–4 which, so far as we know, is the copy that is the most densely illustrated of all the *Lancelot-Grail* manuscripts, boasting a total of 748 illustrations for the entire five-part cycle. But it must also be noted that, even in the sequence considered here, Add. 10292 omits markers at points where Royal and Amsterdam give a miniature or a champie, so the notion of what constitutes a 'complete' picture cycle is variable. Finally, the two Parisian manuscripts show considerable difference from each other and from the rest of the group, despite their textual similarity: BNF, fr. 9123 has nine miniatures, three without placement parallels in other copies, six corresponding to a miniature elsewhere, while BNF, fr. 105 has ten miniatures, six without parallels for placement and four corresponding in position to other copies. These differences are most likely indications that several different selection strategies were at work, even among copies made, as these were, in the same artistic environment or workshop and that observation is further substantiated when the subjects of the illustrations are compared. However, certain scenes are marked in all copies: the opening of the episode (a little later in BNF, fr. 105); Celidoine led away; Nascien at the Turning Island (a little later in Rennes); Nascien on Solomon's Ship, the central precursor to the rediscovery of the Ship in the *Queste*.

I.2. *King Mordrain on the Island*

The island locus is marked at the beginning of the sequence in *Estoire* by a champie initial in Le Mans and Amsterdam, and by an illustration in Rennes, Add. 10292, Royal, BNF, fr. 9123, and a little after the beginning in BNF, fr. 105. Mordrain's miraculous journey – in his own splendidly designed bed, a unique rendering so far as I know – is the focus in Rennes (Plate 1), while his desolation at finding himself alone on the deserted island is what Add. and Royal have chosen to emphasize by showing him sitting on the ground by a cave on the rock, head on hand. In fr. 9123 and fr. 105 Tout-en-Tour's appearance in his white boat, followed by the devil in the form of a horned woman in a black boat are immediately introduced, whereas the other manuscripts place these appearances later in the text. Add. 10292 gives three illustrations, framing Tout-en-Tout and his silver boat with its white sail and red cross (Plate 2)[5] by a double depiction of the devil's black boat which appears before and after the white boat, thus emphasizing pictorially Mordrain's temptation by the devil, whose boat's second appearance has the shields of Mordrain and Nascien on its mast, as the text describes. In the text, the white boat also makes a second appearance which is not illustrated. Rennes and Royal each give a single illustration, choosing Tout-en-tout and omitting the devil,

5   'Cele neif estoit petite mais ele estoit a merueilles bele car li mas estoit ausi blans comme flor de lis et desus en haut avoit vne crois vermeille...' (Add. 10292, f.24). The colour of the sail is not actually mentioned, unless it was assumed to be the same as the colour of the mast.

thus focussing on Mordrain's eventual triumph over the forces of evil. Rennes shows Tout-en-Tout in his boat with a white sail (but no cross), positioning the miniature later than Royal but earlier than Tout-en-Tout's textual appearance. Royal positions its miniature at the very beginning of the boat sequence, emphasizing still more the eventual outcome where Mordrain resists the devil and triumphs thanks to the sign of the cross on the sail of Tout-en-Tout's boat.

Most remarkably, Tout-en-Tout's boat in Royal is shown with a red sail (Plate 3) – an important pictorial variant compared with what is depicted in Rennes and Add. 10292. It depends on a textual variant in Royal, where the colour of the cross has been omitted and the sail itself is described as red, 'Chele nef estoit petite et toute dargent et si estoit li mas dor et li voiles estoit ausi tous viermaus ... Et quant il vit el voile le signe de la sainte crois si fu auques asseures' (Royal f. 36) – and that variant is what the artist has followed, a rare instance in this cluster of manuscripts, proving that whoever specified the subjects of the miniatures (designer, artist, patron?) paid very close attention to what the particular variant in Royal actually says. The picture was not simply copied from an illustrated model.

Such examples are relatively rare in general across the illustrative tradition of the *Estoire del saint Graal*, and a full study of what all the other illustrated copies do at this point in the text, and what their textual variants are, is beyond the scope of this article.[6] However, BNF, fr. 105 and 9123, both illustrated by an artist I call the Sub-Fauvel Master, are two further cases where another textual variant has in part been followed in a picture.[7] Both manuscripts give the same textual variant (not the same variant as in Royal): BNF, fr. 105 on f. 47v says 'cele nef estoit petite toute dargent et si estoit li mas dor et le voile et le voile *sic* estoit ausi blanc comme noiz negiee et si auoit el mi lieu de la nef vne grant crois toute uermeille...' and the rubric preceding the miniature describes the boat and its contents in similar terms, 'Comment li rois Mordrains vit venir dune roche de mer ou il estoit vn moult bel

---

[6]   The Mordrain episode is not always illustrated: there is no picture in this section in BNF, fr. 95, for instance, although the related *Queste,* Yale 229, gives copious illustrations to the Solomon's Ship episode, as I show below.

[7]   BNF, fr. 9123 is a collaborative effort divided between the Sub-Fauvel Master and another Parisian artist known as the Maubeuge Master on the basis of his work in the *Grandes chroniques de France*, Paris, BNF, fr. 10132, sold in 1318 by the Parisian libraire Thomas de Maubeuge. See A. Stones, 'The Artistic Context of *le Roman de Fauvel* and and Note on *Fauvain*', in *Fauvel Studies*, eds M. Bent and A. Wathey (Oxford, 1998), pp. 529–67; R.H. and M.A. Rouse, *Manuscripts and their Makers in Medieval Paris, 1200–1500: Illuminati et uxorati,* 2 vols (London and Turnhout, 2000), I pp. 185–7, 213–15, 248, 373 n. 11, 380 n. 89, 381 n. 103, 391 n. 99, 392 n. 122, II Appendices 7F, 7M, 8D, 9A, ills. 105, 107, 108. Unusually, the text of BNF, fr. 9123 is prefaced by a numbered list of rubrics which correlate with the rubrics accompanying the miniatures. There is no such list in BNF, fr. 105. Rouse and Rouse, I, 106, note the different treatments of Vortiger's election to the throne; and there are many more examples both of similarity and of difference that remain to be explored.

homme en vne nef tout dargent et auoit enmi lieu de cele nef vne crois tout ver-meille.' In the picture, the boat is painted silver, its sail white, its mast gold, and a red cross stands in the boat towards the prow. In BNF, fr. 9123, the text on f. 40 is substantially the same as in BNF, fr. 105 (or vice-versa, since it unclear which, if either, came first or indeed whether one depends on the other): 'Celle nef etsoit moult petite toute dargent et li mez si cstoit dor et li voiles estoit aussi blans comme noif negiee et si auoit el milieu de la nef vne grant crois toute ver-meille...'(f. 40). There are two illustrations for this sequence, on ff. 38 and 41v, whose rubrics, respectively, say 'Comment li roys mordrains vit venir parmi la mer vne nef dargent a gouuernal dor .i. homme dedens et ou mileu de la nef auoit vne crois vermeille Et comment elle ariua a la roche ou li roys estoit' (f. 38, numbered xviij, Plate 4), and 'Comme li roys estoit estoit *sic* en orisons a nostre seigneur et comment la bene nef dargent et lome dedens reuint a lui' (f. 41v, numbered xix). But the illustrations both show Tout-en-Tout handing a large gold cross to Mordrain, an action corresponding neither to text, rubric, nor to any other picture of this episode so far as I know, and unexplained. Both manuscripts continue the sequence by depicting the devil and his boat, but differently: whereas BNF, fr. 105 on f. 53 gives three devils in a boat with shields on the side approaching Mordrain, the devil in BNF, fr. 9123 on f. 43v appears in the guise of a horned woman. Fur-thermore the pictures are differently placed in the text, and their treatment unre-lated to what is in Add., the only one of the Add.-Royal-Amsterdam group to include the devil's boat. At the least, these examples suggest something of the complex and changing nature of text-picture relationships for this episode, to the point that even the same (or closely related) artists were quite capable of produc-ing a different picture if a text variant required it – or even if one did not.

I.3. *Nascien and Solomon's Ship*

Next comes Nascien's discovery of Solomon's Ship. In all seven manuscripts the sequence begins with Nascien in Calafer's prison, marked in Amsterdam by a champie initial and in the others by an illustration, where Rennes (in part), Add. and Royal, and BNF, fr. 105, show Nascien released from prison by a hand seizing him (in the manner of Habakkuk) by the hair. Le Mans shows a slightly earlier moment, when he is thrust into the prison, while Rennes couples the release with Nascien and his son Celidoine both in prison before Nascien's release; and BNF, fr. 9123 shows Nascien in a cloud and flames descending upon Calafer. A second illustration (a champie in Le Mans and Amsterdam) is given in all seven manu-scripts, this time with a focus on Nascien's wife Flegentine, including their son Celidoine again in Rennes and Additional 10292; and BNF, fr 105 has an additional scene focussing on Celidoine. The Turning Island is marked next in all seven man-uscripts (again by a champie initial in Le Mans and Amsterdam), at a slightly later place in Rennes where Nascien approaches the island on horseback, while in Add.

and Royal he lies there dreaming of birds.[8]

At this point Add. once again gives a sequence of illustrations that are without parallel in the other copies, framing the sequence with Nascien on Solomon's Ship at the beginning and end, and marking the history of the three spindles with three explanatory miniatures and two champie initials in between. The first miniature depicts Nascien on the Ship, finding (with hands raised in surprise) its contents of bed with crown and sword, and the three spindles of different colours, white, green and red (Plate 5). Their meaning is critical not only to the story in *Estoire* but also to the reappearance of the ship in the *Queste,* where it marks an important stage in the Grail Knights' understanding of the allegory of the Quest for the Holy Grail in which they are participants. Yet only a few of the illustrations depict the contents of the Ship and the events surrounding Nascien's discovery. In the end, Nascien's curiosity leads to disaster as the ship collapses and he is forced to swim to shore. For the Ship was not intended for him, but for the pure knight yet to come – who in the *Queste del saint Graal* would achieve the Grail Quest along with his companions. Additional 10292 is again alone in depicting the untoward consequence of Nascien's curiosity (Plate 15). Earlier in the text, Add. depicts an episode where another transgression of Nascien is punished: he presumes to look into the Grail, and is blinded as a result. What is depicted in Additional 10292 (f. 20v, and also in Royal, f. 30v) is not actually the blinding of Nascien, nor his subsequent curing, but rather the punishment meted out to Josephé for not having prevented it – Josephé is pierced in the groin with a lance aimed by an angel, a punishment endured for the second time. Josephé had earlier failed to baptise everyone and was lanced in the groin for that.[9] Josephé is subsequently cured, as was Nascien.[10] What is not shown in any of the copies considered here is

[8]   What makes the island turn and where does the motif come from? No hints are given in the text, and there is no mention of this question in M. Szkilnik, *L'archipel du Graal: étude de l'Estoire del saint Graal* (Geneva, 1991). It surely reflects an aspect of scientific knowledge such as the principles of magnetism, and remains to be explored.

[9]   At S I, 77/Pon 159; no illustration either in Add. or in Royal. The second lancing is at S I 80.17/Pon 165.

[10] The curing of Nascien (but not his wounding) is depicted in Bonn, UB, 526. There are obvious parallels with cures effected by relics, such as the near-contemporary case of the future Louis VIII, son of Philippe II and Isabelle, who was cured of dysentery by the touch of relics brought from Saint-Denis: a nail, a thorn, and an arm of St Simeon. On the same day Philippe, abroad and suffering from the same illness, was also cured. This is reported in the historical portion of Yves de Saint-Denis' work on the Life and Miracles of St Denis, found in Paris BNF, lat. 5286, ff. 202v–203 and lat. 13836, ff. 96–97v, and printed by A. Duchesne in *Historiae Francorum scriptores coaetanei, ab ipsius gentis origine, ad Pipinum usque regem, quorum plurimi nunc primùm ex variis codicibus mss. in lucem prodeunt, alii verò auctiores & emendatiores; cum epistolis regum, reginarum, pontificum, ducum, comitum, abbatum & aliis veteribus rerum francicarum monumentis,* 5 vols (Paris, 1639–49), V, pp. 288–9. These references were kindly drawn to my attention by E. A. R. Brown.

a later episode where Nascien and Mordrain are again on Solomon's ship and Nascien presumes to draw the sword, whereupon it breaks and he is inflicted with a wound in the shoulder by another sword, in punishment. King Mordrain reunites the broken sword and returns it to its sheath.

The other six copies all show an aspect of Nascien's initial discovery and some of the contents of the ship, the subject of Add.'s first miniature in the sequence (except for Amsterdam which has a champie initial). In Additional 10292 (Plate 5), all the elements are present in both pictures: the bed with crown (painted in silver or tin), sword and sheath, and the three spindles, two at the front of the bed and one at the back, and the ship has an inscription on the side, reading 'Saches iou ne sui foy non et creanche.' The treatment of the ship in Royal is similar – bed, crown, sword and spindles (all on the near side of the ship) are also present, and there is an inscription on the side of the ship, less easy to read, 'iou ne ai ie my ... iou sui se fe ... non.' These manuscripts are the ones which most faithfully depict the symbolic contents of the ship, whose meaning is elucidated in the text but only partially explained in the pictures, and nowhere, to my knowledge, as explicitly depicted as in Add. 10292. In Royal, Nascien, somewhat incongruously holding his gloves, contemplates the boat from the shore to which he has just swum – and the ship, unlike Add. 10292's final version, is still intact. Rennes and Le Mans each give a less detailed picture of the ship: in Rennes, Nascien looks at the bed with its three spindles which form three corner-posts but the crown and sword are not shown, and companions watch from the shore (Plate 7); in Le Mans, Nascien is alone on the ship (apart from a knight terminal and a cleric terminal above and below) and the bed is present but the crown, sword, and spindles are absent (Plate 6). BNF, fr. 105 and fr. 9123 are both cursory in their treatment of the ship. In fr. 105 the boat is shown twice, the first time with the bed on which is the sword and its decorated sheath and pommel on f. 60, but without the crown and spindle, but shows only the bed on the boat on f. 70; fr. 9123 gives a return of Tout-en-Tout and omits bed, crown, sword and spindles.

I.4. *The Three Spindles*

The intermediary images in Add.10292, and BNF, fr. 105 and fr. 9123, which are similar in content but different in placing, depict highlights of the story of the spindles, grown from the branch taken by Eve at the Explusion from Paradise, and the story is repeated in the *Queste*, with several differences in emphasis, as I show below. The miniatures in Add. begin with the Fall, where the serpent with a female head is coiled around the tree; Adam clutches his throat, having eaten the apple, while Eve holds in her hand a leafy branch, possibly (the image is indistinct) still with an apple attached (Plate 8). In the text this branch, planted outside Paradise, grows into a tree whose wood is white. Depicted in Royal is the sequel, where God commands Adam and Eve to make love beneath the tree, whereupon its wood turns from white to green. Beneath the green tree Cain murders Abel and then the tree turns to red, and offshoots of the tree at each stage retain their original colour, but Add. 10292's trees are all shown as green. The murder in Add. 10292 is achieved with the jawbone of an ass,[11] whereas in BNF, fr. 105 and fr. 9123, the instrument is a spade, and the deed is shown taking place beneath a red tree (Plate 9); in BNF, fr, 9123 the miniature also includes Eve holding the green tree (Plate 10).

Some other manuscripts also focus on the changes in the tree: thus in Paris, BNF, fr. 19162 at the miniature on f. 65 shows the tree in the process of changing colour from white to green, while on the border Eve stands working a butter-churn (Plate 11); in Berkeley, UCB, 106, a two-part miniature shows Cain killing Abel with a spade, with the three trees painted red white and green below (Plate 12a); and Paris, BNF, fr. 95, f. 49v has a historiated initial containing three trees, the middle one with a double blue trunk, the outer two with red trunks, but all with green leaves.[12] One fifteenth-century unillustrated manuscript, Paris, BNF, fr. 1426, left a

[11]   Several scholars have investigated the origins of the jawbone motif. See M. Schapiro, 'Cain's Jawbone that Did the First Murder committed the First Murder', *Art Bulletin,* 24 (1942), pp. 205–12, repr. in *Late Antique, Early Christian and Medieval Art, Selected Papers* (London, 1980), pp. 249–65 at p. 252. The oldest instance cited by Schapiro is in Aelfric's *Heptateuch,* where the text is silent about the instrument but the picture shows a jawbone; and the earliest literary reference Schapiro brings to bear on the subject is the Anglo-Saxon prose Solomon and Saturn, where the jawbone is called a *cinbán* (citing J. M. Kemble, *The Dialogue of Solomon and Saturn* (London, 1848), p. 187), which Schapiro claims would have sounded similar to 'Cain bana' (where 'bana' means murderer). George Henderson, however, points out that differences in pronounciation and other linguistic inconsistencies would have made such a confusion unlikely (G. Henderson, 'Cain's Jaw-Bone', *Journal of the Warburg and Courtauld Institutes,* 24 (1961), pp. 108–14). Henderson agrees with Schapiro that the Aelfric representation is the earliest, and further suggests that the motif may have transferred from Solomon, citing O. F. Emerson, 'Legends of Cain, especially in Old and Middle English', *Publications of the Modern Language Association of America,* 21 (1906), p. 859, referencing Judges 15: 15; or, just possibly, to have been borrowed from a plough coulter as on tenth-century Irish crosses. A.A. Barb, drawing upon a neglected article by Sándor Scheiber, 'Kájin ´s Abel-´ldozati füstjéről szóló legenda életrajza', *Yearbook of the Hungarian Jewish Literary Society IIzr. Magyar irodalmi tdrsukat,* 64 (Budapest, 1942), pp. 127–50, cites ancient Egyptian evidence for the use of flints inserted into the animal's jawbone – and later, into wood – to form a kind of sickle (A. A. Barb, 'Cain's Murder-Weapon and Samson's Jawbone of an Ass', *Journal of the Warburg and Courtauld Institutes,* 35 (1972), pp. 386–9). For the transition from 'primitive jawbone tool' to not only the toothed sickel and the serrated saw but a fearful weapon and status symbol with a venerable history, Barb further cites J. Makkai, 'Early Near Eastern and South East European Gods', *Acta Archaeologica Academ Scient. Hungar,* 16 (Budapest, 1964), pp. 3–64. The same configuration, with a backturned Abel, and the same instrument, are also found in the marginal scene in a devotional book illustrated by the Add./Royal/Amsterdam artist, the hours of Liège (not Maastricht) use, London, BL Stowe 17.

large space on f. 158v preceding the passage starting 'Moult dura lonuemen ceste arbre ... on f. 159, and a note reads ' Cy doit estre larbre de vie paint en /quatre [sic] coulleurs.' And a drawing of three trees is also found in an otherwise unillustrated English thirteenth-century copy of Estoire, London, BL, Add. MS 32125 (f. 205v), at the same place in the text.

No direct reference is made to the Crucifixion either in text or picture, although the presence of Nascien as the discoverer of the ship anticipates the achieving of the Grail Quest by his descendant Galaad, while the descent of Christ from the lineage of Solomon through the Virgin Mary, the new Eve, is hinted at in text and picture, but not elaborated upon. Galaad is in effect a type of Christ, though the link is never made explicit. Similarly the link between Solomon and the wood of the trees grown from Eve's branch may also allude indirectly to the legends about the Wood of the Cross of Christ, grown from seeds obtained from Paradise by Seth which produced three shoots of different trees, cedar, cypress, and pine (no mention of colours) that were discovered by Moses. The three shoots then grew together to form a single tree, which Solomon tried to use for building the Temple (but the planks were always too long or too short) and which eventually served to make the Cross of Christ. Nothing is directly said in the text of the *Estoire* to link the three spindles and their colours to these Cross legends, however. Conversely, so far as I know, there is no reference in any of the Cross legends to the coloured trees of *Estoire* and *Queste* nor to the spindles made from them,

---

[12] In BNF, fr. 19162, Berkeley, UCB, 106 and BNF, fr. 95 these images are placed at S I 130. 6, Pon vol. II, 279. 445, where Add. gives a champie initial; the place is unmarked in the other four manuscripts. BNF, fr. 19162 and its twin, Paris, BNF, fr. 24594 are stylistically related to manuscripts associated with Cambrai, Saint-Omer and Thérouanne: Bonn, UB 526 (written in Amiens in 1286, giving a miniature of Solomon's Ship with only the bier and the spindles) and Paris, BNF, fr. 110, two missals of Cambrai, MM 153 and 154; the Guillaume d'Orange cycle manuscript written in 1295, Boulogne-sur-Mer, BM 192; the Vincent of Beauvais, *Speculum historiale,* Boulogne, BM, 131; and the partial bible, Saint-Omer, BM, 5 and many other related manuscripts. BNF, fr. 95 is particularly close stylistically to the psalter-hours of Thérouanne use, Paris, BNF, lat. 1076 and Marseille BM 111 so emanates from the same diocese in the decade of the 1290s; and it is closely related to Yale 229, whose *Queste del saint Graal* I consider below. See A. Stones, 'The Illustrations in BN fr 95 and Yale 229, Prolegomena to a Comparative Study', in Busby, *Word and Image* (see above at n. 3), 206–83. Berkeley, UCB, 106 is the odd-one out: in a personal communication F. Avril has suggested it is part of a cluster of manuscripts, mostly bibles, associated with Jumièges and other Norman monasteries in the 1270s and 1280s. Given the possibility of monastic production and/or patronage it is interesting to note that in UCB 106 the *Estoire* is preceded by the *Vies des pères* and other material (including Gautier de Coinci's Theophilus Miracle), illustrated by the same artist(s), although the *Estoire* is written in two columns whereas the *Vies des pères* is in three, and the two parts need not always have been together. For further analysis see P. Gehrke, *Saints and Scribe: Medieval Hagiography in its Manuscript Context* (University of California Publications in Modern Philology, 126) (Berkeley, CA 1993).

and the Cross legends are unillustrated apart from the Middle High German Lutwin version, Vienna, ONB 2980.[13]

There is one exceptional depiction of three trees coloured white, green, and red, which may allude to the Cross legends and also, because of the colours, to anticipate the trees of the *Estoire* and *Queste*. These trees are found in the historiated initial to Psalm 118, 33 in the early twelfth-century Psalter of Christina of Markyate (the St Albans Psalter, Hildesheim, Pfarrkirche St Godehard, p. 315, Plate 13).[14] They are placed in a rectangular panel at the bottom of the initial, by a stream outside a structure within which, on the left, a woman holds a leafy branch and a small round object, and faces a man holding a bird on his wrist; a second pair of figures are another man holding a small round gold object grasping a woman (the same woman?) by the hand, as she gestures at him, raising the fingers of her left hand.[15] Geddes interprets this as a depiction of Christina subjected to the temp-

---

[13] The early literature on the Cross legends is summarized in A. S. Napier, *History of the Holy Rood-Tree, A Twelfth Century Version of the Cross-Legend, with Notes on the Orthography of the Ormulum and A Middle English Compassio Mariae* (Early English Text Society, E.A. 103) (London, 1894) and in W. W. Seymour, *The Cross in Tradition, History and Art* (New York, 1898). More recent studies include H. Shields, 'Le bois de la croix: ramifications en français et en occitan', *Mélanges de philologie romane offerts à Ch. Camproux* (Montpellier, 1978), I, pp. 237–48; A. M. L. Prangsma-Hajenius, *La Légende du Bois de la Croix dans la littérature française médiévale* (Assen, 1995); B. Baert, *A Heritage of Holy Wood, The Legend of the True Cross in Text and Image* (Leiden, 2004). To the best of my knowledge, the only manuscript to couple Cross-Legend material with the *Estoire* is Paris, BNF, fr. 95 which opens with *Estoire, Merlin*, and *Suite vulgate*, followed by *Sept Sages* and *Pénitence Adam*. For the latter see E. C. Quinn, *The Penitence of Adam: A Study of the Andrius MS (Bibliothèque Nationale Fr. 95 Folios 380–394v), with a transcription of the Old French and English translation by Micheline Dufau* (Romance Monographs, Inc. 36) (University, Mississippi, 1980). However, Quinn observes that BNF, fr. 95 transmits the Class II version of *Pénitence Adam* in which the Class III interpolation of a rood-tree legend is absent. Quinn refers to the Lutwin version, ONB 2980, on p. 51.

[14] I thank Jane Geddes for drawing my attention to this image and for her views on its significance. See J. Geddes, *The St Albans Psalter: a Book for Christina of Markyate* (London, 2005), Plate 82.

[15] Interpretations of the round objects are given in K. Haney, *The St. Albans Psalter. An Anglo-Norman Song of Faith* (Studies in the Humanities 60) (New York, 2002), p. 592 n. 800, citing A. Goldschmidt, *Der Albanipsalter in Hildesheim und seine Beziehung zur symbolischen Kirchenskulptur des XII. Jahrhunderts* (Berlin, 1895), p. 122: an egg; O. Pächt, F. Wormald, C. R. Dodwell, *The St Albans Psalter (Albani Psalter)* (London, 1960), p. 251: an apple (pl. 77); for Haney, the gold object is a gold coin. She further notes that the trees and water are lacking in the Stuttgart and Utrecht Psalters. For the flowering branch and round objects as Marian attributes see T. A. Heslop, 'The Romanesque Seal of Worcester Cathedral', *Medieval Art and Architecture at Worcester Cathedral* (British Archaeological Association Conference Transactions) (Leeds, 1978), pp. 75–6.

tations of cupidity and lust, based on the commentaries of Ambrose and Augustine.[16] The trees, with their Paradise-Salvation connotations, would add another level of meaning, suggesting that Christina would withstand these temptations.[17] The question remains as to what sources the St Albans image – and the *Estoire* and *Queste* – are drawing upon. The likely date of the St Albans Psalter in the second decade of the twelfth century is a sure indication that some, at least, of the Cross legends, were known in England and at St Albans.

One *Estoire* manuscript has a hint of what might be an allusion to the Cross legends: the Cain-Abel-Trees miniature in UCB 106 is followed by an initial M (Plate 12b) containing a three-part green tree behind which may be seen a vertical brown plank, and three figures in front above a wavy grey motif in the foreground (a boat? water?). Might the vertical plank be an allusion to the Cross and its legends? and might the three figures refer forwards to the three Grail Knights of the *Queste*? If so, the reference is discrete at best, and the manuscript in its present state does not include a *Queste del saint Graal*.

The colour triad of white, green and red no doubt resonated for medieval audiences with additional symbolism not made explicit either in text or rubric in the *Estoire*, nor indeed in the *Queste*. Abundant exegetical literature linked these colours with the precious stones of Exodus and the Apocalypse, the elements, the cardinal virtues, and the colours of liturgical vestments.[18] White, red, and green were even associated with the French monarchy, as by the fourteenth century, threads in these colours were used to attach seals to royal charters.[19]

I.5. *Solomon, his Queen, and the Making and Fitting of the Ship*

What is shown next in Add. 10292 is the making of the ship by carpenters in the presence of King Solomon and his Queen (not named in the text) (Plate 14). It is she, not Solomon, who chooses the objects for the boat and explains for whom they are destined – so she is presented as a parallel for Perceval's sister in the *Queste*. The spindles and the crown, sword and sheath had already been depicted as seen by Nascien and would be shown again in Add. 10292's concluding miniature (Plate 15). Much is made in the text of the symbolism of these objects – the spindles made from the wood of the three trees associated with Adam and Eve and

---

[16] Geddes (see above, n. 14), p. 99.

[17] Geddes (see above, n. 14), p. 105 n. 15.

[18] Useful references are in the *Lexikon der christlichen Ikonographie* under 'Farbensymbolik', cols 7–10. For instance, Bede, Rupert of Deutz, Honorius Augustodunensis all link the four elements to the colours *purpureus, hyacinthus, coccus* and *byssus*.

[19] Many examples were on view at the Archives Nationales in Spring 2007. I thank Hervé Pinoteau for drawing this important feature to my attention. See H. Pinoteau, 'Deux triades de couleurs: Vert, blanc, rouge et bleu, blanc, rouge', *Fonctions de la couleur en Eurasie* (Collection Eurasie, Cahiers de la Société des Etudes euro-asiatiques 9), 2000, pp. 95–107.

Cain and Abel, while the crown and sword are David's and had been kept in the temple. Solomon was to fit out the sword with a new pommel of precious jewels, and a new sheath;[20] Solomon's Queen would take care of the 'renges' or straps, anticipating the need for better ones to be made by Perceval's sister in the *Queste del saint Graal*. It is surprising is that only Add. 10292, BNF, fr. 105, and fr. 9123 have a miniature depicting Solomon; and his wife accompanies him only in Add.

A mixed pattern of relationships between picture and text, and among pictures, emerges from the illustration of these maritime adventures in *Estoire*. Whereas the structure and placing of the miniatures has been most carefully thought out in Add. 10292, the manuscript which also has the largest number of illustrations, it is also clear that the planners/illustrators of Royal, BNF, fr. 105 and fr. 9123 were scrupulous, on occasion, in the attention they paid to the words of the text in those copies. That they chose to omit the contents of Solomon's Ship is surprising, perhaps an indication that symbolic objects other than the cross itself – handed out without textual justification to Mordrain – were of little interest. Indeed, the absence of illustrations of these episodes in copies that were otherwise illustrated suggest that patron interest and patron wealth were also important factors in determining how, and how much, these texts would be illustrated.

[20] '... El temple que vous avez fait en lonor ihesu crist est l'espee le roi david uostre peire le plus merueilleuse qui onques fust forgie et la plus trenchant que onques fust baillie par main de chevalier. prendes la si en ostes le poin et lenheudure et quant uous aures la lemele mis a vne part nous qui connusions les forces des herbes et les uertus des pieres et la matere de toutes coses terrienes faites .i. poin de pieres precieuses si soutilment quil nait apres vous regart domme terrien qui puist connoistre lune de lautre ains quideche chascuns qui le verra que ce soit vne misme piere. apres i faites vne enheudure si merueilleuse que nule ne soit si uertueuse ne si riche. et apres i faites le feure si merueilleuse en son endroit comme lespee sera endroit soi . et quant vous aures toutes ces coses faites si i meterai les renges teiles comme il me plaira....' (Add. f. 34v: S I 133. 19–31). The mention of precious stones suggests knowledge of early bejewelled swords of the Sutton-Hoo or Childeric types, although of course not those particular swords which were unknown in the Middle Ages. See R. L. S. Bruce-Mitford, *The Sutton Hoo Ship Burial*, 3 vols in 4 (London, 1975–83), inv. 95, noting that a sheath with straps ('renges') is also reconstructed; and for Childeric, see *Childeric-Clovis: 1500e anniversaire 482–1982* (Tournai, 1982); and R. L. S. Bruce-Mitford, 'A comparison between the Sutton Hoo burial and Childeric's treasure', *Centenaire de l'Abbé Cochet, 1975* (Actes du Colloque international d'archéologie) (Rouen, 1978), pp. 365–71. Unlike Excalibur, the four other swords in the *Lancelot-Grail* romance – David's sword, the sword drawn from the anvil by Arthur in the *Merlin*, the one drawn from the stone by Galaad, and King Pelles' broken sword mended by Galaad in the *Queste* – are not given a name. In his final speech to Excalibur at the end of the *Mort Artu*, Arthur acknowledges the supremacy of David's sword, 'Ha! Escalibor, boine espee, la millor que len seust el monde, fors seulement cele as estraingnes renges, ore perdras tu ton maistre et ton droit seignor...' (S VI, 379).

II.1. *La Queste del saint Graal*

Of the seven manuscripts examined above for their treatment of maritime adventures in *Estoire,* only the three *Lancelot-Grail* Project manuscripts also contain the *Queste del saint Graal.* I include in addition the Yale manuscript that may have formed part of a *Lancelot-Grail* cycle together with Paris, BNF, fr. 95. Although the maritime adventures form only a small part of the *Estoire* picture cycle in BNF, fr. 95[21] – a surprising omission – the corresponding sequence in the *Queste del saint Graal* is fully illustrated in Yale 229 and offers interesting points of comparison with the three Lancelot-Grail Project manuscripts, particularly as it was made in the same region of eastern Artois or western Flanders a decade or so earlier.

II.2. *Solomon's Ship*

The events surrounding the discovery of Solomon's Ship in the *Queste* link back to Solomon's Ship in the *Estoire* and also point forward to the end of the *Queste* as they anticipate the achieving of the Grail Quest by the three chosen Grail Knights, Perceval, Boort and Galaad, aided by Perceval's sister (nameless, as was Solomon's wife in the *Estoire*). Galaad is to be the eventual winner of the Grail, and it is for him that the Ship was prepared in the *Estoire*. Like Solomon's Queen who tells Solomon what items are to be put in his Ship, Perceval's sister is a seer who knows the meaning of the Ship and its contents which she explains to the knights even before they find the confirmatory letter of explanation in the Ship itself.

Two of the four manuscripts frame the Ship sequence with miniatures emphasising this revelation, most explicitly in a single miniature in Royal where the hand gestures and poses make clear that Perceval's sister is telling the knights about the significance of the Ship (Plate 16), and in two small miniatures in Yale where they are shown first at sea and then entering the Ship. In Add. 10294, Royal and Douce, attention is paid to which knight is which, as they are distinguished by heraldry, painted on surcoats and occasionally ailettes, so that in all three Perceval is shown in an orange surcoat while in Add. 10294 and Royal, Galaad bears the arms *argent* [white] *a cross gules*, referring back to the shield that he wins at the beginning of the *Queste*,[22] and which in turn was King Mordrain's shield, on which Josephé inscribed the cross in his own blood in *Estoire*.[23] Douce curiously gives Galaad the arms normally reserved for Gauvain: *argent* [white] *a canton gules*, a surprising case of heraldic mis-identity. Though they vary across the three manuscripts, these are important instances of the beginnings of heraldry used for the knights, whereas in Yale, made a decade or so before, less attention is paid to using consistent colours for the shields or surcoats of the knights.[24]

[21]   See above at n. 12.

[22]   S VI 22-24; Pau 29-32.

[23]   S I 284. 21; Pon 555. 874. 1.

[24]   See A. Stones, 'Les débuts de l'héraldique dans l'illustration des romans arthuriens', in *Les Armoriaux*, ed. H. Loyau and M. Pastoureau, *Cahiers du léopard d'or,* 8 (1996),

Then follows in all four copies the Adam and Eve sequence, a match for what is shown in *Estoire*, where Add. 10292 marked the story with two champies and two miniatures, of the Fall and the Murder of Abel, the latter shown also in BNF, fr. 105 and 9123 but not illustrated in the other manuscripts. This time all four manuscripts depict the Fall, where Royal concentrates on God's reproach after Adam and Eve have eaten the apple, while the other three show the apple-eating taking place, encouraged in Add. and Douce by a serpent with a female head as in Add. 10292's *Estoire* miniature. Yale has a second part to its Fall miniature, the Sacrifice of Cain and Abel, with details of flames rising and falling (Plate 17), reminiscent of the Sacrifice scene in the Psalter of St Louis, Paris, BNF, lat. 10525. Add. 10294 and Yale both also give the murder of Abel, but at different places in the text, with Cain using different instruments, a short straight knife in Yale and a curved one in Add. 10294 – neither picks up the jawbone motif used by Add. 10292 for the *Estoire* murder. Douce's miniature is an addition, showing the Expulsion, on a page containing a champie initial, while Royal gives a second miniature where God addresses Adam and Eve, this time explaining to them the meaning of the change in the colour of the Tree, from white to green, and the change is also shown in the miniature where the tree has a green crown and white trunk (Plate 18).

All four manuscripts show the Grail Knights and Solomon's Ship, but with different emphases. Indeed this is one of the most frequently represented episodes in *Queste* illustration in general, and there are many variants as to who and what are shown.[25] Perceval's sister is omitted in Douce's miniature (Plate 19) but she is present in the other copies, explaining meanings again in Add. 10294 and particularly in Royal, where Boort turns back to listen to her (Plate 20). The giving and hearing of explanations, from the seeress and from God, is a focus particularly favoured in Royal. In Yale, Perceval's sister is given a more active role as she is shown on the shore, handing to Galaad David's sword with its decorated scabbard and pommel and guard of gold – a subject rarely illustrated, so far as I know (Plate 21). But the 'estranges renges' anticipated by Solomon's wife in the *Estoire*, and made, according to the text of the *Queste*, by Perceval's sister from her own golden hair, are not shown in Yale nor in the other miniatures.

The reading of the letter, found in a decorated purse hanging on Perceval's arm in Add.10294 and Royal, is the main action in Add. 10294, Royal and Douce, and it also figures in Yale where the letter is shown as a scroll (badly rubbed) read to Boort on the boat by Perceval, complementing the sword-giving in the upper

---

pp. 395–420; and for later Arthurian heraldry, M. Pastoureau, *Armorial des chevaliers de la Table ronde* (Paris, 1983).

[25] It is found, for instance, in Brussels, BR 9627-8, BNF, fr. 339, 342, 344, Florence, Laur Ash. 121, Cologny-Geneva, Bodmer 147, Dijon, BM 527, Oxford, Bodl., Rawl. Q. b. 6, Paris, Ars. 3490, BNF, fr. 112, 116, 122, 123, 1423, and no doubt others. The variants are too numerous to discuss here.

part of the miniature and underlining the importance of written proof. Whereas the sword was prominent in Royal's opening Ship miniature, it is not shown again at this point in Royal, nor in the other copies considered here, although other manuscripts do include it. The crown, equally prominent in Royal's opening miniature, is also absent.[26] Here emphasis is given in Add. 10294, Royal and Douce to the bed with its multi-coloured cover (no colours are specified in the text), and to the three spindles, white, red and green, prominently displayed on the front plane of the boat, as they were in the *Estoire* miniatures (Plates 19, 20). The Ship in Yale also has the bed, covered in grey with a green pillow, on a frame painted white with gold finials – but the three spindles and the crown are absent (Plate 21). Other details about the Ship also vary – in Royal there is a sail, absent in the other versions, while Douce's boat has a tiller.

II.2. *Perceval's Sister*

The lower part of Yale's miniature shows the four protagonists setting sail towards the next episode, where Perceval's sister will donate her blood to cure the Leprous Damsel and will die from the bloodletting – and it is notable that none of these manuscripts illustrates the bloodletting incident, only the events that result from it.[27] Add. 10294 is the only manuscript to actually depict the death of Perceval's sister (Plate 22), with an emphasis on her last communion, and Add. 10294 precedes this with a presage heralding divine intervention in the form of the White Stag accompanied by four lions, emblematic of Christ, seen in the forest by Perceval and Galaad. Scenes of destruction precede and follow Perceval's sister's death – in all four manuscripts the Grail Knights see the Leprous Damsel's castle destroyed, in atonement for the death of Perceval's sister, while leading up to her death are variously placed scenes of combat in which the Grail Knights kill a large number of antagonists. In Royal the focus is once again on explanation, by a priest carrying a ciborium, of these deaths and an expiation of them through the Sacrament. Douce marks the place with a champie initial. All four manuscripts depict Lancelot's discovery of Perceval's sister's body on a boat that links back to Solomon's enchanted Ship (if only with a champie initial in Douce, and an added miniature of Lancelot hearing a voice). This time the bed has become a bier, draped in Add. 10294 with the same multi-coloured cover as in Solomon's Ship, and again the pictorial emphasis is on explanatory reading as Lancelot finds the letter left by Perceval which explains who the dead damsel is (Plate 23). Once again the written word is an important witness to the truth. Yale alone continues the pictorial narrative, where Lancelot brings the body to a chapel and is greeted there by a hermit (Plate 24).

[26] The crown is rarely represented at this point.

[27] As I have shown elsewhere, the bloodletting is illustrated in Bonn, UB 526 and Florence, Laur. Ash. 121 (Stones, 'The Illustrations', see above, n. 12). It is a surprisingly rare subject in *Queste* illustration.

II.3. *The Final Scenes*

Another death follows shortly afterwards, that of King Mordrain, a character whose story is mainly played out in the *Estoire*, who dies in the arms of Galaad, physically and psychologically linking the two branches, the two stories, and the two heroes, and marking the succession of Galaad the Grail Winner whose rôle has long been anticipated, as far back as the *Estoire*. After this come two symbolic acts, the joining of King Pelles' broken sword by Galaad, an incident paralelled in the Second Continuation of the *Perceval* of Chrétien de Troyes (where of course Perceval, not Galaad, is the Grail Winner). The illustration in Paris, BNF, fr. 1453, f. 218, the only one among the corpus of surviving Perceval illustrations, shows a valet bringing the two pieces of the sword to the table before Perceval and the Maimed King.[28] Add. 10294 (f.50b) is the only manuscript of the *Queste* manuscripts considered here to illustrate this event, while Yale's illustrative programme culminates in the Grail Liturgy, shown, surprisingly, in a small rather than a large miniature, but one that is remarkable for its depiction – or rather its concealment – of the Grail, hidden from view within a shrine-like tabernacle placed on the altar.[29] It is notable that the other manuscripts omit an illustration of the liturgy, even those where the liturgy in *Estoire* is illustrated with several miniature, not just one.[30]

In Add. 10294, Royal and Rylands, the final miniature depicts the Grail Knights carrying the Grail and the Grail Table, aided by a cripple (who will of course be cured by the Grail).

II.4. *Conclusions*

The illustrations in these romances were not mass-produced from models, nor were the illustrative programmes standard. The stories and their interpretations were multi-valent and patrons, producers and illustrators were well aware of the multiple pictorial possiblities that the stories presented. They capitalized on the many options the texts offered to create products whose illustrations were most likely dictated by a variety of factors, most no longer ascertainable with certainty today, but varied and variable as no two copies, even when produced by the same or closely related craftsmen, are identical in their choice, placement, and treatment of the illustrations.

---

[28] See *Les Manuscrits de Chrétien de Troyes*, ed. K. Busby, T. Nixon, A. Stones, L. Walter, 2 vols (Amsterdam, 1993), II, Plate 407.

[29] For further discussion see A. Stones, 'The Illustrations' cited above, n. 11; and eadem, 'Seeing the Grail', in *The Grail, A Casebook*, ed. D. Mahoney (New York, 2000), 301–66.

[30] It is notable that BNF, fr. 95, most likely the pendant of Yale 229, also illustrates Josephé's liturgy in the *Estoire* as do Royal and Amsterdam but not Add. See Stones, 'The Illustrations', cited in n. 12 and eadem, 'The Grail in Rylands French 1 and its Sister Manuscripts', *Bulletin of the John Rylands University Library of Manchester*, 81–3, (1999), pp. 55–95.

Of the manuscripts considered here, the least expansive are Le Mans and Amsterdam/Douce/Rylands, which so often give a champie where the related manuscripts have a miniature. These manuscripts also simplify, so that the contents of Solomon's Ship found by Nascien are reduced to just the bed in Le Mans, and Perceval's sister is omitted in the important scene of the three Grail Knights on Solomon's Ship in *Queste* in Douce. These omissions suggest that these copies are reductions of more expansive versions, not early simple versions.[31] I still believe Rennes to be the earliest surviving illustrated manuscript,[32] yet its picture-cycle is meagre, with numerous champies. However, it does include unusual details, notably King Mordrain transported in his bed, but this version was not taken up elsewhere, so far as I know. Yale also gives idiosyncratic detail, notably in relation to the Grail Knights and Perceval's sister on Solomon's Ship: and again, so far as I know, its treatment was not repeated. Most thoughtful, in their different ways, are Royal and Add. 10292 and 10294, all taking care to frame important episodes with a 'before' miniature and an 'after' miniature, in Royal especially in relation to the Grail Knights and Perceval's sister on Solomon's Ship and in Add. in relation to the corresponding sequence in *Estoire* depicting Nascien's adventures on the Ship. Yet neither manuscript duplicates the choices that the other (and its makers) has made, and their strategies at times are quite different. So Add. 10292–4 give more miniatures overall, with several appearances of Tout-en-Tout's boat and that of the devil in *Estoire*, and include the Adam and Eve sequence both in *Estoire* and also in *Queste*. Royal's strategy focuses on images of contemplation, reflection and listening, to God in *Estoire* and to Perceval's sister in *Queste,* and both pay careful attention to the details of what is in each text for the treatment of *Estoire's* sail. The strategies in BNF, fr. 105 and 9123 are different from each other, and difficult to fathom. Again, attention was paid at times to what the text says yet at other times the content of the miniatures seems almost random, a strange mixture of deliberate thought and careless inattention. These examples show that there was a great deal of flexibility in what was done, and how: exactly why these particular choices were made we shall probably never know, but the variety and difference in pictorial emphasis these manuscripts represent are indications of how eagerly the texts were embraced by medieval makers and owners alike.

---

[31] For the opposite view in relation to Amst. in *Estoire*, see Meuwese, 'Three Illustrated prose *Lancelot* Manuscripts', cited above in n. 4.

[32] A. Stones, 'The Earliest Illustrated Prose *Lancelot* Manuscript?', *Reading Medieval Studies,* 3 (1977), 3–44.

Gone Fishing: *Angling in the Fitzwilliam Bohun Psalter*

LUCY FREEMAN SANDLER

The opening page of the late fourteenth-century Bohun psalter in the Fitzwilliam Museum has four pictorial units (Plate 1), the most prominent of which is the pair of shields with the arms of Henry VI and Margaret of Anjou and John Stratford, archbishop of Canterbury.[1] These arms were inserted in the mid-fifteenth century and seem to confirm the descent of the manuscript from its original owner, Mary de Bohun or her husband Henry of Bolingbroke, later Henry IV, to their son Henry V, and grandson, Henry VI. The Bohun family arms, together with those of the Edward III and his son, the Black Prince, and of John of Gaunt as king of Castile and his son Henry of Bolingbroke as heir of the duke of Lancaster, are part of the original armorial display on this page.[2]

As for the other pictorial elements, in the upper half of the page are two narratives from the life of David, the first, a doublet. On the left, David, armed with a club, threatens a bear about to devour a sheep; and on the right, David again, now with a slingshot, the stones gathered together in his garment, threatens a lion, here too with a sheep in his mouth. In the historiated initial just below is the second narrative, David raising his sword to decapitate Goliath. As introductory scenes of a David cycle, these subjects are not uncommon, having the most familiar analogue in the Tickhill Psalter of the early fourteenth century.[3] In the Tickhill

---

[1]   Cambridge, Fitzwilliam Museum MS 38–1950; see M. R. James and E. G. Millar, *The Bohun Manuscripts* (London, 1936) pp. 51–9, with reproductions of all illustrations; F. Wormald and P. Giles, *A Descriptive Catalogue of the Additional Illuminated manuscripts in the Fitzwilliam Museum Acquired between 1895 and 1979 (excluding the McClean Collection* (Cambridge, 1982), II, pp. 431–6; L. F. Sandler, *Gothic Manuscripts 1285–1385*, A Survey of Manuscripts Illuminated in the British Isles, V, ed. J. J. G. Alexander (London, 1986), II, pp. 159–61.

[2]   On Bohun heraldry, see L. F. Sandler, 'Lancastrian Heraldry in the Bohun Manuscripts', in *The Lancastrian Court, Proceedings of the 2001 Harlaxton Symposium*, Harlaxton Medieval Studies, XIII, ed. Jenny Stratford (Donington, 2003), pp. 221–32. In that article I identified the royal arms as those of Richard II and his heir apparent, as-yet-unborn, but since then Elizabeth Danbury and Adrian Ailes, whose advice I acknowledge with gratitude, have persuaded me that identification of the arms as those of the father and brother of John of Gaunt is much more likely.

Psalter, however, the scenes of David and the bear and the lion are in the bas-de-page, under the Tree of Jesse that faces the opening page of the text.

The bas-de-page of the Bohun Psalter (Plate 2) is filled with an altogether different kind of pictorial narrative, secular, genre, and parodic, and unique in this manuscript, which otherwise contains only Old Testament subjects from the life of David presented in framed miniatures and historiated initials, and a Last Judgment illustrating the Penitential Psalms at the end of the volume. Except for the first page there are no further bas-de-page illustrations. The psalter is a small manuscript, and the entire bas-de-page area is not more than two and a half inches or so across. Yet in this small space there is considerable highly specific detail.

Like most pictorial narratives, and of course like written words, the sequence of episodes should be read from left to right, and, in general, the composition is processional, all the figures being shown in profile. On the far left, using the page frame as a doorway, an ape enters the scene holding a blackened bowl, which was probably originally silver.[4] Next, on a river bank, an ape with a basket on his back and a fishing rod in his hands approaches the stream, the fishing line with its gold sinker dipping into the water above the head of one of two black fish, and the hook already in the fish's mouth. Then, on the opposite bank, an ape guts the fish laid on a table-top. Next, the fish – at least by inference, the fish – is boiled in a golden pot by two ape-cooks, the one behind the cauldron steadying the legs of the other, who has turned a somersault in order to blow on the flames of the fire. Finally, an ape holding another blackened dish leaves the scene, walking out of the picture in the same way as the first ape had entered.

The only image of its kind, in a prominent position on the opening page of the manuscript, the bas-de-page narrative commands special attention and warrants close study in an effort to 'unpack' its multiple and layered meanings. To this end, the picture may be considered under a number of headings: first, the activity, second the position of the image in the bas de page and at the beginning of the book, and finally, the protagonists in the pictorial narrative.

Fishing and Cooking

In the Bohun psalter vignettes, fishing is depicted as a genre activity devoid of overt symbolic content. Fishing images, as distinct from symbolic, didactic, or heraldic images of single fish, appear in manuscripts in a variety of contexts, including the non-marginal: in the form of miniatures or historiated initials with

---

3   The New York Public Library, MS Spencer 26, f. 6v; see D. D. Egbert, *The Tickhill Psalter and Related Manuscripts* (New York, 1940); also J. J. G. Alexander, J. H. Marrow and L. F. Sandler, *Splendor of the Word, Medieval and Renaissance Illuminated Manuscripts at The New York Public Library* (New York, 2005), no. 41, with more recent bibliography.

4   I thank Dr Stella Panayatova, Keeper of Manuscripts and Printed Books at the Fitzwilliam Museum, for confirming that the black of the bowl has a metallic sheen.

illustrations of biblical subjects or lives of saints, for example, the disciples Peter and Andrew netting fish on the Sea of Galilee;[5] or elaborate calendar scenes developed from the zodiacal sign of Pisces;[6] or bestiary illustrations.[7] Nevertheless, compared to images of hunting, an activity that comes automatically to mind as the counterpart of fishing, medieval fishing images are relatively few in number. In hunting scenes, especially those in the margins, both the hunters and the prey are endlessly varied; humans, both men and women, noble and peasant, as well as dogs, foxes, apes, and hybrids chase hares, stags, and birds; the hunters carry falcons, spears, bows and arrows, even clubs.[8] Hunting was both a necessity and a sport, and was engaged in by professional hunters, by peasants – often illegally – and, for pleasure, by noblemen and women.

Fishing, on the other hand, was a more socially compartmentalized activity.[9] In England, during the Middle Ages, most fishing was commercial, either on the open sea or along the coasts or in estuaries; the salt-water catch was dried or salted; the fishermen were professionals, and the fish were caught in nets. Freshwater fishing too was primarily in the hands of professionals; the main source was the fish-pond, or the mill pond, not the free-flowing river or stream; and again nets were used.[10] Fish was expensive, and was consumed mainly by the aristocracy and the higher clergy. Both these classes replaced the meat in their diet with fish on Wednesdays, Fridays, and Saturdays, and throughout Lent, while the less affluent had to make do with cereals and beans.

[5] See Matthew 4:18, Mark 1:16. For an English example of the 1390s see the Carmelite Missal (London, BL, Add. MS 44892), f. 162, historiated initial for the Introit of the Vigil of St Andrew, with, in addition, a bas-de-page vignette of young men netting fish; see M. Rickert, *The Reconstructed Carmelite Missal* (London, 1952), pp. 111–12, and pl. xxvi.

[6] For an early fourteenth-century English example, see the Queen Mary Psalter (London, BL, Royal MS 2 B. vii, f.73); see G. F. Warner, *Queen Mary's Psalter* (London, 1912), pl. 124.

[7] Although bestiary texts treat numerous fish, most often only one or two illustrations are supplied: the first is usually a composite image depicting many varieties of fish; the second is a pictorial narrative showing sailors landing on the back of the whale (*aspidelone*); for examples, see A. Payne, *Medieval Beasts* (London, 1990), pp. 92–5.

[8] Marginal hunting scenes of all kinds are listed and reproduced under the actors – man, etc. – in L. M. C. Randall, *Images in the Margins of Gothic Manuscripts* (Berkeley, 1966).

[9] On fishing in medieval England, see the following: R. C. Hofmann, 'Fishing for Sport in Medieval Europe: New Evidence', *Speculum*, 60 (1985), pp. 877–92; C. Cyer, 'The Consumption of Fresh-Water Fish in Medieval England', in *Medieval Fish, Fisheries and Fishponds in England*, BAR British Series, 182, ed. M. Aston (Oxford, 1988), pp. 27–38; and G. Lucas, 'A Medieval Fishery on Whittlesea Mere, Cambridgeshire', *Medieval Archaeology*, 42 (1998), pp. 19–44.

[10] For a well-known representation of fish nets in a mill pond see the fourteenth-century English Luttrell Psalter (London, BL, Add. MS 42130), f. 181; see J. Backhouse, *The Luttrell Psalter* (London, 1989), pl. 30, for a colour illustration).

Angling, that is, fishing with a rod and hook, line and sinker, as represented in the Bohun psalter, was uneconomical in terms of commercial food production. It was a sport enjoyed by those by those who had leisure and access to communally or privately held waters. Rod fishing was recognized by medieval writers as providing triple rewards: real food that could be consumed, pleasure in the sport and the skill required for its pursuit, and spiritual refreshment gained from solitude, concentration, and contemplation.[11] Angling scenes appear occasionally in the margins of thirteenth- and fourteenth-century manuscripts, as Lilian Randall's invaluable survey shows.[12] The anglers are either 'ordinary' humans, or else apes parodying humans (Plate 3), and unusually, hybrids (Plate 4). None of the fishermen is identifiably aristocratic. Some of the components of these marginalia have parallels in the Bohun narrative, for instance, the basket to hold the catch (Plate 3). However, I know of no other case in which the activity of fishing is expanded with scenes of cooking the catch,[13] even though in a number of manuscripts showing apes a picture story is created by the addition of a cat or fox stealing the catch from the basket.[14]

Unlike simpler marginal vignettes, the bustling activity in the Bohun psalter emphasizes the tangible results of fishing, not just the catch, but the stages of its preparation for human consumption as food for the table. The silver dishes and golden pot suggest the table of a noble person, like the destined Bohun reader/owner of this book. The fisherman and cooks however suggest the trained servant class, members, so to speak, of the lord's household, like the 'Benoyt de la Quisyne', who was bequeathed one mark on the death in 1361 of Humphrey the sixth earl of Hereford, an earlier member of the Bohun family.[15]

Since cooking is part of the pictorial narrative, the Bohun bas-de-page might be considered in the light of the most famous fourteenth-century English manuscript scenes of food preparation, those in the Luttrell Psalter (Plates 5–8), where Geoffrey Luttrell's servants roast chickens and a suckling pig on a spit, stir stew in

[11] See Hofmann, 'Fishing for Sport', esp. pp. 897–9.
[12] Randall, *Images in the Margins*, lists about thirty instances of marginal fishing as compared to hundreds of scenes of hunting.
[13] Some bestiary illustrations of the whale (see above, n. 7) show the sailors camped on the whale's back fanning a fire and cooking in a cauldron; presumably their meal consists of fish. For a composition analogous to that of the Bohun psalter, but with human actors, see the illustration of the whale in the bestiary cycle of the early fourteenth-century Queen Mary's Psalter (London, BL, Royal MS 2 B vii, f 111), reproduced in Payne, *Medieval Beasts*, p. 94.
[14] See Randall, *Images in the Margins*, s.v. Ape fishing, Man and fish, Man fishing, and figs 44, 45, 47.
[15] For Humphrey's will, see J. Nichols, *A Collection of all the Wills now Known to be Extant of the Kings and Queens of England, Princes and Princesses of Wales, and every Branch of the Blood Royal from the Reign of William the Conqueror to that of Henry the Seventh* (London, 1780), pp. 44–56.

three pots, mince greens, grind spices in a mortar, chop the meat on a cutting board, put it in dishes, and serve the food to the Luttrell family.[16] In the Luttrell Psalter, as in the Bohun psalter, servants work for their lord, who is physically present in the final scene of the Luttrell cycle. Michael Camille suggested that the Luttrell narrative represented a series of 'real' events that culminated in a celebratory Epiphany feast.[17] The Bohun cycle should probably not be interpreted as referring to a specific meal, although the fact that it consists of fish, not flesh, does suggest the Lenten season of self-examination and penance, a time of greatest awareness of the spiritual benefits of recitation of the Psalms.

The Luttrell Psalter food preparation cycle begins on a page whose last line is verse 4 of the second part of Vulgate Psalm 113: 'The idols of the gentiles are silver and gold, the works of the hands of men' and the first scene is directly under the phrase 'opera manuum hominum' (Plate 5). This is a bit of verbal-pictorial word-image play, which responds to the words of the biblical text with images significant to the owner of the book. And the last scene of the cycle (Plate 8), the formal start of the meal, with Geoffrey Luttrell raising his chalice-like cup to his lips, is, as Camille observed,[18] also calibrated with the last text line on the page, from Psalm 114, 'I will call on the name of the Lord', giving the feast a sacramental as well as a secular character.

The Bas-de-Page and the Book

No specific text-image interdependence is evident in the bas-de-page of the Bohun psalter. But the position of the series of fishing and cooking scenes at the beginning of the book is significant. Hunting scenes are often found on the first pages of manuscripts, genre vignettes apparently unrelated either to the sense or the words of the text. In an article of the 1970s however, Howard Helsinger glossed the hunting scenes that appear in the lower margins of the Beatus pages of medieval psalters as allegorical images of the struggle between good and evil.[19] From this vantage point, depictions of fishing too might communicate spiritual truths through the disguise of the secular. And of course, the fish, if not fishing, is one of the earliest symbols of Christ. On one level of meaning then, the fish isolated in the center of the Bohun bas-de-page, about to be gutted, could have elicited associations with the suffering body of Christ, as the fish on the table in

---

[16] The vast literature on the Luttrell Psalter (London, BL, Add. MS 42130) has now been augmented by Michelle Brown's study, with extensive bibliography, which accompanies a full-colour facsimile of the manuscript published by the British Library: M. Brown, *The Luttrell Psalter, A Facsimile* (London, 2006).

[17] M. Camille, *Mirror in Parchment, The Luttrell Psalter and the Making of Medieval England* (Chicago, 1998), pp. 86–9.

[18] Camille, *Mirror in Parchment*, p. 89.

[19] H. Helsinger, 'Images on the Beatus Pages of some Medieval Psalters', *The Art Bulletin*, 53 (1971), pp. 161–76.

scenes of the Last Supper or the Supper at Emmaus alludes to the Sacrament of the Eucharist.[20] Indeed, the Christian Saviour is present in the miniature in the upper part of the page too, in the guise of the central stream of water from which two facing sheep are drinking – a symbolic image of the fountain of life, over which the axial angel of the Lord hovers.[21] The water that separates the two scenes of the Old Testament David has no scriptural basis; it is a multi-functioning device of the artist that doubles the meanings of the miniature itself, and associates the image formally and thematically with the vignettes in the bas-de-page, in this way bringing the two pictorial parts of the page together into a single polyphonic composition.[22]

Helsinger's study of marginal hunting scenes was limited to those on the Beatus pages of psalters. In fact, however, hunting scenes are common on the opening pages of all sorts of late thirteenth- and fourteenth-century manuscripts – Apocalypses, Aristotles, Golden Legends, and romances, for instance.[23] The positioning of such images at the beginning of texts suggests that their meaning relates to books as wholes, that is, to books of any and all types. How can scenes of the hunt be relevant to the concept of the book? I agree in part with Helsinger that they must be understood as metaphors. But their 'lesson' applies to the book and its text as a whole. Put simply, just as you hunt or fish to catch your prey, whether

---

20   See M. Rubin, *Corpus Christi, The Eucharist in Late Medieval Culture* (Cambridge, 1991), 302–16. For pictorial images of Eucharistic fish at the Last Supper and the Supper at Emmaus, see the early fourteenth-century English Psalter of Robert de Lisle (London, BL, Arundel MS 83, ff. 124v and 133), reproduced in colour in L. F. Sandler, *The Psalter of Robert de Lisle in the British Library* (London, 1983, 1999), plates 12, 19.

21   See the wide-ranging discussion of the Fountain of Life by Paul Underwood, 'The Fountain of Life in Manuscripts of the Gospels', in *Dumbarton Oaks Papers*, 5 (1950), pp. 43–138. Based on scriptural passages such as Proverbs 14: 27, Psalms 35: 10, John 4: 14, and Apocalypse 21: 6, Ambrose, among other early Christian writers, said, *Erat fons qui irrigaret paradisum. Qui fons nisi Dominus Jesus-Christus. Fons vitae aeternae est* (*De paradiso* 3: 13).

22   If all the pictorial components are seen as constituting a single entity, it is tempting to identify the two young men seated within the supports of the upper architectural frame – one facing inward and the other outward – as human counterparts of the two apes on the far left and far right of the bas-de-page.

23   An almost random search for examples yields the following (not including psalters or other devotional books): Apocalypse in Anglo-Norman, England, late thirteenth century (Oxford, New Coll., MS 65, f. 1); Aristotle, *Metaphysica and Meteora*, England, c. 1310 (Paris, BNF, MS lat. 6299, f. 2); John Duns Scotus, Commentary on the *Sentences* of Peter Lombard, French scribe, English illuminator, c. 1320–30 (Paris, BNF, MS lat. 3114[1], f. 1); Biblical Concordance, France, first quarter fourteenth century (Vendôme, Bibl. municipale, MS 3, f. 2); Gregory, *Moralia in Job*, France, early fourteenth century (Dijon, Bibl. municipale, MS 172, f. 1); *Roman de la rose*, France, c. 1315–25 (New York, Pierpont Morgan Lib., MS M. 372, f. 1); *Legenda aurea*, France, early fourteenth century (Le Mans, Bibl. municipale, MS 2, f. 1).

flesh, fowl or fish, you hunt for the 'meat' of the text, and just as your catch provides sustenance, so does the text of the book. And in this connection, the image in the Bohun psalter is doubly meaningful. Angling is an activity of quiet concentration, in which pleasure comes from the pursuit as well as the end result of catching the fish. So too with reading and studying the psalms. Cooking also provides sustenance; in the case of its representation in this book, the cooked fish is a metaphor of spiritual and intellectual food. Indeed, it is important to note that the Bohun bas-de-page does not actually include an eating scene. The anglers and the cooks are inviting the reader to the feast, and as he or she turns from page to page, the meal is served.

Mary Carruthers has discussed pictorial images of hunting and fishing in terms of searching the treasure-house of memory;[24] she cites an eleventh century monk's instructions for meditation: 'Be seated within your cell as though in paradise; cast to the rear of your memory everything distracting, becoming alert and focussed on your thoughts as a good fisherman is on the fish. One pathway to this state is through reciting the Psalms; do not neglect this'.[25] The author assumed that his audience would know the Psalms by heart; their recitation was the first step to meditation. This kind of ability to recall the Psalms is not so certain for a lay person at the end of the fourteenth century. Undoubtedly the owner of the Bohun psalter had heard others recite the Psalms, and had recited them with others, but when it came to private, individual recitation as part of devotional practice, *reading* from a psalter text at hand was an aid, if not a necessity. Consequently, I would conclude that in the Bohun psalter, as in other manuscripts where hunting scenes appear at the beginning of the book, the pictorial metaphor is there to encourage to the act of reading, as a first step in digesting the text, and meditating upon it. The book, this same Bohun book, was itself the treasure-house from which food for thought could be extracted.

Ape-Actors

The actors of the Bohun psalter fish story are apes.[26] Marginal apes are human surrogates because they imitate human behaviour, but they are often parodists, casting the human activities in which they are engaged into a negative light, or turning

---

[24] M. Carruthers, *The Book of Memory, A Study of Memory in Medieval Culture* (Cambridge, 1990), esp. pp. 246–7; the design of the dust-jacket of Carruthers' book is based on the fish-hook and fish-swallowing-fish border of the *memoria* of St Lawrence in the well-known fifteenth-century Dutch Hours of Catherine of Cleves (New York, Pierpont Morgan Lib., MS M. 917, p. 266).

[25] M. Carruthers, *The Craft of Thought, Meditation, Rhetoric, and the Making of Images, 400–1200* (Cambridge, 1998), p. 112, Carruthers' translation from Bruno of Querfort's account of the meditational advice of St. Romuald of Camaldoli.

[26] The fundamental study is H. W. Janson, *Apes and Ape Lore in the Middle Ages and the Renaissance* (London, 1952).

serious activities upside down and making them a source of laughter. Ape schools make fun of professors and students; ape bishops make fun of religious practice. Apes are 'low' as opposed to 'high' and indeed their earthy connections are emphasized by the intensity of pictorial focus on their tail-less rear ends, and the frequency with which they are represented in contorted or inverted positions (Plate 9). The question then is why are apes, rather than humans, fishing and cooking in the Bohun psalter? It is certainly amusing to see naked simians acting like human beings, but more can be said. First of all, these are *Bohun* apes, that is, members of the Bohun *familia*. Their activities are servile, and it is significant that the entire cycle of events is set between shields with the arms of the Bohun family as earls of Hereford, Essex and Northampton. The position of the Bohun arms framing the bas-de-page scenes is as calculated an aspect of the page design as the heraldic framework of royal and Lancastrian arms around the upper scene, in which David, the future king of Israel, plays such an important role.

But why apes and not human fishermen and cooks? Can further layers of meaning be recovered? This question can be addressed by examining the representation of apes in other Bohun manuscripts, in particular, the Egerton psalter and hours in the British Library.[27] The Egerton volume was begun around 1360, either for Humphrey de Bohun, the sixth earl of Hereford and Essex, or his nephew, Humphrey, the seventh and last Bohun earl (d. 1373), and completed in the 1380s, probably for Humphrey's heirs. Like the other Bohun manuscripts, the Egerton psalter and hours was designed, written, and illustrated by scribes and artists who worked solely for the Bohun family in their chief residence at Pleshey Castle, Essex. We know that these workers were considered as members of the Bohun *familia*.[28]

The Egerton volume is incomparably rich in its pictorial and decorative program: every psalm and every subdivision of the hours of the Virgin has a historiated initial with an elaborate marginal extension, and all the main divisions of the text not only have large historiated initials but elaborate, often historiated borders that run the full length of the page. The immediate surroundings of the smaller initials are characterized by a wealth of figural and heraldic imagery embedded in the marginal extensions, images that demand reading in conjunction both with the

---

[27] London, BL, Egerton MS 3277; see British Library, *Catalogue of Additions to the Manuscripts 1936–1945* (London, 1970), pp. 376–81; Sandler, *Gothic Manuscripts*, II, pp. 151–4.

[28] On the Bohun artists and their societal position, see L. F. Sandler, 'A Note on the Illuminators of the Bohun Manuscripts', *Speculum*, 60 (1985), pp. 364–72, the identification of the artists cited in the documents with specific illuminators of the surviving manuscripts later amended, see L. F. Sandler, 'Political Imagery in the Bohun Manuscripts', in *English Manuscript Studies 1100–1700, Volume 10, Decoration and Illustration in Medieval English Manuscripts*, ed. A. S. G. Edwards (London, 2002), p. 151, n. 80.

historiations within the initial frames and the words of the text. For instance, in the margin of the page with Psalm 101, the defeated Jean le Bon of France hands his sword to the victorious Edward III after the battle of Poitiers in 1356, and below Edward, Jean reappears, his sword restored to him after the Treaty of Brétigny in 1360.[29] The image in the margin responds to the historiation of the initial, which shows Shimei, who had cursed and thrown stones at David (II Kings 16: 6) kneeling before the king to ask his pardon, and David, with his sword, raising him up and forgiving him (II Kings 19: 16–23). The juxtaposed images in the margin and within the initial project a chivalric concept of noblesse oblige: the great ruler is forgiving toward his enemies.[30]

Among the marginal images of the Egerton psalter and hours are numerous animal actors. It is certain that a good many of them are surrogates for specific human beings, animal nicknames so to speak, the particular animal being based on the coats of arms born by the individual – as the lion of Edward III – or word play on the individual's name, or the individual's personality or physical traits.[31] Adjacent to the text of Psalm 41, for instance, is a hybrid bishop-crane with his beak full of gold balls, his bird 'hands' wielding a broom while clutching more gold balls. He is sweeping up gold and gobbling it down. The reference is, I suggest, to a wealthy bishop, a collector of the 'gold' of ecclesiastical benefices, perhaps William of Wykeham, bishop of Winchester, known as the greatest pluralist of the second half of the fourteenth century.[32]

Among the animals that make more than one appearance in the Egerton manuscript are apes, once with a bear (Plate 10), and another time, with a bear and a lion (Plate 11). It is my belief that these animals represent particular individuals in disguise. The first clue is the bear, since he is shown twice as a scribe, first, in fact, as a kind of scribal colophon at the end of the first text gathering of the manuscript, where he stands and writes on a scroll, 'screbere piers, martin et robinet', a Latin line that includes a bilingual pun, the English word 'bear' (Plate 12).[33] The activity and the position of the bear in the text suggest a reference to the scribe of this manuscript, that is, a scribe working for the Bohuns. The second writing bear

29 London, BL, Egerton MS 3277, f. 68v; see Sandler, 'Political Imagery', p. 125, pl. 5. I owe the identification of the lower king as a second representation of Jean le Bon to Ann Payne. The figure has previously been identified as Charles le Mauvais of Navarre or Richard II of England; see Sandler, 'Political Imagery', p. 124.

30 On the contemporary meaning of this and other marginal images in the manuscript, see Sandler, 'Political Imagery', pp. 114–53.

31 See Sandler, 'Political Imagery', esp. pp. 116–7.

32 See Sandler, 'Political Imagery', pl. 16 on p. 142, p. 143 and notes 70–71.

33 On the writing bear, and other bears in BL, Egerton MS 3277, see L. F. Sandler, 'Bared: The Writing Bear in the British Library Bohun Psalter', in *Tributes to Jonathan J. G. Alexander, The Making and Meaning of Illuminated Medieval & Renaissance Manuscripts, Art & Architecture*, ed. S. L'Engle and G. B. Guest (London, 2006), pp. 269–80.

(he is writing musical notation) is coupled with an ape with a money bag and an owl (Plate 10). The ape-owl pair is the visual echo of a widely circulated couplet, 'Pay me no less than an ape and an owl and an ass'.[34] The ape is a worker for hire, a servant. What kind of servant? I suggest that if the writing bear alludes to the scribe of the manuscript, then his companion, the ape, refers to the artist.

For the Middle Ages, artists could be conceived of as apes, because, like apes, they imitated nature. Such imitation was scorned by theologians up to the end of the thirteenth century as only a simulacrum.[35] Simulacra of nature, that is, works of art, were created, to paraphrase Alexander Neckham, by 'laboring apes', 'prompted by a vile desire for monetary gain'.[36] But this negative attitude was changing in the course of the fourteenth century. As H. W. Janson reported, to Boccaccio, for instance, *simiae naturae* were admirable, *because* they strove to come as close as possible to a great ideal, as Christians strove to imitate Christ.[37] It seems to me however that the representations of the artist in the Egerton Psalter in the guise of apes are still somewhat denigrating, making fun of an animal surrogate for a human being in the same way as the goosing of the scribal bear by a hybrid goose makes fun of scribes (Plate 12). Nevertheless, the artist who painted the ape-artists and the bear-scribes was self-conscious in a sophisticated way about his position and his profession. And while he might have been a 'vile' servant he was also in a position of intimate contact and easy familiarity with his master.

This servant-master relationship is laid out in the marginal image from the Egerton Psalter in which, amidst the foliated extensions of the initial for Psalm 42, three animals, a bear, an ape, and a lion, play together (Plate 11). The lion, of course, is the king of the beasts; that he joins in the game of the bear and the ape, suggests that we should see the 'lord' as allowing his servants to play with him, or himself to play with them. And the lord referred to in this case is a Bohun lord, taking the disguise of his heraldic device, the golden lion. In fact, in contemporary political writing, for instance, John Ergom's commentary on the prophecies of John of Bridlington, the Bohun earls were called 'fulvi glaucique leones', gleaming and golden-colored lions.[38]

Now, to come back to the apes in the Bohun psalter in the Fitzwilliam Museum, if they are Bohun servants in parodic disguise, are they simply surrogates for the Bohun fishermen and cooks? Or, like the apes in the Egerton Psalter, is there any way in which they too can be understood as Bohun artists? I think we

---

34   See M. Camille, 'At the Edge of the Law: An Illustrated Register of Writs in the Pierpont Morgan Library', in *England in the Fourteenth Century, Proceedings of the 1991 Harlaxton Symposium*, ed. N. Rogers (Stamford, 1993), p. 10 and pl. 8, with further bibliography.

35   Janson, *Apes and Ape Lore*, pp. 288–9.

36   Cited in Janson, *Apes and Ape Lore*, p. 289.

37   Janson, *Apes and Ape Lore*, 290–3.

38   See Sandler, 'Political Imagery', p. 116.

can make a case for this. The ape gutting the fish on a table in the central vignette calls to mind the preparation of the pages of a book, the cutting, stretching and scraping of the parchment, as pictured in the well-known historiated initial cycle of the mid-thirteenth-century Hamburg Bible (Plate 13);[39] it is the first stage of making the physical book, to be followed by the succeeding episodes in which cooking pots and serving dishes may also call up associations with the work of makers of manuscripts, as depicted, for example, in the illustration for the entry on colour in the fourteenth-century English universal encyclopedia, *Omne bonum*, showing an artist with his pots of colour (Plate 14).[40]

The painter of the first page of the Fitzwilliam Psalter can be identified as an Augustinian friar, John de Teye, who was mentioned in the 1361 will of Humphrey de Bohun, sixth earl of Hereford and Essex, as 'nostre luminour', and granted ten pounds to pray for his lord.[41] He was still active as an illuminator in the service of the Bohuns at Pleshey as late as 1384, and perhaps even a few year later.[42] The remaining illustrated pages of the manuscript were painted by an anonymous associate who worked with John de Teye on almost all the other surviving Bohun books.[43] It seems worth noticing in this connection that the fishing and cooking

[39] Copenhagen, Kongelige Bibl., MS Gl. kgl. S. 4 2°, three volumes, I, f. 137v, II, ff. 183, 195, III, ff. 165, 208; see E. Petersen, *Living Words & Luminous Pictures, Medieval Book Culture in Denmark* (Copenhagen, 1999), pp. 7–8, with color figs. and A. A. Björnbo, 'Ein Beitrag zum Werdegang der mittelalterlichen Pergamenthandschriften', *Zeitschrift für Bücherfreunde*, 11 (1907/8), pp. 329–35. It may be suggested that the gutting of the fish might also have some connection with fourteenth- and fifteenth-century images and texts metaphorically treating the body of Christ suffering on the Cross as a parchment stretched on a board, wounded by the pen of the scribe, for example, the anonymous fourteenth century *Carta celestie hereditatis*, 'þe parchemyn of þis hevenli chartre is neiþir of scheep ne of calf: but it is þe bodi & þe blessid skyn of oure lord ihesu loomb þat nevere was spottid wiþ wem of synne & was þere nevere skyn of scheep neiþir of calfe so sore & hard streined on þe teynture eiþer harewe of eny parchemyn makere as was þe blessid bodi and skyn of oure lord ihesu crist' (Cambridge, University Lib. MS Ff. 6. 34, f. 72); for this and related 'Charters of Christ', see M. C. Spaulding, *The Middle English Charters of Christ* (Bryn Mawr, 1914), esp. pp. xl–li, 100–2, and Carruthers, *Craft of Thought*, pp. 102–3.

[40] *Omne bonum* (London, BL, Royal MSS 6 E. vi–vii), 6 E vi, f. 329; see L. F. Sandler, *Omne bonum, A Fourteenth-Century Encyclopedia of Universal Knowledge* (London, 1996), II, p. 117.

[41] 'Nous devisons auxint a frere Johan de Teye n're luminour x li. a prier pur nous'; Nichols, *Wills*, p. 50.

[42] See Sandler, 'Note on the Illuminators', 365.

[43] On this collaboration, see L. F. Sandler, *The Lichtenthal Psalter and the Manuscript Patronage of the Bohun Family* (London, 2004), pp. 20–4, 126–9, and for list of manuscripts, pp. 163–5; for a list of the Bohun manuscripts, dating their production and identifying the hands of the artists somewhat differently, see L. Dennison, *The Stylistic Sources, Dating and Development of the Bohun Workshop, ca. 1340–1400*, Ph.D. diss., University of London, 1988, esp. pp. 341–3.

in the Fitzwilliam psalter bas-de-page are the work of not one but two apes. By inscribing himself, perhaps along with his fellow painter, on the first folio of the manuscript in ape disguise, John de Teye left a unique record of the artist's role in the creation of the book.

In sum, the images on the Beatus page of the Fitzwilliam Bohun psalter played an active role in the spiritual life of the owner of the book, encouraging reading and meditation on the text by means of the pictorial narrative of the bas-de-page; they also proclaimed the Bohun position in the sacred and secular economy through heraldry, on the one hand equating the family, with its royal ancestry, with the royal line of the biblical David, and on the other, placing the Bohun servants within the powerful 'embrace' of their lord. The images themselves provided rich materials for Christian meditation: David-as-Christ, the King; the Fountain of Life-as-Christ, the Saviour; and the Fish-as-Christ, the Sacrifice and Redeemer. And finally, the Bohun artist, by representing himself, even symbolically, established his personal presence as creator, his ape disguise the counterpart of the heraldic charges that stand for the noble Bohun family as owner of the book. Through art at least, the servant truly became the master.

Questioning Signs and Symbols:
Their Meaning and Interpretation

† CHRISTA GRÖSSINGER

Medieval people lived in a world filled with symbols, many of which were well known to them. Knowing that, are we in the twentieth and twenty-first centuries in danger of mis- and over-interpretation, in a misguided enthusiasm to find meaning in every detail? We read obscure literature which ordinary citizens in the Middle Ages would never have had access to, we forget that people were largely illiterate, and that priests, who were to instruct their congregations, were not well educated. Thus, we become obsessed with looking for clues to 'hidden' meanings, using theories relevant to us but alien to the medieval mind.

Erwin Panofsky coined the term 'disguised symbolism', and sought meaning in all reality, trying to decipher it by application of an appropriate humanist text. The reader is lulled into accepting his interpretations, since he backs them up with erudite scholarship. It all reads like a fascinating detective story. The prime example of the weakness of Panofsky's methods is the so-called Arnolfini Portrait, 1434, (London, National Gallery) where according to his study, Jan van Eyck had to be an extremely erudite artist.[1] Jan van Eyck may have been a very special artist, close to Duke Phillip, and more educated than other artists. But even he, as it turns out, did not give the profound and agonized attention to the content of the picture that Panofsky and many others expended in trying to decipher its symbolism. As technical tests have revealed, some of the major symbols are not as Panofsky claimed; they were added later. Neither the dog nor the chandelier appears in the underdrawing although, according to Panofsky, they contained essential marriage symbolism.[2] Furthermore, the painting is not a marriage portrait at all, and the male sitter is not Giovanni di Arrigo Arnolfini, with his wife Jeanne Cenami, but probably his cousin Giovanni di Nicolao Arnolfini, who was married by 1434. Giovanni di Arrigo Arnolfini did not marry until 1447.[3]

[1]   E. Panofsky, *Early Netherlandish Painting* (London, 1971), pp. 201–3.
[2]   Other objects not found in the underdrawing were the discarded shoes, the single-lighted candle, oranges, beads, the image of St Margaret, all of which were added at a later stage. R. Billinge and L. Campbell, 'The Infra-red Reflectograms of Jan van Eyck's Portrait of Giovanni(?) Arnolfini and his Wife Giovanna Cenami(?)', *National Gallery Technical Bulletin*, 16 (1995), pp. 47–60.

Although Panofsky's errors have been recognized, his influence is still potent, and some art historians accuse each other of following in his footsteps in spite of their denials. Craig Harbison criticizes Barbara Lane's method of relating all objects closely to a complicated liturgy, with the result that even the most common religious themes, like the Nativity and Adoration are engulfed by complicated constructs to fit contrived associations with that liturgy.[4] He asks whether the artists and the congregation really considered such theological implications when looking at a religious narrative; if they and their patrons were so concerned with them, why, for instance, did they not illustrate the mass more directly in the Last Supper? There were of course commissions – Bouts' altarpiece of the Last Supper in St Peter's, Louvain, for example – which required artists to have been instructed in a specific symbolic programme. But such complicated iconography was rare. Generally speaking, artists would use available patterns, without thinking too hard about their theological and liturgical connotations. In spite of an age of strong personal devotion, church attendance was poor; most people only went to take communion at Easter, and knew little about the sacraments. Priests had to teach their congregations the sacraments and church dogma, but it had to be done simply and clearly, not by complicated and unfamiliar symbols. Many images were based, therefore, on emotional piety rather than knowledge.

Symbols can be double-sided, ambiguous, or have a multi-layered meaning. For example, Bathsheba (Samuel II, ch. 11), who entered into an adulterous relationship with King David, could be seen both as the flirtatious seductress, the tempting Eve, and, having purified herself in the bath, as the spiritual Ecclesia.[5] Different interpretations coexist, and in all cases, both the context and the period have to be considered. Symbols can seldom be slotted into a specific compartment. Artists used workshop patterns, and took inspiration from other works around them. Personal or anecdotal touches might be added, but the narrative remained easily comprehensible.

When Panofsky came to the works of Bosch he gave up in dismay: an artist, thoroughly at home in the medieval tradition, might not in fact be open to decipherment from the standpoint of post-medieval philosophical texts. It has not stopped other art historians having their field day with Bosch, each propounding a pet theory. Foremost was Wilhelm Fränger who made Bosch into a secret heretic, and the high priest of the Adamite sect.[6] Dorinda Dixon believed in

---

3   L. Campbell, *National Gallery Catalogues, The Fifteenth Century Netherlandish Schools* (London, 1998), pp. 196–8.

4   C. Harbison, 'Review of Barbara Lane's The altar and the altarpiece. Sacramental themes in Early Netherlandish Painting', *Simiolus*, 15 (1985), pp. 221–5.

5   T. Kren, *A Masterpiece Reconstructed. The Hours of Louis XII* (London, 2005), pp. 49–51.

6   W. Fränger, *Hieronymus Bosch*, trans. H. Sebba (Newark, N.J., 1999).

Bosch's knowledge of alchemical methods, Cuttler in his witchcraft, Boczkowska in lunar symbolism, and Bax interpreted his work with the help of Dutch proverbs and sayings.[7] Only in the age of Enlightenment was Bosch disregarded altogether. To us, his works have become iconographical puzzles. People at the time did not have such problems: Philip II could not get enough of Bosch's works, and they were avidly copied, or recreated in like manner in the sixteenth century. His paintings are full of monsters, of half-animal/half-human creatures, and of humans in hell fire, as if the medieval world of marginal art had been lifted into the high art of paintings. This medieval world often resists modern ideas of interpretation.

Much time is spent trying to interpret the drolleries of medieval manuscripts. Are they symbolic of the text or is their purpose simply to divert? Do they remind the reader of folly and sin? Some examples from manuscripts illustrate the uncertainties of symbolic meaning. A manuscript from Bruges, before 1388 (Douai, Bibliothèque Municipale, MS 132, f. 129r), a gradual in Latin, has the resurrection as its main scene (Plate 1).[8] Around the margins are: on the right, an archer shooting upwards at a feather-hatted bird-man in the ivy border above; in the bottom margin a bird-catcher drawing in his net, with two free birds being enticed by two caged birds; and the left border has a thrush sitting on top of another ivy border. It is quite possible that the musical text inspired the artist to include the birds. The right hand border can hardly be seen as symbolic of the resurrection; while the scene in the bottom margin would more readily suggest Christ's entombment. Are such interpretations justified or a misguided attempt to make a theory fit? At first glance, these border illuminations bring to mind associations with later artists: the bird-man suggests the figure in the left wing of Bosch's triptych of the Temptation of St Anthony (Lisbon, Museo Antiga), and the bird-catcher evokes Pieter Bruegel the Elder's later Landscape with a Bird Catcher. This latter picture may indicate that the illuminator's object was to create a realistic scene of late fourteenth-century Bruges, and not to convey complicated symbolism.

A Book of Hours with lively, imaginative drolleries is a manuscript made in Ghent, c. 1315–25 (Baltimore, Walters Art Gallery, MS W82). Folio 184 shows the Murder of the Innocents within the initial D of the Hours of the Virgin. The subject is Herod enthroned, and before him, a soldier holding a bleeding child he has killed (Plate 2). In complete contrast to this gruesome scene, there is also com-

[7]   L. Dixon, *Bosch* (London, 2003). C. Cuttler, 'Witchcraft in a work by Bosch', in *Bosch in Perspective,* ed. J. Snyder (Eglewood Cliffs, 1973), pp. 108–17. A. Boczkowska, 'The Crab, the Sun, the Moon and Venus: Studies in the Iconology of Hieronymus Bosch's Triptych The Garden of Earthly Delights', *Oud Holland,* 91 (1977), pp. 197–231; and 'The Lunar Symbolism of the Ship of Fools by Hieronymus Bosch', *Oud Holland,* 86 (1971), pp. 47–69. D. Bax, *Hieronymus Bosch, his Picture-Writing Deciphered,* trans. M. A. Bax-Botha (Rotterdam, 1978).

[8]   *Medieval Mastery. Book illumination from Charlemagne to Charles the Bold 800–1475,* eds L. Preedy and W. Noel (Leuven and Tournai, 2002), cat. no. 66.

edy, especially in the bottom margin, where two apes cater to a large owl dressed in a mitre being presented with a crozier, an obvious parody of the Church and its ceremonies. In the right hand border a noble youth with a falcon on his gloved hand balances on a tendril, while a dragon takes off from above his head. In the left margin, a hybrid figure, human but with furry paws, supports on its head the frame of the initial 'D', steadying it with his right hand.[9] Direct connections between illumination and text are obscure and dubious.

The Luttrell Psalter, c.1335 to 1345, invites symbolic interpretation because of its wealth of marginal scenes of life and hybrid monsters. According to Michael Camille, 'the designer of the babewyns did not place these 'folk' images haphazardly in the text but, as always, with some allusion, even on a metaphorical level, to the psalms'.[10] Half-human, half-animal creatures with tails he believes to represent the English, because by the fourteenth century the English were being satirized as having the tails of vipers, serpents or swine, as a result of Edward I's preparations for war against France in the 1290s: one example, folio 70, is a bald-headed figure with winged, monstrous body and a snake's tail.[11] The Scots were among those known to satirize the English, leading to the assertion that such tailed monsters were not just a formal device but had 'a social meaning for some viewers'; for example folio 149v, showing a hybrid man with club and shield, and a tail between his furry animal legs.

Are not these interpretations a case of reading too much into the images? The mythological hybrids, in particular, can be compared to those carved on misericords, where there is no textual context. Any specific interpretation must be hypothetical. Once prints were available to artists, even manuscript illuminators would copy their images without reference to the text.[12]

It has also been asserted that in the Luttrell Psalter the lack of merriment and paucity of food on the Luttrell table, at folio 208, may reflect the 'anxieties surrounding one particular family's spiritual and social status', or shortages in the land; but most depictions of meals in medieval manuscripts are, in any case, sparse.[13]

The illustrations of the lower margins, especially those showing everyday activities with direct and specific relationship to the text, have attracted attention. For example, it has been argued that the four oxen pulling the plough, at folio 170,

---

[9]   *Medieval Mastery*, cat. no. 54.
[10] Camille, *Mirror in Parchment: the Luttrell Psalter and the Making of Medieval England* (London, 1998), p. 243.
[11] Ibid., p. 294.
[12] E.g. John Rylands Library, Dutch MS 15, where prints by the Master of the Berlin Passion are used on ff. 54v and 57r. C. Grössinger, *Humour and Folly, In Secular and Profane Prints of Northern Europe 1430–1540* (London, 2002), pp. 24–5.
[13] Camille, *Mirror in Parchment*, pp. 87–9.

symbolize the four evangelists leading the way to salvation via the gospels.[14] Perhaps this scene should simply be accepted as a labour of the month, especially as several other labours are illustrated. A similar scene is found on the Lincoln misericords, c.1370, although there, two oxen and two horses pull the plough. The very common motif of a cat playing with a mouse has been thought, in the case of the Luttrell Psalter, folio 190, to symbolize Queen Isabella abusing either her lover Mortimer or royal power.[15] Symbols must be examined in their historical context, but it is difficult to believe that this widely-used motif should be linked to such a specific significance.

Just as marginal illuminations frame the sacred text and historiated initial, so misericord carvings surround the choir and altar. Misericords are closely related to the marginal illuminations of manuscripts. A repertory of lively, cavorting figures, hybrids and animals is at home in both media. Such subjects as centaurs shooting backwards, mermaids, harpies, and strange animals are well known from the bestiaries, and their symbolism is undisputed. What however, of the bawdy scenes and monsters strewn around the choir stalls? How much symbolic value should one allocate to them? Some of the choir stalls required a large number of misericords, and craftsmen were given plenty of scope to fill the spaces and create variety. Very rarely were misericords arranged according to a logical programme. The arrangement is random and many motifs and compositions were taken from whatever patterns were available to the workshops. Half-human monsters are perhaps to be viewed as no more than a reminder to clerics of humanity's part spiritual, part animal nature. English misericords are unique in requiring additional motifs for their supporters. Lions' heads were popular, often with protruding tongues. Did these lions' masks represent good or evil, or were they simply decorative?

Misericords seem to elicit highly imaginative interpretations. The Woman wheeled in a Three-Wheeled Barrow, in Ripon Cathedral, 1489 to 1494 (Plate 3) shows what can happen even when the iconography is known. This motif was copied from a print by the German printmaker known only as 'Master bxg'; it shows a woman, clasping her bottle, obviously too drunk to walk. In the print one can see that she has a goitre, a sign of stupidity, and a barren branch points to Carnival customs. It is obviously a derogative view of the woman. But she has been interpreted as the frail mother of St Cuthman whom he pushed in a wheelbarrow in Steyning, Sussex; when the wheelbarrow broke, he stopped and built a church.[16] Why would a German print that was widely copied, even in Poland, represent such a specific English woman, and why would the carvers of Ripon in the

---

14 M. Brown, *The Luttrell Psalter. A Facsimile* (London, 2006), p. 46.
15 Ibid., p. 48.
16 Guy Wilson, 'Ripon Cathedral: the Oldest Church in England', *Medieval History Magazine,* 9 (May 2002), p. 20. In the text, Steyning is erroneously thought to be in Kent.

north want to represent a very local southern saint who died in the eighth century?

Examples of extreme and ridiculous interpretations are found in commentaries on misericords. In Carlisle, for example, St Margaret is supposed to feature in many of the figural misericords, irrespective of gender. Thus, a man in a tunic holding down two dragons is described as: 'St Margaret on her way to Heaven in full emblematic costume, with small boots, wings behind her raised shoulders and with great emphasis on her wide pregnancy belt. The wyvern biting her leg is unaware of the spirit-form of her body and therefore wastes its time' (Plate 4). A depiction of a hyena devouring a corpse becomes a hyena devouring the corpse of St Margaret of Antioch. The misericord of a wyvern swallowing a man is interpreted as a wyvern eating St Margaret.[17]

Some interpretations become fashionable, driven by discussions on themes pertinent to their times; unfounded deductions are made from otherwise simple, straightforward depictions, given symbolic significance where there is none. This applies in particular when gender and sexuality are involved, often resulting in the application of modern ways of thinking without reference to medieval traditions and workshop practices. Thus, in Diane Wolfthal's *Images of Rape* 'real rape' is seen in almost every embrace, especially in classical subjects, forgetting that many of the classical tales are to be understood in a general allegorical sense, rather than the literal sense in which, for instance, she discusses Pygmalion.[18] Wolfthal, from our modern perspective, attempts to immerse herself into the feelings of the victims, forgetting that works of art rarely tell the true story of life. Many Renaissance artists, like Albrecht Dürer, were more interested in the depiction of the human body stylistically and used classical stories to do it, without pondering the question of rape or justice.

Further extremes of interpretation are found in the depictions of two men standing closely together and touching, conjuring up to the modern mind a homosexual association.[19] But was that the case in the Middle Ages? Homosexual activity is even considered the case in scenes of Christ's Passion when the whips, seen at the crotch, may look like penises. Rude gestures, exposed bottoms and penises were traditional in the depiction of Christ's torments, and the sacred was always juxtaposed to the sexually profane. Such works are full of phallic insults, showing the tormentors as crude, rude and without control over their base passions. Even children expose their private parts before Christ, as in the Carrying of the Cross by Hans Multscher (Berlin, Staatliche Museen), and a bare bottom is pointed at St Apollonia during her martyrdom in the Hours of Etienne Chevalier (Chantilly, Musée Condé). Many examples where in passion scenes a large codpiece is worn

---

17 Thirlie Grundy, *The Misericords of Carlisle Cathedral* (Carlisle, 1991).
18 D. Wolfthal, *Images of Rape* (Cambridge, 1999), pp. 4–5.
19 J. Manca, 'Sacred vs. Profane: Images of Sexual Vice in Renaissance Art', *Studies in Iconography,* 13 (1990), pp. 145–90.

by the tormentors, as in Schongauer's Flagellation, have been interpreted as practicing self satisfaction, but this was the period of large codpieces and they were sported both in religious scenes and in secular portraits – famously of Henry VIII.

Another example is Petrus Christus' St Eligius, 1449 (New York, Metropolitan Museum of Art). The mirror in the bottom right hand corner is cracked, and shows two men, one holding a falcon, usually the symbol of nobility. This has been interpreted as a sign of love, and the relationship between the two men seen as erotic, and thus homosexual.[20] The main figures in the painting are a well dressed couple who have come to ask St Eligius the goldsmith to make them a wedding ring. The man and woman were probably copied from Ouwater's Raising of Lazarus, which is dated to between 1435 and 1445. Petrus Christus' main concern seems to have been the creation of realistic illusionism in imitation of Jan van Eyck. The outside world is seen through the cracked mirror, looking in and sporting the worldly attributes of falcon and fashion; tempted by sin, but not necessarily homosexual.

This interpretation of homosexuality is also given to an image by the Housebook Master (Master of the Amsterdam Cabinet), c. 1485, of two men walking together with their hunting dogs; the slightly older man puts his arm through that of the younger one, and holds onto his jerkin, while the younger man wears a garland on his head, and holds a falcon on his wrist.[21] It is true, as Wolfthal says, that garlands are tokens of love, but in the drypoints by the Housebook Master they are worn by nearly all the young men and women. The Housebook Master is known for his sense of humour, and he often pokes fun at the young men whom he portrays as dandies. To understand these kinds of images one needs to consider medieval society where men and women lived in their separate spaces; young men especially fraternized and joined groups with their male interests. One needs to ask how medieval audiences would have viewed such images. Caroline Walker Bynum in her discussion of mystic marriage as experienced by men and women warns that we must not apply modern notions of sexuality, for in the Middle Ages the line 'between sexual responses and affective responses or between male and female' was much less sharply drawn.[22] To conclude that 'same-sex love was consonant with the courtly ideal' because the dress of the figures appears to be noble would seem unreasonable.[23] A short jerkin and a sword are not neces-

---

[20]   D. Wolfthal, 'Picturing Same Sex Desires: The Falconer and His Lover in Images of Petrus Christus and the Housebook Master', in *Troubled Vision: Gender, Sexuality, and Sight in Medieval Text and Image*, eds E. Campbell and R. Mills (New York, 2004), pp. 23–4.

[21]   Ibid., pp. 31–8. Falconer and His Companion, drypoint, c.1485 (Amsterdam, Rijksmuseum).

[22]   C. Walker Bynum, *Jesus as Mother. Studies in the Spirituality of the High Middle Ages* (Berkeley, 1982), p. 162.

[23]   Wolfthal, 'Picturing Same-Sex Desire: The Falconer and His Lover in Images by Petrus Christus and the Housebook Master', p. 35.

sarily signs of aristocracy. Short jerkins are worn by Dürer in his self portraits; swords can be carried by peasants too, even if illegally, or by those trying to raise themselves up in society; and many in the Kermes prints by the Beham brothers bear swords.

One last example of an image being designated homoerotic is of Christ leaning down from the cross to embrace a knight in the manner of Christ embracing St Bernard, a very popular image in the fourteenth and fifteenth centuries. The text specifically refers to Christ thus rewarding the layman for sparing his father's murderer and not succumbing to anger.[24] One author, however, sees this image as a homoerotic encounter between Christ and a male devotee extending beyond the cell, 'where it seems to have been perfectly acceptable'.[25]

As these examples have shown, it is a temptation to get carried along with a new and exciting theory. There is no symbolic interpretation to fit all motifs and themes. The attempt to explain an enormous variety of disparate motifs as apotropaic, without considering the context and audience, but as addressed to demons only, does not seem plausible. The theory may fit sheelagh-na-gigs and hybrid monsters, but it is difficult to see how it can also be applied to the activities of every day life, to well-known tales such as Reynard the fox, or to entertainers, jester, beggars and churners. Late medieval lead badges with phallic imagery may have been apotropaic, but is it credible that 'demons could be distracted, for example, by portraying activities of everyday life such as games, spinning, hunting, ploughing, and butter making'?[26]

The importance of context for the interpretation of symbolism can be illustrated with the figure of the peasant. The peasant was one of the characters more satirized than condemned, symbolic of the fool upon whom all the worldly and bodily sins were visited. Since the bawdy songs of Neithart in the thirteenth century, the Peasant attained the characteristics of bawdiness, rudeness and extreme sexuality. In the sixteenth century, however, the image of the peasant became more ambiguous; reformers might call him the 'salt of the earth' until the Peasant War changed such a benign notion. Even today arguments over Pieter Bruegel the Elder's representations of the peasants do not cease – are the peasants immoral in their excessive feasting, or are they enjoying themselves deservedly after all

---

[24] A folio from the *Manuel des Péchés*, North French, 1280s (Princeton University Library, Department of Rare Books and Special Collections, Robert H. Taylor Coll., Medieval Manuscript No. 1, fol. 44). This information comes from ch. 4 on St Bernard of my student, Carolyn Muir's PhD thesis, *Saintly Brides and Bridegrooms: The Mystic Marriage in Northern Renaissance Art*, in the John Rylands Library, Manchester.

[25] A. Pearson, *Envisioning Gender in Burgundian Devotional art, 1350–1530* (Aldershot, 2005), p. 120. This, again, was pointed out to me by Carolyn Muir.

[26] R. Mellinkoff, *Averting Demons: the Protective Power of Medieval Visual Motifs and Themes* (Los Angeles, 2004), p. 47.

their hard work?[27] Probably, the peasant was used as a symbol of bad behaviour, as a mirror to humanity, for as Bredero said: 'the presence of the peasants softened the expression of otherwise biting human truths'.[28] Walter Gibson argues that there was much enjoyment and laughter to be gained from observing the feasts of peasants.[29] However, what was the meaning of the peasant in the many designs made by Albrecht Dürer and other artists for table furniture, e.g. fountains and beakers for which the peasant was a popular subject? These tend to be ornamented with plants, fruits, peasants, hunters, as well as satyrs and miners – all figures associated with the earth, and thus, pointing to fertility. Peasants atop beakers are depicted carrying fowl and eggs, just as in the many prints of peasants going to market, from which they are often copied. Is their meaning in table furniture different from that in prints, although still characterized as low class, comic and stupid, with open mouths and grins? An example is a drawing of a Pair of Lovers (Milan, Biblioteca Ambrosiana), attributed to Albrecht Dürer, c.1500 to 1503, where a man in torn clothing carries a basket of eggs, puts out his tongue, ogles a girl and squeezes her nipple, while the girl puts her finger into his mouth; she is slovenly, dressed in a very short skirt, and carrying a round of cheese under her arm. Both are standing on a pedestal, and therefore were meant to be statuettes on top of a table ornament. Thus, although the pair are a lecherous couple, their function is decorative, their eroticism associated with fertility and connected to the iconography of table decorations. According to H.-J. Raupp, didactic symbolism gives way to the decorative element. It becomes less specific, and is used in a more general manner, with increasingly a decorative purpose.[30] The house facades designed by Hans Holbein the Younger, such as the House of the Dance in Basel, c. 1522 to 1524, must have had a decorative function (Plate 5). The scenes do not keep to the storeys of the house. Their purpose was to create a three-dimensional, illusionistic facade, full of movement and life. The designs were chosen for their vitality and exuberance to decorate the facades just as drolleries were to enliven the pages of manuscripts.

A related question is the symbolic meaning or decorative purpose of flowers, once they became naturalistically reproduced. An ability to represent the natural world must have delighted artist and audience alike, and encompassed flowers with well-known Marian symbolism. The very popular depictions of the Virgin and Child in an Enclosed Garden of Paradise included symbolic and non-symbolic flowers.

[27]   For the view of well-earned enjoyment: S. Alpers, 'Bruegel's Festive Peasants', *Simiolus* 6 (1972–3), pp. 163–76, and 'Realism as a Comic Mode: Low-Life Painting seen through Bredero's Eyes', *Simiolus* 8 (1975–6), pp. 115–44. For the moral interpretation, and in answer to S. Alpers: H. Miedema, 'Realism and the Comic Mode: The Peasant', *Simiolus* 9 (1977), pp. 205–19.

[28]   Miedema, *Simiolus* 9 (1977), p. 215.

[29]   W. Gibson, *Pieter Bruegel and the Art of Laughter* (Berkeley and Los Angeles, 2006).

[30]   H.-J. Raupp, *Bauernsatiren* (Niederzier, 1986), pp. 101–3.

At the end of the fifteenth century, the manuscripts of Ghent and Bruges became famous for their illusionistically painted flowers casting shadows in the margins, often enlivened by insects. These paintings were fine examples of the artist's increasingly specialist skill. The margins became more important than the main religious scenes, and the artists seemed to be vying with each other for the accolade of being the second Apelles. In a miniature of a Book of Hours by Simon Bening, the Visitation is set in a landscape which extends into the borders. The bottom margin contains two swans and a prominent stag reflected in the water from which it is drinking.[31] James Marrow calls the landscape lyrical in mood, and so one wonders whether this was the artist's purpose, or whether he also meant to remind one of Psalm 42: 1, 'As the hart panteth after the water brooks, so panteth my soul after thee, O God'. To Jack Goody, the meaning of each flower belongs to the tradition where secular and religious meanings become superimposed in the passage of time. He claims 'flowers do not carry distinctive meanings since there is so much overlap'. He gives the example of Catholic painters like Jan Breughel and Daniel Seghers who do not mention symbolism in their writings, for in their flower pieces, he believes, they were more interested in form and colour, and in their 'commonplace significances of luxury, vanity and the passing beauty of earthly things'.[32]

The question is relevant to the so-called market pieces by Joachim Beuckelaer which do not have religious scenes in the background. Here, vegetables are piled up – cabbages, carrots, parsnips or fruits – all tended by a buxom young woman, often with a man in tow. They can be interpreted as phallic symbols, the round shapes of cabbages associated with the female womb, the carrots and parsnips with the male member. But were such pictures bought mainly for their symbolic value and for their moral messages, or would patrons whet their appetites with the luscious fruit so beautifully arranged in all its abundance? It was probably a combination of both. An enticing depiction certainly helped sales. Van Mander tells of an Antwerp mintmaster who was so enamoured by the realism that he kept bringing in more fowl, fish, meat, fruit and vegetables for the painter to add.[33]

Medieval workshop practices, too, can throw light on the question of symbolism since patterns, first drawings, and later prints, were widely used. Thus a seated St Magdalene from a Lamentation (The Hague, Mauritshuis) by the School

[31] J. Marrow, *Pictorial Invention in Netherlandish Manuscript Illumination of the Late Middle Ages* (Leuven, 2005), p. 15, Ill. 41.

[32] J. Goody, *The Culture of Flowers* (Cambridge, 1993), pp. 175–6.

[33] C. van Mander, *Het Leven der Doorluchtighe Nederlandsche/en Hoogh-duytsche Schilders* (Haarlem, 1604), fols. 279v–280r, and Miedema, H., *Karel van Mander. The Lives of the Illustrious Netherlandish and German Painters,* (Doornspijk, 1994), pp. 210–11. *Joachim Beuckelaer. Het markt-en keukenstuk in de Nederlanden 1550–1650,* exhib. cat. (Ghent, 1986), p. 34.

of Rogier van der Weyden was translated into a woman on the left of the Feeding of the Ten Thousand attributed to the Master of St Catherine (Melbourne National Gallery of Victoria), although her outstretched left arm, originally attempting to support the dead Christ, and the right hand on her breast, with her head tilted in sorrow, no longer make sense symbolically in the new context.[34] This happened to many figures whom artists considered interestingly posed, and illustrates how flexible they were in meaning.

Once engravings and woodcuts became available, craftsmen in all media looked to them as patterns. Engraved playing cards illustrate that flowers, birds, animals and figures were created as patterns; what was important to artists were forms and positions, rather than their symbolic meanings. One example is Master P.W. of Cologne's round playing cards.[35] Sometimes artists would extract motifs that took their fancy. The artists of the Harley Hours (BL, Harley MS 1662) painted between 1463 and 1468 to 1476, copied heavily from both religious and secular prints of the Master of the Berlin Passion: including thirty three marginal figures, such as birds, grotesque heads, animals and ornamental foliage, attached to flourished ascenders or the top lines of text folios.[36] For instance, the front part of a dog with its paws crossed and tongue hanging out has been extracted from a print of three dogs licking one another in joyful greeting.[37] Artists had available to them a repertory of patterns to be copied in manuscripts and in other media. They could be used in narrative and as decoration. Patterns and their symbolism could be plundered, transferred, or modified.

It is essential to look at what is seen, without imagining what may be concealed. Pictures rarely tell a real life story in every detail. Conspiracy theories are very much a phenomenon of our age. Since many motifs were copied from patterns and used in different contexts and media, we must be wary of attributing to them profound symbolic significance. That is not to say that there is no meaning, but the meaning may be general, well-known, without specific significance to a given text. Art was then less prudish; what we would now call obscene was depicted with glee. Why should not pure laughter be allowed, as on the misericord depicting fools using cats as bagpipes, in St Botolph's church, Boston, Lincolnshire (Plate 6)? The period, the characteristics of the artist, and the audience must always be taken into consideration. Beuckelaer's kitchen pieces may not have been for general public consumption, but for a small group of initiated art

---

[34]   M. Davies, *Roger van der Weyden* (London, 1972), pl. 119. *Central panel from triptych of the Miracles of Christ,* in U. Hoff and M. Davies (eds), *Les Primitifs Flamands, National Gallery of Victoria, Melbourne* (Brussels, 1971), pl. I.

[35]   C. Grössinger, *Humour and Folly* (2002), pl. 173, p. 149.

[36]   U. Weekes, *Early Engravers and Their Public: the Master of the Berlin Passion and Manuscripts from Convents in the Rhine-Maas Region, ca. 1450–1500* (London, 2004), p. 47.

[37]   Ibid., p. 48, fig. 44, and BL, Harley MS. 1662, f. 6v.

lovers.[38] Even if the patrons and audience were very learned, like Ortelius and other friends of Pieter Bruegel the Elder, would Bruegel himself, as Walter Gibson asks, have had the same knowledge and been equally versed in classical literature?[39] Often, we must accept that a symbolic meaning is no longer within our grasp, that it is ambiguous, or even, that there is no symbolic meaning at all.

[38]   *Joachim Beuckelaer,* p. 34.
[39]   Gibson, *Pieter Bruegel and the Art of Laughter,* p. 73.

The Published Writings of Janet Backhouse
(1938–2004)

ANDREW PRESCOTT

Books, Facsimiles and Edited Volumes

John Scottowe's Alphabet Books (Ilkley: printed for the Roxburghe Club at the Scolar Press, 1974)

The Madresfield Hours: a Fourteenth-Century Manuscript in the Library of Earl Beauchamp (Oxford: printed for presentation to the members of the Roxburghe Club, 1975)

(with Mirjam Foot and John Barr) *William Caxton: an Exhibition to Commemorate the Quincentenary of the Introduction of Printing into England [held in the] British Library Reference Division, 24 September 1976–31 January 1977* (London: British Museum Publications Ltd for the British Library, 1976)

The Illuminated Manuscript (Oxford: Phaidon, 1979)

Books from the Age of Bede: [catalogue of an exhibition held at] *Jarrow Hall May 28th–June 17th* [and] *The British Library June 22nd–Sept 2nd 1979* (Hebburn: Bede Monastery Museum, 1979)

(with François Avril, Françoise Baron and Pierre Bazin) *Trésors des Abbayes Normandes* (Rouen: Musée des Antiquités, 1979). [Catalogue of an exhibition held at the Musée des Antiquités, Rouen, 27 April–22 July 1979, and also at the Musée des Beaux-Arts, Caen, 12 August–4 November 1979]

The Lindisfarne Gospels (Oxford: Phaidon in association with the British Library, 1980)

(with D. H. Turner and Leslie Webster) *The Golden Age of Anglo-Saxon Art 966–1066* (London: British Museum Publications for the Trustees of the British Museum and the British Library Board, 1984). [Catalogue of an exhibition held at the British Museum, 9 November 1984–10 March 1985]

Books of Hours (London: The British Library, 1985)

(with Christopher de Hamel) *The Becket Leaves* (London: The British Library, 1988)

The Luttrell Psalter (London: The British Library, 1989)

The Bedford Hours (London: The British Library, 1990)

(with Leslie Webster) *The Making of England: Anglo-Saxon Art and Culture, AD 600–900* (London: British Museum Press, 1991) [Catalogue of an exhibition held at the British Museum 8 November 1991–9 March 1992]

The Isabella Breviary (London: The British Library, 1993)

(with Y. Giraud) *Pierre Sala: Petit Livre d'Amour* (Luzern: Faksimile Verlag, 1994)

(with James D. Marrow and Gerhard Schmidt) *Biblia Pauperum: Kings MS 5, British Library, London* (Luzern: Faksimile Verlag, 1994)

The Lindisfarne Gospels: a Masterpiece of Book Painting (London: The British Library, 1995)

The Lindisfarne Gospels [video] (London: The British Library, 1995)

Medieval Flowers and Plants: The British Library Engagement Diary for 1996 (London: The British Library, 1995)

Medieval Flowers and Plants: The British Library Address Book (London: The British Library, 1995)

The Hastings Hours (London: The British Library, 1996)

The Medieval Year Engagement Diary 1997 (London: The British Library, 1996)

The Lindisfarne Gospels Postcard Pack (London: The British Library, 1996)

The Illuminated Page: Ten Centuries of Manuscript Painting in the British Library (London: The British Library, 1997)

Pictures from the Past: Using and Abusing Medieval Manuscript Imagery, Leicester University Medieval Research Centre Texts and Studies 1 (Leicester: Leicester University, 1997)

A Medieval Illuminated Book of Days [with illustrations from the Hastings Hours] (London: The British Library, 1997)

A Medieval Illuminated Address Book [with illustrations from the Hastings Hours] (London: The British Library, 1997)

The Lindisfarne Gospels Book of Days (London: The British Library, 1997)

The Lindisfarne Gospels Address Book (London: The British Library, 1997)

Medieval Feasts and Festivals Engagement Diary 1998 (London: The British Library, 1997)

Medieval Feasts and Festivals Address Book 1998 (London: The British Library, 1997)

The Burdett Psalter and Hours: Lot 50 in the Sale of Western Manuscripts and Miniatures [at Sotheby's, 23 June 1998] (London: Sotheby's, 1998)

The Sherborne Missal (London: The British Library, 1999)

The Lindisfarne Gospels: Turning the Pages [CD ROM] (London: The British Library, 2000)

Medieval Rural Life in the Luttrell Psalter (London: The British Library, 2000)

Medieval Birds in the Sherborne Missal (London: The British Library, 2001)

The Medieval English Cathedral: Papers in Honour of Pamela Tudor-Craig [Proceedings of the Harlaxton Symposium, 1998], Harlaxton Medieval Studies 10 (Donington: Shaun Tyas, 2003)

Illumination from Books of Hours (London: The British Library, 2004).

Articles and Contributions to Exhibition Catalogues

'Delius Letters', *British Museum Quarterly*, 30 (1965–6), pp. 30–5

'Two Books of Hours of Francis I', *British Museum Quarterly*, 31 (1966–7), pp. 90–6

'A Victorian Connoisseur and his Manuscripts: the Tale of Mr Jarman and Mr Wing', *British Museum Quarterly*, 32 (1967–8), pp. 76–92

'Manuscript Sources for the History of Mediaeval Costume', *Costume*, 1 no. 2 (1968), pp. 9–14

'The Spanish Forger', *British Museum Quarterly*, 33 (1968–9), pp. 65–71

'Pioneers of Modern Calligraphy and Illumination', *British Museum Quarterly*, 33 (1968–9), pp. 71–9

'Forgeries', 'Modern Calligraphy and Illumination', 'Autographs', 'Correspondence and Papers of Eric Millar' [contributions to catalogue of the Eric Millar Bequest to the Department of Manuscripts, British Museum], *British Museum Quarterly*, 33 (1968–9), pp. 40–2, 50–2

'Bourdichon's "Hours of Henry VII"', *British Museum Quarterly*, 37 (1973), pp. 95–102

'A Miniature Masterpiece by the Spanish Forger', *Quarto: Abbot Hall Art Gallery Quarterly Bulletin*, 12 no. 4 (1973), pp. 8–15

'Gold in the Medieval Book', *Mining Survey,* 83 no. 4 (1973), pp. 10–17

'An Illuminator's Sketchbook', *British Library Journal*, 1 (1975), pp. 3–14

'An Elizabethan Schoolboy's Exercise Book', *Bodleian Library Record*, 9 (1978), pp. 323–332

'Acquisitions', *Friends of the National Libraries: Annual Report for 1980*, 5 [description of British Library, Additional MS. 61725, a 13th cent. drawing of the

Sacrifice of Isaac cut from a copy of the chronicle of Peter of Poitiers]

'A Reappraisal of the Bedford Hours', *British Library Journal*, 7 (1981), pp. 47–69

'An English Calendar, *circa* 1330 [British Library, Additional MS. 61887]', in *Fine Books and Book Collecting: Books and Manuscripts Acquired from Alan G. Thomas and Described by his Customers on the Occasion of his Seventieth Birthday*, ed. Christopher de Hamel and Richard A. Linenthal (Leamington Spa: James Hall, 1981), pp. 8–10

[Contributions to] *The Vikings in England (and in their Danish Homeland)*, ed. Else Roesdahl, James Graham-Campbell, Patricia Connor and Kenneth Pearson [Catalogue of an exhibition held in York, 1981] (London: Anglo-Danish Viking Project, 1981)

'French Manuscript Illumination 1450–1530', in *Renaissance Painting in Manuscripts: Treasures from the British Library*, ed. Thomas Kren (New York: Hudson Hills; London: The British Library, 1983), pp. 145–80 [Catalogue of an exhibition held at the John Paul Getty Museum, Malibu, 6 October 1983–8 January 1984, and afterwards at the Pierpont Morgan Library, New York, 20 January–29 April 1984, and the British Library 25 May–30 September 1984]

'A Book of Hours by a Contemporary of Jean Bourdichon: a preliminary note on British Library, Yates Thompson MS 5', in *Manuscripts in the Fifty Years after the Invention of Printing: some papers read at a colloquium at the Warburg Institute on 12–13 March 1982*, ed. J. B. Trapp (London: Warburg Institute, 1983), pp. 45–9

'An Anthology in Miniature', *British Museum Society Bulletin*, 46 (1983), pp. 20–3

'The Making of the Harley Psalter', *British Library Journal*, 10 (1984), pp. 97–113

[Contributor to] *Age of Chivalry: Art in Plantagenet England 1200–1400*, ed. Jonathan Alexander and Paul Binski (London: Royal Academy of Arts in association with Weidenfeld and Nicolson, 1987) [Catalogue of an exhibition at the Royal Academy, 6 November 1987–6 March 1988]

'Devotions and Delights: the Illuminated Books of Gothic England', *History Today*, 37 no. 11 (1987), pp. 25–31

(with Shelley Jones) 'D. H. Turner (1931–1985): a Portrait', 'Bibliography of the Writings of D. H. Turner', *British Library Journal*, 13 (1987), pp. 111–7

'The Tilliot Hours: Comparisons and Relationships', *British Library Journal*, 13 (1987), pp. 211–31

'Founders of the Royal Library: Edward IV and Henry VII as Collectors of Illuminated Manuscripts', in *England in the Fifteenth Century: Proceedings of the 1986*

Harlaxton Symposium, ed. Daniel Williams, Harlaxton Medieval Studies 3 (Woodbridge: The Boydell Press, 1987), pp. 23–41

'Birds, Beasts and Initials in Lindisfarne's Gospel Books', in *St Cuthbert, His Cult and His Community to AD 1200*, ed. Gerald Bonner, D. W. Rollason and Clare Stancliffe (Woodbridge: Boydell and Brewer, 1989), pp. 165–74

'Illuminated Manuscripts and the Early Development of the Portrait Miniature', in *Early Tudor England: Proceedings of the 1987 Harlaxton Symposium*, ed. D. T. Williams, Harlaxton Medieval Studies 4 (Woodbridge: Boydell and Brewer, 1989), pp. 1–19

'A Psalter from the Diocese of York', *The Art Quarterly of the National Art Collections Fund*, 4 (1990), pp. 24–9

'Arms and Manuscripts: The King's [i.e. Henry VIII's] Illuminated Books', *History Today*, 41 no.6 (1991), pp. 43–7

'The Making of England', *History Today*, 41 no. 11 (1991), pp. 7–12

'Illuminated Manuscripts and the Development of the Portrait Miniature', in *Henry VIII: A European Court in England*, ed. D. Starkey (London: Collins and Brown in association with the National Maritime Museum, 1991), pp.88–90 [catalogue of an exhibition held at the National Maritime Museum 1 May–29 September 1991; JMB also contributed catalogue entries for the illuminated manuscripts]

'Sir Robert Cotton's Record of a Royal Bookshelf', *British Library Journal*, 18 (1992), pp. 44–52 [reprinted in *Sir Robert Cotton as Collector: Essays on an Early Stuart Courtier and his Legacy*, ed. C. J. Wright (London: The British Library, 1997), pp. 230–7]

'Early Renaissance Manuscripts: Illuminations from the Collection of Miss Violeta Harris', *National Art Collections Fund Review for 1992*, pp. 18–22

'A Salute to the Tudor Rose', in *Miscellanea Martin Wittek: Album de Codicologie et de Paléographie offert à Martin Wittek*, ed. Anny Raman and Eugène Manning (Louvain: Peeters, 1993), pp. 1–14

'The Helmingham Breviary: the Reinstatement of a Norwich Masterpiece', *National Art Collections Fund Review for 1993*, pp. 23–5

'Aethelwold', 'Anglo-Saxon Art', 'Eadui', 'Jean Poyet', and 'Lindisfarne Gospels' in *The Dictionary of Art*, ed. Jane Turner (London and New York: Macmillan Grove, 1996)

'The So-Called Hours of Phillip the Fair: an Introductory note on British Library Additional MS 17280', *Wiener Jahrbuch für Kunstgeschichte* 46–47 (1993–4) [a festschrift for Gerhard Schmidt], pp. 45–54

'Sir John Donne's Flemish Manuscripts', in *Medieval Codicology, Iconography,*

Literature and Translation: Studies for Keith Val Sinclair, ed. Peter Rolfe Monks and D. D. R. Owen (Leiden: E. J. Brill, 1994), pp. 48–57

'"Outward and Visible Signs": the Lindisfarne Gospels', in *The Sense of the Sacramental: Movement and Measure in Art and Music, Place and Time*, ed. David Brown and Ann Loades (London: S.P.C.K., 1995), pp. 103–21

'Illuminated Manuscripts Associated with Henry VII and Members of his Immediate Family', in *The Reign of Henry VII: Proceedings of the 1993 Harlaxton Symposium*, ed. Benjamin Thompson, Harlaxton Medieval Studies 5 (Stamford: Paul Watkins, 1995), pp. 175–87

'The Sale of the Luttrell Psalter', in *Antiquaries, Book Collectors and the Circles of Learning*, ed. Robin Myers and Michael Harris, Publishing Pathways 10 (Winchester: St Paul's Bibliographies; Delaware: Oak Knoll Press, 1996), pp. 113–28

'Pennarum Nitor: a Jacobean Scribal Patternbook', in *Books and collectors, 1200–1700: Essays Presented to Andrew Watson*, ed. J. P. Carley and C. G. C. Tite, British Library Studies in the History of the Book (London: British Library, 1996), pp. 413–28.

'The Royal Library from Edward IV to Henry VII', in *The Cambridge History of the Book in Britain*, vol. 3 (1400–1557), ed. Lotte Hellinga and J. B. Trapp (Cambridge: Cambridge University Press, 1999), pp. 267–73

'Charles of Orléans Illuminated', in *Charles d'Orléans in England 1415–1440*, ed. Mary-Jo Arn (Cambridge: D.S. Brewer, 2000), pp. 157–64

'The Lady Margaret Beaufort hours at Alnwick Castle', in *England and the Continent in the Middle Ages: Studies in Memory of Andrew Martindale: Proceedings of the 1996 Harlaxton Symposium*; ed. John Mitchell, assisted by Matthew Moran, Harlaxton Medieval Studies, 8 (Stamford: Shaun Tyas, 2000), 336–48

'"A Very Old Book": The Burdett Psalter-Hours, Made for a Thirteenth-Century Hospitaller', in *Studies in the Illustration of the Psalter*, ed. Brendan Cassidy and Rosemary Muir Wright (Stamford: Shaun Tyas, 2000), pp. 55–66

'Manuscripts on Display: Some Landmarks in the Exhibition and Popular Publication of Illuminated Books', in *The Legacy of M. R. James*, ed. Lynda Dennison (Donington: Shaun Tyas, 2001), pp. 37–52

'Memorials and Manuscripts of a Yorkist Elite', in *St George's Chapel, Windsor, in the Late Middle Ages* ed. Colin Richmond and Eileen Scarff, Historical Monographs relating to St George's Chapel, Windsor Castle 17 (Windsor: Dean and Chapter of Windsor, 2001), pp. 151–60

'The Hours of Charlotte de Bourbon at Alnwick Castle', in *'Als Ich Can': Liber Amicorum in Memory of Professor Dr. Maurits Smeyers*, ed. Bert Cardon, Jan Van der Stock, Dominique Vanwijnsberghe, et al (Peeters: Leuven, 2002), pp. 71–90

'A Further Illuminated Devotional Book for Lady Margaret Beaufort', in *Reading Texts and Images: Essays on Medieval and Renaissance Art and Patronage in honour of Margaret M. Manion*, ed. Bernard J. Muir (Exeter: University of Exeter Press, 2002), pp. 221–35

'The Lovel Lectionary: a Memorial Offering in Salisbury', in *The Medieval English Cathedral: Papers in Honour of Pamela Tudor-Craig: Proceedings of the 1998 Harlaxton Symposium*, ed. Janet Backhouse, Harlaxton Medieval Studies 10 (Donington: Shaun Tyas, 2003), pp. 112–25

'Art and Patronage in Late Medieval England', *History Today*, 53 no. 10 (2003), pp. 11–19

'Lady Margaret Beaufort' [and other contributions] in *Gothic: Art for England, 1400–1547*, ed. Richard Marks and Paul Williamson, assisted by Eleanor Townsend (London: V&A Publications, 2003) [Catalogue of an exhibition held at the Victoria and Albert Museum 9 October 2003–18 January 2004]

'The Psalter of Henry VI [London, British Library, Cotton MS. Domitian A. xvii]' in *The Illuminated Psalter: Studies in the Content, Purpose and Placement of its Images*, ed. F. O. Buttner (Turnhout: Brepols, 2004), pp. 329–36

'Jean Bourdichon and the Hours of Louis XII' in *A Masterpiece Reconstructed: the Hours of Louis XII*, ed. Thomas Kren with Mark Evans (Los Angeles: The J. Paul Getty Museum; London: The British Library, 2005), pp. 1–20

'The Case of Queen Melisende's Psalter: An Historical Investigation' in *Tributes to Jonathan J. G. Alexander: The Making and Meaning of Illuminated Medieval and Renaissance Manuscripts, Art and Architecture*, ed. by Susan L'Engle and Gerald B. Guest (London: Harvey Miller, 2006), pp. 457–70

'Patronage and Commemoration in the Beaufort Hours', in *Tributes to Lucy Freeman Sandler: Studies in Illuminated Manuscripts*, ed. Kathryn A. Smith, and Carol H. Krinsky (London: Harvey Miller, 2007), pp. 331–44

(with James Carley) '"Greater erudition and judgment than any previous monarch": King Henry VIII's Libraries and their Contents', in *The Inventory of Henry VIII,* vol. IV, *Decorative Arts and Everyday Objects*, ed. Maria Hayward and Philip Ward (Harvey Miller [Brepols], for the Society of Antiquaries of London, forthcoming).

Select Reviews and Review Articles

A. Engelbregt, *Het Utrechts Psalterium. Een eeuw wetenschappelijke bestudering (1860–1960)* (Utrecht: Haentjens Dekker and Gumbert, 1965): *Burlington Magazine*, 108 (1966), pp. 326–7

'Reichenau Illumination: Facts and Fiction' [review of C. R. Dodwell and D. H.

Turner, *Reichenau Revisited: a reassessment of the place of Reichenau in Ottonian Art*, Warburg Institute Surveys II (London: Warburg Institute, 1965)]: *Burlington Magazine*, 109 (1967), pp. 98–100

Rafaele Arnese, *I codici notati della Biblioteca Nazionale di Napoli* (Firenze: Olschki, 1967): *The Library*, 5th Ser., 23 (1968), p. 258

'The Trinity College Apocalypse' [review of Peter H. Brieger and Marthe Dulong, *The Trinity College Apocalypse* (London: The Eugrammia Press, 1967)]: *Burlington Magazine*, 111 (1969), pp. 35–6

The Caxton Ovid. A Complete Facsimile of William Caxton's Translation of Ovid's Metamorphoses, 1480: *Burlington Magazine*, 112 (1970), pp. 55–6

N. R. Ker, *Medieval Manuscripts in British Libraries, 1 (London)* (Oxford: Clarendon Press, 1969): *The Library*, 5th Ser., 25 (1970), pp. 253–4

Wolfgang Speyer, *Bücherfunde in der Glaubenswerbung der Antike mit einem Ausblick auf Mittelalter und Neuzeit* (Gottingen: Vandenhoeck and Ruprecht, 1970): *The Library*, 5th Ser., 25 (1970), pp. 355–7

M. B. Parkes, *English Cursive Book Hands 1250–1500* (Oxford: Clarendon Press, 1969): *The Library*, 5th Ser., 26 (1971), pp. 67–8

S. C. Cockerell and John Plummer, *Old Testament Miniatures* (London: Phaidon Press, 1969); Jean Longnon, Raymond Cazelles and Millard Meiss, *Les Très Riches Heures du Duc de Berry* (London: Thames and Hudson, 1969): *Burlington Magazine*, 113 (1971), pp. 279–80

Alfred Fairbank, *The Story of Handwriting: Origins and Development* (London: Faber and Faber, 1970): *The Library*, 5th Ser., 26 (1971), pp. 174–5

'Recent Literature on Illuminated Manuscripts' [reviews of: Angela Daneu Lattanzi and Marguerite Debae, *La Miniature Italienne du Xe au XVIe siècle* (Brussels: Bibliothèque Royale Albert Ier, 1969); J. J. G. Alexander and A. C. de la Mare, *The Italian Manuscripts in the Library of Major J. R. Abbey* (London: Faber, 1969); Otto Pächt and J. J. G. Alexander, *Illuminated Manuscripts in the Bodleian Library, Vol. II: The Italian Schools* (Oxford: Clarendon Press, 1970); Peter Brieger, Millard Meiss and Charles Singleton, *Illuminated Manuscripts of the Divine Comedy* (London: Routledge, Kegan and Paul, 1969); Csaba Csapodi and Klára Csapodi-Gárdonyi, trans. Z. Horn and A. West, *Bibliotheca Corviniana* (Shannon: Irish University Press, 1969); Ilona Berkovits, trans. Z. Horn and A. West, *Illuminated Manuscripts in Hungary XI–XVI centuries* (Shannon: Irish University Press, 1969); J. J. G. Alexander, *Norman Illumination at Mont St Michel 966–1100* (Oxford: Clarendon Press, 1970); George Galavaris, *The Illustrations of the Liturgical Homilies of Gregory Nazianzenus* (Princeton: Princeton University Press, 1969); James H. Beck, *Mariano di Jacopo detto il Taccola: Liber tertius de* *ingeneis ac edifitiis non usitatis* (Milan: Edizioni il Poifilo, 1969)]: *Burlington Magazine*, 115 (1973), pp. 167–70

'The Hours of Englebert of Nassau' [review of J. J. G. Alexander, *The Master of Mary of Burgundy: a Book of Hours for Engelbert of Nassau* (London: Phaidon Press; New York: George Braziller, 1970)]: *Burlington Magazine*, 115 (1973), pp. 684–5

O. Pächt and J. J. G. Alexander, *Illuminated Manuscripts in the Bodleian Library, Oxford, Vol. III (British, Irish and Icelandic Schools)* (Oxford: Clarendon Press, 1973): *Burlington Magazine*, 116 (1974), pp. 417–18

'Medieval Manuscript Treasures' [reviews of: Bezalel Narliss, *Golden Haggadah. A fourteenth-century illuminated Hebrew manuscript in the British Museum* (London: Eugrammia Press, 1970); Marcel Thomas, *Les Grandes Heures de Jean Duc de Berry* (London, Thames and Hudson; New York: George Braziller, 1971); Claude Schaefer, trans. Marianne Sinclair, *The Hours of Etienne Chevalier* (London, Thames and Hudson; New York: George Braziller, 1972)]: *Burlington Magazine*, 116 (1974), pp. 479–80

'"Monumenta Annonis" at Cologne' [review of the exhibition *Monumenta Annonis* at the Schnütgen Museum, Cologne, 30 April–27 July 1975]: *Burlington Magazine*, 117 (1975), pp. 426–7

S. Der Nersessian, *Armenian Manuscripts in the Walters Art Gallery* (Baltimore: Walters Art Gallery, 1973); S. Der Nersessian, *Etudes Byzantines et Arméniennes* (Louvain: Imprimerie Orientaliste, 1973): *Burlington Magazine*, 117 (1975), p. 675

A. Putaturo Murano, *Miniature Napoletane del Rinascimento* (Naples: Libreria scientifica editrice, 1973); Anna Rosa Calderoni Masetti and Gigetta Dalli Regoli, *Sanctae Hildegardis Revelationes* (Lucca: Cassa di Risparmio, 1973)]: *Burlington Magazine*, 117 (1975), p. 814

Gatherings in Honor of Dorothy E. Miner, ed. Ursula E. McCracken, Lilian M. C. Randall, Richard H. Randall (Baltimore: Walters Art Gallery, 1974): *Burlington Magazine*, 118 (1976), pp. 237–8

Mendel Metzger, *La Haggada Enluminé, Vol. I* (Leiden: E. J. Brill, 1973): *Burlington Magazine*, 118 (1976), p. 524

Charles Sterling, *The Master of Claude, Queen of France: A Newly Defined Miniaturist* (New York: H. P. Kraus, 1975): *Burlington Magazine*, 118 (1976), pp. 524–6

Werner Abraham, *Losbuch in Deutschen Reimpaaren* (Graz: Akademische Druck- u. Verlagsanstalt, 1973); Reiner Hausherr, *Bible Moralisée* (Graz: Akademische Druck- u. Verlagsanstalt, 1973); P. Bloch, *Reichenau Evangelistar* (Graz:

Akademische Druck- u. Verlagsanstalt, 1972); Kurt Holter, *Hrabanus Maurus: Liber de Laudibus Sanctae Crucis* (Graz: Akademische Druck- u. Verlagsanstalt, 1973); Wolfgang Hilger, *Das ältere Gebetbuch Maximilians I* (Graz: Akademische Druck- u. Verlagsanstalt, 1973): *Burlington Magazine*, 118 (1976), pp. 708–10

L. F. Sandler, *The Peterborough Psalter in Brussels and Other Fenland Manuscripts* (London: Harvey Miller, 1974); C. M. Kauffman, *Romanesque Manuscripts 1066–1190* (London: Harvey Miller, 1975): *Burlington Magazine*, 118 (1976), pp. 710–11

Otto Pächt and Dagmar Thoss, *Die Illuminierten Handschriften und Inkunabeln der Öster-reichische Nationalbibliothek; Französische Schüle I* (Vienna: Ostereichischen Akademie der Wissenschaften, 1974): *Burlington Magazine*, 119 (1977), p. 509

Millard Meiss and Elizabeth H. Beatson, *La Vie de Nostre Benoit Sauveur Ihesuscrist & La saincte Vie de Nostre Dame,* (New York: New York University Press, 1977): *Burlington Magazine*, 120 (1978), p. 243

Jaroslav Folda, *Crusader Manuscript Illumination at Saint-Jean d'Acre, 1275–91* (Princeton: Princeton University Press, 1976): *Times Literary Supplement*, 12 May 1978, p. 534

Robert Branner, *Manuscript Painting in Paris during the Reign of St Louis: a study of styles* (Berkeley: University of California Press, 1977): *Burlington Magazine*, 121 (1979), p. 390

J. J. G. Alexander, *Insular Manuscripts: the 6th to the 9th century* (London: Harvey Miller, 1978): *Burlington Magazine*, 121 (1979), pp. 802–3

M. B. Parkes, *The Medieval Manuscripts of Keble College, Oxford* (London: Scolar Press, 1979): *Medium Ævum*, l (1981), pp. 107–9

Karen Gould, *The Psalter and Hours of Yolande of Soissons* (Cambridge, Ma: The Medieval Academy of America, 1978): *Burlington Magazine*, 123 (1981), p. 173

S. Osley, *Scribes and Sources: Handbook of the Chancery Hand in the Sixteenth Century* (London: Faber and Faber, 1980): *History*, 66 (1981), pp. 126–7

Jenny Stratford, *Catalogue of the Jackson Collection of Manuscript Fragments in the Royal Library, Windsor Castle* (London: Academic Press, 1981): *Times Literary Supplement*, 17 September 1982, p. 1019

R. Marks and N. J. Morgan, *The Golden Age of English Manuscript Painting 1200–1500* (London: Chatto and Windus, 1981): *Burlington Magazine*, 125 (1983), pp. 363–4

Roger S. Wieck, *Late Medieval and Renaissance Illuminated Manuscripts in the Houghton Library* (Cambridge, Ma: Harvard College Library, 1983) [catalogue of an exhibition in the Houghton Library 15 March – 3 June 1983]: *Burlington Magazine*, 125 (1983), p. 755

English Court Culture in the Later Middle Ages, ed. V. J. Scattergood and J. Sherborne (London: Duckworth; New York, St Martin's Press, 1983): *The Library*, 6th Ser., 6 (1984), pp. 406–8.

J. Plummer, *The Last Flowering: French Painting in Manuscripts 1420–1530* (New York: Pierpont Morgan Library; London: Oxford University Press, 1982): *The Antiquaries Journal*, 65 (1985), pp. 193–4

Rowan Watson, *The Playfair Hours: a Late Fifteenth Century Illuminated Manuscript from Rouen* (London: Victoria and Albert Museum, 1984): *The Antiquaries Journal*, 66 (1986), pp. 206–7

Thomas H. Ohlgren, *Insular and Anglo-Saxon Illuminated Manuscripts: an iconographic catalogue, c. AD 625–1100* (New York, London: Garland, 1986): *The Library*, 6th Ser., 9 (1987), pp. 58–9

Christopher de Hamel, *A History of Illuminated Manuscripts* (Oxford: Phaidon, 1986): *The Library*, 6th Ser., 9 (1987), pp. 282–4

Otto Pächt, trans. Kay Davenport, *Book Illumination in the Middle Ages* (London: Harvey Miller, 1986): *The Antiquaries Journal*, 67 (1987), pp. 435–6

Suzanne Lewis, *The Art of Matthew Paris in the Chronica Majora* (Aldershot: Scolar Press, 1987): *The Antiquaries Journal*, 68 (1988), pp. 167–8

N. J. Morgan, *A Survey of Manuscripts Illuminated in the British Isles, vol. 4: Early Gothic Manuscripts (II), 1250–1285* (London and Oxford: Harvey Miller and Oxford University Press, 1988): *The Antiquaries Journal*, 68 (1988), pp. 364–5

Raphael Lowe, *The Rylands Haggadah* (London: Thames and Hudson, 1988): *Apollo*, 130 (1989), p. 360

The Book of Hours in Medieval Life and Society, ed. R. S. Wieck (London: Sotheby's Publications, 1988); Nigel Thorp, *The Glory of the Page: Medieval and Renaissance Manuscripts from Glasgow University Library* (London: Harvey Miller, 1987); Georges Dogaer, *Flemish Miniature Painting in the 15th and 16th Centuries* (Amsterdam: B. M. Israel, 1987): *Apollo*, 130 (1989), pp. 428–9

Lilian M. C. Randall, *Medieval and Renaissance Manuscripts in the Walters Art Gallery: France, 875–1420* (Baltimore and London: John Hopkins University Press, 1989): *Apollo*, 131 (1990), pp. 278–9

Henri Defoer, Anne S. Korteweg, Wilhelmina Wüstefeld, James H. Marrow, *The Golden Age of Dutch Manuscript Painting* (Stuttgart: Belser, 1989): *The Library*, 6th Ser., 13 (1991), pp. 158–9

Avril Henry, *The Eton Roundels: Eton College MS 177* (Aldershot: Scolar Press,

1990): *The Book Collector,* 41 (1992), pp. 405–7

Alain Arnould and Jean Michel Massing, *Splendours of Flanders: Late Medieval Art in Cambridge Collections* (Cambridge: Cambridge University Press, 1993): *The Library,* 6th Ser., 16 (1994), pp. 236–9

John Williams, *The Illuminated Beatus: A corpus of Illustrations of the Commentary on the Apocalypse* (London: Harvey Miller, 1994): *The Antiquaries Journal,* 75 (1995; Book Review Supplement), pp. 58–9

Carolingian Culture: Emulation and Innovation, ed. Rosamond McKitterick (Cambridge: Cambridge University Press, 1994): *International Journal of Heritage Studies,* 1 (1995), pp. 187–8

The Hours of Mary of Burgundy. Codex Vinobonensis 1857 Vienna, Österreichische Nationalbibliothek. Commentary by Eric Inglis (London: Harvey Miller, 1995): *The Antiquaries Journal,* 76 (1996), pp. 300–1

Marie-Helene Tesnière and Prosser Gifford, *Creating French Culture: Treasures from the Bibliothèque Nationale de France* (New Haven and London: Yale University Press, 1995): *Apollo,* 145 (1997), pp. 60–1

William Noel, *The Harley Psalter* (Cambridge: Cambridge University Press, 1995): *Antiquaries Journal,* 77 (1997), p. 423

Liber Vitae of the New Minster and Hyde Abbey, Winchester, ed. Simon Keynes, (Copenhagen: Rosenkilde and Bagger, 1996); Walter Cahn, *Romanesque Manuscripts: the Twelfth Century* (London: Harvey Miller, 1996); Kathleen Scott, *Later Gothic Manuscripts, 1390–1490* (London: Harvey Miller, 1996): *Antiquaries Journal* 78 (1998), pp. 495–7

Alison Stones, *Le Livre d'Images de Madame Marie* (Paris: Editions de Cerf): *Burlington Magazine* 140 (1998), p. 755

M. Budney, *Insular, Anglo-Saxon and Early Anglo-Norman Manuscript Art at Corpus Christi College, Cambridge: an Illustrated Catalogue* (Kalamazoo: Western Michigan University, 1997): *The Antiquaries Journal,* 79 (1999), pp. 417–18

Michael Camille, *Mirror in Parchment: The Luttrell Psalter and the Making of Medieval England* (London: Reaktion Books, 1998): *Burlington Magazine,* 141 (1999), pp. 173–4

John B. Friedman and Jessica M. Wegmann, *Medieval Iconography: a Research Guide* (New York and London: Garland Publishing, 1998): *Journal of Ecclesiastical History,* 51 (2000), pp. 133

G. Cavallo and R. Chartier, *A History of Reading in the West* (Cambridge: Polity Press, 1999); *Incunabula: Studies in Fifteenth-Century Printed Books Presented to Lotte Hellinga,* ed. Martin Davies (London: The British Library, 1999): *History*

Today, 50 no. 6 (2000), p. 58

Roger S. Wieck, William M. Voelke and K. Michelle Hearne, *The Hours of Henry VIII: a Renaissance Masterpiece by Jean Poyet* (New York: George Braziller with the Pierpont Morgan Library, 2000): *Burlington Magazine*, 143 (2001), p. 375; *Scriptorium*, 55 (2001), pp. 316–18

John Lowden, *The Making of the Bibles Moralisées [1: the Manuscripts; 2: The Book of Ruth]* (University Park: Pennsylvania State University, 2000): *Journal of Ecclesiastical History*, 53 (2002), pp. 356–7

John Williams, *The Illustrated Beatus: a Corpus of the Illustrations of the Commentary on the Apocalypse*, 4 (11th and 12th centuries) (London: Harvey Miller, 2002): *The Antiquaries Journal*, 83 (2003), p. 505

Christa Grössinger, *Humour and Folly in Secular and Profane Prints of Northern Europe, 1430–1540* (London: Harvey Miller, 2002): *The Antiquaries Journal* 83 (2003), p. 516

Christopher de Hamel, *The Book: A History of the Bible* (London: Phaidon, 2001): *History Today*, 52 no. 4 (2002), p. 61

C. M. Kauffman, *Biblical Imagery in Medieval England 700–1550* (London: Harvey Miller, 2003): *Antiquaries Journal* 84 (2004), pp. 449–50.

Memoirs and Obituaries of Janet Backhouse

'Janet Backhouse': *The Times*, 29 December 2004

Michelle P. Brown, 'Backhouse, Janet Moira (1938–2004)', *Oxford Dictionary of National Biography* (Online edition: Oxford University Press, Oct 2008) [http://www.oxforddnb.com/view/article/94459, accessed 15 June 2009]

Christopher de Hamel, 'Janet Backhouse', *Burlington Magazine*, 147 (2005), p. 554

Pamela Porter and Shelley Jones, 'Janet Backhouse, Colleague and Friend', in *Illuminating the Book: Makers and Interpreters: Essays in Honour of Janet Backhouse*, eds M. P. Brown and S. McKendrick (London: The British Library, 1998), pp. 11–16

A. Ward, 'In Memoriam Janet Backhouse (1938–2004), *Ephemerides Liturgicae*, 119 (2005), p. 258

Roger S. Wieck, in review of *The Illuminated Page: Ten Centuries of Manuscript Painting in the British Library* in *Speculum* 74 (1999), p. 1026.

INDEX

1 (Ailes). Cocket seal (Edward III) for delivery of wool and hides at Boston depicting the three lions passant guardant (or 'leopards') of England (TNA E 43/649).

2 (Ailes). Custom counterseal (Edward III) for delivery of wool and hides at Boston depicting a lion passant guardant (or 'leopard') of England and a bust of the king (TNA E 43/649).

3 (Ailes). Privy seal (1333) of Richard Airmyn, keeper of the house of converts, featuring a single lion's head at the centre of a cross and a *fleur-de-lis* on each arm (TNA E 43/59).

4 (Ailes). Signet of Richard II depicting the royal crown (TNA CP 51/1/4). Reproduced from Tout, *Administrative History of Medieval England*, 5, p. 202, pl. iv.

5 (Ailes). Seal (1313) of the Great Wardrobe depicting two crossed keys (TNA E 43/559).

6 (Ailes). Seal (1315) of Ralph Giffard, sheriff of Cambridgeshire and Huntingdonshire, featuring a gatehouse or castle between his initials (TNA E 43/669).

7 (Ailes). Seal (1330) of office of Richard de la Pole as the king's butler featuring the broad arrow badge (TNA E 43/63).

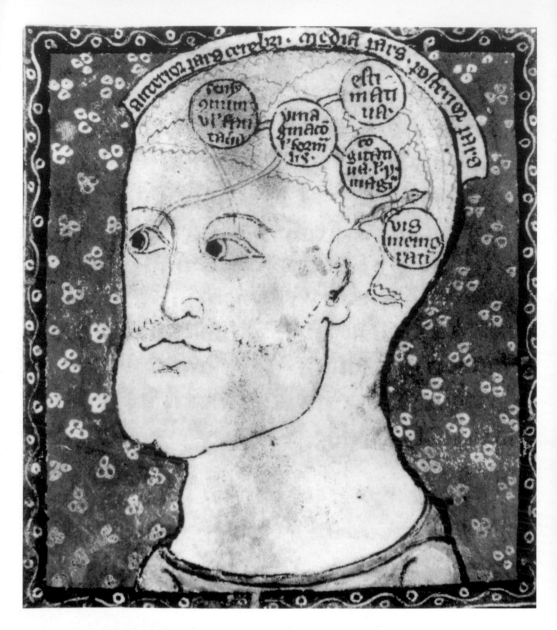

1 (Carruthers). Cambridge University Library MS Gg 1.1, f.490v:
diagram of brain functions. English, c.1330.

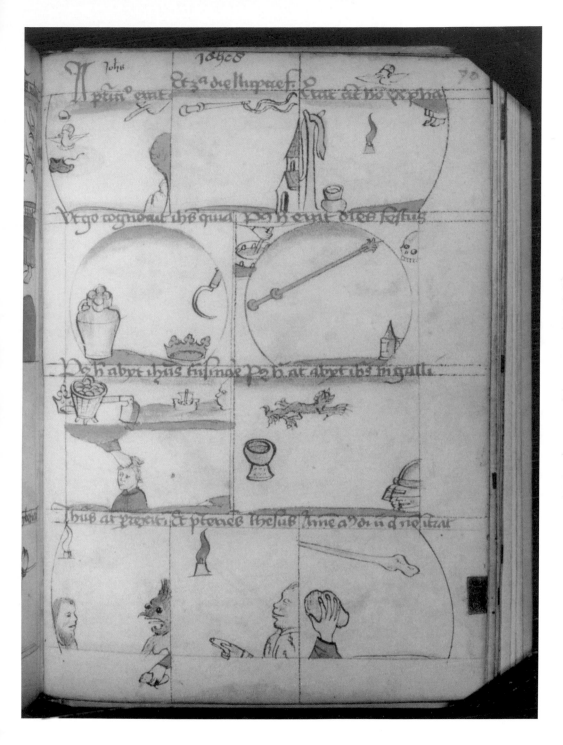

2 (Carruthers). Cambridge, Fitzwilliam Museum, MS Fitzwilliam 11, f.70.
Mnemonic notae in a late 15th-century German, Rhineland (?) bible.

3 (Carruthers). Oxford, Bodleian Library MS Douce 366, f. 147v:
Ormesby Psalter. Norwich, betw. 1310 and 1320.

4 (Carruthers). London, British Library, Add. MS 54782, ff. 55v–56:
Hastings Hours, 1480–83. Flemish.

5 (Carruthers). Oxford, Bodleian Library MS Douce 366, f. 9v.
Beatus page in the Ormesby Psalter, Norwich, c.1325.

1 (Cherry). Drawing of the chantepleure in Villard de Honnecourt's notebook.
Paris, BN ms fr. 19093, f.17. French, between 1225 to 1235.
Reproduced from Hahnloser, *Villard de Honnecourt*, Tafel 17e.

2 (Cherry). The Corpus Christi silver-mounted mazer. English, fourteenth century.

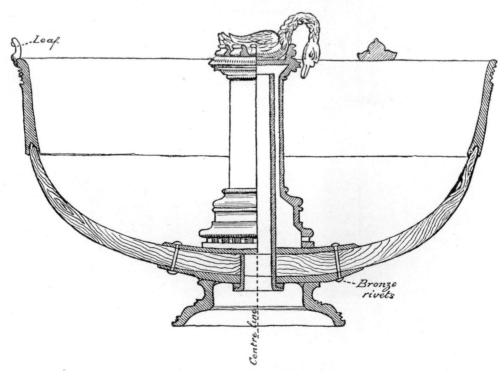

3 (Cherry). Drawing of the Corpus silver mazer with bird. English, fourteenth century.
Reproduced from *Catalogue of Plate Exhibited in the Fitzwilliam Museum* (1895), no. 11.

4 (Cherry). White-painted pottery chantepleure. English, fifteenth-century. British Museum.

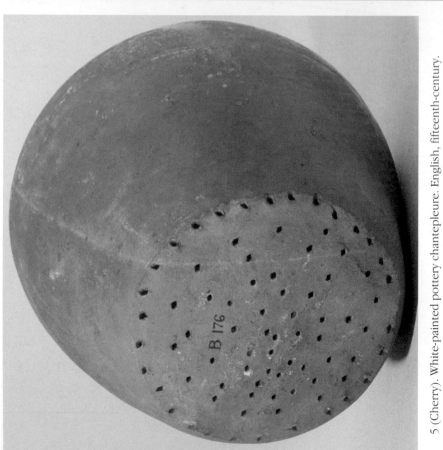

5 (Cherry). White-painted pottery chantepleure. English, fifteenth-century.
British Museum.

6 (Cherry) (opposite). Ipswich ware. English seventh to eighth century
Ipswich Museum.

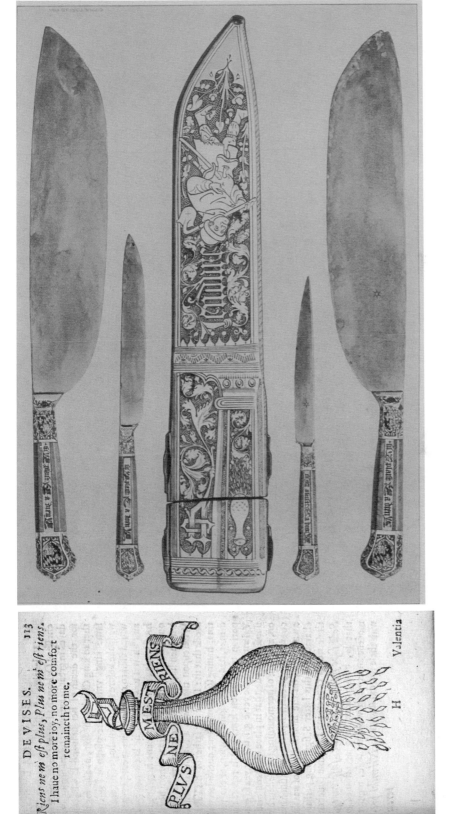

8 (Cherry). Sheath and set of knives. French, early fifteenth-century. Watercolour published in *Archaeologia* 60, pt 2 (1906).

DEVISES.   113

R_iens ne mⁱ eſt plus, Plus ne mⁱ eſt riens.
I haue no more ioy, no more comfort remaineth to me.

MEST RIENS

NE PLVS

H   H

Valentia

7 (Cherry). The Chantepleure from PS's edition of Paradin's *Devises* (1591).

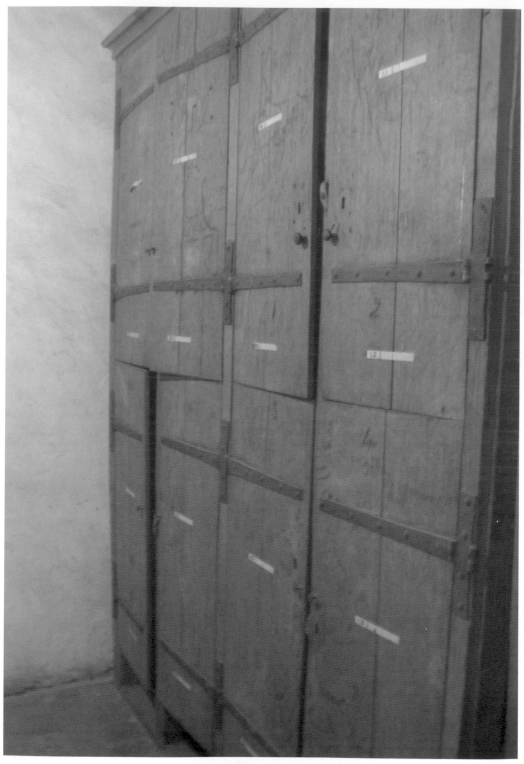

1 (Danbury). Armoire made in 1413 by William Ickenham, the Winchester College carpenter, Exchequer Room, Winchester College.

2 (Danbury). Two muniment chests made 1396–7 for Winchester College, Lower Muniment Room, Winchester College.

3 (Danbury). Markings on the inside of the lid, Treaty Chest, Chapel of the Pyx, Westminster Abbey.

4 (Danbury). Label on the front of a pyx, Muniment Room, Magdalen College, Oxford.

5 (Danbury). Lid of Bruce chest, The National Archives TNA E 27/9.

6 (Danbury). Front of Bruce chest, The National Archives TNA E 27/9.

7 (Danbury). Lid of Calais chest, The National Archives TNA E 27/8.

8 (Danbury). Front of Calais chest, The National Archives TNA E 27/8.

1 (Grössinger). A page from a Gradual, Bruges, before 1388,
Douai, Bibliothèque Municipale MS 132, f. 129.

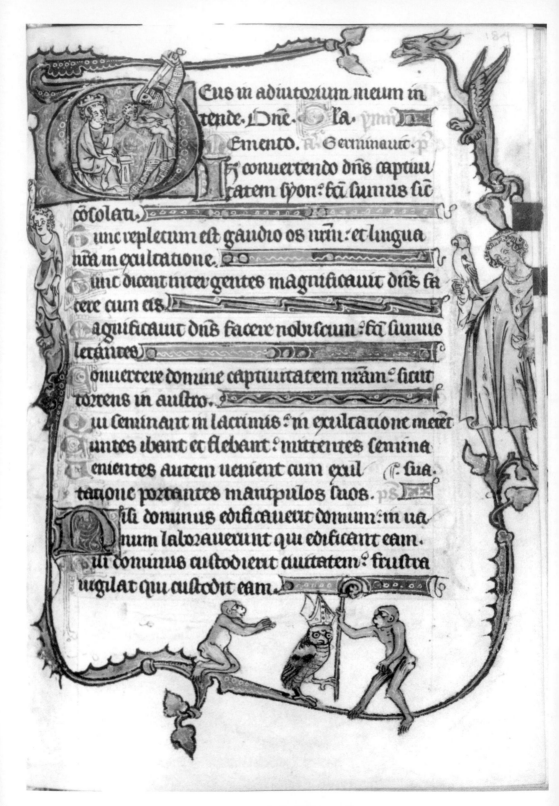

2 (Grössinger). A page from a Book of Hours, Ghent, c. 1315 to 1325, Baltimore, Walters Art Gallery, MS W.82, f. 184.

3 (Grössinger). Misericord of a Woman wheeled in a Three-Wheeled Barrow.
Ripon Cathedral, 1489–94.

4 (Grössinger). Misericord of a Man in a tunic holding down two Dragons.
Carlisle Cathedral, *circa* 1420.

5 (Grössinger). Drawing for the facade of the House of the Dance in Basel, by Holbein the Younger, c. 1522 to 1524, Basel, Kunstmuseum, Kupferstichkabinett.

6 (Grössinger). Misericord of Two Fools playing Bagpipes on Two Cats. St Botolph, Boston, 1390s.

1 (Luxford). Mendlesham, Suffolk: 'God's eye' view of the church.

2 (Luxford). Colchester, Essex: facade of the surviving gatehouse of the Benedictine abbey of St John.

3 (Luxford). Long Melford, Suffolk: detail of south side of the clerestorey.

4 (Luxford). Swannington, Norfolk: inscription 'ihc NAZARENUS' over south porch.

5 (Luxford). Great Witchingham, Norfolk: south porch with Marian motifs in flushwork over the portal.

6 (Luxford). Worlingworth, Suffolk: Marian monogram with host over, south porch.

7 (Luxford) (above). Hunworth, Norfolk:
crowned letter L and gridiron for St
Lawrence, the church's patron saint.

8 (Luxford). Woodbridge, Suffolk:
chalice and host motif on the south porch.

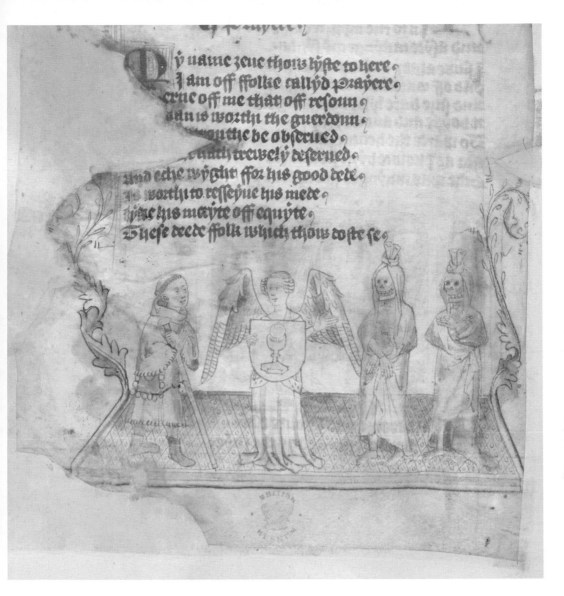

9 (Luxford). BL, Cotton MS Tiberius A. vii, f. 102v (Lydgate's *Pilgrimage of the Life of Man*): Prayer presents Pilgrim with a chalice and host on a shield, in the presence of two cadavers.

10 (Luxford). Southwold, Suffolk: flushwork 'tabernacles' with 'image plinths' flanking the west door.

1 (Morgan). Jesus and Mary monograms, Thornford, St Mary Magdalene (Dorset).

2 (Morgan). Tower base with Jesus, John and Mary monograms, Garboldisham, St John Baptist (Suffolk).

3 (Morgan). Mary monogram surrounded by roses and lilies, Great Chart, St Mary (Kent).

4 (Morgan). Jesus and Mary monograms, Ropsley, St Peter (Lincolnshire).

5 (Morgan). Mary monogram, Bitchfield, St Mary Magdalene (Lincolnshire).

6 (Morgan). Mary monogram, Steeple Ashton (Wiltshire).

7 (Morgan). Mary monogram on a shield held by an angel, Glastonbury, St John (Somerset).

8 (Morgan). Mary monogram, Ashill, St Nicholas (Norfolk).

9 (Morgan). Mary monogram with Annunciation brooch or morse, New College, Oxford.

10 (Morgan). Entrance porch with Mary monograms, Great Witchingham, St Mary (Norfolk).

11 (Morgan). Entrance porch with Mary monograms, Yaxley, St Mary (Suffolk).

12 (Morgan). Tower parapet with Mary monogram, Little Stonham, St Mary (Suffolk).

13 (Morgan). Tower parapet with Mary monogram, Rougham, St John Baptist (Suffolk).

14 (Morgan). Clerestory parapet with 'STSM', Wortham, St Mary (Suffolk).

15 (Morgan). Swords of sorrow, Bury St Edmunds, St James (now Cathedral) (Suffolk). c. 1500.

16 (Morgan). Heart of Mary roof boss, Bristol, Cathedral. c. 1475–1500 (from C. J. P. Cave, *Roof Bosses in Medieval Churches*, Cambridge, 1948, p. 45, pl. 298).

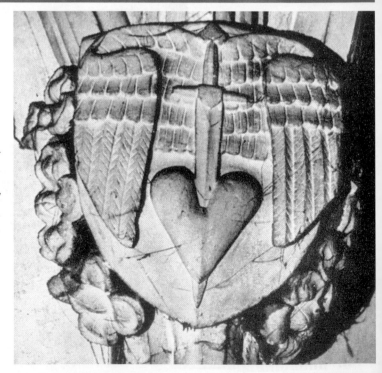

17 (Morgan). Heart of Mary roof boss, Beverley, St Mary (Yorkshire). c. 1475–1500 (from C. J. P. Cave, *Roof Bosses in Medieval Churches*, Cambridge, 1948, p. 45, pl. 297).

18 (Morgan). Heart of Mary shield, Butcombe, St Michael (Somerset). c. 1475–1500.

19 (Morgan). Heart of Mary badge,
Museum of London.
c. 1450–1500.

20 (Morgan). Marian shield,
Sugar Chantry,
Wells Cathedral. c. 1489
(from *Antiquaries Journal*,
11 (1931), pp. 286–8).

1 (New). Sacred Monogram (Cambridge, Fitzwilliam Museum MS 2–1957, f. 41v).

2 (New): Five Wounds on a shield with the lance, spear and nails (Cambridge, Fitzwilliam Museum MS 2–1957, f. 46r).

3 (New): Wounded Heart, hands and feet of Christ, with Calvary cross, scourges and nails (Cambridge, Fitzwilliam Museum MS 2–1957, f. 78).

4 (New): Head of Christ (Cambridge, Fitzwilliam Museum MS 2–1957, f. 50).

5 (New): 'Arms of the Virgin Mary', with eagle in pen flourishing (Cambridge, Fitzwilliam Museum MS 2–1957, f. 37v).

6 (New): ES monogram, crozier and Shelford rebus (Cambridge, Fitzwilliam Museum MS 2–1957, f. 34).

7 (New): Shelford pen-flourished 'caricature' (Cambridge, Fitzwilliam Museum MS 2–1957, f. 43v).

8 (New): Brass of Gwen More, mother of Elizabeth Shelford,
Bramley, Hampshire.

Of yo̅ charite pray for ye̅ soule of Gwen y̅ one sime tyme ye̅ wyf of John
Shelton of ye̅ cite of Herford elquier & moder to dame Elizabeth Shelton de
Abbes of the monastery of Shaftsbury the which Gwen dyed the vij
day of august y̅ yere of our lord M̅ cccc lxxxij on whose soule Ihu have mcy

1 (Rogers). Sidney Sussex MS 37, f. 133v, Sacred Heart with Divine Eye.

2 (Rogers). Sidney Sussex MS 37, f. 94v, Man of Sorrows.

3 (Rogers). Sidney Sussex MS 37, f. 116v, Virgin and Child with Holand lady.

4 (Rogers). York, Borthwick Institute, MS Staple 2, f. 5v.

5 (Rogers). York, Borthwick Institute, MS Staple 2, f. 8.

6 (Rogers). York, Borthwick Institute, MS Staple 2, f. 15v.

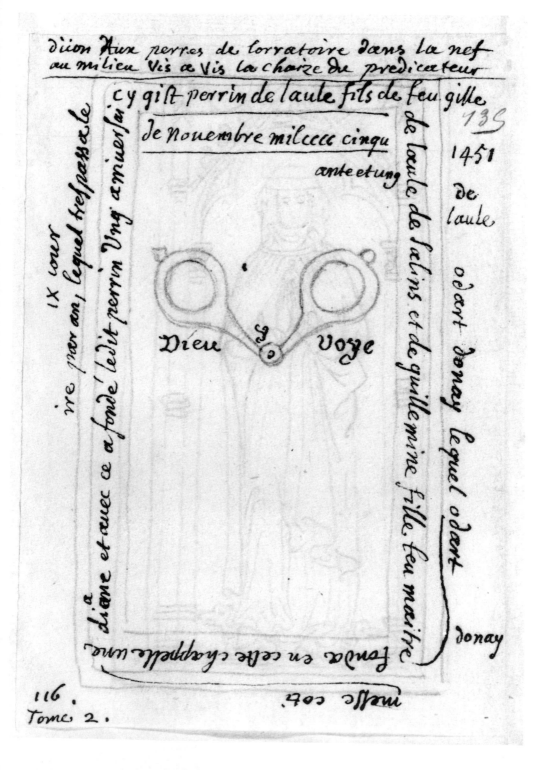

7 (Rogers). Drawing of the incised slab of Perrin de Laule, d. 1451, formerly in the Oratorian church, Dijon, from the collection of Roger de Gaignières (d. 1715), Paris, BnF MS fr. 8226, p. 135.

10 (Rogers). Painted panel of St. Isidore, with Trinitarian Eye, Carinthian, early 19th-century. Maria Saal, Propstei, Möbelsammlung, Austria.

8 (opposite, top) (Rogers). Matteo de' Pasti. Divine Eye, reverse of Alberti medal.

9 (below) (Rogers). Reverse of Great Seal of the United States, from one dollar bill.

1 (right) (Sandler). Bohun Psalter, Psalm 1 (Cambridge, Fitzwilliam Mus. MS 38–1950, f.1).

2 (below) (Sandler). Bohun Psalter, Psalm 1, bas-de-page (Cambridge, Fitzwilliam Mus. MS 38-1950, f. 1).

3 (opposite, top) (Sandler). Amiens Missal, bas-de-page (The Hague, Meermanno-Westreenianum Mus. MS 78.D.40, f. 44).

4 (opposite, below) (Sandler). Psalter and Hours of Yolande of Soissons, Hours of the Virgin at Prime, bas-de-page (New York, Pierpont Morgan Lib. MS M. 729, f. 268).

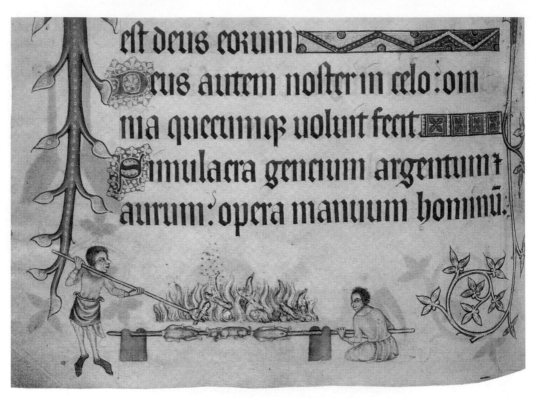

5 (Sandler). Luttrell Psalter, Psalm 113, detail (London, British Library, Add. MS 42130, fol. 206v). Photo after J. Backhouse, *The Luttrell Psalter* (London, 1989) fig. 43.

6 (Sandler). Luttrell Psalter, Psalm 113, detail (London, BL, Add.MS 42130, f. 207). Photo after Backhouse, *The Luttrell Psalter*, fig. 44.

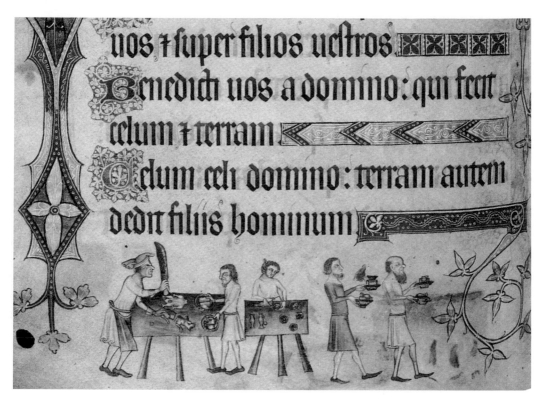

uos ⁊ super filios uestros.
Benedicti uos a domino : qui fecit
celum ⁊ terram.
Celum celi domino : terram autem
dedit filiis hominum

7 (Sandler). Luttrell Psalter, Psalm 113, detail (London, BL, Add. MS 42130, f. 207v).
Photo after Backhouse, *The Luttrell Psalter*, fig. 47.

chi : ⁊ in diebus meis inuocabo.
Circumdederunt me dolores mor
tis : et pericula inferni inuenerunt me.
Tribulacionem ⁊ dolorem inueni : ⁊
nomen domini inuocaui

8 (Sandler). Luttrell Psalter, Psalm 114, detail (London, BL, Add.MS 42130, f. 208).
Photo after Backhouse, *The Luttrell Psalter*, fig. 48.

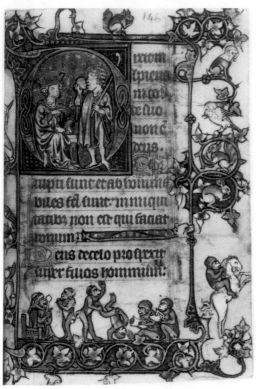

9 (Sandler). Flemish Psalter, Psalm 52 (Oxford, Bodleian Lib. MS Douce 5, f. 146).

10 (Sandler). Bohun Psalter and Hours, Psalm 118k (London, BL, Egerton MS 3277, fol. 84, detail).

11 (Sandler). Bohun Psalter and Hours, Psalm 42 (London, BL, Egerton MS 3277, f.32v, detail).

12 (Sandler). Bohun Psalter and Hours, Psalm 16 (London, BL, Egerton MS 3277, f.13v, detail).

13 (Sandler). Hamburg Bible, Prologue to Daniel (Copenhagen, Kongelige Bibl. MS Gl.kgl.S.4 2°, II, f.183, detail). Photo after C. de Hamel, *Medieval Craftsmen, Scribes and Illuminators* (London, 1992), fig. 8.

14 (Sandler). Omne bonum, 'Colour' (London, BL, Royal MS 6 E vi, f. 329, detail).

3 (Stones). London, BL MS Royal 14.E.III, f. 36.

Estoure conte ci en
droit que li roys d
uordrains fu por
tez loing de son
regne · bien · xvij
iornees · Et quât
vint orendroit leure de nonne
que li roys ot veu dessous lui to

il encore vn autre ensoine pcoil
ne pot aler deliurement ce fu quil
ne lauoit mie acostume Ensi q̃ nac
ciens fu c̃ .j. nef vt .iij. fnsiaus et .j.
espe. et .j. couroune dor fuxent.

5 (Stones). London, BL, Add. MS 10292, f. 31.

Lors erra tant quil uit
tout apertement la
cose quil auoit des le
matin veue en la mer
li sot urmement que ce estoit vne
neif mout riche ⁊ mout bele si en
fu mout lies· si seffozcha tant da
len quil en̄ux̃ en uuer· ⁊ si

mere. Et coument li fuissel estoi
ent de naturel coulour sans nule
painture. Si retourne aconter de
nasaen dont il est grant pieche
teus

dut li con
tes q grant
pieche rer
garda nas
aens les
iij. fuisiax
dont lilis
estoit 7 por
sauoir se

6 (Stones). Le Mans, MM 354, f. 110.

il peust la connoistre de quoi il
estoient si coulouret. kar cou ne
quidoit il nue legierement que
il fuissent de naturel coulour. Dont
il dut lors a soi mesmes vn mot

7 (Stones). Rennes, BN 255, f. 46.

Rdit li conte
que grant pi
ece regarda
flacienc les
trois fuisse
aus dont lilis
estoit auiro
net 7 clos por sauoir sil peust la co
noistre decoi il estoient ensi colore.

ment & por col le pee til miuet
mile. Si sen tait ore li contes a p
ler si v̅ dirons dune autre cose.
En si q̅ cue et adam sunt p̅ ev̅ar lar
bre et adã se pient par le geule.

8 (Stones). London, BL, Add. MS 10292, f. 31v.

hi endroit dist li con
tes que el milieu du
lit sour quoi lespe o
lisoit ot · iij · siuliaus ·

9 (Stones). Paris, BNF fr. 105, f. 65v.

ment caym occist abel so frere xxiiij

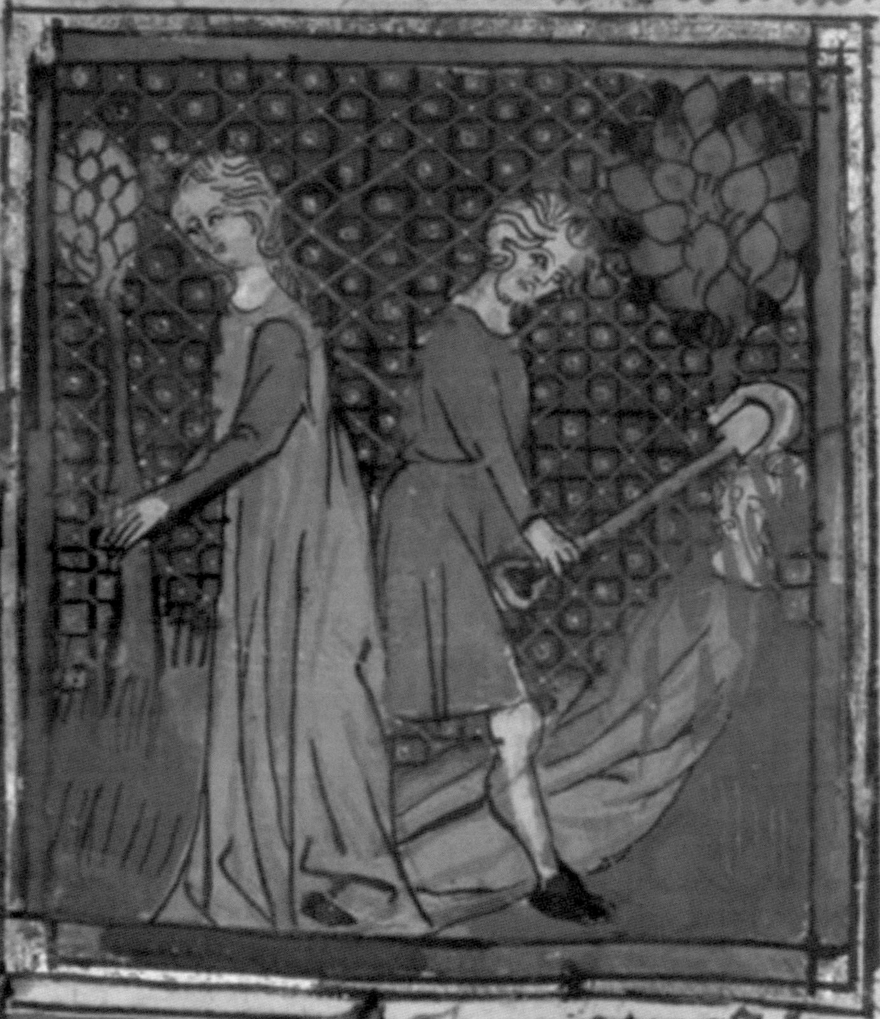

Tant se taist li contes en cestui point de lespee et del kierre et li parole dune chose. car il dist q

11 (Stones). Paris, BNF fr. 19162, f. 65.

10 (Stones). Paris, BNF fr. 9123, f. 53v.

crut tant ⁊amenda· que ce estoit li plus bi
aul arbret de tout le monde·

12a (Stones).
Berkeley,
UCB 106,
f. 145v, col. a.

12b (Stones).
Berkeley,
UCB 106,
f. 145v, col. b.

lt dura louguement al arbret
en tel color· ⁊ en tel biaute co
me vos aues oi deniser· el conte
ne onques ne uelli ne ne chan
ja· ne ne secha· ne de nule
riens nempira· fors detant
seulement· c.il ne porta ne floz ne fruit·v)

Via mandatoys tuoys cucurri :
cu dilatasti cor meum ·

13 (Stones). Hildesheim, Sankt Godehard, St Albans Psalter, p. 215.

enit ance auferens tauoite vne
nef, et salemos et la feme le regñ
zent.

lendemain si tost cō
me li iours aparut
tramist salemons
ses messages z loing
z pres por querre carpentiers · z
quant il furent tout assamble de
uant lui si loz omanda que il li

14 (Stones). London, BL, Add. MS 10292, f. 34.

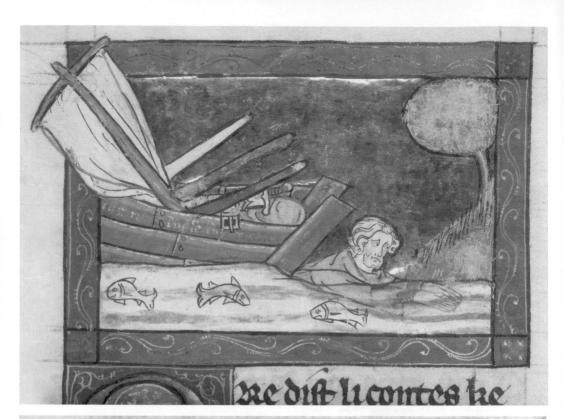

17 (Stones). New Haven, Yale University, Beinecke Library 229, f. 253.

15 (opposite, above) (Stones). London, BL, Add. MS 10292, f. 35v.
16 (opposite, below) (Stones). London, BL, Royal MS 14.E.III, f. 125v.

tages restores qui perdus es
toit al tans de lores.

Re dist ⁊ repaire li con
tes al rainsiel q̃ estoit
remes en tre ⁊ dist quil

Re dist li contes ho avant vie

nule painture · Si sen taist a tāt
li contes ⁊ pole dautres choses ⁊

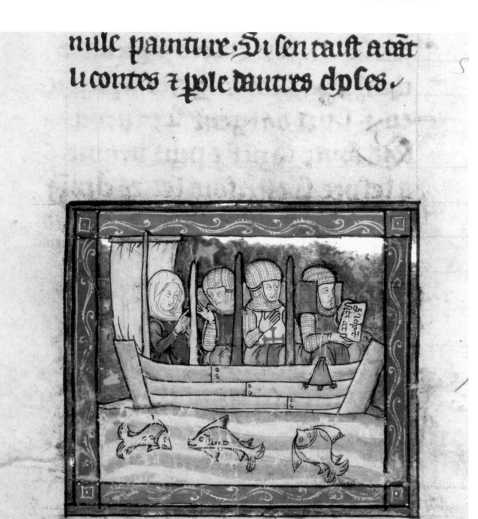

Ke dist li contes ke grāt
pieche regarderent li · iij ·
ⱳpaignon le lit ⁊ les · iij ·
fusiaus · ⁊ tant qͥl trouuerent

20 (Stones). London, BL, Royal MS 14.E.III, f. 130v.

18 (opposite, above) (Stones). London, BL, Royal MS 14.E.III, f. 128.

19 (opposite, below) (Stones). Oxford, Bodleian Library, Douce 215, f. 35.

21 (Stones). New Haven, Yale
University, Beinecke Library 229,
f. 257v.

R dist li contes que gnt piere
regarderent li tivi copaigno
le tit. les fuifiaus. 7 tanral

23 (Stones). London, BL, Add. MS 10294, f. 47v.

24 (Stones). New Haven, Yale University, Beinecke Library 229, f. 262v.

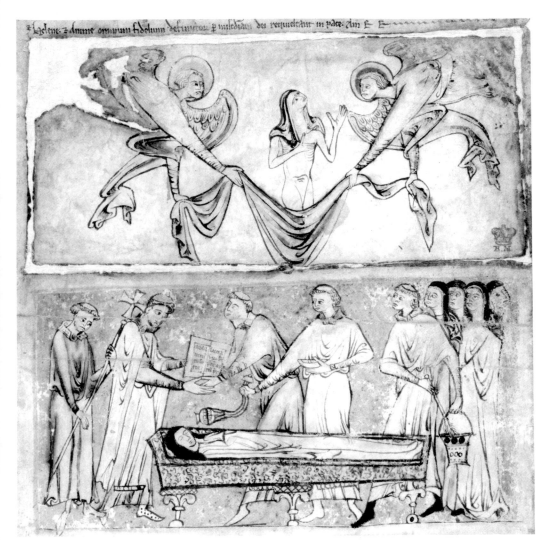

1 (Tudor-Craig). Mortuary Roll of Lucy de Vere. British Library, Egerton MS 2849.

2 (Tudor-Craig). Sir John de Wautune and wife. Wimbish, Essex 1347.
Brass rubbing by L. A. S. Waller, 1848.

FROM A BRASS
late in Ingham Church Norfolk.

n.8 Etched by Charles A. Stothard Jun.t F.S.A. Sept.r 1820.

London, Published as the Act directs Nov.r 25.th 1815 by Mrs. F. Bray.
4 Rodney Buildings, New Kent Road, and by Mess.rs Arch, Corn.

3 (Tudor-Craig). Sir Miles de Stapleton and wife, 1364, formerly Ingham, Norfolk.
From Stothard, *Monumental Effigies*, 1819.

Lord John Harsick and Lady, South Acre, 1384.

4 (Tudor-Craig). Sir John Harsick and wife, 1384. Southacre Norfolk.

5 (Tudor-Craig). Peter Halle and wife, c. 1430. Herne, Kent.

Sir Walter Mauntell, 1487, and his wife Elizabeth.

6 (opposite) (Tudor-Craig). Sir William Mauntell and wife, 1487. Nether Heyford, Northamptonshire.

7 (Tudor-Craig). Sir John de la Pole and wife, c. 1380. Chrishall, Essex.

8 (Tudor-Craig). Robert Hatfield and wife Ada, 1409. Owston, Yorks.